The Audubon
Society
Field Guide
to the
Natural Places
of the
Mid-Atlantic States:
Coastal

Other titles in this series
include:

The Audubon Society
Field Guide
to the Natural Places
of the Mid-Atlantic States:
Inland

The Audubon Society
Field Guide
to the Natural Places
of the Northeast:
Coastal

The Audubon Society
Field Guide
to the Natural Places
of the Northeast:
Inland

The Audubon Society Field Guide to the Natural Places of the Mid-Atlantic States: Coastal

Susannah Lawrence

A Hilltown Book
Pantheon Books, New York

Staff for this volume

Editor: Caroline Sutton
Reporters: Susannah Lawrence and Barbara Gross
Cartography: Rebecca Lazear Okrent and Gene Gort
Consultant: Richard Plunkett

Library of Congress Cataloging in Publication Data

Lawrence, Susannah.
    The Audubon Society field guide to the natural places of the Mid-
Atlantic States.

    Bibliography: p.
    Includes index.
    Contents: Coastal—Inland.
    1. Natural areas—Atlantic States—Guide-books.
I. Gross, Barbara. II. National Audubon Society.
III. Title.
QH76.5.A87L39   1984   917.4'0443   83–21417
ISBN 0–394–72279–5 (v. 1)
ISBN 0–394–72280–9 (v. 2)

Text design: Clint Anglin

Manufactured in the United States of America
First Edition

The National Audubon Society

For more than three-quarters of a century, the National Audubon Society has provided leadership in scientific research, conservation education, and citizen-action programs to save birds and other wildlife and the habitat necessary for their survival.

To accomplish these goals, the society has formally adopted the Audubon Cause: TO CARRY OUT RESEARCH, EDUCATION, AND ACTION TO CONSERVE WILD BIRDS AND OTHER ANIMALS, TREES AND OTHER PLANTS, SOIL, AIR, AND WATER, AND ALSO TO PROMOTE A BETTER UNDERSTANDING OF THE INTERDEPENDENCE OF THESE NATURAL RESOURCES. To carry out the Audubon Cause, the society's programs are structured around five specific missions that encompass the tremendous scope of the organization:

—Conserve native plants and animals and their habitats
—Further the wise use of land and water
—Promote rational strategies for energy development and use
—Protect life from pollution, radiation, and toxic substances
—Seek solutions for global problems involving the interaction of population, resources, the environment, and sustainable development.

Our underlying belief is that all forms of life are interdependent and that the diversity of nature is essential to both our economic and our environmental well-being.

Audubon, through its nationwide system of sanctuaries, protects more than 250,000 acres of essential habi-

tat and unique natural areas for birds and other wild animals and
rare plant life. The sanctuaries range in size from 9 acres around
Theodore Roosevelt's grave in New York State to 26,000 acres of
coastal marsh in Louisiana. Most of the sanctuaries are staffed by
resident wardens who also patrol adjacent natural areas not owned
by Audubon.

Audubon's 500,000 members provide the underpinning for all the
society's programs and activities. Two-thirds of our members also
belong to local Audubon chapters, now numbering more than 480,
which serve in their communities as focal points for conservation,
nature education, and citizen action on environmental issues.

We also maintain ten regional offices, each staffed by two or more
full-time professional conservationists who advance Audubon programs throughout the fifty states.

Our staff conducts wildlife research to aid such endangered species
as the bald eagle, whooping crane, eastern timber wolf, and bog
turtle and to provide knowledge of the ecologically sound management of our sanctuaries. The society also publishes the award-win-
ning *Audubon* magazine and *American Birds* magazine.

For further information about the society, write or call:

National Audubon Society
950 Third Avenue
New York, N.Y. 10022
(212) 832-3200

Contents

Acknowledgments

This was an enormous project, requiring the contributions of great numbers of people. I would first like to thank all those who bravely tried out the directions and the maps.

Without the sponsorship of the Audubon Society this project would never have been undertaken. I would especially like to thank Richard Plunkett for his suggestions and corrections.

Special thanks to Meredith Wilder and Robert McWilliams, who contributed the descriptions of Thousand Acre Marsh and Woodland Beach; Cecil Frost, who wrote the description of the Zuni Pine Barrens; and June Zampolino, for her work on the Timber Beaver Swamp. The staffs of the national wildlife refuges, national, state, and local parks, and hunting and fishing areas described in this book have universally been helpful and supportive. The staff, stewards, interns, and supporters of the Nature Conservancy have provided assistance and encouragement in covering Conservancy preserves. I would also like to thank the Virginia Society of Ornithologists, the New Jersey Audubon, the Delmarva Ornithological Society, the Delaware Nature Education Society, and the Maryland Ornithological Society for their help in compiling information.

The following people provided invaluable aid in reviewing material and answering innumerable questions and in some cases even acting as guides. Rick Dolish, Patuxent River Park; John Gregoire; Tolly Peuleche; William Portlock, Chesapeake Bay Foundation; Gary Roisum,

Huntley Meadows Park; Hank Schneider, National Park Service; Eric Seed, Maryland Department of Natural Resources; Dr. Stan Shetler, Smithsonian Institution; William Sipple, Environmental Protection Agency; Dr. Frank Whitmore, Smithsonian Institution; Hal Wierenga; Dr. Norbert Psuty, Center for Coastal and Environmental Studies, Rutgers University; Dr. Jerry Schubel, Marine Sciences Research Laboratory, SUNY; Dr. William Reifsnyder, Department of Environmental Studies, Yale University; Ralph Eshelman, Calvert Marine Museum; Henry Armistead; Brian Harrington of the Manomet Bird Observatory; Karl Anderson, Rancocas Nature Center; Wade Wander; Chris Pague; Dr. Gerald Johnson, Department of Geology, College of William and Mary; Dr. Thomas Pickett, Delaware Geological Survey; Joe Lomax, Stockton State College; Peggy Jahn, Delaware Audubon Society; Lorraine Fleming, Delaware Nature Education Society; Dr. Shep Krech; Rusty Holger and Peter Martin of Delaware Wildlands, Inc.; Charles Mohr; Dr. Richard Forman, Department of Botany, Rutgers University; Joe Fehrer; Jim Stasz; Dr. Evelyn Maurmeyer, Marine Science School, University of Delaware; Dr. Charles Blem, Biology Department, Virginia Commonwealth University; Dr. Donna Ware and Dr. Stewart Ware, Department of Botany, College of William and Mary; William Sheehan; Tony Florio, Delaware Division of Fish and Game; Dr. Eugene Vivian, Conservation Environmental Studies Center.

I particularly wish to thank two people without whom the book would never have been completed. Barbara Gross not only authored five site discriptions but assisted with the organization, research, and editing of the volume. Caroline Sutton has been editor, friend, and supporter. She persuaded me that anything is possible. I have been extremely lucky in having excellent editorial help from David Frederickson, who scoured and polished the manuscript, and from my editors at Pantheon, who spurred me on. I would also like to thank Dan Okrent for allowing me to do this book. Finally, I owe a special debt to all the friends and relations who fed, sheltered, and encouraged me on my travels.

How to Use This Book

The aim of the Audubon Society Field Guides is to enable the reader to explore and enjoy the natural history and ecology of selected natural areas in the United States. Unlike any other guide to the outdoors, this series describes the interaction of plants, animals, topography, and climate so that the hiker, birder, or amateur naturalist will be able to understand and more fully appreciate what he or she sees. Today, almost all the sites presented in these guides, whether in public or private ownership, are maintained for public education and enrichment. All offer geological, botanical, or biological points of interest, as well as the beauty, excitement, and tremendous variety of the outdoors.

This guide is one of an initial set also including a Mid-Atlantic inland volume, a Northeast coastal volume, and a Northeast inland volume. The areas covered in each guide have been determined, as often as possible, according to geological rather than governmental boundaries. The separation of coastal and inland volumes in the Mid-Atlantic series, for example, is clearly indicated by the *fall line*. This roughly north–south demarcation running from New York City into Georgia occurs where the flat Coastal Plain rises to meet the rolling hills of the Piedmont.

Each guide contains descriptions of over a hundred natural areas, and each site description pinpoints what is most significant, intriguing, or unusual about that area. More important, it explains *how* the site came to look as it does, and *why* certain species of vegetation and wildlife can be found there. Thus, while one narrative unravels the geological history of a region as it is revealed in the rock outcrops along a trail, another centers on a rare and ancient stand of Atlantic white-cedar, and still another highlights the waterfowl that gather in an area, explaining their feeding, breeding, and migratory habits. Indeed, if the diverse entries about a particular area such as the Chesapeake Bay are read as a group, the visitor can reach a fuller understanding of both the existing biotic climate and the workings of human and natural history. Furthermore, the sites have been organized by geological and ecological regions, each prefaced by an introductory essay providing a general look at the geology, vegetation, and wildlife in that region and the human influence on it. Since the Coastal Plain from New Jersey to North Carolina is part of one discrete geological region, this volume contains only one such essay.

All sites are numbered, and a system of cross-referencing throughout enables the reader to locate the most thorough discussion of a particular species or geological formation. For example, ospreys may be mentioned briefly in one description, but there will also be a reference to a fuller discussion elsewhere in the book. Each site opens with precise directions to the area and ends with a section called *Remarks*. Here is included such practical information as the length and difficulty of a recommended walk; what equipment to bring; possible activities such as swimming, fishing, and skiing; the availability of boat rentals; nearby places to camp; and best times of the year to visit.

Most site descriptions include a map, keyed by letter to the narrative, which leads the visitor along a suggested walk or boat trip. A sample map follows, along with a key to the various symbols that appear throughout the book.

The back of each guide includes a brief glossary, a bibliography of works on related subjects, and an extensive index. The Index is cross-referenced to enable the reader to find a particular site of interest, whether because of a species or geological formation or because of certain sports and other activities.

It may be useful to read about a site before visiting, to learn the length of the trip and what equipment to bring. While principal species of vegetation or wildlife are identified in the entries, others are mentioned in passing, and the amateur birder or botanist may therefore wish to bring along a field guide to birds, trees, or wildflowers. Recommended supplementary guides are listed in the Bibliography.

Finally, it is important to remember that natural sites are never unchanging places, but rather always in flux. Wind and wave action alter the profile of the coast; bogs fill in with vegetation; some animals learn to adapt to the influx of civilization while others vanish.

Wooded area

Paved road

Dirt road

Brook or stream

Secondary trail

Tidal flat

Shore line

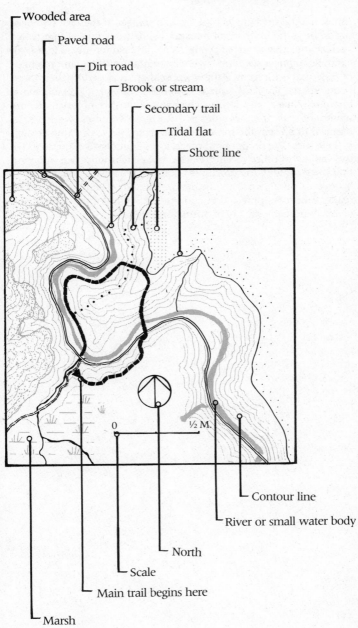

Contour line

River or small water body

North

Scale

Main trail begins here

Marsh

Many natural areas reflect the human impact of the past two centuries, be it the draining of marshes or the reseeding of forests. No such change is an isolated event. As an old field returns to forest, for example, pioneer seedlings give way to mature forest, and the birds of prey that once hunted the open field are replaced by their forest counterparts. Similarly, our knowledge about such phenomena is interdisciplinary, and forever changing as further observations are made and past theories uprooted. In these volumes, we have attempted to present the most widely accepted geological and ecological theories. We do not presume to be comprehensive, nor to judge the validity of other recent theories and conclusions. Our aim is to introduce some of the processes botanists, biologists, and geologists believe to be at work in the natural world, thereby offering the reader a deeper appreciation and understanding of the complexity, beauty, and vulnerability of our natural areas.

The Audubon
Society
Field Guide
to the
Natural Places
of the
Mid-Atlantic States:
Coastal

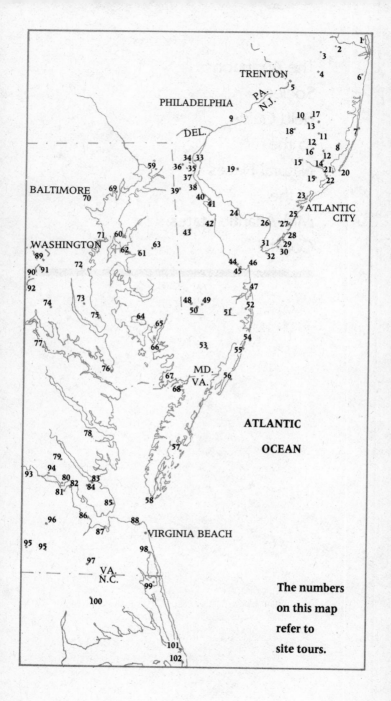

The numbers on this map refer to site tours.

Introduction

By the Edge of the Sea

From New Jersey south to the Gulf States, North America is ringed by a broad plain that falls gently off into the Atlantic Ocean and continues out 100 miles or so before finally reaching the lip of the continent. Almost imperceptibly it slopes upward from the dune-lined beaches of the shore to the old oak woods at the edge of the Piedmont Province to the west. Even at its highest elevation the plain is rarely more than 300 feet above the sea. From the flat, sandy Pine Barrens to the densely wooded swamps of the Nottoway and the stately trees of the York River, the Coastal Plain is a region of unexpected diversity. At the same time it not only has a common geological history but also many similarities of climate. Humidity, temperature, length of growing season, and other climatic indicators change very gradually from north to south. Because of this and because of its low topography the Coastal Plain has been an important corridor for the movement of plants and animals both north and south. Only part of the Coastal Plain Province is covered in this volume, the part that runs along the Atlantic from New Jersey down to the mouth of the Roanoke River, in northern North Carolina.

This is young land, a plain of sediments still largely unconsolidated into rock. Like a beach as the tide ebbs, the plain carries few marks. Time and time again the ocean has swept in, drowning the shore and depositing new layers of sediment. Time and time again the ocean has retreated, and rivers have deposited silt and sand in broad deltas across the plain. Only with the retreat of the

1

Wisconsin ice sheet, about 10,000 years ago, did the Coastal Plain as it appears today emerge.

Its formation, however, began about 180 million years ago. It was then that the vast ancestral continent, known as Pangaea, began to break apart along a line paralleling what is now our eastern seacoast. This rift widened gradually, was invaded by the sea, and became the Atlantic Ocean. Borne on the moving plates of earth's crust, the land masses of Africa, Europe, and America drifted apart. As the continents drew away, shallow marine and near-shore sediments were deposited on the margin of the old continental crust, which consists of layers of ancient metamorphic and igneous rock.

By 135 million years ago, rivers flowing down to the new shore had begun laying down a thin wedge of sediments. These sediments were tiny pieces of ancient rock worn away from the Appalachian highlands to the west. Since then the oceans have risen and fallen, the land has been lifted and eroded, and layers of sediment have accumulated. Some strata are light-colored marine sands; some are riverine gravels; and still others are the fine sediments of a calm bay. Today, while still little more than a shallow covering at its westward edge, the wedge of Coastal Plain sediments is thousands of feet thick along the outer rim of the continental shelf.

Where the sandy sediments meet the uplands of the Piedmont Province, those ancient metamorphic and igneous rocks form a distinct boundary between the two provinces. This division is most clearly revealed as a line of falls and rocky rapids along the streams flowing eastward onto the Coastal Plain. This "fall line" (as it was called in colonial America) marks the upper limit of navigation on the coastal rivers. Along it great commercial centers developed, where water power was available, and where land routes met oceangoing vessels.

About 2 million years ago, great sheets of ice spread across much of the earth. Geologists are not certain how this came about. It was probably the cumulative effect of many small changes, such as slight shifts in weather patterns, a minute decrease in solar radiation, an increase in cosmic dust, a change in the orbit of the earth, or a rise in the levels of particulates and carbon dioxide in the atmosphere. Combined, such changes caused summers to cool just a few degrees, so that in certain key locations the winter snow did not melt completely. Each year more and more snow collected, compacting the layers below into ice. A glacier was born.

Once begun, the glaciers fed themselves, for the ice reflected sunlight away from the earth, making the climate even colder. Air flowed from the edge of the ice sheet to the uncovered land and back, going through rapid shifts in temperature and humidity, creating turbulent weather and frequent storms. These storms dumped more snow on the ice mass. The ice spread over North America from a center in Canada (not, as one might expect, from the North Pole). When the sheet reached south to about New York, it could go no further; at that point the melting of the ice each summer balanced the winter's advance. Four times the ice crept south, binding up such quantities of water that the oceans dropped hundreds of feet. Each glacial period was followed by a warm time when the ice melted and seas rose again. The most recent ice sheet, the Wisconsin, was probably not the last. Geologists suspect that we are in the midst of another interglacial period, due to end in another 90,000 years or so.

The ice sheets never reached the Coastal Plain, but they were world-shaking events and the face of the province was shaped by them as surely as the course of modern Europe was shaped by World War II. It was the glacially caused rhythmic advance and retreat of the ocean across the Coastal Plain which has given it the face we recognize today. In southeastern Virginia the sea's dance across the land has clearly left its mark, a pattern of ridges or scarps that were once coastal beaches. In New Jersey, with its coarser sediments, the scarps are much more subdued. With each fall in sea level, the rivers of the Coastal Plain eroded deeply into their beds, gouging out wide valleys, leaving great escarpments. With each new rise, the river valleys flooded again, creating the estuaries of the Chesapeake and the Delaware. Other streams winding across the Coastal Plain filled with sediment, oozed over their banks, and became low-lying swamps like those of the Nottoway and Blackwater rivers and the Dismal Swamp.

There were more subtle effects as well. The wall of ice was thousands of feet high. It cooled the environment for hundreds of miles to the south. Southern New Jersey resembled today's northern Canada, cloaked in heavy forests of spruce and fir. As the glaciers retreated and the climate warmed, the spruce and fir gave way to pines, hemlocks, and aspen, the species of the New England woods. Then they too gave way to deciduous forests of mixed oaks. Eventually, the pitch-pine forests of the Pine Barrens took over, shaped by frequent fire into a unique habitat. However, scattered over the plain, in the cool bogs of the New Jersey Pine Barrens, one can still find curly-grass fern, broom crowberry, and a few other remnants of those ancient northern forests.

The rising seas and the dumping of millions of tons of glacial debris into the oceans also gave birth to a lacy chain of barrier islands hugging the Atlantic shore. Scientists still do not know exactly how the islands first formed. Some islands are little more than shell-littered beaches, a few hundred feet wide, coming alive each June with riotous colonies of terns and gulls. Others stretch for miles, their interior a patchwork of high old dunes and pine-oak forest. The barrier islands now protect the coast from the full brunt of ocean storms. Behind them lie shallow sounds and estuaries fringed with salt marsh. In these sheltered waters many species of fish, crustaceans, mollusks, and other marine animals spend part or all of their life cycle.

Some islands, particularly those along the Gulf Coast, may have started as sandbars that migrated landward as the sea level rose with the melting of the ice sheet. Others perhaps began as long spits of sand laid down by longshore currents (see **#25**). As these lengthened into peninsulas, great storms breached them, creating inlets and dividing them into islands. Still another theory is that the islands originated as dunes along an ancient coastline far to the east. As the sea level rose, the dunes became islands. Tides, waves, and currents then moved the islands westward to their present position.

Determining the exact age of any of the island deposits is extremely difficult because of the constant movement of the sand. One thing is clear, though: for the moment only small amounts of sediment are being fed into the barrier system. Some of the islands may move and grow, but the system as a whole is shrinking.

The barrier islands are constantly changing. Sea level rises several inches every 100 years on this part of the coast. Over time the islands all along the Atlantic are migrating westward. As long as the mainland shore retreats at a similar rate, the islands maintain their distance. In some places, however—such as Cape Henry, in Virginia, and the northern coast of New Jersey—high ground along the coast slows the sea's encroachment. Here the barrier island has become part of the coast itself.

The ocean is both destroyer and builder. While it wears away at the coast, eroding it westward inch by inch, its huge reservoir of minerals and dissolved oxygen replenish the coastal waters and marshes. It is the sea that softens the coastal climate, warming the winter and cooling the summer. The Gulf Stream, a current of turquoise tropical water, is swirled northeastward along the Atlantic coast by the spinning of the earth, a phenomenon called the *Coriolis effect* (see **#7**). Its warmth counters the cold winds blowing over the continent. The vast reservoir of the ocean itself helps to temper the swing of the seasons. Slow to gain or lose heat, the waters act as a giant storage unit, slowly absorbing the sun's heat in summer and slowly giving it back through the cold winter. The effect of this warmth is enormous. From the Virginia Tidewater to the highlands of the Piedmont there is a difference of several degrees in average winter temperatures. These few degrees are vividly reflected in the distribution of many southern animals and plants whose ranges bulge northward along the coast.

The flocks of birds that migrate north and south along the Atlantic flyway find food and shelter along the temperate Mid-Atlantic coast. In early fall, insects, seeds, and berries provide food for tiny warblers, thrushes, swallows, vireos, and other landbirds. Later in the cold November days, while the inland fields and trees are bare, the marshes are still lush with plants, the waters full of marine animals and aquatic vegetation. Now flights of geese and ducks are at their height. The diving and dabbling ducks that breed on the freshwater potholes of the Great Plains move south along the coast, dropping into each pool and tidal creek and river mouth. At the Chesapeake Bay the wintering grounds begin. From here southward, the waters are open all or most of the winter. Around the bay, where mechanical reapers harvest corn and other crops, geese gather all winter long to feed on waste grain. Some species like the red-winged blackbird and Virginia rail come eastward from freshwater wetlands to winter along the coast, where food will be plentiful and the waters open.

On any site in the Coastal Plain, water more than any other factor determines the interrelationships of plants and animals, including man. Living cells must stay wet in order to survive and to function, but some plants and animals can survive in dry climates. Too much water can be a problem, depriving plants and animals of oxygen; but some organisms have been able to adapt to saturated environments. Rainfall is plentiful in the Coastal Plain, from 40 to 48 inches per year. Even so, every moisture regime—from very dry *(xeric)* to very soggy *(hydric)* and everything in between *(mesic)*—can be found. Where soils are sandy and porous, rainwater filters rapidly through them, leaving the upper layers dry and poor in nutrients. Water is seldom far away, however, even on the driest soils, for the water table is often just below the surface. The driest sites are found on the dunes of the coastal edge. Here the sands have yet to become soils, the rain drains away, and the plants are exposed to the constant winds. The porous sandy soils of the pine plains in the New Jersey barrens are also xeric.

On the inner, oldest portions of the plain, soils are better developed, richer in organic material, better able to retain moisture. On these mesic soils, agriculture has flourished. South of the Chesapeake Bay the topography becomes flatter; in many lowland, swampy sites, soils are very poorly drained or hydric. Although there are no high hills rising from the Coastal Plain, the fierce strength of the Susquehanna River and its tributaries has carved out high bluffs along the western edge of the Chesapeake Bay. These are well-drained sites, which support stands of older trees and of species like mountain laurel, more reminiscent of the rolling Piedmont Province to the west.

Most of the area covered by this volume falls within a forest type called oak-hickory. This means that on a mesic site, where soils are moist but well drained, a mature or climax forest of various oaks will dominate the canopy or the top story of trees. Hickories tend to be slightly less important and to come into the canopy later. The term *climax forest* is used to describe an association of trees and other vegetation that tends to replace itself, presumably because it is the type of forest best suited to local conditions. This at least is the theory. In practice, the picture is much more confusing. Many ecologists mistrust the term *climax*, believing that habitats are always evolving and changing, no matter how slowly. They prefer the term *mature* to describe the later stages in a forest's evolution.

Succession is the process by which one stage of vegetation gives way to another. When a bare dune by the sea is first colonized by beach grass, *primary succession* is occurring. When plant cover has been burned or logged or storm-damaged, the new cycles of growth that follow are called *secondary succession*. Succession has been described in the past as a neat progression from one stage to another. As each stage grows it changes the habitat by providing more shade, more moisture, more moderate temperatures, more nutrients to the soil. Theoretically, each stage comprises a different set of plants. In practice, sometimes all the climax species may be present in one of the early stages of the succession. Sometimes early succession species linger on into the climax canopy. Chance must largely determine which seeds happen to fall in a forest clearing or which plants have managed to survive disturbance.

No natural disturbance can begin to rival the reckless, headlong pace of human activity on the Coastal Plain. Since the colonists first arrived along the Virginia coast and found it pleasing, the Coastal Plain has been more heavily used than any other province in North America. Repeatedly cleared, cut over, and built upon, much of its forest is third and fourth growth. Its more fertile soils were heavily farmed up to the time of the Civil War. Then, as labor grew scarce, fields were abandoned. Secondary succession began, probably as it does today on old fields. First came weedy vegetation such as crabgrass and horseweed; then asters moved into the open ground. Mixed with the asters, broom sedge began to appear, gradually taking command of the old field. With the broom sedge came the first pines, commonly pitch pine and Virginia pine in more northern areas, loblolly and shortleaf pine to the south.

Timber had replaced field crops as a cash crop by the 1920s. In the southern Coastal Plain especially, pines were harvested regularly. Pines continue to be common throughout much of the region due to frequent cycles of lumbering and frequent burning. Fires have been a by-product of industry, commerce, and agriculture since the English landed in Virginia. Pines are favored by frequent fire. They sprout best in the open and often survive fires that destroy other species.

Left to evolve, the pine forest gradually changes. After 80 years, the pines may still be present, but oaks, hickories, and a mix of other deciduous species eventually take over.

Farming and development have taken their toll around the edges of the Chesapeake Bay (although the growth of agriculture has inadvertently extended the wintering range of Canada geese and whistling swans far north of where it once was). Little forested land of any significance remains on Maryland's Eastern Shore, and animals like the Delmarva fox squirrel and river otter, which once ranged over the entire peninsula, have nearly vanished.

The marshes have also suffered. Drained to combat mosquitoes, filled in to increase land, polluted by agricultural and industrial wastes, marshes are in danger all up and down the coast.

Only the impenetrable tupelo and cypress swamps of southeastern Virginia have survived largely unchanged since colonial times. These swamps, the outliers of the vast river swamps of the south, begin at the very southern boundary of the area covered by this book. Protected by constant flooding, they are havens for animals such as bobcat, beaver, river otter, and mink that have become rare elsewhere on the Coastal Plain.

Human activity has created habitats as well as destroyed them. Grassy fields, forest edges, and open pine woods are perfect habitat for many of the Coastal Plain creatures. Eastern cottontail, raccoon, opossum, white-tailed deer, gray and red foxes, gray squirrel, southern flying squirrel, and white-footed mouse are found in many habitats. Reptiles and amphibians become increasingly varied and numerous as you travel south where winters are warmer and less arduous, and food supplies are available longer. Southeastern Virginia marks the northern border for a number of species, among them the squirrel treefrog, the pine woods treefrog, and the little grass frog.

At first glance, the flat sloping terrain of the Coastal Plain hints at a uniform ecosystem with few surprises, but that glance is deceptive. The shifting balance of the shoreline and sea, the rolling bluffs above the Chesapeake Bay, the deep river swamps of the Nottoway and the Blackwater, the orchid bogs of the Pine Barrens, the wide coastal marshes are all part of an unfolding tale—rich and complex and unfinished.

1.

Sandy Hook

━━━━━━━━━━━━━━━━━━━━━━━━━━━━━━

Directions: **Monmouth County, N.J. From New York City take the New Jersey Turnpike to Exit 11. Follow the Garden State Parkway south about 12 miles to Exit 117. Drive east on Route 36 about 13 miles to Sandy Hook. Designated parking areas are scattered all along the peninsula. The nature trail begins at the parking area for the visitors' center (A).**

Ownership: **Part of the Gateway Recreation Area, National Park Service.**

The long point of land known as Sandy Hook is a place of surprising wildness and beauty, though it guards the polluted waters of New York Harbor. About 6 miles long, it includes salt marshes, back-dune forests, freshwater ponds, and long stretches of open beach where piping plovers and colonies of least terns breed each summer in sight of the towers of the city to the north. This barrier spit, like the rest of the Atlantic shore, took shape in the thousands of years following the last glacial period (see **Introduction**). The northern movement of the longshore current along the coast here and the action of tides and waves have created the curving peninsula (see **#25**). If you look at a map of the hook, you will see the remnants of other, earlier curving spits at Spermaceti and Horseshoe coves. Each of these spits was once the northernmost point of land; Sandy Hook subsequently grew out of them and extended farther northward. The hook appears to have taken shape in a series of fits and starts. This is probably the result of the opening and closing of inlets in the barrier beach. When a passageway was clear, sediments eroded off the Navesink highlands to the west were washed out through the inlet and swept north onto the spit. Then the inlet closed again and much smaller amounts of sediment were added to the spit. Over the last 200 years, Sandy Hook has grown 1.5 miles. The curving of the hook is created in part by the bending of the waves as they approach the spit and in part by sediments as they are deposited. The two processes reinforce each other. At **B** several jetties or groins and a seawall, which stops just to the south, have resulted in severe erosion (see **#6**). If left to itself, this might become a breach in the peninsula. The stones of the groins and of the seawall do provide home for mollusks, and this

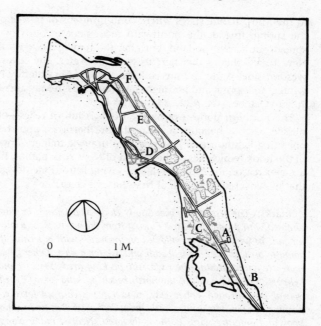

attracts a number of diving ducks and other waterfowl in the winter. Stop to look for red-throated and common loons, rare red-necked grebes, scoters, and oldsquaws (see **#6** and **#20**).

A highlight of Sandy Hook is the holly forest (**C**). Although it is still part of an active coast guard facility, tours are made into it on scheduled weekends and holidays. Holly is the climax species here, and one of these trees is estimated to be 150 years old. The holly is well suited to the very dry conditions of the spit. Its roots reach down to the water table about 5 feet below the surface, while its thick-skinned, glossy leaves reduce water loss. Elsewhere on the interior portions of the island, redcedar and black cherry are particularly abundant. These species come earlier in the succession and will eventually be shaded out by the hollies (see **Introduction**).

A well-marked nature trail leads north from the visitors' parking area. This is a good birding trail during spring and fall migrations because it touches a variety of habitats: thickets, forest, fields, and freshwater ponds. Many species of landbirds migrate through the area, for like Cape May to the south, Sandy Hook extends invitingly out into the open waters of a wide estuary, and it provides diverse habitats well stocked with food. Sandy Hook is one of the few places in the Mid-Atlantic states where concentrations of hawks occur in the spring. Inland, the northward movement of birds of prey is spread out across the land, but after the hawks move up through New Jersey, they gather here to cross the water. The coves on the western side of the spit are collecting points for waterfowl in fall, winter, and spring and for migrating shorebirds in May and again in July to October (see **#22, #41,** and **#42**).

The northern portion of Sandy Hook is full of relics—old Nike missile pads, a heliport, a radar station, barracks, and the oldest operating lighthouse in America. The strategic military importance of the hook, which lies at the mouth of New York harbor, has been a major reason for its preservation, saving it from the development that has covered almost all of New Jersey's coast.

Remarks: *The best time to visit Sandy Hook is off-season. In summer it is jammed with people and cars. Fishing from the groins is especially good in the fall. In winter fires are allowed on the beach with a permit. If you are going to bird, stop at the tollbooth and ask for a pass. Other good birding spots are found around the radar-site parking area (***D***), around the old heliport (***E***), and north of the north beach parking area (***F***). From Memorial Day through Labor Day, a user fee is charged for ocean beach parking. The visitors' center has a great deal of written information on the hook and organizes visits to the holly forest. Nearest public camping is at Cheesequake State Park (see ***#2***). The hook is ideal for bicycling. In warm weather take plenty to drink and insect repellent. For further information contact Gateway National Recreation Area, Sandy Hook Unit, P.O. Box 437, Highlands, N.J. 07732, (201) 872-0115; visitors' center, (201) 872-0092.*

2.

Cheesequake
State Park

Directions: **Middlesex County, N.J. From New York City take the New Jersey Turnpike to Exit 11. Follow the Garden State Parkway south about 6 miles to Exit 120. Go to the end of the exit ramp and turn south (right) on Laurence Pkwy and go 0.2 mile. Turn west (right) on Cliffwood Ave. and go 0.3 mile to a T intersection. Turn north (right)**

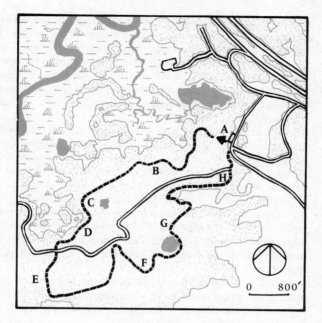

on Gordon Rd. and drive 0.3 mile to the park entrance on
the right. Drive in past the tollbooth to the Nature Trail
Parking Area (**A**).

Ownership: **New Jersey Division of Parks and Forestry.**

Dry, upland pitch-pine woods, rich mixed hardwood stands of large
American beeches, hickories, and oaks, freshwater marsh, salt marsh,
and white-cedar bogs lie mixed together on the rolling topography
of Cheesequake State Park. This surprising array of habitats sits on
the inner Coastal Plain just 30 miles from New York City. Here, the
pine-barrens vegetation of southern New Jersey mingles with the
deciduous forest of the northern part of the state.

The inner Coastal Plain, which stretches from the Raritan Bay to
the Delaware Bay, is made up of deposits of sand and clay laid down
70 to 160 million years ago during the Cretaceous period. The soils
that have developed from these deposits are generally much more
fertile than the younger, very sandy soils of the outer Coastal Plain.
This is principally due to the clay in the soil, which helps to hold

nutrients and moisture. Ever since the colonists first arrived, the inner Coastal Plain has been prized for agriculture, and the clay has been dug for making stoneware and bricks. More recently, though, the inner Coastal Plain has been turned into the major transportation zone of the state and the focus of heavy industrial development. Very little natural plant cover remains in the region. The woodlands at Cheesequake State Park hint at the former richness and variety of the inner Coastal Plain.

Begin at the parking area and walk along the Yellow Trail, a guided nature trail, which follows a stream lined with swamp azalea and skunk cabbage. Skunk cabbage is often the first plant to appear in the spring, pushing up through the snow and icy ground in February or March. The strong, unpleasant odor of skunk cabbage is apparently a lure to carrion flies, which act as pollinators, carrying the male pollen from one plant to the ovary of another (see #15 on pollination). On the right side of the trail is a dry ridge covered with white, red, black, and chestnut oaks. In spring, pink lady's slippers form a carpet across the ground in one of the largest displays in New Jersey.

After about 300 yards turn left along the Red Trail. At **B**, pitch pines become prominent in the canopy and the woods are similar to the pine-barrens forests to the south. The shrubs, which include several species of huckleberry, blueberry, sheep laurel, and mountain laurel, belong to the heath family. In the dry woodlands of the park, clumps of trailing arbutus come into flower in early spring. This is an evergreen woody vine with tiny white or pink, sweet-scented blossoms. It is pollinated by queen bumblebees, which fly from flower to flower to gather food for their brood. The queen bee is fertilized in the fall, hibernates over the winter, and lays her eggs in the spring. Until the first batch of worker bees hatch out, she is solely responsible for feeding her offspring.

Cross Perrine's Rd. and continue on the Green Trail. (If you turn right on Perrine's Rd., you will come to brackish marshes bordering Cheesequake Creek; see below.) At **C** a boardwalk passes over a section of freshwater marsh merging into wooded swamp. Running through the marsh is one of several streams that drain off the uplands surrounding Cheesequake Creek. At their highest these bluffs are about 160 feet above sea level. Because the region drained by the creek is small (only about 1000 acres), undeveloped, and cut off from the heavy industrial area to the west, it has remained relatively clean and unpolluted. The freshwater species along the boardwalk are dominated by cattail and cinnamon fern, with elderberry, buttonbush, and southern arrowwood around the edges. Jewelweed is also common. It is entwined with dodder, a parasitic yellowish vine that wraps itself around the host. Suckers penetrate the stem of the host and extract its sap.

Just beyond, the trail moves into a young white-cedar bog (**D**). Such bogs are common in the Pine Barrens (see **Pine Barrens**) but rare in the north. These trees are large, and though no borings have been done, they are probably about 50 years old. In the acid soil of the bog, highbush blueberry and swamp azalea fill the shrub layer, while sphagnum moss and a variety of sedges form the ground cover. Sweetbay magnolia, red maple, and blackgum grow among the cedars. Eventually they may replace the cedars as the dominant species, just as they have in some of the white-cedar bogs of the Pine Barrens.

After crossing Museum Rd., the trail rises onto higher ground and enters a stand of white pines mixed with a deciduous forest of white, red, scarlet, and black oaks, hickories, American beech, red maple, and black birch (**E**). The understory and shrub layer in this part of the park are completely different from other parts of the park. Instead of heath shrubs, you will find flowering dogwood, ironwood, sassafras, and persimmon in the understory, together with spicebush, witch-hazel, and serviceberry in the shrub layer. All of these species, common in the richer soils of the Piedmont to the west, indicate that better soils lie below. Gypsy moths have done significant damage to the oaks of the canopy in recent years, and as a result sassafras—an understory species that needs sunlight—has become much more abundant throughout the park. In the woods, watch and listen for ruffed grouse, a fairly common bird throughout much of the region. This pudgy-looking brown bird is more often heard than seen, exploding noisily into the air from under your feet. The male "drums" during the breeding season by standing on a log and rapidly beating his wings. He does so to establish his territory and to attract females.

The Green Trail now turns east. As it drops to cross the stream at **F** and **G**, it enters small floodplain habitat with sycamore, tuliptree, and river birch. River birch is a southern species whose range extends into southern New York and southwestern Connecticut. The distinctive flaking of the sycamore's outer bark is due to the fact that the bark cannot stretch as the tree grows.

Spring brings a variety of wildflowers to the park. At **H** masses of wild lily-of-the-valley carpet the forest floor, and star flowers are abundant just to the north of Museum Rd. Throughout the deciduous woods look for false solomon's seal, wood anemone, wild geranium, sessile bellwort, a variety of violets, and many others. These early flowers are called ephemerals because their flowering is short-lived. They must bloom before the leaves of the trees and shrubs have cast the forest floor into deep shade.

With the many types of habitat come many species of birds. Warblers are plentiful during migration, especially in the fall. Look for them throughout the park. All year long you can observe many of the more familiar species of woodland and forest edge, birds that are found throughout most of the region covered by the Mid-Atlantic volumes. Blue jays, crows, robins, starlings, cardinals, chickadees, and the other common species are of limited interest to most of us because we see them so often. They are species which have adapted well to life in the temperate zone, the cold winters and warm summers, by eating foods which are found all year long. They all have very broad tastes, eating mixtures of nuts, seeds, fruits, and insects. Some species consume snails, spiders, and worms as well. Crows and blue jays will eat almost anything. These species have also been able to adapt to human activities. Clearing land for agriculture or development destroys the original woodland habitat, but around the edges of fields and towns, hedgerows and shrubby thickets grow up, which provide new habitat for many species such as mockingbirds, catbirds, brown thrashers, and a variety of sparrows. Crows, blue jays, robins, and chickadees gather in gardens, town parks, and backyards. Crows are particularly interesting, for they can solve problems, remember, mimic human speech, and even learn to count to 3 or 4. Crows also develop complex social hierarchies within the flock.

Both the black-capped and the Carolina chickadee are found within the park, which lies at the intersection of their respective ranges. To the south you will find only the Carolina chickadee and to the north only the black-capped. The two are rarely found in the same territory, for their habitat and food source are identical. Where they do meet, they sometimes crossbreed. Although they look very similar, their voices are different. The Carolina chickadee gives a four-note whistle sounding like "fee-bee, fee-bay," instead of the two-note whistle of the black-capped species.

From the parking area at **A** drive to the parking area by Hooks Creek Lake. A trail leads out into the salt marsh here, a miniature version of Tuckerton (see **#21**) with salt-marsh cordgrass along the creek and salt-meadow cordgrass on the higher marsh. If you take a canoe up Hooks Creek toward the lake, you will see a transition from salt marsh to brackish marsh with big cordgrass, reed grass, American three-square, Olney three-square, narrow-leaved cattail, switch grass, marsh hibiscus, and other species. Because of the high quality of water in the creek, aquatic life flourishes. Eels, bluefish, and flounders come up the channel to spawn and feed. Fiddler and blue crabs make their home here, and in early summer diamondback terrapins crawl onto the banks to lay their eggs (see **#64**). Muskrat, red fox, gray fox, and long-tailed weasel also use the marsh. Your best chance to see both animals and birds is very early in the morning.

Remarks: *A circuit of the Red and Green trails may take about 1.5 hours. Walking is easy. Do not pick any wildflowers in the park, particularly the trailing arbutus, which is easily destroyed. Camping is available at the park all year. The park is open daily from 8:00 a.m. till dusk. Activities include swimming, crabbing in Hooks Creek in late summer and early fall, and fishing in the creek and in the lake (license required). Facilities for basketball and softball are available. Rowboats for rent in the town of Morgan along Route 35. For further information contact Cheesequake State Park, Matawan, N.J. 07747, (201) 566-2161.*

3.
Helmetta

Directions: **Middlesex County, N.J. From New York City take the New Jersey Turnpike south to Exit 8A, about 45 miles from the Lincoln Tunnel. Go east on Route 32 for 2.3 miles and turn north on Gatzmer Rd. Drive 0.3 mile and turn east (right) onto Lincoln Ave. This feeds into Helmetta Rd. Follow it 2 miles to Maple St. in Helmetta. Turn north (left). Canoes can be launched at the parking area by the lake, which is 0.1 mile up the road. Continue on 0.3 mile, turn left, and drive 0.3 mile to the dirt road running into the forest on the left.**

Ownership: **Jamesburg County Park, Middlesex County Commission.**

Well north of the Pine Barrens, in the midst of the fertile inner Coastal Plain, are scattered outliers of the sandy pitch-pine woods and acid cedar bogs. Helmetta is one of the few remaining examples, an island of Pine Barrens vegetation isolated by the extensive development of the area. Southern species like the carpenter frog and northern fence lizard continue to exist here, cut off from the rest of their species, but the Pine Barrens treefrog has not been reported at Helmetta in years. It is unclear what will happen to these and other Pine Barrens species in these islands without the genetic variety provided by a large population.

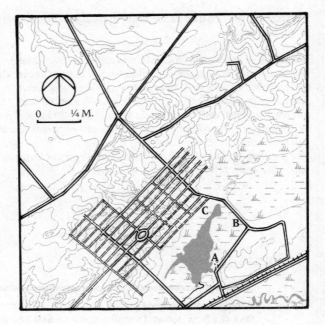

Although Helmetta lies in the inner Coastal Plain, an area of generally richer soils (see **#2**), the conditions here parallel those of the Pine Barrens (see **Pine Barrens**). On the high ground, just a few feet above the water of the bog, the soil is sandy and porous and supports a pitch-pine forest. The wetlands along the Manalapan River indicate a high water table, such as that which exists in the Pine Barrens.

From the first stop (**A**) you look out over a bog, ringed by dead and dying Atlantic white-cedars, with open water in the middle and floating mats of sphagnum moss. Blackgum is very common here, along with sweetgum, red maple, and some sweetbay magnolia, and represents the next stage of swamp forest, which is replacing the cedars. On the hummocks along the border of the open water are typical bog plants, including sundews, cranberry, and marsh St. Johnswort. Out on the hummocks, a variety of orchids have been found in the past, but their current status is uncertain. Slender-leaved ladies' tresses, yellow-fringed orchis, and white-fringed orchis have recently been reported in the area. Back in the pine woods (**C**) are pockets of wet, boggy soil where some orchids may persist. Look for floating plants on the surface of the water such as fragrant water

lily and various species of bladderworts, including purple bladderwort. (see **#17**).

From point **A** drive north along Maple St. 0.3 mile. Turn left and
follow the shore of the bog. Stop at **B.** Here there is a thick growth
of water willow, or swamp loosestrife, and Virginia chain fern. Water willow is one of the plants that is instrumental in turning open
water into bog by providing an increasingly stable substrate on which
vegetation can grow. Its tough branches grow out over the surface
of the water, and sphagnum moss then catches hold in the dense
network of the branches. Watch for poison sumac, which also grows
in this section of the bog.

A variety of amphibians breed in and around the wet areas of
Helmetta. The carpenter frog is at the extreme northern limit of its
range here. Its chorus, best heard at night, sounds like an army of
carpenters hammering away (see **#100**). Chorus frogs, spring peepers, and pickerel, green, and southern leopard frogs are all common
here, and Fowler's toads are particularly numerous (see **#90**). Chorus
frogs and spring peepers, both related to treefrogs, are heard much
more easily than seen. In this area they begin to sing with the first
warm rains in spring, from early to mid March, while farther south,
they sing during the cool rains of winter. The spring peeper is a small
brown or gray treefrog marked with a crude "X" on its back. It sings
from a perch in low bushes and trees by the water's edge. By exploring with a flashlight at night you may catch sight of its small
iridescent vocal sac, inflated like a balloon on its throat. In his *Field
Guide to Reptiles and Amphibians*, Roger Conant describes the treefrogs' distant chorus as the sound of sleigh bells. The chorus frog
does not climb very high, preferring a clump of grasses out in the
open marsh. Dr. Conant describes its call as something similar to
that produced by strumming the small teeth of a comb with your
fingernail, hitting the shortest teeth last to make the sound rise at
the end. The best time to hear these frogs is in the evening.

From **B** drive 0.2 mile and park (**C**). Walk in to the pine woods
to the left of the road. This is very similar to the woods of Lebanon
State Forest (see **#13**), with pitch pines forming the canopy and a
variety of shrubs of the heath family below. The northern fence
lizard, another southern species near the northern limit of its range,
still lives in these woods. It has the rough pointed scales typical of
the genus of spiny lizards. The male has a blue throat and bright
blue patches along its sides, while the female has horizontal stripes
down its back. Like most reptiles, the fence lizard basks on old
stumps and logs in sunny areas when it is cold and hides under logs
and rocks when it is too hot. When approached, it makes for the
nearest tree and climbs around to the side away from the intruder.

If you circle the tree, the lizard will dart around so that the trunk is once more between you and it. Its diet is primarily insects. Like other reptiles, it hibernates in winter.

In the dry pine woods, one can find pine warbler, rufous-sided towhee, ovenbird, scarlet tanager, and ruffed grouse. Around the lake, great blue heron, belted kingfisher, and swallows are common.

Going back to the car, drive 0.3 mile to Port Rd. Turn left. Continue along this road, which turns left sharply and becomes Washington Rd. On a May evening at about 7:30, the air over this road hums with whip-poor-wills, which breed here in great numbers. To return to Maple St., take the first left.

Remarks: *Nearest camping is at Cheesequake State Park. Other activities include fishing and boating on the lake. License required; no rentals nearby. Unfortunately, the shores of the lake are badly littered.*

4.

Assunpink Wildlife Management Area

Directions: **Monmouth and Mercer counties, N.J. From New York City take the New Jersey Turnpike to Exit 8, about 50 miles from the Lincoln Tunnel. Turn west on Route 33 and go 1.0 mile to the light in Hightstown. Bear left immediately on Route 539 south and drive 4.5 miles to Herbert Rd. Go east (left) 2.0 miles to Imlaystown Rd. Turn north (left) and drive 1.3 miles to the parking area on the shore of Lake Assunpink.**

Ownership: **New Jersey Division of Fish, Game, and Wildlife.**

This patchwork of man-made lakes, open fields, lowland forest, marsh, upland woods, and hedgerows lies midway between the Atlantic Ocean to the east and the Delaware River to the west, right in the middle of the state. Surrounded by farms, development, and highways, it is a magnet for birds of all sorts; 253 species, both rare and common, have been recorded here. Because each season brings different species, frequent visits throughout the year can be rewarding.

The first stop is the parking lot **(A)** by Lake Assunpink. From here you can scan the lake for an astonishing variety of waterfowl from March through April and again from late October through December. Diving ducks such as common mergansers, lesser scaups, and pintails flock here in large numbers. More ring-necked ducks have been seen here than anywhere else in the state. The common loon is frequently reported in May and again in October and November, while pied-billed, horned, and red-necked grebes are sighted annually. Each March and April, bands of whistling swans stop over on the lake on the way north. From May through August, black and Caspian terns, graceful birds that are rarely spotted this far from the coast, may be observed flying over the lake. A number of shorebirds stop to feed along the shore; pectoral sandpipers (April) and greater yellowlegs (April–May and August–October) are especially numerous. In autumn look for another coastal migrant, the merlin, a swift dark falcon that feeds heavily on small birds (see **#32**). The endangered peregrine falcon is also seen from time to time. Over the lake and the nearby fields, thousands of swallows hunt for insects from March through April and September through October. Most are tree swallows, their backs and wings a glistening green-blue, but purple

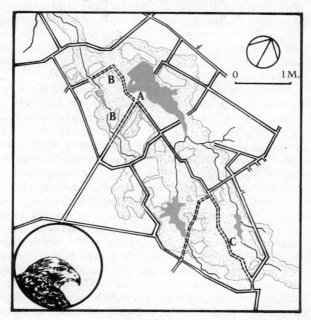

Inset: Red-tailed hawk

martins, and bank, barn, and rough-winged swallows are also common. Occasionally a cliff swallow may appear; it is uncommon because of its nesting requirements.

To the south and west of the lake are fields (**B**) administered by the Fish and Wildlife staff. Kept open for small-game hunting, these grassy areas provide nesting habitat for the grasshopper sparrow, a threatened species in New Jersey. The sparrow is named for its call, which sounds remarkably like the metallic clicking of a grasshopper. It also lives in the same habitat of dry open fields and relies on the insect as a major source of food. When flushed, the bird will fly a short way and drop once more into a clump of grass.

To the east of the parking lot are shrubby thickets used by nesting blue grosbeaks, orchard orioles, and yellow-breasted chats. The blue grosbeak is a southern bird which for reasons not well understood has become increasingly common in New Jersey. Look for it throughout the area in bushy hedgerows along roadsides. Listen for the melodious song of warbling vireos in the treetops near the parking area; it sounds something like "brigadier, brigadier, brigadier" repeated over and over.

Drive east from the parking lot to the office and turn north (left) toward the lake. This dirt road takes you out to the southeastern end of the lake. The marshes here, best explored by canoe, provide nesting grounds for king rails and wintering grounds for dabbling ducks (see **#64**). Along the shore is a lowland woods of blackgum, sweetgum, red maple, and tuliptree. Hooded and Kentucky warblers, both southern wetland species, nest in the undergrowth.

Continue east from the office and go straight at the crossroads beyond. The dirt road rises onto high ground. Stop here and walk around. The woods at **C** are very different from the lowland forest by the lake. You are now on a *cuesta*, an irregular ridge of land that runs from the Atlantic highlands just south of Sandy Hook southeasterly toward the Delaware Bay separating the inner and outer Coastal Plains. The cuesta exists because the Coastal Plain sediments here have been cemented together into ironstone, which is more resistant to erosion than the sediments to the east or the west. On this higher and drier ground black and white oaks and hickories are the main canopy species, while blackjack and scrub oak, huckleberry, and blueberry are the main shrubs. (For further discussion of the inner Coastal Plain, see **#2**.) By turning right at the crossroads, you will come to a woodland where a number of species nest, including the scarlet tanager, eastern wood pewee, black-and-white warbler, and ovenbird. The next right beyond the woods leads to Stone Tavern Lake, another collecting point for migrant waterfowl in early spring (March and April).

In winter a variety of birds of prey are seen throughout the area. Most common are the red-tailed hawk, American kestrel, and northern harrier. Rough-legged hawks down from the Arctic tundra are seen regularly each winter. At dusk look for short-eared, long-eared, and barn owls gliding over the fields. During the day look for great horned, long-eared, and saw-whet owls in the numerous evergreen plantings scattered through the area. Equipped with silent wings, good vision, and acute hearing, owls are great hunters. The long outer feather of the wing, the first primary, has a saw-toothed edge, which cuts the noise of the feather moving through the air. The central vane of the flight feathers tends to be downy, which also muffles sound. Their enormous eyes enable owls to see well at night. Several species including the short-eared owl hunt regularly in daylight. Owls have two ear openings, one on each side of the head. Each is surrounded by a deep layer of feathers, which can be spread open to catch sound and guide it to the ears. A number of owls are also fitted with a leathery flap of skin along the front edge of the ear opening, which when erect catches sound coming from behind the bird. In many species the size and configuration of the ear openings are asymmetrical. This enables the owl to pinpoint the direction and distance of the sound's origin. All owls have concave facial discs surrounding the eyes. Shaped like radar receivers, they too help focus sound. But the long feathery tufts of the great horned and long-eared owls have nothing to do with their ability to hear.

When hunting for owls in the daytime, look for the white stains of droppings and for pellets at the base of the evergreens. Owls tend to roost close to the trunk of the tree. Their streaked and mottled plumage and motionless pose helps them blend into the bark.

Remarks: *Nearest camping is at Allaire State Park due east near the Garden State Parkway. Activities include fishing in the four lakes; license required. Remember that there is hunting here in fall except on Sundays. Along Herbert Rd. are Reed's sod farms. The open flat fields attract a number of rare shorebirds during migration: the upland sandpiper in July and August, and the buff-breasted sandpiper and golden plover in September and October. The short grass and plowed fields lure flocks of horned larks from fall to spring. A spotting scope is useful for scanning the lake.*

5.

Trenton Marsh

Directions: **Mercer County, N.J. From New York City take Route 1 south into Trenton, where it becomes the Trenton Freeway. Exit at Route 206 (S. Broad St.) south and travel for about 1.5 miles to Sewell Ave. (in the 1800 block, 1 block past Holy Angels Church). Turn right and go to the end of the paved road. Turn left on the dirt road and park in the large parking area at the marsh.**

Ownership: **Roebling Memorial Park, Mercer County Park Commission.**

Alongside the Delaware River, just south of Trenton and right at the inner edge of the Coastal Plain, lies one of the largest and most diverse freshwater marshes in central New Jersey. Similar to the larger Tinicum Marsh in Philadelphia (see **#9**), Trenton Marsh consists of over 300 acres of swamps, tidal marshes, shallow ponds, and creeks. This is the northern limit of the tides. To the north, the river must cut its way through the harder rocks of the Piedmont. Here it can spread out across the gentler contours of the Coastal Plain. The current slows and sediments collect in the shallows, encouraging the development of the marshes (see **Chesapeake Bay**). Trenton Marsh has long been a popular area among birders. The principal attraction is a wide variety of marshbirds. The wooded areas harbor many migrant and resident landbirds.

From the parking area, walk along the causeway toward the woods. The cattail marsh on the right (**A**) attracts common snipes, common gallinules, and sora, Virginia, and king rails. The last four species nest at Trenton Marsh and are best seen from late April through June. The snipe is a migrant most often observed in March and April. Though the secretive rails are maddeningly difficult to glimpse, the best way to lure them into the open is to play a recording of their calls at dawn (see **#67**). The shallow pond to the left of the causeway (**B**) draws waterfowl and pied-billed grebes in early spring. The marsh plants are similar to those at Tinicum and supply a variety of foods to birds. Principal species include broad-leaved and narrow-leaved cattails, bur-marigolds, smartweeds, common arrowheads, and wild rice. Buttonbush and alder are the most common shrubs.

As one enters the woodland at the far end of the causeway, two

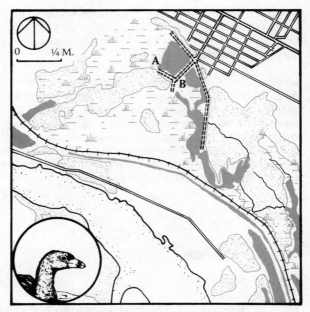

Inset: Pied-billed grebe

trails begin. The trail to the right travels through a swamp dominated by pin oak, silver and red maples, river birch, arrowwood, and spicebush. Migrant warblers, vireos, and thrushes are commonly seen here from late April through May. The trail to the left leads to another pond frequented by least and American bitterns. The soft cooing of the least bittern reminds one of the song of the black-billed cuckoo. But the voice of the American bittern is unlike that of any other North American bird. It takes air into its esophagus and emits it in groups of three syllables, producing a hollow, booming sound that can carry for over a half mile (see **#67**).

After about 150 yards this trail intersects a crossdike. Turn right here and look for willow flycatcher, marsh wren (long-billed), yellow warbler, common yellowthroat, and swamp sparrow, all of which are common nesters here (May to July). Other interesting birds that can be seen here and elsewhere in Trenton Marsh include wood duck, greater and lesser yellowlegs, northern harrier, osprey, belted kingfisher, eastern kingbird, and rusty blackbird. The rusty blackbird is one of the first spring migrants, arriving when the spring peepers begin to call sometime in late February or March. The birds stop to feed on aquatic animals along pond edges before continuing north to Canada and northern New England. Wood ducks prefer to nest in wooded swamps and are often difficult to observe. This is not true here, for the dike provides a good view of the area. Bald eagles are also occasionally seen.

Remarks: *Another area to check for migrants and resident land birds is the picnic area in Roebling Memorial Park (see map). To get there drive straight ahead for 0.7 mile from the central parking area. The deciduous woods and shrubby areas here can be explored via several paths. Carolina wrens, northern orioles, and scarlet tanagers are just a few of the birds often observed here. Fishing and picnicking are permitted in the area but camping is prohibited. Camping is available at Timberlake Campground, 6 miles south of Allentown, N.J., on Route 539.*

6.
The North Shore
Ponds and Inlets

Directions: **Monmouth County, N.J. From New York City take the New Jersey Turnpike south to Exit 11 and the Garden State Parkway to Exit 98, about 55 miles in all. Go south on Route 34 (which becomes Route 35 south) across the Manasquan River, about 6.4 miles. Turn left after the bridge toward the ocean. It is 7.3 miles to the beach. Manasquan Inlet is on the left.**

Ownership: **Various.**

The barrier islands that lie along the Jersey coast vanish north of the Manasquan Inlet. From there to Sea Bright, where the long spit of Sandy Hook begins, the sea strikes upon the mainland. Along this part of the shore are the Atlantic highlands. As they erode, the longshore currents carry sand north into the basin of New York Harbor, where it forms Sandy Hook (see #1) and south to the barrier islands that hug the shore (see #25). When the seacoast lay far to the east thousands of years ago, barrier islands may have existed all along the New Jersey shore, but as the seas rose and the shore retreated westward, the coastline changed shape and gradually the islands along this stretch of New Jersey disappeared. All along this section of coast are a series of freshwater ponds, often just a few feet from the sea. They are magnets for an array of waterfowl from fall to spring.

Manasquan Inlet is the first stop. Gulls collect in the sheltered waters on the inlet. Small numbers of glaucous and Iceland gulls arrive each winter at Manasquan, Shark River Inlet to the north, and scattered locations along the shore (see **#22**). The lesser black-backed gull, a European species seen in increasing numbers along the Atlantic Coast, is sighted from time to time. Mixed in with the flocks of the tern-like Bonaparte's gulls are little and black-headed gulls, a few of which are found off the northern Atlantic Coast each year. The best time to look for them is in late winter to early spring.

From November through April, Manasquan Inlet is a good place to see sea ducks—all three scoters, oldsquaws, and red-breasted mergansers—also common and red-throated loons and horned grebes. From October through April, gannets and black-legged kittiwakes are seen here.

All along the New Jersey coast, stone jetties or groins form a fringe along the beaches. These groins, built to trap sand and to protect the beaches, have instead contributed to their erosion (see **Cape May** and **#1**). Mollusks cling to the rocks of the pier and attract a variety of sea ducks during the winter months. Immature king and common eiders are regularly seen in small numbers all along the coast; most adults winter farther north. The plumage of the male king eider is arresting: its back is black and its chest snowy white, with a soft gray cap on its head, a startling orange bill, and a face patch edged in black. The common eider is the only duck in these regions with a white back and black belly. It has a very long sloping bill. These birds are known for their thick layers of down feathers. With this insulation they are able to survive temperatures down to $-70°F$ along the Arctic coasts. The eider dives deep for marine food; king eiders have been recorded at depths of 150 feet. Mollusks, sea ur-chins, starfish, sea cucumbers, and other animal life are the staples of their diet. Blue mussels clinging to the rocks of the stone piers are a particular favorite. An eider can swallow a mussel whole, breaking it apart with the grinding action of its gizzard. All birds have gizzards, which serve in place of teeth to break up their food. Many species eat sand or gravel in order to provide the grindstone for the gizzard. The muscular contractions of this organ then macerate the food so that it can be digested more readily.

Another rare species is the harlequin duck. The male boasts a beautiful combination of steel-blue back, chestnut flanks, white face, and varied white markings on the back of its head. The harlequin nests across the north of Canada from Labrador west to Alaska and Asia, living by the side of mountain streams. Wintering along the coast, it hunts for crustaceans among the rocks.

From Manasquan Inlet drive west on Broadway to Route 35 and turn north (right). Go 0.7 mile to Route 71 and turn north (right). Drive 1.5 miles to Washington Blvd. in Sea Girt. Turn east (right) at the light. After 0.5 mile the road curves left past a grove of American holly trees. Washington Blvd. becomes First Ave. Turn east (right) after 3 blocks on New York Ave. and drive to the ocean.

As you patrol the winter beaches, look for gannets diving into the sea just offshore. Nesting in the rocky cliffs along the North Atlantic, the gannet is the pelagic or oceanic species most often seen from shore, especially from the Manasquan and Shark River inlets (see **#54**). The adult gannet is a large white bird with black wingtips and a long bluish bill. In flight it looks pointed at head and tail, which distinguishes it from gulls and other sea birds. It generally flies with its bill pointing downward. When the gannet spots a fish, it plummets out of the sky at speeds of around 60 feet per second. Underwater, it grabs the fish on the way up, rather than spearing it or scooping it up from above like other species. The neck and breast of the gannet are lined with special tissue that automatically fills with air before it dives to cushion the bird's body on impact. The very heavy bill and skull also protect the bird from the repeated shocks. Another adaptation is closed nostrils. Instead, the gannet has openings along the side of its mouth. These are fitted with horny lids which automatically close when the bird is diving. (Cormorants, which are also diving birds, are similarly equipped.) Gannets, like many other white birds such as gulls, storks, and snow geese, have dark wingtips. The dark pigment contained in these feathers makes them stronger and more durable than the white ones.

In winter, purple sandpipers search the rocks of the groins, hunting for small mollusks and crustaceans. Dunlin sanderlings and black-bellied plovers are the only other shorebirds usually seen here in winter. As a general rule birds of northern climates are larger than their counterparts from warmer habitats. In the cold, their greater mass helps them conserve heat. The purple sandpiper is much larger than the least sandpiper, for example. All three species of scoters are common winter visitors along the Jersey coast. They are all dark sea ducks and can be seen flying in shaggy lines up and down the coast.

Return to First Ave., turn north (right), and then left at "Ridge-wood House" just before the bridge. This dirt road follows the south side of Wreck Pond. Make a circuit of the pond by turning right on Beacon Rd., then right on 7th St., right on Shore Rd., and right again on Ocean Rd. Turn left on Union Ave., proceed to Ocean Ave., and turn left. Wreck Pond and the other ponds along this stretch of the shore attract both diving and dabbling ducks (see **#64**). On any given day in winter you may see an interesting mixture of species. Some of the more uncommon ones include bufflehead, red-breasted merganser, greater scaup, ruddy duck, gadwall, and American wigeon. The first four species are diving ducks; the red-breasted mergansers are particularly adapted to fishing and swimming underwater. Mergansers have long, slender bills with serrated edges which enable them to grasp and hold onto slippery fish. Although close to the sea, the ponds stay fresh. Salt water is denser and heavier than fresh and will tend to sink to the bottom, while fresh water floats on top.

Continuing north on Ocean Ave., you can stop frequently to look for seagoing species. After 1.7 miles, Lake Como appears on the west. From there to the Shark River Inlet is 1.4 miles. This inlet, edged with rocks, has sometimes harbored alcids and harlequin ducks. Alcids are small pelagic birds, generally seen out on the open sea. From time to time they are blown in to shore by storms (see **#54**).

Another excellent spot for birding is the marina on the Shark River estuary. To reach it drive south again to 5th Ave., and turn right along the shores of Silver Lake. Bear left on N. Lake Dr. 0.5 mile to 8th Ave., turn right on 8th Ave., and cross Route 35 to the marina. During recent years one male Barrow's goldeneye has passed the winter here. This bird looks very much like the common goldeneye, a large duck with white sides and a dark back, a conspicuous golden iris, and a white patch on the face. The common goldeneye has a glossy green head; the Barrow's has a purple cast to its head and more black on its back. The Barrow's goldeneye, more common along the New England coast, breeds in Iceland and western North America.

A favorite place for waterfowl is a small cove at the end of Marconi Rd. To reach it drive south on Route 35 for 0.8 mile and go right on Belmar Blvd. Go 0.4 mile to Marconi Rd. Turn right and drive to the water. This spot is known as a haunt of the Eurasian wigeon. It is usually found along with American wigeon on fresh and brackish marshes and lakes. These two dabbling ducks are similar in appearance. The male American wigeon has a gray-brown head with a broad green patch, a gleaming white forehead, and rusty sides. The male of the Eurasian species has a buff-colored forehead, a chestnut brown head, and gray sides. The females of all species of duck are much drabber than the males and are therefore more difficult to distinguish.

To reach the Garden State Parkway return to Belmar Blvd. Continue straight across Belmar Blvd. and go 0.2 mile to Route 38. Turn west (right), and go 2.7 miles to the parkway.

Remarks: *There are a number of other lakes all along the coast both to the south of Manasquan Inlet and to the north in Avon, Asbury Park, and Long Branch. Ocean Ave. will lead you to them. Camping at Allaire State Park just west of Exit 98. A spotting scope will be useful at Shark River and the pier at Barnegat.*

7.
Island Beach
State Park

Directions: **Ocean County, N.J. From New York City take the New Jersey Turnpike south to Exit 11 and the Garden State Parkway south to Exit 82, about 70 miles in all. Go east on Route 37 for 6.7 miles. Then turn south on Route 35 for 2.7 miles to the park entrance. Park at any designated area within the park.**

Ownership: **New Jersey Division of Parks and Forestry.**

The close-packed development of the Jersey shore stops abruptly at the entrance to Island Beach State Park, and for 10 miles this is a wild beach, a place without jetties, houses, or concrete retaining walls. Here the forces of tide and wind and wave still shape and reshape the shore both daily and seasonally. If left to themselves, beaches are always in flux. Many of the changes are subtle, occurring over long periods of time, but on many beaches a dramatic shift occurs each year. In summer, Island Beach is a wide, gently sloping strand. This gives way to a short, steep beach of coarse sand as winter storms pound the shore. On a cold February day, when the wind shrieks in from the northeast, hurling up clouds of sand, and the waves shatter against the beach, this change seems to be happening before one's eyes. It is hard to believe that the cold, bitter wind that drives the waves and the sand is a manifestation of the sun's energy striking the earth.

The waves that shape Island Beach in winter are born in storms out at sea, sometimes thousands of miles away. Storms form when two air masses of different temperatures, pressures, and humidities converge. Air masses and the winds that drive them are created by the unequal heating of the earth by the sun. Because the earth is round and rotates on a tilted axis as it revolves around the sun, the sun strikes different parts of the globe at varying angles and for varying periods each day. There are seasonal variations too. We know that in winter the tilt of the earth keeps the sun low on our southern sky, while in summer the sun rises much higher. Vast global patterns of circulating air are created as heated air rises up at the equator and flows north and south toward the poles, there cooling and sinking back to earth. As the cold air over the poles sinks, it flows back toward the equator. This circulation of warm and cold air accounts for the prevailing winds that move across the earth's surface. These winds would move in straight lines north to south and south to north if the earth did not rotate as it orbits the sun; but the spinning of the earth causes the winds to arc, moving the air in large circles. This is called the Coriolis effect, and it influences tides and currents as well as winds. In the Northern Hemisphere the prevailing winds are the polar easterlies (meaning they blow from the east), the mid-latitude westerlies that drive across the continental United States, and the northeast trade winds just north of the equator. These winds account for the major movements of air masses across the Northern Hemisphere, accounting for much of our weather.

This apparently simple pattern of movement is distorted and confused by an infinite number of local variations. The disparate surfaces of the oceans and the continents absorb and radiate heat at very different rates, and mountain ranges play havoc with the orderly movement of the winds. The ocean breeze on a sunny summer afternoon at any beach along the Atlantic is one example. The land heats up more quickly than the ocean, so that by 10:00 or 11:00 a.m., the warmed air above it is rising, creating a low-pressure zone. Cooler, heavier air over the ocean pushes in to replace the rising air, producing a welcome onshore breeze. At night the opposite cycle occurs, with warmer air rising above the sea and cooler air from the land flowing offshore.

Air masses are vast pools of air that have acquired more or less uniform temperatures and humidities characteristic of the land or the ocean over which they lie. Once formed, an air mass moves as a body. In the northeastern United States, weather is largely determined by the movements of three air masses: a dry continental polar air mass that forms over Canada, a moist polar air mass that forms over the North Atlantic, and a very wet air mass that begins in the subtropics and moves north. Generally, these air masses are high-pressure systems. Air is moving out from the center of the mass into zones of lower pressure. Because of the Coriolis effect, high-pressure systems in our hemisphere spin in a clockwise direction. The air mass is like a vast spinning wheel throwing off streams of air. Thus, when two air masses begin to approach each other, a zone of insta-bility arises where the winds of each system swirl against each other. An irregularity or bubble in the pattern can occur and a pocket of air begins to move counterclockwise, forming a low-pressure system. It is the beginning of a storm.

The greater the difference in temperature between one air mass and another, the more turbulent will be their meeting. In winter when the Arctic region is locked under snow and ice, the tempera-ture difference between polar and tropical air masses is at its greatest. This accounts for the frequent storms of the season, including the destructive northeasters that pound the Mid-Atlantic shore each winter. The center of the low-pressure system is to the south and east of us. We are thus in the northern portion of the storm, where the coun-terclockwise circulation brings winds from the northeast.

How ocean waves begin is not fully understood, but the changes in pressure as wind moves over the water play some part. Once the wave is formed, the wind pushes against it, imparting its energy to it. Three factors determine the size of the waves that hit the coast: the velocity of the wind, the distance the wave travels, and the depth of the water.

A wave is a pulse of energy passing through the water. The mol-ecules of water and anything floating in the water or on the surface essentially do not change position as the wave passes. A gull or duck floating on the sea, for example, will rise and fall with each passing wave and end up in the same place. The wave moves through the water in a series of circles. The circles are largest at the top of the wave, becoming smaller and more elliptical at the bottom of the wave. Although the visible portion of the wave may only be a few feet on the open ocean, the pulse of energy may be moving at a depth of 30 feet or more below the surface. As the wave begins to strike the shallow bottom close to shore, friction slows the forward motion and the wave begins to rear up out of the water and grows a sharp crest. Then movement at the bottom of the pulse slows, while the top of the wave continues forward even faster. As the water grows shallower, the wave grows higher and steeper, and the bottom of the wave moves more and more slowly, until the lower portion of the wave can no longer support the crest. When the depth of the water is about 1.3 times the height of the wave, the wave breaks, releasing all the pent-up energy of the storm wind at once. In winter the wave breaks first on an outer sandbar, re-forms, and breaks again on the beach. The beach, made up of billions of sand grains each separated by a tiny air space, acts as a cushion to absorb the immense, incessant pounding of the surf. The energy of waves breaking on the shore is vast, measured in tons per square foot. With the breaking of the wave, the molecules of water move forward for the first time, rather than in a circular motion. The swash, as it is called, sweeps over the surface of the water and up onto the beach, carrying sand and debris with it.

The size of the waves and frequency with which they break on the shore are factors that vary seasonally and create the seasonal differences in the beach. In summer, when storms at sea are less frequent, the waves that strike the shore are generally spaced far apart and are moderate in height. Coarse, heavy particles settle at the line of the breaking waves, while finer sand is carried up the beach by the swash. In the long interval between waves, much of the swash sinks into the face of the beach. The remaining water moves back down the beach, but the flow is reduced by friction against the sand. This means that more sand is deposited on the surface of the beach than is carried away, with the result that the beach becomes wider and wider.

In fall and winter, heavier storms cause waves that hit the coast more strongly and more frequently. If the height of the storm coincides with high tide, the waves will be especially powerful. The rapid sequence of the waves tends to saturate the lower face of the beach so that the swash carries suspended sand up the beach and deposits it on a ridge called the berm. (Summer beaches can have a berm too, which is often so gentle as to be imperceptible.) The backwash, which is heavier in winter, sweeps back down the face of the beach, carrying finer sand with it. Thus, while the top of the berm is built up, the face of the beach is cut back. The finer sand is swept out as far as the line of breaking waves and forms a sandbar. This bar helps protect the shore from the full force of the winter seas. After a heavy storm, the beach is often shaped into a series of small headlands and embayments called *cusps*. The higher areas that project into the sea are made up of coarser sands. No one understands how these shapes form, but they are associated with storms.

The backdune vegetation of Island Beach is typical of barrier islands (see **#55**) and includes holly, bayberry, redcedar, poison ivy, winged sumac, and catbrier, all of which provide abundant food and shelter for migrating songbirds in early fall. Warblers and a selection of uncommon sparrows are seen here every year, including the lark sparrow, the clay-colored sparrow, the vesper sparrow, and, in winter, the Ipswich race of the savannah sparrow. Winter birding is also excellent. Gannets dive offshore (see **#6**), and scoters and oldsquaws fly up the ocean edge, using the troughs of the waves as flyways. Other diving ducks feed at the Barnegat Inlet at the southern tip of Island Beach; there, king and common eider and harlequin duck dive for mollusks clinging to the rocks of the jetties, while purple sandpipers skitter among the stones. The Barnegat jetty, on the south side of the inlet, is a well-known spot for eider and harlequin duck in the winter (see **#6**).

Remarks: *The bay side of Island Beach is a sanctuary and is closed to the public. Birding for migrating songbirds can be done from the road. To reach the inlet, either walk south along the beach or drive to the last parking area and walk 1½ miles along the ORV access road. Walking can be very tiring because of the soft sand. Other activities include surf fishing from the beach and jetties; bluefish and striped bass are the specialities. Nature walks into the restricted areas are held spring through fall. In summer no reservation is required. Spring and fall trips are largely for school groups and must be set up in advance. New Jersey Audubon makes regular trips to the area. Their address and telephone number: P.O. Box 693, Bernardsville, N.J. 07924, (201) 766-5787. For further information contact Island Beach State Park, Seaside Park, N.J. 08752, (201) 793-0506. A spotting scope is useful for seeing ducks out on the ocean.*

8.
Manahawkin Swamp

Directions: **Ocean County, N.J. From New York City drive south on the New Jersey Turnpike to Exit 11 and take the Garden State Parkway to Exit 63, about 90 miles in all. Go east on Route 72 about 1.5 miles to Route 9 north and turn left. One block past the traffic light, turn east (right) on Stafford Ave. Go 1 mile to Hillard Rd. and turn south (right). Drive about 1 mile and park.**

Ownership: **Manahawkin Wildlife Management Area, New Jersey Division of Fish, Game, and Wildlife.**

The woods to your left (**A**) are a National Natural Landmark typifying the bottomland forest that once covered lowlands of the outer Coastal Plain in New Jersey. The main species here are sweetgum and red maple, with blackgum and some white oaks. The biggest trees are 3 feet in diameter and well over 100 years old. Beneath the canopy the main shrubs are sweet pepperbush, highbush blueberry, and a scattering of other species including large black alder or winterberry, fetterbush, and sassafras. Cinnamon fern and sphagnum moss cover the ground. All the vegetation here is adapted to wet ground. There is little evidence of disturbance, no stumps or logging trash and few windfalls; these woods are apparently a natural, undisturbed stand. Hurricane damage many years ago might account for the absence of very old, large trees.

Several unusual species of birds are found in the woods and at the marsh edge (**B**). The tall deciduous trees of the bottomland forest are ringed by mature pitch pine and mixed oaks, providing a habitat that is increasingly rare in New Jersey. Hooded and prothonotary warblers nest here, along with Acadian flycatchers. The Acadian flycatcher is a small, greenish bird with a white throat. It is a southern species that has recently expanded its range to New Jersey. Small flycatchers are often very difficult to tell apart except by song. The Acadian flycatcher has an emphatic two-note call "ka zeep" with the second note higher than the first. It builds a small hanging nest suspended in the fork of a tree. From mid-May to early June, olive-

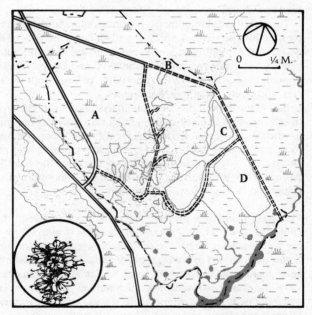

Inset: Sweet pepperbush

sided flycatchers frequent the wood margins. Whip-poor-wills are are abundant in the pine-oak woods bordering Stafford Ave., and you can hear them calling at night in May and June. Listen also for the chuck-will's-widow, a close relative of the whip-poor-will, which is extending its range north into this area (see **#11**).

From the intersection of Stafford Ave. and Hillard Rd. drive east 1.5 miles. The brushy edge of the marsh and the woods (**B**) is where you are likely to see migratory olive-sided flycatchers in late spring as well as nesting prothonotary warblers. A dull, dark olive green, with a white "zipper" down the middle of its breast, the olive-sided flycatcher at rest is extremely difficult to spot, for it sits motionless in the tops of the trees. The clear, whistling call sounds something like "drink three beers" or "hip-three cheers." Look for it chasing insects at the forest edge. To find the prothonotary warbler, watch for a flash of brilliant yellow-orange darting through the shrubbery (see **#53**). This southern warbler is close to the northern limit of its range here. Short-billed marsh wrens have been recorded here from time to time. This bird has become increasingly rare in its former breeding range along the Atlantic Coast.

A series of seasonal freshwater pools, maintained by the Division of Fish, Game, and Wildlife, is one of the best places in New Jersey to see least bitterns. The pools also attract herons and egrets, waterfowl and shorebirds.

To reach the impoundments continue on Stafford Ave. 1 mile and park beside the road. A series of trails follows the tops of the dikes between the impoundments. Rare species are sometimes found, especially in the first two impoundments (**C** and **D**): you may be lucky enough to see cinnamon teal and white pelican, both western species, and white ibis, a southern species.

East of the impoundments a salt marsh takes over. The broad plain of salt-meadow and salt-marsh cordgrasses provides nesting habitat for the tiny black rail (see **#65**). Like the whip-poor-will, this bird is more easily heard than seen on warm, calm nights in May and June. During the day, northern harriers swing over the marsh in low patrols, while in summer ospreys fish in the impoundments. Winter brings rough-legged hawks down from the Arctic.

Remarks: *Camping is available at Bass River State Forest. Mosquitoes, biting flies, and ticks are abundant in the warm weather. Spring and fall are the best seasons. Trails atop the dikes are overgrown. Activities include fishing and crabbing in Barnegat and Manahawkin bays. Boat rentals can be arranged at the marina in Barnegat on East Bay Ave. and along Route 72 on the eastern and western shores of the bay. The bays are large, and winds can make the water very rough. It is also easy to be stranded by low tide in the shallow marsh creeks. The marsh creeks are excellent for canoe-*

ing. Barnegat National Wildlife Refuge lies to the north and to the south. The best way to explore it is by boat. For further information contact the NWR manager at P.O. Box 544, 686 E. Bay Ave., Barnegat, N.J. 08005, (609) 698-1387. The largest pitch pine on record in the state of New Jersey is located on Hillard Rd., just west of Route 9. This tall, large-crowned tree is 8 feet in circumference.

9.

Tinicum National
Environmental Center

Directions: **City of Philadelphia, Pa. From the intersection of I-95 with I-76 drive south on I-95 about 5 miles. Go north on Island Ave. about 0.5 mile to Bartram Ave. and turn west (left). Go 0.3 mile to 84th St. and turn north (right). Go 0.7 mile to Lindbergh Blvd. and turn west (left). Go 0.2 mile to the entrance on your right. This area has been under construction for several years and detours are par for the course.**

Ownership: **U.S. Fish and Wildlife Service.**

Lying within the city limits of Philadelphia at the very edge of the Piedmont Province is the Tinicum National Environmental Center, 1200 acres of freshwater marsh, tidal creek, old fields, and second-growth forest. At its eastern edge is a shallow impoundment where thousands of ducks gather in the fall and winter; each summer, herons and egrets nest in a rookery at the southern end; flights of migrating warblers throng the thickets and woods around its rim. Two hundred and eighty-eight species have been recorded here. The wetlands at Tinicum are an island of green along a heavily developed portion of the Delaware River, one of the main passageways for birds moving up and down the Atlantic flyway (see **Chesapeake Bay**). Once part of extensive wild-rice marshes lining the tidal rivers of the Atlantic Coast, the impoundment at Tinicum is now sealed off from tidal fluctuations by a dike that separates it from the Darby Creek and the Delaware River. Diking of the marshes in this region began with the Dutch in the seventeenth century, but the main dike which encircles the impoundment was constructed in the 1930s.

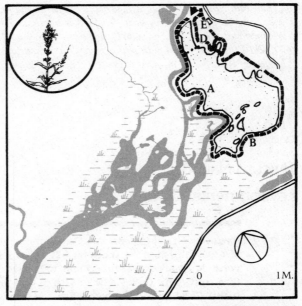

Inset: Purple loosestrife

A foot trail begins by the parking lot and runs around the impoundment. Vegetation within the impoundment consists mostly of floating and emergent plants. Submerged vegetation is minimal due to a large population of carp. By roiling up the mud along the bottom, these fish deprive the plants of light. The tiny green leaves of duckweed, so called because of its value as a wildlife food, cover much of the surface of the water. Duckweed has long, straight slender roots, which dangle, acting as stabilizers to keep the leaves upright. Around the edges of the water are many emergent species including spatterdock, pickerelweed, bur reed, cattails, and creeping willow primrose, as well as several species of sedges and rushes (see **#34**). A large colony of purple loosestrife—a European import—is threatening to take over from the other emergent species. Like many other alien plants, it is so aggressive that it often chokes out native species. Its woody stalks shade the earth below so that other plants cannot sprout. All these plants are a rich source of food for the ducks that glide into the marshes each autumn. Most species of dabbling ducks and diving ducks are seen here (see **#64**), including the less common redhead, canvasback, and ring-necked duck. Among the rafts of green-winged teal, look for the European race of the species, distinguished by a white stripe along its flank. The tower at **A** is an excellent vantage point for observing waterfowl.

In late summer, the impoundment shrinks, exposing wide flats of mud. Knots of migrating shorebirds gather to feed here in April and May and from July through September. Although some coastal species like the marbled godwit and ruddy turnstone are rarely if ever seen, a wide variety of coastal and inland shorebirds find their way here. Some of the rare birds regularly sighted at Tinicum are the ruff, both the Wilson's and northern phalaropes, solitary sandpiper, and American golden plover; keep in mind, however, that these birds are not seen every year.

In summer, tall stands of cattail hide the nests of Virginia and king rails and their close relative the sora (see **#67**). Common gallinules and American coots also nest in the reeds. Gallinules and coots are both related to rails, but whereas rails are extremely secretive, these birds are readily found on the open water. They are good swimmers and look somewhat alike: both are dark birds with small heads and shields of horny material on their foreheads. The common gallinule has a bright red shield, the American coot a whitish one.

The heron rookery at the end of the impoundment (**B**) is one of the few in the area. It is used by great blue herons, black-crowned night herons, great egrets, and snowy egrets (see **#28**). Green herons also nest here, but are generally not colonial nesters, preferring woodlands, reeds, and grasses.

The warm shallow waters of the impoundment support a thriving turtle population. Red-bellied and painted turtles are apt to be seen basking in the sun. The red-bellied is listed as endangered in Pennsylvania, and this is one of the few places where it is easily spotted. Neither of these is overly shy and you should be able to get quite close to them. Snapping turtles also live in the impoundment (see **#100**). Their bite can be extremely painful. Box turtles are the most familiar to us, as they are more apt to be found on land, though they spend much of their time soaking in water or mud. Their name comes from their ability to fit the hinged bottom of their shell tightly against the upper shell to make a virtually impenetrable seal, an efficient defense against predators.

Along the eastern edge of the impoundment there are old fields (**C**). Look for sparrows in the meadows and bordering thickets. Savannah and vesper sparrows are casual visitors, while chipping and white-throated sparrows are quite common. During the summer the fields are full of blackberry, milkweed, bindweed, bladder campion, aster, New York ironweed, common mullein, ragweed, yarrow, Queen Anne's lace, and other perennials typical of the old-field stage of succession (see **Introduction**). This area is being kept at this stage by the managers in order to maintain habitat diversity.

Butterflies are attracted to the flowering plants, and, like bees, they have a special relationship with them. While probing for nectar, the sweet liquid which is apparently produced by the plant only to attract insects, the butterflies become covered with a dusting of male pollen and carry it to the female ovaries of the next flower they visit. As with bees, different species of butterflies become associated with different plants, which ensures that pollen will not be wasted on the wrong flower. Twenty-five species have been photographed at the refuge. Those more commonly seen include the red admiral, painted lady, red-spotted purple, viceroy, aphrodite fritillary, and monarch.

The wet thickets and young trees at **D** by the end of the boardwalk are becoming a lowland forest. The thick viburnums offer excellent cover for wildlife, and a variety of berries provide food. Fox and white-crowned sparrows frequent this area from autumn to spring, and the willow and alder flycatchers are present in summer. Spring and fall warbler migrations are exciting at Tinicum and this is a favorite spot for a number of species. Farther on at **E** the thickets give way to a young lowland forest of red maple, sweetgum, green ash, white ash, and blackgum, with an understory of sassafras, flowering dogwood, and staghorn sumac.

The orchard oriole, a southern species of the forest edge, and the warbling vireo, which is uncommon due to its preference for mature forests, nest in the woods at Tinicum. Both the yellow-billed and rarer black-billed cuckoos nest in the woods as well, their numbers varying from year to year in tune with the populations of caterpillars on which they feed. Cuckoos are skulkers, keeping to the deep shade and dense shrubs. Migratory warblers, flycatchers, and vireos pass through the woods; even the uncommon yellow-bellied flycatcher is occasionally seen each fall.

Loggerhead shrikes are rare visitors at Tinicum, most often seen perching on telephone wires and bush tops. The bird is about the size of a robin, with a gray back, black wings, a black mask, and white throat. It has the unique habit of impaling its prey on a thorn or sharp branch. The principal range of the shrike is to the west and to the south of Tinicum. Each winter a few birds appear along the Mid-Atlantic coast from Delaware to Connecticut. The birds apparently come south from the region of the St. Lawrence River. Once the loggerhead bred in New England and along the coast but has since disappeared from the region. Today, even in the south, its numbers are falling rapidly.

Remarks: *The walk around the entire impoundment is 3½ miles. For a shorter trail, you can cross the impoundment at the boardwalk. The Tinicum Environmental Center is open from 8:00 a.m. to sunset, free of charge.*

The visitors' center is open daily from 8:00 a.m. to 4:30 p.m. Bird lists as well as other information are available there. There is a canoe launch onto Darby Creek by the visitors' center. Fishing with a license is allowed in the impoundment. There are carp, sunfish, perch, catfish, crappie, and gizzard shad. For further information contact the Refuge Manager, Tinicum National Environmental Center, Suite 104, Scott Plaza 2, Philadelphia, Pa. 19113, (215) 521-0662; visitors' center, (215) 365-3118.

Close by the airport are open fields of short grass which are a favorite winter haunt of such northern species as the short-eared owl, rough-legged hawk, water pipit, snow bunting, and Lapland longspur. Other birds of prey—such as the northern harrier, American kestrel, and Cooper's, sharp-shinned, red-shouldered, and red-tailed hawk—also patrol the short grass for rodents and small mammals. These may also be seen at the center. To reach the area return to Island Avenue and follow the signs for I-95 north. Drive straight through all the intersections until you reach a sign for Fort Mifflin on the left. Bear right here to the ARCO tanks, 0.5 mile down the road on the left.

The Pine
Barrens

Directions: This region covers most of southern New Jersey. A good starting point for explorations is Lebanon State Forest. From New York City drive south on the New Jersey Turnpike to Exit 11 and the Garden State Parkway to Exit 67, about 85 miles in all. Turn west on Route 534. After about 4 miles it feeds into Route 72. Continue on Route 72 about 16 miles to the forest entrance, which will be on the right. Or take the New Jersey Turnpike south to Exit 7, about 60 miles. On U.S. 206 drive south 16.8 miles to Red Lion. Turn east on Route 70 and drive 8.3 miles to a traffic circle. Take the first right, Route 72, and turn left into the forest entrance almost immediately.

Stretching for 2000 square miles, the Pine Barrens are a vast region of sandy pine and oak forests, dense cedar swamps, quiet brown streams, and bright green bogs brilliant with orchids. It is a garden of rare and endangered botanical species, a meeting place where 14 northern species of plants reach their southern limit, and 100 southerners reach their northern limit. Others that grow sparsely elsewhere may be seen here in great profusion. In all, about 800 kinds of plants have been identified. Some 23 species of orchids have been recorded, some so unusual that only a few people know where to find them, some so common that their blossoms lay a pink haze over the bogs in June. One may see several forests of dwarfed pitch pines, whose origins have intrigued scientists for over a century. Geology, climate, fire, and human activity have interacted to produce a remarkable region, and a mysterious one, for the evolution of the Pine Barrens is a very complex history that is still being unraveled.

One hundred and thirty-five million years ago the land now known as the Pine Barrens was part of a dynamic seashore. As the sea level fluctuated over time, the area was covered by the ocean, coastal lagoons, and salt marshes. Over millions of years thousands of feet of clay, silt, and sand were deposited. Only in the last few million years has the Coastal Plain emerged from the sea (see **Introduction**). The surface soils of the Pine Barrens are coarse, sandy, and very porous; rain filters through rapidly. Deep below the surface are layers of impermeable clay, which traps rainwater. A stratum of either rock, gravel, or sand through which water can flow is known as an *aquifer*. Here the aquifer lies just below the surface of the ground, sometimes so close that it emerges to form slow-moving streams, bogs, and swamps. Rainfall is abundant in southern New Jersey, about 45 inches per year. As a result, the Pine Barrens sits over a vast reserve of pure water. The aquifer is very vulnerable to pollution, however, because the porous surface soil fails to strain out impurities. Preservation of this irreplaceable resource is a major consideration in efforts to protect the Pine Barrens.

In some places the sandy soils are capped by coarse, more gravelly materials, which are much younger. After a period of uplift 5 million years ago, material eroded off the higher lands to the west. Carried down by streams, it was deposited over the Coastal Plain. These gravels contain large air spaces that allow water to pass through even more readily than the sandy soils. As a result they more successfully resisted the massive erosion by runoff from the glaciers to the north and the Arctic winds that swept the area during the Ice Age. Thus, the very same material that once lay on the bottom of river valleys now sits on the highest points of the Pine Barrens, such as Apple Pie Hill, Beacon Hill, and parts of the Pine Plains.

The soils of the Pine Barrens are highly acidic and poor in nutrients. This is in part because the surface soils contain very little clay, which helps retain nutrients. The soils are also porous, and the abundant rainfall quickly leaches any nutrients that result from decaying organic material. Although the Coastal Plain sands once lay on the ocean floor, fossils of marine life, rich sources of calcium, are virtually absent. Calcium would neutralize the acidity somewhat. The acidity of the soil largely determines the plant and animal life that can flourish here: earthworms and snails are rare, for example, while shrubs of the heath family such as blueberry, huckleberry, sheep laurel, dangleberry, and leatherleaf do very well.

Fire has shaped the face of the Pine Barrens for perhaps thousands of years. Dry surface soil and resinous pines create highly flammable conditions; in most upland regions, serious fire occurs three or four times a century and in some areas as often as ten. With the arrival of the colonists the vast majority of these fires have been man-made. The settlers logged and cleared the trees four to six times to make charcoal and glass, to forge iron, and to build roads. Sparks from forges, smudge fires to keep off the bugs, and cooking fires often escaped and set the woods ablaze, where trash from logging and clearing provided dry fuel. Today about 1100 fires flare in the Pine Barrens each year, most of them due to carelessness.

The vegetation here has adapted to thousands of years of harsh conditions. By looking at the composition of a section of forest, it is possible to tell how often fires occur there. Throughout most of the region, one finds pitch pine mixed with patches of shortleaf pine and a variety of oaks. Pitch pines are better equipped to withstand frequent burning. They have thick insulating bark, which protects the inner, living layers. If the fire is not too fierce, the tree will sprout new needles almost immediately from dormant buds on the trunk and branches. Young pitch pines are able to resprout at the roots, but they gradually lose this ability as they grow. Since resinous pines are very flammable, a fire can tear through a pine forest, laying bare the soil and making it inhospitable for most species. Pitch pines, on the other hand, will readily resprout and their seedlings grow best on bare-soil. Shortleaf pine can also sprout needles from trunk and branch, but apparently becomes less vigorous with very frequent fires. It is scattered through the Pine Barrens, but not in the Pine Plains, which burn every 10 years or so. Virginia pine, which does not resprout this way, is found only on the outer edges of the Pine Barrens.

Although all species of oaks can resprout at the root, they weaken and die if burned too often. None is able to sprout from the trunk. White oaks, chestnut oaks, and scarlet oaks are most sensitive to fire. They are found in areas of the Pine Barrens which burn least frequently. Post oaks and to a lesser degree black oaks are hardier and will be found where fire is more frequent, perhaps every 25 years. Blackjack oak and scrub oak are the strongest of all; their growth may even be stimulated by regular burning. They are the only oaks which grow on the Pine Plains.

Where fire occurs rarely, oaks begin to outnumber the pines for several reasons. Litter accumulates on the forest floor, forming a nursery for oak seedlings. When strong wildfires do break out in mature stands, they roar through the tops of the tall trees, killing off the pines. The oaks are able to sprout again from the root of their crowns, but such resprouted oaks do not produce top-grade lumber.

Climatological changes connected to the Ice Age and the warming period that followed have also affected the types of vegetation growing here. The last glacier stopped about fifty miles to the north. From pollen samples, botanists have determined that the Pine Barrens were then covered with northern forests of spruce, pine, and birch. Many northern species of plants grew here. As the climate gradually warmed and the ice retreated to the north, these northern species also retreated northward, in part because of competition from species that are more vigorous in a milder climate. In a few places, a scattering of northern species hung on, becoming relics of their former and much wider distribution. They are found in the harsh conditions of the Pine Plains or the highly acidic bogs where competition from other species is minimal.

Following the retreat of the glacier came several cycles of warming and cooling. During warm periods, southern species spread northward. Pockets of these southern species were able to hang on along the Coastal Plain as the climate grew colder again, in part because winters here are tempered by the sea (see **Introduction**). This accounts for the extraordinary number of southern species which reach their northern extent in the Pine Barrens. Although the Pine Barrens have been heavily used by people since the colonists arrived, the region has not been paved over, industrialized, or buried by houses. The habitats for these relic species have survived. Some human activity has even provided new habitats for these species. The rare curly-grass fern, for example, grows on the stumps of cedar trees that have been cut down.

Animal life, like the vegetation, responds to the singular conditions of the region. Burrowing snakes and small mammals are plentiful in the loose, sandy soil. Bass and bluegills, freshwater fish common elsewhere in New Jersey, cannot breed in the acidic streams and lakes. Two other species, the Pine Barrens treefrog and the carpenter frog, have shown an ability to live in the highly acidic streams where other amphibians cannot. The distributions of some animals, like those of some plants, reflect the moderate climate in this section of New Jersey, for a number of insects, snakes, and frogs reach their northern limit here.

Ninety-one species of butterflies have been identified. Of these, the most commonly seen are the mourning cloak, with deep maroon wings, and several species of swallowtail. Six species of butterfly are northern: the eyed brown, blue-eyed grayling, meadow fritillary, red-spotted purple, hoary elfin, and bog cooper. The pearly eye, Lakehurst satyr, southern woodnymph and variegated fritillary are southern species.

Throughout the dry upland areas are scattered the crescent-shaped mounds of the leaf-cutting ant. The ants collect fresh leaves and process them inside the mound by chewing them up into small, moist pieces. The leaf bits are fertilized by fecal matter and planted with bits of fungus from existing supplies. The fungus grows rapidly and is harvested by the colony for food. The ants are selective about the species of fungus and weed out unwanted varieties. The mounds themselves are unlike other ant colonies in that they have many entrances. It is thought that this adaptation helps to ventilate the nest. The pile of rotting leaf bits gives off tremendous heat, which rises through the center of the mound, pulling fresh air in through the entrances around the outer edges.

Six of the eighteen species of snakes found here are at the northern limit of their range—the scarlet snake, corn snake, coastal plain milk snake, eastern kingsnake, rough green snake, and northern pine snake. The pine snake was once widespread in the Pine Barrens. It is now uncommon and found mostly in dry upland sites. Like the eastern hognose, the eastern worm snake, and the scarlet snake, it is a burrowing snake and the sandy soils are a perfect home. Not being poisonous, it has adopted a frightening act to ward off attack. When threatened, the pine snake vibrates its tail, hisses like a punctured tire and may even strike. Being secretive, this species is rarely seen. It and the corn snake are threatened species in New Jersey. The hognose also puts on an amazing show. When encountered, it rears up as if about to strike, flattening its head to look like a viper and puffing out its body. If the observer stands ground, the snake rolls over on its back, throws up its last meal, and goes limp. At this point one can pick it up and it will dangle, limply, over the hand. Place it on its stomach and the snake will turn over on its back again. Eventually, if left alone, the snake will right itself and disappear into the underbrush. The only poisonous snake in the Pine Barrens is the timber rattlesnake, which shows some characteristics of the canebrake rattlesnake of the south. Like its southern relative, it prefers the damp lowlands along the banks of Pine Barrens streams. It is very rarely encountered.

Like burrowing snakes, small burrowing mammals are common. Look for the tunnels of the eastern mole, pine mouse, and white-footed mouse in the dry upland areas. White-tailed deer are everywhere, for the rich shrub layer provides them with plentiful food. Red squirrels are abundant but gray squirrels, which eat chiefly acorns, are not. Gray foxes and raccoons, which eat all sorts of plant and animal life, are numerous, while the more carnivorous red fox occurs in smaller numbers. Mink, river otter, and long-tailed weasel are found along the waterways; elsewhere in New Jersey most of their habitat has been destroyed. These animals are most active at night and the best time to look for them is very early in the morning. Once extinct in the mid-1800s, beavers have been reintroduced and flourish in several Pine Barrens streams.

In the acid streams of the region, relatively few species of fish can survive. They are dark-colored like the water they inhabit, and often strikingly marked. The color of the water derives from tannin leached from the peat bogs, white-cedar bark, and needles, and from iron in the soil. The blackbanded and banded sunfish are common in the upper reaches of the streams and do not occur outside the Pine Barrens. Downstream, near the mouth of the rivers, the waters are less acidic and different species begin to appear, including golden and spotted shiners, white catfish, and mummichogs. It isn't clear how acidity affects the fish, but one possibility is that it inhibits reproduction.

The extensive pine forests that cover most of the region provide a limited variety of food and habitat for birds. The spectacular warbler flights of northern New Jersey do not occur here. Many species, the hairy and downy woodpeckers for example, prefer to nest in deciduous trees, and insect eaters like vireos and flycatchers find more food in deciduous forests. Thus, where oaks are more abundant in the Pine Barrens, a greater diversity of birds also exists.

In the upland pine forest, common nesting species are the rufous-sided towhee, ruffed grouse, bobwhite, and pine and prairie warblers. Others include the Carolina wren, white-breasted nuthatch, Carolina chickadee, ovenbird, and tufted titmouse, all common in southern New Jersey. The black-throated green warbler, usually associated with the conifer forests of the north, is one surprising resident species; it nests in white-cedar swamps.

The prothonotary warbler, a southern species, together with the yellow warbler, yellowthroat, and redstart, breeds along the streams and swamps. Migratory waterfowl use the ponds and flooded cranberry bogs of the Pine Barrens in spring and fall. Wood ducks nest in the swamps.

The birds of prey most often seen are turkey vultures, red-tailed hawks, American kestrels, and broad-winged hawks. In winter, nesting great-horned owls and screech owls are common, and the saw-whet owl, unusual in New Jersey, is sometimes heard. Common nighthawks and eastern bluebirds are sometimes found nesting in recently burned areas. Nighthawks do not build a nest, however; the female merely chooses a spot on the barren ground. Day and night, the nighthawk hunts on the wing, sometimes high in the air, sometimes skimming the ground, its wide mouth open to catch insects. The chuck-will's-widow, a southern species that is moving north, occasionally catches small birds in the same manner. Both chuck-will's-widows, found in coastal areas of the Pine Barrens, and whip-poor-wills hunt by night in the Pine Barrens.

Only recently have the Pine Barrens received any protection from development and destruction. In 1979 Governor Byrne of New Jersey signed a bill setting aside 370,000 acres to be preserved and 1,000,000 additional acres to assume a semiprotected status. Much of the land is still privately owned, and schemes for developing the region for vacation homes do not die easily. One of the greatest dangers to the area is the enthusiasm of professional and amateur naturalists. Rare botanical sites are destroyed by human traffic, eager collectors, and photographers whose pursuit of the perfect shot leads them to move delicate orchids to improve the setting. The entries below describe some of the interesting plants one may see but not the locations of the rarest species. Any exploration of bogs and streams should be done from the water. When walking in bogs, stay in the wettest spots, and avoid the hummocks where most of the special and rare plants grow. Do not, of course, pick or uproot anything. All this may seem obvious, but something happens to the most sensible people when face to face with a dragon's-mouth orchid.

Remarks: *Camping is available at several locations including Lebanon State Forest, Wharton State Forest, Bass River State Forest and Parvin State Park. The best and least damaging way to see the bogs, cedar swamps, and lowland areas of the barrens is by canoeing the rivers. There are many canoe-rental outfits which will drop you off and pick you up. Be prepared to haul the boat over snags especially in the smaller branches. Spring and fall are especially beautiful and very crowded on weekends. The summer can be very hot, but that is when most species of orchids are in bloom. A winter expedition on a sunny day in February can be magical, silent, and solitary. The flat, sandy roads that crisscross the dry uplands are ideal for biking. Be warned that it is easy to get lost on the smaller sand tracks, many of which are not on any topographic map. These smaller roads have patches of soft, deep "sugar" sand to trap your wheels. Other activities include hiking, swimming, and fishing for pickerel in old cranberry-bog impoundments. The ocean beaches are nearby. Cranberries are cultivated in man-made bogs throughout the region and harvested in the fall.*

10.

Whitesbog

Directions: **See general directions for the Pine Barrens. From the traffic circle by the entrance to Lebanon State Forest go northeast on Route 70. Go 6.8 miles to Route 530 and**

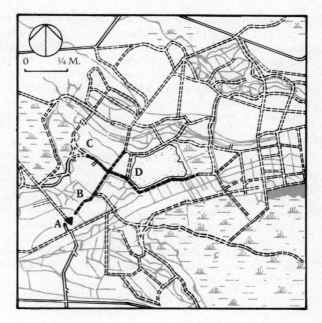

turn west. **Look for the sign to the Conservation Environmental Studies Center, 1.2 miles on your right. Drive into the tiny community of Whitesbog and park.**

Ownership: **Lebanon State Forest, New Jersey Division of Parks and Forestry.**

Whitesbog covers approximately 3000 acres and contains many Pine Barrens habitats. There are pine forests, cultivated fields of blueberries, commercial cranberry bogs, old fields reverting to forest, and white-cedar bogs. The flooded cranberry bogs and reservoirs attract numerous species of migratory waterfowl and wading birds.

A network of sandy roads winds through the area. At **A** walk northeastward in the direction of the old crop duster landing strip. The road begins in a lowland pitch-pine forest (see **#17**). Here the water table lies only 15 to 30 inches below the surface of the ground, depending on the rainfall. Sheep laurel, fetterbush, and staggerbush are common shrubs, and leatherleaf appears where the water is closest to the surface. At **B** another road angles in sharply from the left. Between the two roads, beneath the pines, you can find sand myrtle, a plant unique to the Pine Barrens (see **#11**).

Beyond the woods the road passes through cultivated blueberry fields and on into old fields. There is a scattering of houses here known as Old Florence, a summer village for migrant workers. Red maple, blackgum, sweetgum, sassafras, shining sumac, and gray birch are invading the open ground. These species are typical of the early stages of succession on cleared land in the Pine Barrens, where the surface soil is not wet but where the water table is just below ground. Further out by the old landing strip (**C**), a low mat of pyxie moss, sand myrtle, and bearberry covers the ground.

The reservoir at **D** attracts many shorebirds during late summer and early fall. At that time, after several months of heavy water consumption, the water level has fallen, exposing extensive mud flats—an ideal feeding ground for the birds (see **#42**). To the south of the reservoir are flooded cranberry bogs where migrating Canada geese and dabbling ducks such as mallards, black ducks, wood ducks, pintails, and teal gather in spring and fall. In late March and early April bands of whistling swans, a rare sight in New Jersey, collect here on their way north. The swans feed so rapaciously on cranberry vines in commercial bogs that local growers have taken to scaring the birds away with blank shot.

11.

Pine Plains

Directions: **From New York City drive south on the New Jersey Turnpike to Exit 11, then south on the Garden State Parkway to Exit 67, about 100 miles in all. Turn west on Route 534 about 4.4 miles. Continue west on Route 72; after 4.1 miles, turn south on a dirt road. Drive 1 mile and stop.**

Ownership: **New Jersey Department of Environmental Protection.**

In every direction a forest of stunted pine stretches to the horizon. This is the West Plains, one of three such areas in the Pine Barrens. Whether one walks five minutes or an hour into these woods, the vegetation remains the same; the pitch pines grow to an average height of only five feet; below them one finds scrub oak and black-jack oak. The shrubs are predominately black huckleberry and lowbush blueberry. The plains have looked this way for hundreds of years—since the days when the colonists arrived and recorded what they saw, and possibly for centuries before this. Poor soil, toxic minerals, and wind have all been offered as explanations for the forest's unusual appearance. Today only one theory is accepted as the major cause of this pygmy forest: regular and frequent fires, occurring roughly every 10 years.

On the east side of the road for many miles is evidence of a fairly recent fire. As you walk among the trees, you can see that many have sprouted new needles from the trunk. The roots have sprouted as well (see **Pine Barrens**). The trees have adapted to fire in other ways. Examine the cones on both sides of the road. Where the forest has not burned, the pine cones are closed; in the burn zone, the heat of the fire has released the cones. This means that fire stimulates the trees to bring forth seedlings. The oaks up on the plains have also adpated genetically by rapidly producing acorns after a fire and by sprouting energetically from the roots. Scrub oak is a northern species and blackjack oak a southern species. They meet here and cross-breed, as do many of the oaks. The ground of the burn is already being covered with lichens and various heath shrubs.

It is not clear why fires burn so frequently in the Pine Plains. Wind is part of the answer. The plains, about 150 feet above sea level in this area, are higher than the surrounding forest and thus exposed to stronger winds, which dry the vegetation and fan the flames once they begin.

Other interesting plants of the plains include sand myrtle, pyxie moss, and Pine Barrens rattlesnake root. Two species of sand myrtle grow in the Pine Barrens: one exists only in the barrens; the other is found in similar barrens in the Carolinas and Kentucky. The two can be distinguished only by the absence or presence of gland dots on the tiny flower stalk. Pyxie "moss" is not a moss at all but an evergreen, flowering plant. Like the sand myrtle, it is disjunct in its distribution, for the main range of the species lies from southeastern Virginia to South Carolina. Its presence here dates from a time thousands of years ago when the climate was considerably warmer (see **Pine Barrens**). It covers the ground with tiny pink blossoms in spring. Pine Barrens rattlesnake root is also a southern species. Broom crowberry is a northern species found only on the Pine Plains, in the Shawangunks of New York, and along the coast from Massachusetts to Maritime Canada. Like curly-grass fern it established itself in the south when the glaciers transformed this part of New Jersey into a cold, barren land where little could grow. It grows vigorously after burning, which must be one reason for its success in this fire-dominated landscape.

12.
White-Cedar
Bogs

Throughout the Pine Barrens, lines of tall, dark-green trees break out above the light-green canopy of the pines. These dense stands of white-cedar mark the stream courses. Once, white-cedar forests covered thousands of acres, but the wood, valued for construction because it is sturdy and rot-resistant, was cut again and again. White-cedar grows in even-aged stands. This is due to its selectivity. The conditions for sprouting must be just right: not too much moisture and not too little. The seedlings are very intolerant of shade, so once a set of seedlings starts to grow, no second generation will sprout below the first. Often when a stand of white-cedar has been cleared, it is replaced not by a new growth of cedar but by red maples, blackgum, and sweetbay. This may be due partly to browsing by deer, which love to eat the cedar seedlings. The maple, gum, and bay forest also grow around the edges of white-cedar stands, where the swamp forest merges into the drier pine-oak forest. As you explore a white-cedar bog, you will see that the trees do vary in thickness. These differences reflect slight variations in the amount of light, moisture, and nutrients available to each tree. Some shrubs common beneath the cedars are sweet pepperbush, swamp magnolia, and three members of the heath family: fetterbush, clammy azalea, and highbush blueberry. Virginia chain fern, netted chain fern, and sphagnum moss are abundant, along with a variety of bog species. The black-throated green warbler, the Acadian flycatcher, and the brown creeper, birds uncommon to this part of New Jersey, are sometimes associated with the cedar bogs.

Where to find white-cedar bogs:

Shinn's Branch

Directions: **Follow general directions for the Pine Barrens. From the entrance to Lebanon State Forest, drive 0.3 mile to Shinn's Branch Rd. Turn right and go 0.9 mile to the crossroads. Go left and drive 0.5 mile. Park by the bridge.**

Ownership: Lebanon State Forest, New Jersey Division of Parks and Forestry.

Absegami Nature Trail

Directions: From New York City take the New Jersey Turnpike south to Exit 11. Then follow the Garden State Parkway south to Exit 52, about 100 miles. Go to the end of the exit ramp and turn west (right) on Stage Rd. Go 1 mile, bear right, and continue 0.8 mile to the entrance to the forest on the left.

Ownership: Bass River State Forest, New Jersey Division of Parks and Forestry.

The nature trail leads through a young white-cedar bog.

Oswego River

Directions: From the Pine Plains (see #11 for directions) continue south about 8 miles to Lake Oswego. Follow the road around the end of the lake to Little Hawkin Rd. Turn south (left) and drive 0.3 mile to the outlet of the lake. The canoe trip down the Oswego or East Branch of the Wading River begins here and passes through Martha Furnace, a boggy area with many fascinating plants. There is an extensive white-cedar bog north of Martha Furnace.

Ownership: Bass River State Forest and private lands border the river.

13.
Lebanon State
Forest

Directions: See general directions for the Pine Barrens. Enter the Lebanon State Forest, drive 0.3 mile, and turn right on Shinn's Branch Rd. Drive 2.2 miles to Buzzard Hill Rd. to the old glassworks site, where camping areas have been laid out. Turn north (left) and go 1.3 miles.

Walk around this area and explore northwards on the dirt roads. The forest is mostly pitch pine, with occasional shortleaf pine, post oak, black oak, scrub oak, and some small patches of dwarf chestnut oak. One colony of dwarf chestnut oak is growing just opposite the concrete bathhouse by the first camping area.

The canopy of this forest type is more varied than the wetland woods, but the herb layer is skimpy by comparison. Several hundred species of grasses, flowers, ferns, and such are found in the lowlands, but less than a hundred in the uplands. Moisture is the determining factor. The uplands are drier because the water table is farther down. Bracken fern, asters, clovers, broom sedges, goldenrods, and little bluestem are typical plants. In spring pink lady's slippers bloom throughout the upland woods.

The woods here are a favorite nesting site for red-headed woodpeckers, a species that has been declining.

Remarks: *There is a seasonal nature center here, which is open from June to October.*

14.
Stafford Forge

Directions: **From New York city take the New Jersey Turnpike to Exit 11 and the Garden State Parkway south to Exit 58, about 95 miles in all. Turn west on Route 539N for 0.3 mile. Turn north (right). Drive 1.4 miles and turn left into the Stafford Forge Wildlife Management Area. Park by the pond and walk along the dirt road. The road can be driven but is very rough.**

Ownership: **New Jersey Division of Fish, Game, and Wildlife.**

The highlight of this site is the oak-pine forest that borders the roadside (**A**). The mixed oak forest here is made up of black, white, scarlet, and chestnut oaks. Pines are few. In the Pine Barrens, only a few such nearly pure oak stands exist. These occur in the vicinity of old villages. The abundance of fire-sensitive oaks suggests that settlers protected the forests around their homes, allowing the oaks to

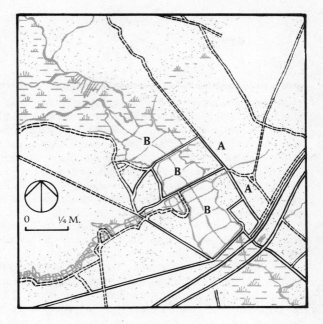

mature. Beyond the settlements, where the forest is dominated by pitch pine and blackjack oak, it is clear that fires burned unchecked.

Also of interest at Stafford Forge are the cranberry bogs (**B**), which contain many typical Pine Barren bog species. The bogs are beginning the transition to wooded swamp. Red maples, some white-cedar, and sassafras are now growing on the high ground of the hummocks. At the far end of the bog is an old cedar swamp that has been flooded, the trees killed. The activity of beavers, the flooding of land for cranberry production, draining of agricultural land, and logging have all contributed to the disappearance of white-cedar stands.

15.
Bogs

Unlike bogs in northern New Jersey and Pennsylvania that date from glacial times, the bogs of the Pine Barrens occur because the water table intersects the ground surface, creating an area that is constantly wet with little if any outflow. The natural acidity of the soil and water of the barrens is intensified by sphagnum moss, which absorbs nutrients from the water, thereby increasing the water's acidity. If left to themselves, these bogs will eventually fill in with shrubby vegetation and become wooded with lowland species of trees (see **#89**). Many of the special and rare plants of the Pine Barrens are found in the bogs. Because a number of these are on federal and state endangered lists, their specific locations are not given, but you are free to explore on your own and look for them.

Most spectacular are the orchids. They come in many forms, from tiny, inconspicuous flowers to large, exuberant magenta blossoms. Orchids from both north and south occur here, some of them exceedingly rare. For example, a very small number of southern yellow orchis, which is almost extinct in this state, grows here in the Pine Barrens. In spring and summer the bogs startle the eye with the pink flowers of the dragon's-mouth or arethusa orchid, the calopogon or grass pink, and the rose pogonia. The dragon's-mouth orchid does not have a strong root system and is especially vulnerable to disturbance. It is disappearing from most of its habitats south of Canada. The white-fringed orchis, showy and abundant, is found in a number of habitats including bogs, damp roadsides, and savannahs, open wet meadows that often mark the site of old commercial cranberry bogs. All orchids are sensitive to too much traffic, easily destroyed by inadvertent footsteps, and almost impossible to transplant. Their habitats are often wetland areas that are drained or filled in to make way for development. While a species may be locally common, few orchids are really abundant.

Among the other rare plants of the Pine Barrens is the bog asphodel, which occurs only here and in some parts of Delaware. Its yellow flowers appear in the end of May. Unique to the Pine Barrens of New Jersey is goldencrest, with its flat-topped cluster of small blossoms in summer.

Many of the species of interest to botanists are inconspicuous grasslike plants that are very difficult for the amateur to identify. Often found in bogs and swamps of the region, these species include pipeworts, beaked-rushes, spike rushes, sedges, nut rushes, and horned rushes.

In the slow-moving streams, ponds, and wet edges of the bogs, one can find several species of bladderworts. These plants are botanically quite sophisticated. Several species are aquatic and, when in bloom, float on the surface of the water with a tiny stem and flower held erect. This is accomplished by means of small air-filled sacs, which are attached to a network of rootlike leaves at the base of the flower stalk (see **#17**).

Webb's Mills Bog

Directions: **From Lebanon State Forest drive east on Route 72 about 14 miles to Route 539. Turn north and drive 6.2 miles and park by the bridge. A rickety boardwalk extends into the bog. Walk on the white sand between the hummocks.**

From New York City take the Garden State Parkway south to exit 67, about 85 miles, and go west on Route 534 about 4 miles until it runs into Route 72. Continue west on Route 72 about 2 miles to Route 539 and turn north. Drive 6.2 miles and park by the bridge.

Ownership: **New Jersey Department of Environmental Protection.**

Webb's Mills is an accessible example of a typical Pine Barrens bog. Hummocks of evergreen leatherleaf and sphagnum moss perch on a base of white sand partially covered with peaty muck. From spring to fall something of interest is always in bloom here, primarily on the hummocks, which serve as miniature nurseries. Sphagnum moss creates these hummocks as it grows; the hummocks then become sponges for rainwater. They are only a few inches high, at most a foot from base to crown, and yet very specific communities occupy different elevations in response to changes in moisture. On the wet, sandy soil at the lowest level grow marsh St. Johnswort and spatulate-leaved sundew, an insectivorous plant (see **#89**). On the edges of the hummock itself, a little up out of the water, round-leaved sundews, sphagnum moss, and cranberry appear. Although similar to the naked eye, several species of sphagnum moss live here, each with different moisture requirements. Sphagnum moss has special moisture-retaining cells that allow it to absorb several times its weight in water. This maintains the plant through dry weather. Cranberry is more tolerant and grows over all the hummocks. Slightly higher than the round-leaved sundew, you will find thread-leaved sundew, a Coastal Plain species that grows from New Jersey up into Massachusetts. In its company are usually other interesting plants. The curly-grass fern, a tiny bright green corkscrew that looks nothing like fern, is one of the best known plants of the Pine Barrens. Elsewhere, it is found only in Nova Scotia and Newfoundland. It is a relic of the colder glacial period when northern plants moved south in front of the ice sheets. The Carolina club moss, on the other hand, is a southern species, which occurs only in patches on the Coastal Plain in Maryland and Virginia. From North Carolina south to Florida it is more common. It is a primitive member of a primitive family. Pockets of it occur all over the Southern Hemisphere in South America, Australia, New Zealand, Sri Lanka, South Africa, and elsewhere. This species has not changed since the continents were one large landmass, over 200 million years ago.

On top of the hummock where conditions are driest, one will see orchids, dwarf huckleberry, leatherleaf, and bog aster, short-leaved milkwort, and others.

Around the perimeter of the bog, the forest is made up of pitch pines with a rich assortment of shrubs such as clammy azalea, sheep laurel, dangleberry, and several species of blueberry and huckleberry. These are all members of the heath family, well suited to acidic, nutrient-poor soil. Local nonheaths include sweet pepperbush, inkberry and winterberry hollies, and swamp magnolia.

As you leave the bog, walk a few minutes south along the road to the dirt road, which turns east. The soil is now very dry, and the forest is an upland type characterized by pitch pines, and dryland shrubs including golden heather, black huckleberry, sand myrtle, bearberry, staggerbush, scrub oak, and bayberry, which is usually a seaside shrub. Little bluestem grass, panic grasses, and bracken fern are common herbs in this habitat.

Forge Pond

Directions: **From New York City take the New Jersey Turnpike south to Exit 3. Go southeast on the Atlantic City Expressway to Exit 28 for Hammonton, approximately 23**

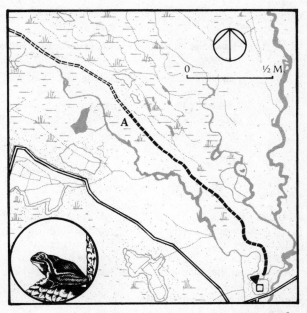

Inset: Treefrog

miles. Go north on Route 54 for about 2 miles to Route 542
and turn east (right.) Go 8 miles to Pleasant Mills Church
and turn left into the parking lot. A dirt road runs north
from the parking lot. Forge Pond Bog is along the left side
of this road (A).

Ownership: **Wharton State Forest, New Jersey Division of
Parks and Forestry.**

Lying along the Nescochague Creek, Forge Pond has filled in to
become a fine example of a Pine Barrens bog. A large colony of Pine
Barrens treefrogs thrives here. This endangered species is found only
in the Pine Barrens and in isolated colonies in the south. Part of the
treefrog's success here is no doubt due to its ability to survive and
breed in especially acidic conditions.

Continuing east along Route 542, you will come to Batsto historical village. The deep-indigo flowers of the pine-barren gentian appear along the roadside here in October. This is one of the rarities of
the barrens; it ranges from South Carolina to southeastern Virginia,
and then skips north to New Jersey.

Oceanville Bog

Directions: **From New York City take the New Jersey Turnpike to Exit 11 and the Garden State Parkway south to
Exit 48, about 105 miles. Turn south onto U.S. 9; go about
7 miles to Oceanville. When you reach Great Creek Rd.
opposite the entrance to Brigantine National Wildlife Refuge, turn west and go 0.4 miles. Park beside the road. The
bog lies adjacent to the road, so there is no reason to actually go into it.**

Ownership: **Private property.**

The glory of this bog is the display of dragon's-mouth orchid and
grass pink at the end of May. Other orchids include the rose pogonia,
white-fringed orchis, and the woodland green orchis. The beautiful
stripes and dots on the orchid help to guide insects into the heart of
the flower so that they will carry a load of pollen to the next plant.
The insect is searching for nectar, the sweet substance produced by
most flowers solely to entice insects. Orchids apparently do not produce
nectar, but generations of insects have "learned" that if they enter
the heart of the flower, they will find nectar. Though they are continually disappointed, the insects continue to be lured into the orchid. Orchids gain some of their nutrients in this inhospitable environment with the help of special fungi called mycorhizae, which
grow along their roots. Pitcher plants, which are insectivorous, bloom
here in May (see **#89**).

16.

Rivers

The rivers of the Pine Barrens—the Mullica, the Batsto, the Oswego,
and the Wading, plus Cedar Creek and others—are all navigable
depending on recent rainfall and your willingness to get your feet
wet. Because of the great quantities of water trapped below the
surface of the barrens, the rivers never dry up, even in drought, but
during the driest months, usually February and October, they become very shallow. These streams move slowly across the low relief

of the Coastal Plain. Because they originate in the region, the streams are never swollen with rainwater from other areas, and the porous soil effectively prevents local flooding. Snags are abundant because the streams cannot flush them out.

The waters of the Pine Barrens are tea-colored. One source of the color is iron. As rainwater filters through decaying organic matter in the soil, it becomes acidic. The acid water dissolves iron in the soil and carries it down into the aquifer. The dissolved iron reemerges in the streams; when it comes into contact with the air, it oxidizes, forming red deposits on the banks and oily slicks on the surface of the water. Iron deposited on the sandy shore eventually becomes cemented into a form of sandstone known as bog iron. From the latter part of the seventeenth century into the middle of the nineteenth, bog iron was mined for forges in the barrens. Most of the ponds and many of the bogs in the area originated as forge ponds for this industry.

Because rainfall is the sole source of water in the Pine Barrens, the streams and ponds are very pure, far better than most New Jersey water. High acidity inhibits bacterial growth. The water was prized on long ocean voyages of the nineteenth century because it stayed pure for months on end.

Along the streams you will see much of the distinctive vegetation of the Pine Barren wetlands (see following entries). In the streams themselves, vegetation is limited. One common plant is the swaying rush, its long delicate green strands floating beneath the surface of the water. Because its stems are flexible and smooth, it offers little resistance to the current. A stiff species would constantly be battered by the stream.

Remarks: *Campsites are available to canoeists along several of the streams. Contact the Wharton State Forest office—R.D. 1, Batsto, Hammonton, N.J. 08037, (609) 561-0024—to obtain permits and further information. There are many canoe rental businesses in the area. The most well known is probably Mick's Canoe Rental in Jenkins along Route 563, (609) 726-1380. Their season is March through November.*

Some sample running times for Pine Barrens rivers:

—*The west branch of the Wading River: From Speedwell on Route 563 to Evans Bridge on Route 563: 6 hours. There are take-out points above and below this.*

—*The east branch of the Wading River (Oswego River): From Oswego Lake to Harrisville Lake: 4 hours.*

17.

Pakim Pond

Directions: **Follow general directions for Pine Barrens. From the entrance to Lebanon State Forest drive 0.3 mile to Shinn's Branch Rd. and turn east (right). Drive 2.2 miles to Buzzard Hill Rd., turn north (left), and drive 0.5 mile to Pakim Pond.**

Ownership: **Lebanon State Forest, New Jersey Division of Parks and Forestry.**

A small, deep-blue lake fringed by pitch pine and white cedars, Pakim Pond is an old man-made lake, like the majority of ponds in the Pine Barrens. Left to themselves for many years, they have acquired their own characteristic Pine Barrens vegetation. An upright, spiky plant called bayonet rush and clusters of white water lilies grow in the shallow waters by the shore. Look also for small floating plants called bladderworts. The rootlike leaves float just below the surface and are covered with small sacs. When a tiny aquatic animal such as a water flea touches the sensitive hairs at the opening of the bladder, the bladder opens and sucks in the creature along with water. The bladder closes, trapping the insect inside, where it is digested. Other hairs inside the bladder take up the digested material and pass it into the plant. The flower (often yellow) rises above the water on a short stem, held afloat by the bladders. At the southeastern end of the pond (**A**) are a scattering of white-cedars and a boggy area where marsh St. Johnswort, orchids, and other bog plants grow. The southwestern shore of the pond is edged by lowland forest shading back into upland pine forest. Red maples and blackgum, with an understory of sassafras and young maples and gums, form the lowland portion. Dangleberry, sweet pepperbush and clammy azalea are among the heaths in the shrub layer. Chain fern, cinnamon fern, and royal fern are found along the shore, while just a few feet back, in drier soil, bracken fern begins to appear.

At the northeastern end of the pond is a wet, open meadow, which stretches to the water's edge. Such meadows are common around Pine Barrens ponds, where drainage is poor and the land is flat (**B**). Here, look for a number of bog species such as pitcher plants, sundews, several species of club moss, and cranberry. A low land woods of pitch pines borders the meadow. Where pitch pines grow in soggy conditions they form a transition habitat between wetland and upland. Sheep laurel is the dominant shrub in this forest type. Along the dam over the north end of the pond (**C**) you will see turkeybeard in bloom in early summer. This plant is found in sandy pine woods in New Jersey, Delaware, and southeastern North Carolina and in the mountains from Virginia to Georgia.

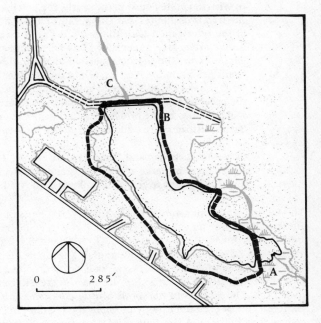

Other Pond Habitats

Lake Absegami in Bass River State Forest: **Take Exit 52 off the Garden State Parkway and turn west (right) at the end of the exit ramp. Bear right after 1 mile. The forest entrance is 0.8 mile up the road on the left.**

Lake Oswego: **Take Exit 63 off the Garden State Parkway. Drive west 9.7 miles on Route 72. Turn south on a wide dirt road and go 8.2 miles to the lake, which is on the left.**

18.

The Batona Trail

Directions: **The Batona Trail runs from Lebanon State Forest (see general directions for Pine Barrens) in the north to Wharton State Forest in the south. The northern end of the trail is on Route 72 at Ong's Hat, 1.5 miles northwest of the intersection with Route 70. It passes through the headquarters area of Lebanon State Forest and alongside Pakim Pond. The southern portion of the trail begins at Evans Bridge on the West Branch of the Wading River. To reach it, take Route 72 east 2.6 miles from the entrance to the Lebanon State Forest and turn south on Route 563. Go south 6 miles to the bridge. The trail passes through the Batsto Historical Area, and can be picked up there.**

Ownership: **Lebanon and Wharton State Forests, New Jersey Division of Parks and Forestry, and private. The Batona Hiking Club oversees the upkeep of the trail.**

The Batona Trail winds through all the main forest types of the Pine Barrens. Forty-one miles from end to end, it can be easily broken up into shorter hikes. It crosses Routes 72, 563, and 532, then the Friendship Rd. past the Caranza Memorial. The Apple Pie Hill fire tower can be reached by walking the trail or by driving 2.5 miles east of Chatsworth on Route 532. A dirt road on the left leads south to the hill. The view from the top is a wide panorama of the Pine Barrens. You can see the canopy of pines, the tall dark lines of the cedars. The hill is 205 feet high, one of the unusual high points protected from erosion by the riverbed gravels (see **Pine Barrens**).

Remarks: *There are several camping sites along the route. Apply for a permit and a map of the trail at the Lebanon State Forest office, New Lisbon, N.J. 08064, (609) 726-1191.*

19.

Parvin State Park

Directions: **Salem County, N.J. From New York City take the New Jersey Turnpike south to Exit 1. On U.S. 40 go east 19.6 miles. Just beyond the town of Elmer turn south (right) on Route 553; go 5.1 miles to Centerton. Turn east (left) on Route 540 and go 1.3 miles to the sign for the Second Landing Parking Area and pull in.**

Ownership: **New Jersey Division of Parks and Forestry.**

Lying at the edge of the Pine Barrens, Parvin State Park harbors many of the trees and plants typical of that region. It also has species common to the Piedmont and the inner Coastal Plain (see **#2**), for the soils tend to be richer here than in other parts of the Pine Barrens. The topography is rolling instead of flat, shifting rapidly from lowland forest to drier uplands.

Surrounding the parking area (**A**) is a stand of mixed oak, including white, black, Spanish, and chestnut oaks. Hickories, mostly pignut, are scattered throughout, and flowering dogwood is abundant in the understory. Hickory, chestnut oak, and dogwood are absent from even the least disturbed Pine Barrens forests; while Spanish oak only appears at the fringes of the barrens (see **#14**).

A nature trail begins on one side of the parking area and leads down into lowland woods (**B**). The vegetation changes abruptly. Numerous white-cedars are interspersed with red maple, blackgum, and some sweetbay magnolia—all species common to the areas of the Pine Barrens where white-cedar is giving way to the next stage in the succession (see **#12**). Shrubs and herbs are also familiar, including sweet pepperbush, highbush blueberry, swamp or clammy azalea, and Virginia chain, cinnamon, and royal ferns. Spicebush is here as well, marking a transition to Piedmont species.

Cross over the bridge at Muddy Run and turn left off the trail back up onto the high ground (**C**). The dry, sandy conditions and the pitch-pine forest, with huckleberry, blueberry, scrub oak, and blackjack oak, are reminiscent of the forest at Lebanon State Forest. Here there are other anomalies: extensive stands of mountain laurel, a shrub more common in the valley and ridge provinces to the west, and an occasional willow oak, another Piedmont species. You can

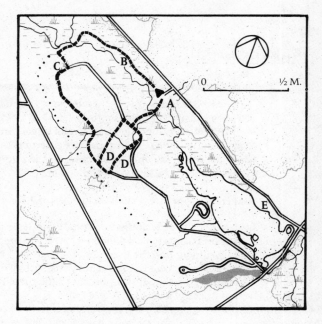

make a circuit of the woods on the macadam road or cross back to the parking area on small trails through the woods (**D**).

Most of the park has been cut over many times, but some older oaks, which appear to be well over a hundred years old, persist in the vicinity of the park office (**E**).

Remarks: *The terrain is easy and the walk will take about an hour. There is camping at the park. Canoe rentals are available; the trip down Muddy Run is a good way to see the lowland forest there. Other activities include swimming, fishing (license required), nature programs, and hiking along many miles of trails. Spring is particularly lovely here, for in May the mountain laurel is covered with white or pink-tinted flowers. The spring landbird migration is especially good at Parvin.*

20.
Long Beach
Island—Holgate

Directions: **Atlantic County, N.J. From New York City take the New Jersey Turnpike south to Exit 11. Continue south on the Garden State Parkway about 69 miles to Exit 63 at Manahawkin. Turn east on Route 72 to Ship Bottom, 6.8 miles. Turn south on Bay Ave. and go 9 miles to the end of the road. In summer you must pay a fee to park in the lot, but parking is free on the side streets. From here it is a long walk of about 2.5 miles to the mud flats at the end of the spit. The dune area is off limits, to protect breeding birds.**

Ownership: **Holgate Division, Brigantine National Wildlife Refuge, U.S. Fish and Wildlife Service.**

Beyond the last house, the curving tip of Long Beach Island extends for several miles, covered by low dunes, beach grass, and tidal flats. Protected from development, the end of the island lies open to the sea. Storm tides wash over it, razing the vegetation and sweeping sand into the bay. As sea level rises and currents shift, the island moves and changes shape, gradually retreating westward (see **#25** and **#30**). Just a handful of such places are left along the Jersey shore. Because of the storms, succession is continually interrupted, and the dunes never grow very large. American beach grass, which thrives on being regularly buried in sand, is particularly abundant (see **#55**). The open shell-cobbled beach is a prime nesting ground for certain species of birds. Every summer large colonies of least terns and black skimmers occupy the area; piping plovers and oystercatchers nest on the sands (see **#30**). Do not walk across the nesting area; both the eggs and the baby birds are extremely difficult to see and adults are easily disturbed.

In the bay are wide mudflats that lie exposed at low tide. Migrating shorebirds such as black-bellied plovers, willets, red knots, short-billed dowitchers, and small sandpipers or "peeps," use them extensively in May and again from July into October. To see the flats you must walk to the very end of the designated nesting area and then follow the southern edge of it to the bay.

65

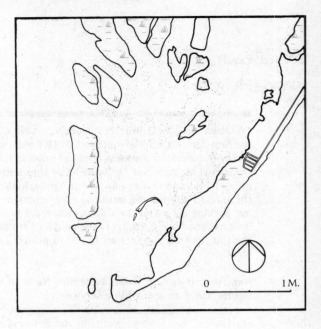

0   1 M.

A mild winter day can be the best time of all to take this walk on the beach. Oldsquaws, diving ducks which have distinctive black-and-white plumage and long, pointed tail feathers, move up the coast in tumbling, wheeling flight. Both the red-throated and the common loon can be seen. Loons are not related to any other genus. They are a very old group of birds, dating back 65 million years. They are superb divers and swimmers, but their feet are placed so far back on their bodies that walking is almost impossible. Their diet is mostly made up of fish. Not all their bones are hollow as in most species of birds; this added weight helps them dive. Loons also have large amounts of the substance myoglobin in their muscles that allows them to store greater amounts of oxygen. Loons have several other physiological adaptations that enable them to stay submerged a considerable time.

All three varieties of scoters are seen off the beach, diving for mussels and other mollusks. The best time to see waterfowl moving over the ocean is in the morning from about 7:00 to 10:00.

In the bay large concentrations of brant, bufflehead, common goldeneye, and other species gather to feed on submerged vegetation. The brant is a coastal species of goose, seldom found far from the sea. Until the 1930s its diet was almost entirely made up of eelgrass. Then a blight virtually wiped out the eelgrass for a time. The brant suffered a great decline in population before turning to sea lettuce, a species of algae.

Remarks: *A hot, tiring expedition on a sunny summer day. Take water. A trip to Long Beach can be rewarding at any time of year. A spotting scope is useful in winter.*

21.

Tuckerton Salt Marsh

Directions: **Ocean County, N.J. From New York City take the New Jersey Turnpike south to Exit 11, then the Garden State Parkway to Exit 58, about 95 miles. Go south on Route 539 for 3.5 miles to U.S. 9 and turn southwest. After 0.2 mile bear left on Great Bay Blvd., a small two-lane road that stretches 7 miles through the marsh.**

Ownership: **New Jersey Division of Fish, Game, and Wildlife.**

Between the Great Bay of the Mullica River and Little Egg Harbor is a broad salt marsh, one of the largest and least disturbed stretches of marshland in New Jersey. The beauty of Tuckerton is subtle, its colors soft gold, rust, and tawny brown in fall and winter, glowing shades of green in late spring and summer. Deceptively uniform in appearance, salt marshes, as well as the brackish marshes of the Chesapeake estuary and the freshwater marshes at Troy Meadows, are a gigantic food factory, churning out tons of organic material that supports an amazing parade of animal life, from microscopic bacteria to thousands of shorebirds, waders, and songbirds. All along the Great Bay Blvd. stretch vast flats of salt-meadow cordgrass cut by tidal guts marked by the taller, coarser salt-marsh cordgrass. These plants and a handful of others are the only ones that can survive here, due to the heavy concentrations of salt. The reward for these plants and for the animal life of the marsh that feeds on them is the rich and continuous supply of nutrients, such as

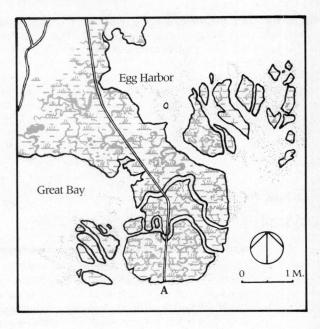

potassium, phosphorous, and calcium, which are trapped and recycled here.

The gently shelving coast of the Mid-Atlantic, with its many bays and estuaries, is ideal for marsh formation. The rivers wash down great loads of nutrient-rich sediments that have been eroded off the uplands. When they meet the sea, the river currents slow, and some sediments are deposited in the estuary (see **Chesapeake Bay**). More sediment is deposited by a process called flocculation. As the fresh water comes in contact with salt water, a chemical reaction takes place because of electrically charged mineral salts in the seawater. Particles of sediment coagulate, become heavier, and drift to the bottom. The daily high tides also bring sandy sediments into the estuary or the sheltered bay behind a barrier beach. As the incoming tide is stronger than the falling tide, some of that load of material remains behind on shoals in the mouth of a barrier beach inlet and on the shores of the bay. These sediments form muddy or sandy shallows where vegetation can sprout. Submerged plants like eelgrass and wigeon grass act as traps for sediments by slowing the currents of the tidal flow.

In the intertidal zone, on muddy or sandy banks exposed at low tide, salt-marsh cordgrass takes root. Once it begins to grow, it continues to build the marsh by also trapping sediments with its network of stems and leaves. Salt-marsh cordgrass bears seeds, but its main method of propagation is by means of rhizomes, specially adapted stems that spread out horizontally underground from the parent plant and then sprout. This is a very efficient system, which allows the plant to stay protected all winter long below the surface of the marsh and to grow as soon as temperatures are warm enough. The tough, fibrous root and rhizome system of the cordgrass helps to bind the marsh together into a spongy layer of live plant material, muck, and partially decayed vegetation called peat. The marsh will continue to grow upward until it is just above the mean high-tide level. At this height the marsh will be flooded only by the spring tides, which occur twice a month with the new and full moon, and by storm tides (see **#29**).

Seawater contains on the average 35 parts of salt to 1000 parts of water. This may not sound like very much, but anyone who has been rolled by the surf and inadvertently swallowed a mouthful knows how salty this is. Most landplants die if exposed to seawater. The high concentration of salt destroys the moisture balance in the plant, drawing all water out of its cells. Water is a key ingredient in all the essential chemical reactions that carry out the life processes of the plant, the medium that transports food and removes wastes. To survive, the plant must maintain the proper moisture balance.

A key to understanding the movement of water in and out of the plant is the semipermeable membrane, which surrounds the cells of the plant. Water moves easily back and forth across the membrane; larger salt molecules move less easily. If there is more water than salt on one side of the membrane and more salt than water on the other side, water will move through the membrane until the concentrations are equal on both sides.

Salt-marsh cordgrass, a tall lush species that edges the tidal creeks and bays, has a variety of mechanisms to maintain the proper levels of salts and moisture in the main body of the plant. The root cells of the plant contain higher concentrations of sodium chloride than the surrounding seawater, which means that water molecules will pass into the root cells, not out of them. Also at work is a chemical pumping system that allows the inner cells to take in the salty water and pump out the salt at the same time. As a result the inner sap of the cordgrass has very low salinities. Other parts of the plant isolate excess molecules of salt and transport them to salt glands on the undersides of the leaves, where salt is excreted in crystals. The next high tide or rainstorm washes the crystals away. A waxy layer on the leaves prevents additional water loss through transpiration in the hot summer sun. Other salt-marsh plants use these as well as a variety of other devices to survive in their inhospitable home. Most of these mechanisms require tremendous amounts of energy that freshwater plants do not need to expend. It is not surprising that given the chance, salt-marsh cordgrass will grow better in fresh water, but fierce competition from freshwater plants generally prevents this.

The lush stands of salt-marsh cordgrass indicate the most productive part of the marsh. It is here that fresh deposits of sediment and nutrients are left with each high tide. Blue-green algae on the surface of the marsh capture inorganic nitrogen, turning it into a compound usable by the marsh grasses (see #31). Other algae attach themselves to the stems of the cordgrass or are swept in with each high tide. In winter when the cordgrass has died back, the algae are still growing, converting sunlight to sugar and starch. Decaying vegetation and algae are constantly consumed and broken down by bacteria (see #23). Together they become a nourishing food called detritus, which is avidly consumed by snails, clams, oysters, crabs, and other creatures. They in turn deposit their wastes, containing many nutrients, back in the marsh. The marshes produce several tons of organic material per acre per year using the sun's energy to convert inorganic chemicals, carbon dioxide, and water into vegetation. About half of the nutrients contained in this material are recycled to the marsh itself and about half go into the surrounding waters to feed the mollusks, crustaceans, fish, and other life of the estuaries and bays.

Several feet back from the edges of the creeks begins a zone of poor drainage. Here the peaty muck is saturated with water; even the tiniest spaces are filled. Oxygen cannot penetrate the sodden material and nutrients cannot be replaced. Nitrogen is in especially low supply in this zone. This may be the saltiest part of the marsh, for the daily tides do not flush the area as fully as they do the creek banks. As drainage is poor, rainwater cannot wash the salts out of the soil. In this stressful environment the salt-marsh cordgrass is less vigorous, dwarfed.

The high marsh is the area that is flooded only during the highest or spring tides, which occur twice a month, and storm tides. The grasses here are finer and less stalwart, often lying in wind-flattened whorls on the ground. The two dominant species are salt-meadow cordgrass and salt grass, both often referred to as salt hay. Since colonial times, salt hay has been harvested as fodder for domestic animals. Here the grasses form a dense mat that keeps the surface of the marsh moist. This probably helps keep the plants from drying out. The thick cover also benefits small animals, protecting them from the hot sun and from the eyes of predators. It is an ideal nesting ground for the secretive sharp-tailed sparrow.

Throughout the high marsh are shallow depressions where water collects after spring and storm tides. Then, in the weeks that follow, the water evaporates and leaves behind a salty residue. Over time these depressions, or salt pannes, become so salty that almost nothing will grow in them. Around the fringes of the pannes, one group of plants, the glassworts, manages to flourish. These plants are succulents, storing great amounts of water in their stems in order to dilute the salts they take in. The small, fleshy fingers of the glassworts turn deep red in autumn, making fierce points of color in the dune marshes. Juicy and somewhat salty, this plant is good to eat.

Other common high-marsh plants include sea lavender, a delicate plant that bears tiny lavender blossoms from July to October, and seaside goldenrod, marsh elder, black rush, and hairy seablight, found toward the landward border of the high marsh.

Scattered across the marsh are many small ponds, which can develop in a number of ways. A flock of snow geese feeding heavily in a small area can destroy all the vegetation, allowing a small pocket of water to collect there. Or a depression in the marsh may become dammed off with a deposit of plant debris or sediment at high tide so that it never completely drains at low tide. Whatever its origin, once a pool is established, it continues to deepen as the marsh plants and the underlying peat below rot away. The marsh plants cannot stand permanent flooding. Once they decay, the peat below is attacked by bacteria. The movement of water in the pond keeps oxygen supplied to these minute scavengers. Marine plants such as wigeon grass and various algae and small fish thrive in the ponds, making them rich feeding grounds for such shorebirds as greater and lesser yellowlegs, spotted sandpiper, black-bellied and semipalmated plovers, and whimbrel during the spring and fall migrations. Herons, egrets, and glossy ibis also hunt in the pools and the tidal creeks in the breeding season (see **#28**).

The roadside provides another type of habitat. Higher than the marsh, it is drier and less salty. Redcedar, holly, bayberry, high-tide bush, and poison ivy in its shrub form make a thick border that provides excellent cover and a source of food for migrating songbirds. Such cover is important, for many migrating hawks prey on smaller birds (see **#32**). In August, thousands of tree swallows light in the bayberry to eat the small waxy fruits, which are indigestible to most other species of birds. August and September are the time to see clouds of monarch butterflies as they migrate thousands of miles to Central America. They are attracted to the seaside goldenrod; sometimes a dozen of them gather on a single plant. While a single generation accomplishes the southward flight, the movement northward in spring is apparently achieved by several generations of monarchs, each flying further north before laying its eggs on a milkweed plant.

At the end of the road, extensive mudflats lie exposed at low tide (**A**). Dying marsh plants and rotting peat, drowned by the rising sea level, and microscopic marine animal and plant life provide food for myriad creatures: clams, mussels, insect larvae, worms, snails, etc. Bacteria attack the decaying plant matter here too, and begin to break down the tough indigestible cellulose that gives the plant its shape. The next high tide sweeps these substances back into the marsh where they fertilize the living marsh. Attracted by this wealth of food, shorebirds flock to the mud flats at Tuckerton (see **Cape May** and **#28**). The rare curlew sandpiper has been known to stop here. American oystercatchers nest on the marsh by the mudflats. A southern species that has been steadily pushing its territory northward, the oystercatcher is common only at certain locations along the coast. Their flat, dagger-shaped bills help them to pry oysters, mussels, and clams off rocks and pilings and out of the mud, and then to open them. Look, too, for the boat-tailed grackle over the marsh; it reaches its northernmost distribution on the southern New Jersey coasts.

Remarks: *At low tide you can walk out onto the marshes but high boots or old sneakers are advisable. There is good crabbing in warm weather from the seven bridges on Great Bay Blvd. Spring and fall are more pleasant than summer, when biting insects are at their fiercest. Bug repellent is essential from May through the first frost.*

22.

Brigantine National
Wildlife Refuge

Directions: **Atlantic County, N.J. From New York City take the New Jersey Turnpike south to Exit 11, then the Garden State Parkway south to Exit 48, about 105 miles. Take U.S. 9 south for 5.5 miles to Oceanville and turn east (left)** on Great Creek Rd., which leads directly to the refuge. Stop at the refuge office for bird lists and to look at the log in which visitors note interesting sightings.

Ownership: U.S. Fish and Wildlife Service

From spring to fall and back to spring again the marshes, open waters, and uplands of Brigantine quicken with the skittering flights of shorebirds, the exuberant colors and songs of spring warblers, and the thrust and sweep of skeins of migrating geese. Over 275 species of land and water birds have been identified here, many of them rarities. Like the other classic birding areas, Cape May and Bombay Hook, Brigantine encompasses a range of habitats. Salt, brackish, and freshwater marshes, freshwater impoundments and open salt bays, cleared fields, brushy woods, and hedgerows offer refuge to migrants and nesting species.

The 8-mile wildlife drive around the refuge begins with a stop at the Gull Pond (**A**). This old gravel pit has filled in with water and is a collecting area for gulls and waterfowl. Large numbers of gulls gather in winter, the most common being the herring, greater black-backed and ring-billed gulls. The greater black-backed gull is gradually pushing its range southward. Large and aggressive, it not only robs other gulls of food but occasionally kills other birds. Laughing gulls with their dark heads and red bills take over as the most common species in summer. Gulls are not strong fliers; they rely instead on their ability to glide on updrafts off the water's surface. Their flight pattern distinguishes them from terns, whose long, pointed wings make them strong, swift fliers. Terns flap almost continuously and hover in the air above the water like a kestrel hunting over land. Gulls are not good swimmers either; instead they snatch fish off the surface of the water, scavenge along the beach, forage for rodents, insects, grain, and shellfish. This all-inclusive diet has enabled them to flourish in a variety of habitats, many of them man-made such as dumps, landfills, and harbors. They have learned to follow fishing fleets to feed on waste fish. In spring, swirling clouds of gulls follow the farmers as they plow in order to feed on the grubs and other insects turned up in the new earth. The herring gull, the most common type over most of the Atlantic shore, is remarkable for its ingenuity in cracking open shellfish. It will take a clam or mussel into its beak, fly over a hard surface—rocks or concrete for example—and drop the shellfish so that it cracks on impact.

Two major attractions for birds are the West Pool (**B**) and East Pool (**C**), two freshwater impoundments. The levels of water in these pools changes seasonally, which in turn alters the vegetation in

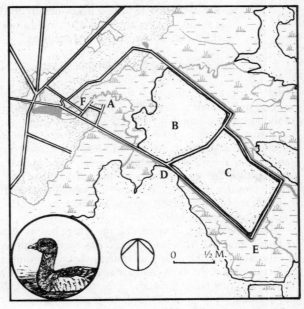

Inset: Brant

them. In winter the ponds are full of water and attract great numbers of waterfowl from fall to early spring. Approximately 150,000 ducks and geese winter in the refuge. Many species of dabbling duck are common here in fall, including species such as American black duck, northern pintail, gadwall, northern shoveler, and blue-winged and green-winged teal. The lesser snow goose is abundant here from October through December. Some are a bluish-gray color; this color phase of the species is apparently increasing. Flocks of whistling swans also come to the pools in late fall (see **#60**). Diving ducks such as ring-necked, canvasback, greater scaup, and hooded merganser can be seen, especially in fall and early spring. The lesser scaup also visits the pools, though in smaller numbers than the greater. It apparently prefers sites further inland (see **#9**).

In May, and again from July through September, the water in the impoundments is lowered, creating extensive mudflats. Migrating shorebirds arrive in great numbers, the southward migrations bringing the greatest variety of species (see **#42**). Some of the more unusual species found here include the ruff, northern and Wilson's phalaropes, curlew, white-rumped stilt, western and Baird's sandpipers, marbled and Hudsonian godwits, and whimbrel. Along with the common snipe and black-bellied plover, which are also seen at Brigantine, the whimbrel is found along nearly every coast of every sea in the world. Although it inhabits marine environments while on migration and in winter, in summer it nests by fresh water in coniferous forests of the far north. The most conspicuous shorebird is the large and noisy willet.

At Turtle Cove (**D**) sea ducks, including the white-winged, surf, and black scoters, oldsquaw, bufflehead, and common goldeneye, are frequent visitors in winter. Look here also for brant, small dark geese with white necklaces. One of the chief goals in establishing the refuge was to provide a feeding ground for this species, whose population was decimated during the 1930s due to a blight which killed its principal food, eelgrass. Their diet has now shifted to sea lettuce, a variety of seaweed, and the population of brant has been largely restored. As much as 90 percent of the entire population appears at Brigantine from fall to spring. These geese nest far north in the Arctic, where severe weather late into summer occasionally prevents the laying of eggs—another factor limiting its population.

The eastern impoundment (**C**) is an excellent duck-breeding area. The birds like the small hummocks of grasses that dot the pool. Gadwall, ruddy duck, northern shoveler, and black duck nest here regularly. This is an excellent area for waders in the spring, beginning in April. Eleven species of herons, egrets, and bitterns and an abundance of glossy ibis appear on the refuge (see **#28**).

At the southeast corner of the East Pool (**E**) is an area called Godwits' Corner, where marbled and Hudsonian godwits, along with American avocets, gather in late summer on their way south. American avocets are striking birds: white, buff, and black with long, stilt-like legs and long upward-curving bills. They swing their bills back and forth through shallow water to strain out small bits of food. As they often feed in stagnant, muddy environments, their food supply includes dead and decaying material. This may explain why the species is susceptible to tapeworms. Their striking appearance is unusual among shorebirds, most of which have muted coloring or are patterned to provide good camouflage on their nesting or wintering grounds.

Over the impoundments and the surrounding marshes, look for the northern harrier throughout the year. During the cold months rough-legged hawks and short-eared owls down from the Arctic tundra patrol the marshes and the open uplands; and in the summer ospreys are common residents. Bald eagles are occasionally seen at any time of year, joined from time to time by golden eagles. You may also see the endangered peregrine falcon. The Peregrine Fund at the Cornell Laboratory of Ornithology has erected "hacking" towers for the release of young captive-reared peregrines (see **#58**). In some winters snowy owls may appear along the coast, here and at Manahawkin, Tinicum, Tuckerton, and Island Beach. Their usual home is the far north, and their incursions southward are tied to the cyclical rise and fall of the lemming populations in the Arctic. When the lemmings abruptly die off, food is scarce and the snowy owls show up far south of their normal wintering range.

Along the western edge of the West Pool are uplands, with woods and open fields, areas of heavy brush, and scrub pines. Landbird migration peaks here in the first three weeks of May, and again in August and September, with nineteen species of warblers shown on the checklist as common or uncommon and another ten as occasional or rare. Over the open fields in winter look for snow buntings, horned larks, and Lapland longspurs, which are occasionally seen. Snow buntings move across the open ground in flocks. In flight, their winter plumage appears mostly white marked with bits of black and buff.

Doughty Creek is bordered by a freshwater marsh (**F**) where king, sora, and Virginia rails and American and least bitterns nest. These species are all very shy and difficult to spot as they skulk through the marsh grasses (see **#67**). At low tide, watch the edges of the tidal creeks for clapper rails.

Remarks: *This is only a sketch of the immense variety of birdlife to be found at Brigantine. Further information may be obtained by contacting the Refuge Manager, Brigantine National Wildlife Refuge, Great Creek Rd., P.O. Box 72, Oceanville, N.J. 08231. See also the* **Bibliography.** *Along the western shore of the West Pool are a number of trails leading through the upland region and along Doughty Creek. Other activities include photography from a number of blinds along the causeway between the two impoundments, and fishing in the creeks of the refuge. Small motor boats can be rented nearby at Chestnut Neck Marina off Route 9 on the Mullica River, and offshore charter fishing is available from Atlantic City. The Pine Barrens and the Atlantic beaches are nearby. The refuge is open to the public free of charge from sunrise to sunset. Weather can be changeable in winter and there is often a strong wind. In the warmer weather mosquitoes and biting flies can be a nuisance. Nearest camping is at Bass River State Forest (see* **#12***). A spotting scope is especially useful for scanning the pools.*

23.

Longport
Sod Banks

Directions: **Atlantic County, N.J. From New York City take the New Jersey Turnpike to Exit 11 and the Garden State Parkway south to Exit 30, about 125 miles from Lincoln Tunnel. On Route 52, go southeast 1.2 miles to the traffic circle. Go three-quarters around the circle to Shore Rd.; go north 0.8 mile to Maryland Ave. and turn right. After 2.4 miles the road from Ocean City joins from the right. Either turn right to the parking lot just before the Ocean Drive bridge or turn left and park the car on the side of the road just beyond the bridge crossing the small creek. Scan the sodbanks with a scope or binoculars and explore the creek for snails and hermit crabs.**

Ownership: **Privately owned.**

The ragtag remnants of an old salt-marsh stand seaward of the beach and are exposed at low tide. Salt-marsh cordgrass and wisps of algae cling stubbornly to the spongy hunks of peat, binding this ancient meadow mat and dissipating storm-generated waves. In among the cordgrass and algae, blue mussels, mud snails, and periwinkles litter the surface. Great numbers of shorebirds collect here in the spring and fall, attracted by the abundant food. The rare bar-tailed godwit has been seen here in May for several consecutive years.

The rising sea level has drowned much of the Great Egg Harbor river basin and the marshes that once edged this estuary sheltered behind the barrier islands to the east. If continually submerged, salt-marsh grasses die and the peat beneath them begins to fall apart. Some vestiges of salt-marsh cordgrass now survive because the area is exposed as the tide ebbs. But as the sea continues to rise, it too will disappear. The dying plant material is attacked by microscopic bacteria, tiny creatures whose few cells are so small that they must digest their food outside the cell and draw in the nutrients as they are released. The bacteria and the partially broken down plant material, or detritus, are a main source of food for many small marine organisms that cannot digest the living plant fibers. Algae, which clings to the grasses and the peat, is the other prime source of food for these organisms. Most algae is so small that it is invisible to the naked eye or is seen only as a wash of color which can be green, blue-green, or yellow.

The species of mollusks found here are attracted by the decaying marsh. Mussels, which are filter feeders, draw in water laden with detritus and algae and expel wastes. Food particles and oxygen are filtered out by their gills as the water passes over them. Basically sedentary creatures, blue mussels attach themselves to any firm surface such as stone jetties, pilings, or hummocks of peat by means of an intriguing system. The mussel extends its foot, a fleshy appendage used for locomotion in other species of mollusks, so that it touches the anchoring material. Then a special gland secretes a substance which flows down a narrow groove in the foot and hardens immediately on contact with the water. By repeating this process many times, the mussel becomes anchored by a series of tough stringy filaments called byssal threads and can go about the business of eating and reproducing.

Snails have a different system. Moving around the surface of the peat by means of their foot, they scrape tiny morsels of food off the surface with a special filelike tongue called the radula. Equipped with minute teeth angled toward the creature's mouth, the radula can be extended and retracted to convey scraps of food to the mouth. The radula is a common feature of many mollusks.

Mollusks are a very ancient group of animals, dating back 500 million years. Their shells of calcium carbonate are secreted by a unique attachment, the mantle, which is a layer of tissue lying between the shell and the internal organs. The horny protuberances of the giant clam, the pearly delicate shell of the nautilus, the tiny spirals of snails and the elegant symmetry of the scallop are all created by the mantle.

The ancestor of snails and whelks had a flat, coiled shell, one coil wrapped neatly in the next. At some point, the coil twisted, became asymmetrical and turned into the familiar turban shape seen today. The change apparently provided the creature with greater protection from its predators, for the flat coil did not allow the snail to withdraw its head first. Its foot got in the way. The angled spiral, on the other hand, allows the snail or whelk ample room for a safer retreat.

The bar-tailed godwit, which has been seen here in spring for several years, was originally a Eurasian species that has drifted across the Bering Sea to nest in Alaska. Occasionally, individuals find their way south along the Pacific and Atlantic coasts. In summer piping plovers nest along the high-tide line, one of a few such sites in New Jersey (see **#28**).

Remarks: *Spring, late summer, and fall are the best times to see large numbers of shorebirds. In winter the jetties in the town of Longport just to the east are good for eider and harlequin duck. Go south on the road to Ocean City and pull over by the inlet just before the bridge. Brant, oldsquaw, scaup, and scoter collect here during the cold months. Camping at Belleplain State Forest south of Belleplain on Route 550. Other activities: fishing from the barrier beaches, swimming, deep-sea charters from Ocean City.*

24.

Fortescue Wildlife Management Area

Directions: **Cumberland County, N.J. From New York City follow the New Jersey Turnpike south about 120 miles to Exit 1. Go south and southeast on Route 49 to Bridgeton, about 27 miles. About 3 miles beyond Bridgeton, turn south (right) on Route 553 and drive about 9 miles to Newport. In Newport turn south and go about 5 miles to Fortescue at the end of the road. The turns are well marked with signs.**

Ownership: **New Jersey Division of Fish, Game, and Wildlife.**

Every March tens of thousands of greater snow geese arrive on the Delaware Bay off Fortescue, N.J. Since before records were first kept, the birds have gathered here, their strange nasal calls filling the air. Geese are creatures of precise habit, and snow geese are no exception. They form lasting family bonds and may even mate with the same partner for the whole of their long lives. Unlike other species of migratory birds, the adults and their offspring stay together during the fall migration, a small unit within the larger flock. Year after year they follow the same migratory routes, stopping at the same resting places, and breeding on the same patch of Arctic tundra far to the north. As a result of these patterns of bonding and migration, two races of snow geese have emerged—the greater snow goose, which is mainly an Atlantic Coast migrant, and the lesser snow goose with both a white and a blue phase, which moves north and south through the interior of the continent (see **#22** and **#98**).

Greater snow geese winter from the Chesapeake Bay south to Back Bay and Currituck Sound in North Carolina. After arriving in the Delaware Bay, they stay a few weeks to feed and rest before moving north about the second week in April to their next stopping ground, St. Joachim on the St. Lawrence River, not far from Quebec. Safe from hunters in spring, the birds fly into the marshes during the day to feed on salt-marsh cordgrass. Out on the bay in March, rafts of diving ducks gather and scoters are frequent visitors to the area (see **#99** on feeding habits). The geese stop at Fortescue on their way south too. Arriving in November, they move on as the waters freeze up. During hunting season the birds stay out on the river in the daytime, moving into the marshes at night to feed.

Remarks: *Camping is available at Belleplain State Forest south of Belleplain on Route 550. The best way to really see the birds is to hire a local powerboat at Fortescue or one of the other small towns in the area. You can spend the day exploring the creeks and marshes along the shore. September is also a marvelous time here. Although the snow geese have not arrived, there are migrating shorebirds, nesting gadwalls and teal, and herons and egrets. Be prepared for biting insects. Wear a heavy long-sleeved shirt and a hat. These same boats are available for fishing trips in the bay.*

25.
Corson's Inlet

Directions: **Cape May County, N.J. From New York City go south on the New Jersey Turnpike to Exit 11. Then take the Garden State Parkway south to Exit 25, about 125 miles in all. Go east on Route 623 about 2 miles to Ocean Drive, also called Central Ave. Turn south (right) and go about 2 miles to 55th St. Turn west (right) on 55th St. and follow it for 1 mile. Park on the left and walk out to the ocean (A). From there continue to drive south, stopping frequently to look for birds. Just before the toll bridge, pull off to the right to look over the salt marsh (B). Drive over the bridge into Strathmere and take the first left. Drive to the end and park. Walk up Whale Beach to the inlet for a different perspective (D).**

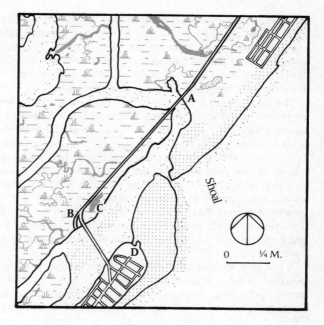

Ownership: **Corson's Inlet State Park, New Jersey Division of Parks and Forestry; town of Ocean City, and town of Strathmere.**

All along the Jersey coast, developers and the Army Corps of Engineers have attempted to fix the capricious shoreline of the barrier beaches, building jetties to immobilize the inlets, stone piers or groins to trap the sand, seawalls to stop erosion. Corson's Inlet is the last free inlet remaining. It is allowed to wander at will, to fill with shoals, to close or widen. At its mouth turbulent lines of waves intersect, collide, and overtake each other, marking the positions of shoals and sandbars. The inner bay is calm, serene. The sandy beaches, mudflats, and salt marsh that border the inlet bring shorebirds, waterfowl, herons, and other waterbirds throughout the year. Even in summer this is quiet place, for thanks to the shifting shallows, the power boats keep away.

The barrier-island inlets are created by storms, often by hurricanes which sweep down on the coast from time to time. During a big storm, the wind piles waves up against the shore. If the storm coincides with a very high tide (see **#29**), it sends tons of water through an existing inlet into the bay behind the barrier. Then as the hurricane moves on, the winds come from the opposite direction and may force the water in the bay to break through in a new place. Once formed, the inlet will be shaped by two forces: the daily tides flushing in and out of the opening, and the longshore current bringing a constant supply of new sand along the coast.

The tides deposit sediments in tidal deltas at the inner and outer entrances to the inlet. Because the rising tide entering the bay is stronger than the falling tide, it brings more sand into the bay than is taken away. Some of the sand is swept onward to the salt marshes, helping to build up the height of the marsh (see **#21**). A steady supply of sand may keep the marsh from eroding as sea level rises (see **Introduction**). The incoming tides also bring in nutrients such as potassium, calcium, nitrogen, and phosphorous (see **Chesapeake Bay** and **#21**), and carry marine organisms into the bay. The constant influx of salt water maintains the growth of the cordgrasses on the marsh. Without it, brackish marsh species would take over.

If you sit at the beach and watch the waves roll in, you will usually perceive them as striking the beach head-on. Although it may be imperceptible, the waves almost always approach from an angle, even though it may be slight. The direction of the waves is determined by a complicated combination of underwater topography, winds, the shape of the shoreline, the flow of large rivers such as the Hudson, and offshore landmasses such as Long Island and Cape Cod.

Although the waves approach the beach at an angle, the backwash which runs back down the beach after the wave has broken takes the quickest route, straight down the beach (see diagram). As a result, sand carried by the waves actually moves along the beach. At Corson's Inlet, where the waves generally approach from the northeast, the net movement is southward. This longshore current is also called *littoral drift*.

The southbound current accounts for the migration of the inlet southward. Sand is continually being deposited at the northern side of the inlet and being removed from Whale Beach at the southern side. If left to themselves, all of New Jersey's barrier islands would have this characteristic shape, pointed at the southern end where sand is being added, blunt at the northern end where sand is being removed. Although the tidal flow interrupts most of the longshore current, some sand continues to move south and is deposited in the middle of the channel. This is why jetties have been built to guard the inlet channels elsewhere. These sandbars are constantly shifting as the strength and direction of the waves change (see **#7**). The sandbars protect the bay from the full force of the sea and are a main source of sand for the marshes.

At some point, the inlet will probably close. Another hurricane may dump vast quantities of sand here all at once, or the inlet may simply fill up with sand over time. In either case, a new inlet will open up somewhere else, for inlets are a crucial part of the barrier-island system, providing a safety valve through which the power of storms is channeled.

The path to the beach from the parking area (**A**) leads through typical back-dune vegetation of bayberry, poison ivy, and panic grass. This is an excellent place to see migrating warblers and a variety of sparrows. In winter, search the bushes for the Ipswich sparrow, an uncommon subspecies of the savannah sparrow. Look also for horned larks and snow buntings. Crossing the primary dune, you will find goldenrod on the back of the dune, giving way to American beach

Longshore Current

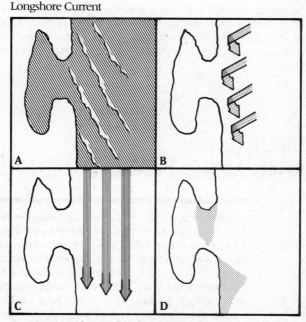

A. Direction of waves breaking on the shore
B. Action of the sand
C. Direction of the longshore current
D. Eventual effect

grass on the top and front of the dune (for barrier-island vegetation see #31 and #55).

Least terns nest on the beach in summer. Be careful when walking on the beach at this time; the eggs and the young are very hard to see (see #30). Look for many species of waterfowl in the inlet during the fall and winter (see #20). In summer, willets, clapper rails, and seaside and sharp-tailed sparrows nest in the marshes (B). At the small pool to the east of the road just north of the toll bridge (C), piping plovers have nested regularly in recent years. These shorebirds are becoming rarer and rarer in New Jersey due to loss of habitat (see #30). The small whitish birds are so well matched to their sandy habitat, in spite of the black ring around their neck, that they seem to disappear when motionless. Shorebird migrations in May and again from late July through September bring great numbers of birds to feed on the mudflats and sandbanks (see #21 and #22).

Remarks: *Camping is available at Belleplain State Forest south of Belleplain on Route 550. Other activities include fishing, swimming, and sailing in the inlet. Swimming is unsupervised. Be careful, as currents can be strong. Mosquitoes can be fierce in summer on the marsh side of the inlet.*

26.
Beaches of the Delaware Bay:
Reed's, Moores, Thompsons

Directions: **Cape May and Cumberland counties, N.J. From New York City go south on the New Jersey Turnpike to Exit 11 and then on the Garden State Parkway to Exit 13 (about 140 miles from Lincoln Tunnel). Exit west 0.4 mile to U.S. 9. Turn south (left) on U.S. 9 and go 0.8 mile to Swainton. Turn west (right) onto Route 646 and go 3.3 miles toward Goshen. Turn south (left) on Route 615, Goshen-Swainton Rd., and go 0.4 mile. Turn south (left) on Route 47 and go 1.7 miles to Bidwell's Ditch, a tidal creek. Here you can put in a small boat or canoe and ride the tide down through the marsh and back. Continue on 0.6 mile to Reed's Beach Rd., which comes in from the** west (right). Follow it 1.6 miles to the end and park. Do not go into the private marina on the right. Walk out along the jetty and the beach.

To reach Moores Beach get back onto Route 47 going north then west; about 13 miles beyond Goshen turn south (left), at the sign for Moores Beach. Drive to the water's edge and park.

To reach Thompsons Beach continue on Route 47 northwest 0.5 mile and turn west (left) toward Heislerville. Go 1.6 miles and turn south on Thompsons Beach Rd. Drive to the end of the road.

Ownership; Beaches are public land below the high-tide line.

Every May when the spring tides rise along the protected shores of the Delaware Bay, thousands upon thousands of horseshoe crabs make their way up the beaches to lay their eggs. The shallows heave and ripple; the shoreline is littered with these strange armor-plated creatures. Scudding back and forth through the sky, and blackening the beaches, thousands of shorebirds arrive, while flocks of raucous laughing gulls perch on the stone jetties and wait on the sand. As the tide falls, millions of tiny green eggs lie exposed, and the birds feast.

Horseshoe crabs are an ancient species that has remained essentially unchanged since the first dinosaurs evolved 200 million years ago. Not crustaceans at all, these "crabs" are related to spiders. Their only living close relatives are in Asia, a reminder that the continents were once united. For most of the year the crabs live on the ocean floor, moving slowly along the bottom, eating mollusks and worms. The flow of tides and currents passing over their curved shells help to hold them on the bottom. The crabs shed their shells as they grow, just as a snake sheds its skin. The shell splits at the front and the crab walks out in its new suit. It is often the empty shell, not a dead crab, that people find along the high-tide line. During the breeding season, however, many crabs do become stranded on the beach and die. Frequently, the crabs are flipped onto their backs in the surf. Some manage to right themselves by using their spikey tails; others are attacked by bands of seagulls, which devour their soft inner parts.

The height of the breeding activity falls during the high tides of the full or new moon in the second half of May. Then one can see the crabs swimming, upside down, waving their legs feebly in the air. Right side up they sink to the bottom. They have two large compound eyes and seven inconspicuous eyes around the edge of their shell. These smaller eyes are sensitive to ultraviolet light and may help them navigate to shore. The mating sequence begins when the male, which is considerably smaller than the female, grasps the female's shell with specially adapted pincers. Once on the beach the female scrapes a small depression in the intertidal zone and lays a clutch of thousands of eggs. Then she drags the male across the eggs so that he can fertilize them. Afterwards, the female covers the eggs with sand. The female may return to the beach several times during the short breeding season to lay more eggs. Because there are so many horseshoe crabs in the Delaware Bay, they are constantly digging up each other's eggs, exposing them for the birds.

At Reed's Beach great flights of ruddy turnstones and red knots partake of the bounty with the gulls. Virtually the entire North American population of red knots may pass through the Delaware Bay. Over a period of several days the birds gorge on the eggs, building up a layer of fat. From the Delaware Bay they will travel north perhaps 2500 miles to their Arctic nesting grounds. There is some evidence to suggest that the birds make this flight almost non-stop, fueled by the food stored as fat in Delaware Bay. This fat may also help them survive the first weeks on the tundra, when food may still be scarce. Other shorebirds, primarily sanderlings and semi-palmated sandpipers, also eat the crab eggs, but they tend to congregate further up the bay at Moores and Thompsons beaches.

The shorebirds make their long journey north because the tundra habitat provides a perfect nursery. Harsh winters exclude reptiles and reduce populations of other predators. In summer the frozen tundra becomes a soggy plain of pools and bogs, which offers further protection and creates breeding grounds for countless insects. Twenty-four hours of sunlight allow the birds to forage all day long and spurs the growth of plant and insect life. This abundance of food is helpful to young birds once they hatch. Because the season is short, the birds' breeding cycle is much faster than in species farther south. By late summer, the young birds are fledged and ready to start their travels toward the wintering grounds.

Remarks: *The best time to see the birds feeding is from just after high tide to low tide in the second half of May. There is camping at Belleplain State Forest just north of Moores Beach. For other activities, see* **Cape May**.

27.

Timber Beaver

Swamp

Directions: **Cape May County, N.J. From New York City go south on the New Jersey Turnpike to Exit 11 and on the Garden State Parkway about 140 miles to Exit 13. Turn west (right) onto Avalon Rd. and then left immediately onto U.S. 9 south. Drive 0.8 mile and turn west (right) onto Goshen-Swainton Rd. Drive 1.6 miles and turn northwest (right) onto Route 657. Drive 1.3 miles to point A, where a corduroy road cuts through the swamp. In summer this is heavily overgrown. Continue on 1.6 miles to point B, where Beaver Dam Rd. goes east into Clint Millpond. To reach Route 83, drive north on Gravel Hole Rd. from intersection of Beaver Dam Rd., Gravel Hole Rd., and Route 657. Turn east (right) on Route 83 and drive 1.9 miles to the dirt track (C). Park by the bridge and walk to your right down to the track. Walk south about 1 mile for a good overview of the swamp.**

Ownership: **New Jersey Division of Fish, Game, and Wildlife.**

On the rolling surface of the swamp is a stand of mature lowland forest, thick and impenetrable at its heart. Once the area drained directly into Sluice Creek, a tidal stream that empties into the Delaware Bay. Beavers and man dammed the headwaters of the creek at Clint Millpond. Upstream the waters are fresh; below the dam they become brackish.

Walk into the swamp along the corduroy road (**A**). At the start of the road the canopy is sparse, for this area has been heavily timbered, and gypsy moths have badly damaged the remaining trees. Southern red oak (Spanish oak), willow oak, and loblolly pines, along with scattered red maple and sweetgum, make up the canopy.

Gypsy moths will strike oaks first. The caterpillars hatch out in summer and feed voraciously on the leaves. The first year's defoliation does not injure the tree too badly, for the most important period of growth is in the spring when the leaves first come out. During

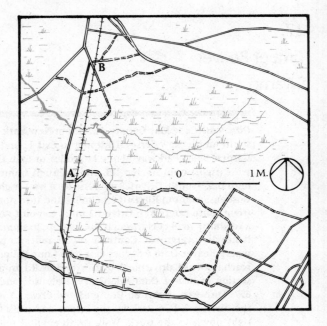

those early weeks the tree makes most of the food that will last through the following winter. After a second year of defoliation, however, the tree begins to weaken. The caterpillars eat constantly. They are laying up a vast store of energy which will power their transformation into adult moths. During the time they are in the cocoon, they will have nothing to eat. In late summer the moths emerge to lay their brown egg masses on the trunks of the trees. The new generation of caterpillars will hatch out the following spring.

Like many other pests, gypsy moths were imported from abroad. Originally they were to be our answer to the silkworm, the foundation of a new industry. Infestations break out about every ten years. There is a population explosion of moths, which may last several years. Trees are devastated. Then, almost as quickly, the population subsides again, as disease, predators, and too much competition take their toll.

Light shining through the open canopy has encouraged a thick carpet of ferns and orchids on the swamp floor. Shrubs are also abundant and include black huckleberry, lowbush blueberry, sweet pepperbush, swamp azalea, and catbrier. If many of the oak trees are killed, the woods may revert to an earlier successional stage of loblolly pine and red maple. Loblolly is close to the northern edge of its range here.

Further into the swamp, the trees close in, the understory crowded with young red maples. Tiny streams cross the road to the Sluice Creek. A heavy layer of herbaceous plants hides these small channels. Timber Beaver Swamp is a fine place for birds. A variety of owls and woodpeckers nest in the vicinity.

Take Beaver Dam Rd. (**B**) into Clint Millpond. Downstream from the pond the brackish river edge of Sluice Creek is lined with salt-marsh cordgrass and salt-meadow grass (see **#21**). Here, deep in the midst of the swamp, look for beaver, river otter, and muskrat. The muskrats prefer to build their lodges in the fresh water farther upstream. Mallard, black duck, wood duck, and teal nest in the hidden recesses of the swamp, well protected against disturbance. Here there is also one lone baldcypress, far north of its expected range. The tree is about 60 feet tall and 5 feet in circumference (see **#73**).

Remarks: *Allow a whole day to explore this swamp from different angles. From fall to spring is the best time to visit, when the mosquitoes and ticks are less ferocious. Other activities include birding at Cape May and Stone Harbor (see* **Cape May** *and #30), deep-sea fishing out of Cape May, surf fishing along the shore.*

Cape May

Directions: **Cape May County, N.J. From New York City drive south on the New Jersey Turnpike to Exit 11, then on the Garden State Parkway to the end, about 155 miles in all. There it runs into Lafayette St. (Route 109). Follow Lafayette into the center of town, where it forms a T with Perry St.**

Soaring overhead, clustering on the branches of trees and shrubs, floating on the bay, sweeping over the ocean, birds, thousands upon thousands, surge into Cape May during the fall migrations. Hawks, eagles, warblers, shorebirds, sparrows and finches, thrushes, flycatchers, vireos and kinglets, ducks, geese, swans—hundreds of different species collect on this narrow point of land, waiting for the right weather for crossing Delaware Bay. A legendary event to all birders, the fall flights are an extraordinary spectacle for anyone to see.

There are always birds at Cape May. Spring begins in March when the ducks and geese begin to move northward along the Atlantic Coast and companies of common and red-throated loons join the overwintering waterfowl. As April and May progress, shorebirds converge in ever-increasing numbers: twelve species of sandpipers, yellowlegs, red knots, dunlins, whimbrels, dowitchers, plovers, oystercatchers, willets and perhaps a Wilson's phalarope. Egrets, herons, terns, skimmers, and gulls breed and raise their young through the spring and summer, and by July, the autumn migrations have begun again with the first sandpipers already passing south en route from the muskeg and tundra far to the north. From mid-September to mid-October the hawks own the skies. An average of a thousand per day may be seen, squadrons of sharp-shins and kestrels and many less common species. The height of the migration coincides with that of the songbirds on which they prey. Many songbirds migrate at night, primarily to avoid the hawks, and rest and feed during the day. Seventeen species of hawks, eagles, and vultures are regularly found at Cape May.

Winter belongs to the waterfowl. Scoters, eiders, and oldsquaws ride the Atlantic and shelter in the lee of the stone jetties. In milder winters, bay ducks raft on the bay and dabbling ducks use the fresh-water ponds. The Christmas count of birds regularly records approximately 150 species at Cape May.

The key to this avian parade is geography. The tip of New Jersey is a narrow finger pointing southwestward across the Delaware Bay. The far shore is several miles away across open water. During the fall migrations, birds funnel down into the cape following the line of the land. The prevailing northwest winds of autumn blow the birds southward along the east coast; if they do not expend tremendous energy to fly against it, they may be blown out to sea. When the wind blows strongly from the northwest, the birds are reluctant to cross the Delaware Bay, and they stack up at the cape like commuters waiting for a rush-hour train. This is a good time to see great numbers of songbirds and raptors (or birds of prey).

In part because it is only a few miles wide, Cape May is a meeting ground for many habitats: woodlands, open fields, seacoast, fresh-water and saltwater wetlands, and estuaries. Such diversity of food and shelter brings diversity of insect life, reptiles, mammals, amphibians, and aquatic creatures, and they in turn attract the 360 species of birds found here.

The southern part of New Jersey is undergoing tremendous change. Development is eating up open space, posing questions about the future of the cape and its wildlife populations. Although many of the following sites have been designated as preserves, construction in surrounding land will remove important buffer zones and make these sites more vulnerable to pollution and disturbance.

Remarks: *Peak birding months:*

Shorebirds	*April–May*	*July–October*
Songbirds	*April–May*	*August–September*
Birds of prey	—	*September–October*
Waterfowl	—	*October–March*
Waders	*April–September*	—

Be forewarned that fall warblers are not in breeding plumage, and the various species can be very hard to distinguish, one from another.

At the end of the parkway, just across the Cold Spring Canal bridge, is the South Jersey Fishing Center, with deep-sea fishing boats for hire. There is frequent ferry service to and from Lewes, Del., on the far side of the bay. Cape May itself is full of wonderful Victorian houses, many of them open to overnight guests. A selection of private campgrounds lies along U.S. 9 just north of the cape. The nearest state campground is at Belleplain State Forest, due west of the parkway on Route 550. An excellent resource is the Cape May Bird Observatory, New Jersey Audubon Society, P.O. Box 3, 707 E. Lake Dr., Cape May Point, N.J. 08212, (609) 884-2736.

28.
Stone Harbor
Heronry

Directions: **Cape May County, N.J. From the intersection with Perry St. in Cape May, take Lafayette St. north to the Garden State Parkway. Go to Exit 10, about 12 miles. Go east on Route 657 (Stone Harbor Blvd.) and cross two bridges. At the first light, 3rd Ave., turn south. Go about 1 mile. Parking is on the left (east) side of the street (A).**

Ownership: **Borough of Stone Harbor.**

Consisting of 27 acres in the midst of a summer beach colony, the Stone Harbor Heronry is one of the most important on the entire Atlantic Coast. At sunset in the breeding season the sky is a tumult of birds. Black-crowned and yellow-crowned night herons are flying out to feed in the marshes. Glossy ibis, common, snowy, and American egrets, and little blue, Louisiana, and green herons are sailing in to roost in the trees. This patch of back-dune forest, mostly black cherry, redcedar, and holly, has been a rookery for a long time, well before there were any houses along the beach. Year after year the birds return, apparently undisturbed by the proximity of thousands of people.

Nesting colonies probably evolved as a means of protection. When a predator is nearby, one bird calling an alarm can alert all the others. Often, birds will band together to drive off the intruder.

Communal living also has its problems, though. Competition for nest sites and material is fierce. At Stone Harbor the observer has a clear view of striking mating displays and vigorous disputes, which provide insight into social behavior and the birds' efforts to deal with habitat shortages.

The extensive wetlands to the west of the heronry are a rich hunting ground where the birds search for small fish, crustaceans, small mammals, amphibians, and even insects. The abundance of food is one reason why the rookery became established here, and the relatively tall trees providing apartmentlike living are another. But why the herons came to this pond and these trees in particular, no one really knows.

These wading birds are especially adapted to a life divided between trees and marsh. Their long gangling legs, long sinuous necks, and dagger bills are perfectly suited to prowling through the tidal creeks and pools. They can stand immobile for long periods of time and then suddenly dart their heads forward, grabbing, not spearing, their prey. They often use their feet to gently stir the mucky bottom, snatching fish and crustaceans as they move away. Unlike ducks and geese whose rapid flight and webbed feet limit them to life on the

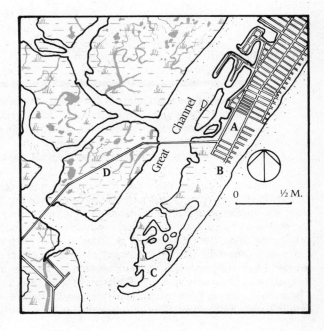

water, herons and egrets have a slow, flapping flight which allows them to land in the trees, while their long agile toes enable them to roost securely.

By the 1900s, the number of herons and egrets had declined alarmingly because they were hunted for their long, delicate breeding plumes, which were used for decades to embellish ladies' hats. The snowy egret has particularly beautiful feathers growing from its breast, head, and back. Since then, strict wildlife laws have changed fashions, and protection of the birds and their nesting colonies has allowed their numbers to recover.

Great blue herons do not nest at this rookery. They do winter on the surrounding marshes in considerable numbers, catching fish and perhaps small mammals such as the marsh vole. The great blues do not use the heronry for roosting at night; they remain in the marshes.

Remarks: *Dawn and dusk from late April to the end of August are the prime time to visit. Toward the end of the summer, the young birds are learning to fly, an amazing and hair-raising adventure. Walk around to the east side of the heronry for another view.*

29.

Nummy's Island

Directions: **Cape May County, N.J. Follow directions to Stone Harbor Heronry and continue south on Third Ave. bearing right across first bridge through the salt marsh (D, p. 93).**

Ownership: **New Jersey Green Acres Program, private.**

The dominant species on this small island is salt-marsh cordgrass (see **#21**). Drive slowly, stopping to scan the numerous ponds for a diversity of waterbirds, especially waders and terns during the breeding season and shorebirds and waterfowl during migration. Herons and egrets come from the rookery at Stone Harbor Point to feed here, and some even nest on the island. Boat-tailed grackles, red-winged blackbirds, common and Forster's terns, American oyster-catchers, and black skimmers are all present in spring and summer. The roadside grasses shelter sharp-tailed and seaside sparrows, birds whose habitat makes them difficult to observe. At high tide they can be seen hunting for insects on the upper leaves of the grasses, where the insects take refuge from the high water. Northern harriers and short-eared owls sweep over the marshes in winter, searching out rodents and small birds.

The daily tides that flush Nummy's Island and all the marshes along the coast are caused by the gravitational pull of the moon as it orbits around the earth, and, to a lesser extent, that of the sun. Every 24 hours and 51 minutes, the moon passes over Nummy's Island. At this point, it pulls the oceans toward it, and a high tide occurs. When the moon is on the other side of the earth another high tide rises here because the waters, which are also spinning with the earth, are pulled outward by centrifugal force. Low tides occur when the moon is a quarter of a globe away. Twice each month the moon is in line with the sun: during the new moon, the sun and moon are on the same side of the earth; during the full moon, the earth is between the moon and the sun. Now the added gravitational pull of the sun brings especially high tides, called spring tides. The moon takes about a month to complete its elliptical orbit of the earth. Once a month the moon's orbit brings it closest to the earth, and its gravitational pull is strongest. This is the perigee, when spring tides occur at the same time as perigee, the tides are at their highest. When the moon is farthest from the earth it is in apogee, and tides are very low.

Remarks: *High tide is the best time to visit Nummy's Island. The birds are forced off the mudflats and into the salt marsh and ponds close to the road.*

30.
Stone Harbor
Point

Directions: **Cape May County, N.J. From the intersection with Perry St. in Cape May, take Lafayette St. north to the Garden State Parkway. Go about 12 miles to Exit 10 and take Route 29 (Stone Harbor Blvd.) east 3.5 miles to 2nd Ave. Turn south and go to the end (B, p. 93).**

Ownership: **Boroughs of Stone Harbor and Avalon.**

On the low sandy spit of Stone Harbor Point, the dynamics and landward migration of a barrier island are laid out in miniature (see **#55**). Standing at the parking lot and looking south, you can see in one glance the pattern of surf, beach, foredune, dune, salt marsh, and bay. On the shell-cobbled area of the point lies one of the few remaining nesting sites for least terns and piping plovers in all of New Jersey.

Along the beach at Stone Harbor and all along the coast of New Jersey, a series of stone piers or groins push out into the sea. As the longshore currents, which move southward carrying massive loads of sand, hit the jetties, the speed of the water slows and some of the sand is dropped (see **#25**). As a result the beaches in the lee of the jetties grow larger and the beaches to the south shrink, robbed of the sand that otherwise would replenish them. The beaches of both Cape May and Stone Harbor Point have felt the sand depletion; the beaches at Cape May have virtually vanished, while Stone Harbor Point has migrated a third of a mile westward since 1970.

Other changes are in progress. Ocean tides and currents are washing over the middle of the spit, carrying the beach to the bay side. A new barrier island has formed at the end of the point. On a windy day the sand hurtles across the point in clouds, and huge breakers pound through the inlet. It is easy to see why barrier islands are unstable.

In the middle of the point are shrub-covered dunes, which are continually being destroyed by storms. The lack of new supplies of sand intensifies the problem, preventing the dunes from building when the fine weather breezes are blowing (see **#55**). Exposed at low tide along the bay side of the end of the point are lumps of salt-marsh peat, reminders of the changing shape of the point. As the sands migrate westward they cover and kill off sections of marsh.

In summer the band of shells and sand at the tip of Stone Harbor (**C, p. 93**) becomes a crowded colony of nesting terns and black skimmers. The least tern lays its eggs in a small depression in the sand, making no attempt to build a nest. The adult terns sit on the eggs not to warm them but to shade them from the hot sun. The camouflage coloring of the eggs and the young birds protects them when the adults are away from the nest. They are so well disguised that the most careful hiker may inadvertently step on them. The only way to avoid this is to stay clear of nesting sites and observe the birds from a safe distance. Black skimmers and common terns, which also use the point hollow out more substantial nests, but all are vulnerable to human beings, rats, cats, dogs, raccoons, and other predators. The terns will vigorously defend their nests against attack, and for them, the colony is clearly a protective strategy. The piping plover, a solitary nester and a shy bird, very sensitive to human encroachment, is now declining rapidly in New Jersey. Together with the least tern it has been the most severely affected by the rapid development of the New Jersey coast.

Black skimmers may be observed flying gracefully just above the surface of the near shore ocean and bays, hunting for small fish that come up to the surface at dusk. The skimmer is equipped for fishing with a huge, thin red-and-black bill. The lower mandible is considerably longer, and grows faster than the upper, to counter the greater wear it receives. The skimmer flies with its bill open, the lower half slicing through the water. When it strikes something, the bird clamps the upper mandible shut, pulls its head down and back, then tips it up, swallows the fish or small crustacean, and begins all over again, all without missing a wingbeat.

During the spring and fall migrations, a traveling circus of shorebirds streams through, feeding on the beach or on the mudflats in the bays. Ruddy turnstone, dowitcher, whimbrel, willet, least sandpiper, marbled godwit, oystercatcher, black-bellied plover, and an occasional golden plover are among the birds you may see (see **#26** and **#42**).

In winter look for sea ducks in the inlet (see **#21**). Diving ducks and brant also inhabit the bay during this season and often seek shelter in the lee of the jetties when the bay freezes.

North of the point, Seven Mile Beach stretches to Townsend's Inlet. From fall to spring the beaches are nearly deserted except for beachcombing gulls and the gleaming white flocks of sanderlings massed like clouds on the beach or skittering along the edge of the water. The birds poke the wet sand for tiny mollusks and crustaceans, which come to the surface to feed when the waves wash over the beach. Brownish dunlins flash over the shore; their feats of formation flying are stupendous. Many species of shorebirds share this ability to zigzag in unison, alert to some unseen signal. The mechanism of communication is not fully understood by scientists. At times the movement appears to begin at the head of the flock; at others it passes from one side of the flock to the other. There are clear advantages for birds living in flocks. Like the nesting terns, they protect each other by sounding an alarm if danger approaches, and this tends to confuse a predator. They also help each other find food. If one bird is seen feeding, others will come and join it.

Around 50th St. is the remnant of a high dune system which, at 48 feet high, is the tallest known in New Jersey. The bands of vegetation from the ocean edge to the secondary dune system are similar to those at Higbee Beach. This is one of the best places along the New Jersey shore to see this transition. This dune has been carefully preserved by the Borough of Avalon, which has recognized its value in protecting the community from the ocean during hurricanes and northeast storms. Be sure not to walk on the dune except at designated crossings.

Remarks: *Along Stone Harbor Blvd. is the Wetlands Institute, a coastal museum and education center that is open to the public. Programs, nature trails, and natural history information are available to the visitor year round.*

31.
Higbee Beach

Directions: **Cape May County, N.J. From the intersection with Lafayette St. in Cape May, go northwest (right) on Perry St., which becomes Sunset Blvd. At the second traffic light, 0.3 mile, go north (right) on Broadway. Drive 1.6 miles and turn west (left) on New England Rd. just before the bridge. Go to the end of the road and park.**

Ownership: **New Jersey Division of Fish, Game, and Wildlife.**

At Higbee Beach a forest of wind-sculptured trees, thickly covered with vines, blankets a series of old dunes. Such forests were once characteristic of the barrier islands along the Jersey shore, offering an endless source of berries, seeds, and shelter for their wildlife. Now only remnants of these stands survive.

Higbee Beach has been set aside as a wildlife management area because of its importance as a migratory rest stop for a myriad of birds, including several threatened or endangered species of birds of prey. The birds feed and gather strength here before their flight across the bay. A combination of upland forest, old field, freshwater pond and marsh, as well as dune woodlands and beach, ensures a healthy supply of small mammals, reptiles, amphibians, and smaller birds as well as numerous roosting sites. Ospreys, bald eagles, Cooper's hawks, peregrine falcons, and northern goshawks are regular visitors.

Walk from the parking lot toward the bay. Just before reaching the open beach, turn south (left) along an old pathway through the dunes. The sand in these dunes comes from the continental shelf, transported here by ocean currents sweeping around Cape May Point. Winds and tides have completed the task of forming the dunes.

After a short walk, you will find yourself in the heart of the old dune forest (**A**). Partially protected from the sea by a sandy foredune barrier, black cherry, redcedar, persimmon, American holly, and hackberry grow here. The bark of these trees is porous and provides little defense against the salt. Therefore, windborne salt effectively prunes the upper branches by drying them out, limiting their height and creating interesting shapes. Although this area seems very dry, the trees are able to obtain adequate water because the water table is close to the surface. Virginia creeper, wild grape, and Japanese honeysuckle grow rapaciously among the trees and shrubs. In the shrub layer, bayberry, beach plum, and poison ivy are most abundant. Almost every plant in this zone produces edible fruits, enjoyed by a variety of wildlife.

At **B** the trail moves out of the dune forest and onto the primary dune. Here the vegetation is closer to the sea and therefore more vulnerable to salt. Most of the trees have disappeared. Bayberry and beach plum predominate. Bayberry is a particularly important species because it is one of the few plants which can convert gaseous nitrogen into a form usable to other plants. Actually, it is bacteria

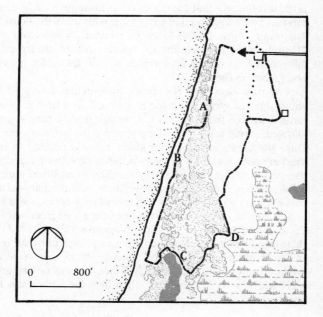

living in small nodules on the roots of bayberry and wax myrtle (a southern relative) which make the transformation. The nitrogen is now "fixed" in the form of ammonia. Most of it goes into the host plant, for the bacteria do not store it. The plant has more nitrogen than it can use and passes the surplus into the surrounding soil. This surplus may be picked up by other plants. Nitrogen is crucial to all plants and animals, because it is needed to form amino acids, which in turn are the building blocks of proteins. Bayberry produces thousands of small waxy berries which are indigestible for most birds; however, tree swallows find them irresistible, flocking to the bushes by the thousands in September.

Between the dune and the sea lies the foredune, an area still above the normal high-tide line. Herbaceous plants like seaside goldenrod, sea rocket, seaside spurge, salt-marsh cordgrass, and above all American beach grass are the dominant vegetation here. They must be much more salt-tolerant than the shrubs of the primary dune, and they have developed special mechanisms to handle this problem as well as shifting sands (see **#21**). The beach grass is vital to the formation and continued existence of the dune system (see **#55**).

Along the beach, look for shining jewels in the sand, "Cape May Diamonds." These are pieces of crystal quartz that have been washed and polished by the estuarine currents and the rise and fall of the tides. It is thought that the stones come from the Ice Age deposits of sand and yellow gravel that cover large portions of the Coastal Plain. The outer yellow stain is limonite, a common iron-oxide product. This has worn off, revealing the quartz underneath. In spring and fall this is a good spot from which to look for ducks, geese, loons and grebes on the bay.

Now turn eastward. The dunes surrounding Davey's Lake (**C**) show signs of wear, open places where four-wheel-drive vehicles have destroyed the vegetation. Although driving here is no longer allowed, it will take a very long time for the plants to grow back. Once the vegetation has been killed, there is nothing to hold the sand in place. Blowouts develop in this dune system, carrying away the nutrients that had been deposited by plant litter. Further, the sand blows eastward, covering wetlands, and the painstaking process of primary succession must begin all over again (see **#93**).

Standing at (**D**), you can look out over a vast freshwater marsh, Pond Creek Meadow, filled with phragmites. Prior to 1917 this was tidal marsh. The area was drained, and phragmites took over (see **#32**). Muskrats, egrets, herons, bitterns, ducks, and geese use this wetland, and it is an excellent hawk lookout because you are at eye level with the tops of the trees. (It is here the author saw her first goshawk.)

The path back to the parking lot follows the hedgerows and the edge of the upland forest. Fall and spring warblers come here in great numbers.

Remarks: *The trail is an easy walk of about one hour, but should be avoided in summer, when it becomes unbearably hot. On the way back along Broadway stop at the railroad tracks and walk south. This spot is renowned for a variety of songbirds—especially warblers—in spring and fall.*

32.
Cape May Point
State Park

Directions: **Cape May County, N.J. From the junction of Perry St. and Lafayette St. in Cape May, go west on Perry St. (which becomes Sunset Blvd.). After 2 miles, turn left on Lighthouse Rd. and go 0.7 mile to the park.**

Ownership: **New Jersey Division of Parks and Forestry.**

This is one of the best locations for watching the fall hawk migration. A raised viewing platform provides an unobstructed view to the north and east. The most abundant species here are the sharp-shinned hawk and the American kestrel; both are strong, fast flyers. The former has evolved the ability to catch smaller birds on the wing; the latter often hovers above the ground hunting for large insects and rodents. Crossing the open bay poses no problem for them or for the merlins and peregrine falcons that fly through in smaller numbers. Merlins breed in the northern coniferous forests of Canada, near ponds, streams, lakes, and bogs. Shorebirds, insects, rodents, and crayfish are all part of their diet on migration. Due to the destruction of habitat and the presence of pesticides in their foods, these birds have dwindled in numbers.

Peregrine falcons are now one of the rarest birds in America. Forty years ago they nested all over the United States, wherever cliffs and water were found together. Then abruptly from 1950 onward they began to disappear at an alarming rate. The peregrine is high on the food chain, feeding chiefly on larger birds. Residues from DDT and other chlorinated hydrocarbon pesticides on plants become concentrated in the flesh of the small mammals and birds that consume them. As these animals in turn are eaten by larger birds, the pesticides are absorbed and concentrated again. A peregrine dining on a pigeon or a tern can accumulate enough of these toxic substances to interfere with calcium production. As a result, peregrines, merlins, ospreys, and other birds of prey produced eggs with such thin shells that they could not support the weight of the adult bird. The clutches of eggs were destroyed. Virtually extinct as nesting species in the eastern United States, peregrines are seen regularly during migration along the coasts. An effort is under way to establish a breeding population in central Cape May County and all along the Atlantic coast (see #58).

These hawks are prodigious hunters. While flying thousands of feet up in the air, a peregrine will spot a smaller bird in flight and plummet at speeds up to 200 mph, hitting the prey a tremendous blow with its large feet before snatching it from the air. They can also approach a bird from below, flip over on their backs, and grab the victim with their talons.

The awesome flights of broad-winged hawks of the inland routes are not usually seen at Cape May. The broadwings cannot soar out over the bay where there are no updrafts to sustain them. Occasionally a strong northwesterly wind blows them down to the cape, and they circle aimlessly, stymied by the open water. They must head north again to find a way over the Delaware before heading south along the western shore.

The park has a network of trails that leads through freshwater marshes, hardwood islands, ponds, and old fields. At one time the lowlands here were tidal marsh. Dikes were built so that crops of salt-meadow cordgrass, also called salt hay, could be grown as fodder. As the habitat became less saline, cattail marsh developed. Then, the wetlands were drained to reduce mosquito-breeding grounds (see #52). As the water level dropped, the cattails died out and phragmites or reedgrass, a tall, beautiful, and rapacious reed, took over. It has limited use for wildlife, while cattail is widely used by birds and marsh animals for food and nesting material. Also, cattail does not prevent other plants from coexisting. Phragmites is very difficult and expensive to eradicate. Cutting and the use of selective herbicides combined with raising the water level of the marsh are two methods that have been successful.

The ocean to the east and the bay to the west act as heat radiators during the winter, modifying the climate. The temperature of the winter ocean rarely falls below 36°F, while the air temperature

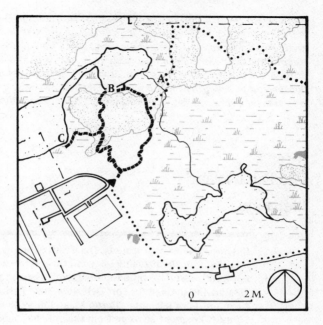

is often much colder. Heat from the ocean, passing into the air, tempers the climate and extends the growing season, thus allowing a variety of southern species to grow farther north here along the Coastal Plain than they do inland.

At **A** is a grove of tall wax myrtles, a southern coastal shrub with a delicately mottled gray bark, found here at its northern limit. Associated with it is the southern gray treefrog, also at its northern limit in Cape May County. Southern species of flowering plants include blue boneset and rattlesnake master, which bloom in late summer and early fall. Two southern oaks, Spanish and willow, grow on hummocks along the trail, mixed with white oak and hickory. These stands are a favorite haunt for warblers.

The sourgum and persimmon woods at **B** attract flights of huge, pale-green luna moths on early summer evenings.

Summer is when you will hear the rap-rap-rapping croak of the carpenter frog by the freshwater pond (**C**). Cape May and the Pine Barrens farther north are the only areas in New Jersey where this southern coastal species is found. The pond is also a nesting ground for secretive rails and bitterns.

Remarks: *The small museum by the parking lot is open all year from 8:30 a.m. to 4:30 p.m. A naturalist is on duty from spring to fall. On the beach an abandoned bunker provides a good lookout from which to view seabirds and geese. Several hundred yards to the east, you can look north across a cow pasture where shorebirds, waterfowl, and waders collect in the appropriate season. The field is owned by the Nature Conservancy and is open to the public. A parking area is provided along Sunset Blvd.*

33.
Pea Patch Island
Heronry

Directions: **New Castle County, Del. From Wilmington take U.S. 13 south; about 10 miles beyond the intersection with I-295, turn east (left) onto Route 72, which becomes Route 9, following the sign for Fort Delaware State Park, and go 2.6 miles. Turn left onto Clinton St. and drive to the end, 0.7 mile. Frequent boats go from the gray building on the right across to the island park and heronry from 11:00 a.m. to 6:00 p.m. on weekends and holidays, from late April through the end of September. In 1982 the fare was $2.25 for adults, $1.25 for children.**

Ownership: **Delaware Division of Parks and Recreation.**

In the small circle of trees and shrubs on this island is the largest heronry in Delaware and one of the most important in the Mid-Atlantic states. About eight to nine thousand birds nest here during the breeding season, flying out to feed along the Delaware Bay marshes and across into New Jersey. Eight species of herons and egrets congregate in the rookery, the most common being the cattle egret. Cattle egrets are native to Africa and Europe. From there they have spread over every continent. Arriving first in South America during the nineteenth century, the species has made its way northward. In the past twenty years, cattle egrets have established colonies from Florida up into Canada. The key to their success is apparently the special ecological niche they fill. Their favorite foods are grasshoppers and crickets, and their favorite feeding ground is in the midst of cattle. Several of them will follow one cow, catching the insects put to flight by its passing.

Snowy egrets and glossy ibis are also numerous, followed by little blue herons and black-crowned night herons. Great blue herons, yellow-crowned night herons, and tricolor Louisiana herons are present in small numbers. The Louisiana heron is a southern species, which is gradually extending its range northward; Pea Patch is at the edge of its current range (for a discussion of heronries see **#28**).

The heronry is located on fill deposited by the Army Corps of Engineers in the early 1900s. The principal species of vegetation are typical of succession on fill: trees include red maple, sweetgum, blackgum, pin oak and willow oak; the chief shrubs are American alder, southern arrowwood, and highbush blueberry. During the mid-1970s a study of the colony was conducted which showed that after one season the trees and shrubs used by the birds were severely damaged, due to a highly alkaline guano that the birds produced in enormous quantities. The following season the birds moved on to a new patch of trees and shrubs, only to repeat the destruction. It was feared that once the birds had made the rounds of the island, the colony would disperse, having no adequate area in which to nest. Fortunately, this has not happened; there is enough vegetation on the island so that by the time the birds return to a nesting area, the trees and shrubs have regenerated.

The overall population has remained stable for several years, but certain species have fluctuated greatly, decimated in some years by nematodes. Periodic infestations of these marine worms attack small fish called mummichogs. Herons and egrets, which feed on these fish, ingest the worms as well and even pass them on to their off-spring. Snowy egrets have been the most vulnerable to these worms, while the cattle egrets, which feed on insects, toads, and frogs, have not been affected. The infestations generally come after a warm spring.

Remarks: *A short nature trail leads out to an observation platform from which you can look out at the heronry. Camping is available at Lum's Pond State Park. Follow signs on Route 72 west of U.S. 13.*

34.

Dragon Run
Marsh

Directions: **New Castle County, Del. From Wilmington, drive south on U.S. 13. About 10 miles beyond the intersection with I-295, turn east onto Route 72 and go 1.4 miles. Turn south opposite the Getty Oil Co. and go 0.8 mile to the creek. Park beside the road (A). A canoe or small boat can be launched east of the weir. For another view of the creek stay on Route 72 until it crosses the creek. Parking is difficult here.**

Ownership: **Getty Refining and Marketing Co., New Castle–Gunning Bedford School District, private farms, and Delaware City Park along the eastern edge.**

A narrow creek, perfect for boating, winds through rich freshwater marshes where wood ducks, bitterns, and pied-billed grebes nest in the thick vegetation, and herons and egrets feed. The creek itself is impounded by three weirs built for mosquito control. As in the salt marsh, small changes in water depth are accompanied by distinct changes in vegetation (see **#21**). The variety of species found in freshwater wetlands, however, is much greater. Yellow pond lily, or spatterdock, is the dominant species in the deeper parts of the channel. Closer to shore extensive colonies of emergent plants take over; these include pickerelweed, smartweed, arrow arum, and fragrant water lily. In the shallows, broad-leaved cattails and hummocks of buttonbush are common, with some extensive stands of phragmites. At the edges of the marsh, wetland tree species such as red maple, silver maple, and black willow are encroaching.

Purple gallinules are not common birds, even in the far south where they are year-round residents, but in 1975 and for several years afterwards, a pair of gallinules was recorded nesting in the marsh—the first known pair breeding this far north. Related to rails (see **#67**), these birds have such long toes that they can support themselves on lilypads floating on the water.

Many dabbling ducks use the marshes during the fall migration, attracted by the abundant supply of food. Most of the plants here produce wildlife food, sometimes from several parts of the plant.

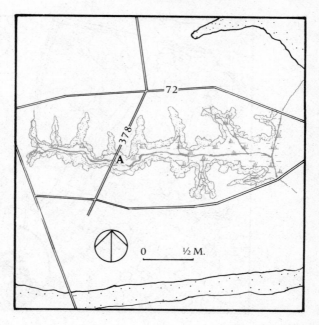

Each arrow arum plant produces quantities of seeds, but these are so high in oxalic acid that only the wood ducks eat them as a staple diet.

Remarks: *The creek is about 2 miles long from Route 378 to Route 72. Best times are spring and fall. Canoe rentals in Wilmington (see* **#40**). *Fishing is allowed in the creek; hunting is not. This site is very close to the launch dock for the boat to the Pea Patch Island Heronry. Nearest camping is at Lum's Pond State Park (see* **#33**).

35.

Thousand Acre

Marsh

Directions: **New Castle County, Del. From Wilmington, drive south on U.S. 13; about 10 miles beyond the intersection**

Inset: Marsh hawk

with I-295, turn east onto Route 72 and go 1.7 miles. Turn south onto Route 9 and travel 4 miles, crossing the Chesapeake and Delaware Canal on the Reedy Point Bridge. To the right from the bridge is a grand view of the marsh. Park on the shoulder of the road. For another view of the marsh, turn right from Route 9 onto Dutch Neck Rd. (Route 417). The marsh is on the left for 1.5 miles. Although this road has no shoulder, it is lightly traveled, and you can park on the side of the road.

Ownership: **Fourteen private owners.**

From the Reedy Point Bridge, Thousand Acre Marsh spreads southward in an alluring patchwork of shimmering water and lush vegetation. To the west of scenic River Rd. (Route 9), towering phragmites obscures the life of the marsh from the passing motorist. This is the largest freshwater marsh in the state, and 80 percent of it is open water during the spring wet season.

Large numbers of waterfowl and shorebirds breed and feed in this habitat. Ospreys, common egrets, and great blue, little blue, and green herons make their nests here. These birds find fishing relatively good in the marsh, although the water level fluctuates due to natural cycles and human intervention. Fishing is better in the Dragon Run Marsh farther north.

In late spring, northern harriers can be seen soaring above and hunting for prey in the marsh grasses, while long-billed marsh wrens, clapper, king, and sora rails are preparing their nesting sites in the weeds and grasses of the marsh. Purple martins return to nest in boxes on the perimeter. In the fall, the waterfowl arrive in great numbers. Canada geese, mallards, blue-winged and green-winged teal, wood ducks, and whistling swans rest during their migration. Some of the geese and ducks will remain throughout the year, becoming permanent residents. Millet, smartweed, and duckweed are the main food plants for the birds. Geese also forage in nearby fields (see **Chesapeake Bay**). Carp, the principal fish in the marsh, control the growth of the sparse, submerged vegetation. As they feed, they stir up muck, which clouds the water and reduces the light available to underwater plants. Cattails, sedges, and numerous wildflowers grow along the edge of the water.

The primary furbearing inhabitant of the marsh is the muskrat. Muskrat lodges (locally called "houses") can be seen in large numbers from the road. They are located near the marsh grasses, which are the muskrat's main source of food and building material. The Thousand Acre Marsh was once the prime muskrat-trapping area of the state, but now this enterprise is minimal. The muskrat population has declined, mostly due to the continuing encroachment of phragmites, which now covers 80 percent of the marsh where once cattail was dominant. Phragmites is of little use as a wildlife food, and muskrats have difficulty pushing through its thick and sturdy stems. At its peak, Thousand Acre Marsh supported fifty muskrats per acre; in the last 30 years the average has declined to one per acre. Other furbearing mammals located in the marsh in limited quantities are the otter, mink, and weasel.

Among the common reptiles are snapping turtles and northern water and black rat snakes, while the marsh's amphibian population includes chorus frogs and spring peepers (see **#3**).

What was once one of the finest freshwater marshes on the East Coast now struggles for its existence. Originally a brackish marsh connected to the Delaware Bay, Thousand Acre Marsh was diked off sometime before 1875. From time to time the marshes were drained to supply water for farming. After World War I, water levels were raised to encourage muskrats. Since then a battle has developed over the management of the marsh. Sluice gates that maintain the water level of the marsh are opened mysteriously in the dead of night, apparently by duck hunters who hope to encourage the growth of wild millet. Unfortunately, this has only aided the growth of more phragmites. Muskrat hunters want the marshes flooded, hoping to drown out some of the phragmites. Multiple ownership makes any organized approach difficult. Meanwhile, the marsh continues to decline.

Remarks: *The best time of year to visit the marsh is in the late spring. Access to the area for canoeing is possible by permission of landowners. Just stop and ask; the system is informal. Canoes can be rented in Wilmington (see #40). In nearby Port Penn, the Port Penn Museum (open from May to October by appointment) depicts old marsh life-styles. Fall usually brings a marshland festival in the area, which includes a feast of snapper soup, muskrat meat, and other marsh delicacies. Closest camping area is Lum's Pond State Park. Other activities include hunting and fishing in season. Indian artifacts of the Lenape tribe have been found in the area.*

36.
Chesapeake and Delaware
Canal Fossil Beds

Directions: **New Castle County, Del.** *First Stop:* **From Wilmington drive south on U.S. 13 to St. Georges, about 14 miles. Just before the bridge over the Chesapeake and Delaware Canal, turn right and go 0.2 mile, paralleling the bridge. Jog right, then left, make a left and then right onto the dirt road closest to the canal. Drive west 3.2 miles to the end.** *Second Stop:* **Go north on U.S. 13 back toward Wilmington 1.3 miles. Turn west (left) onto Route 72 and go 1.4 miles to Route 71. Go south (left) 3.3 miles on Route 71 and turn left. Drive 0.4 mile to the end and turn left. Go 0.4 mile to the end. You are now at the top of the bank. A steep path leads down to the water's edge.**

Ownership: **U.S. Army Corps of Engineers.**

This bank of fossil-bearing marine sediments dates back roughly 70 to 100 million years. Exposed by the excavation of the canal, four formations lie neatly stacked like the layers of a cake. The materials composing the layers, the types of fossils found in each, and most of all the texture of the sediments tell a story of the origins of each band of deposit. The exposed, sandy cliff provides an ideal nesting site for bank swallows, a species that is unusual because of its very particular nesting requirements. All spring and summer, these graceful birds hawk for insects by the canal.

The first stop is at a point of land directly opposite the cut. The view from there will give you a sense of the whole formation. The western portion was destroyed in 1982 by the corps, but much of the bank still remains. The future of the site is uncertain due to natural erosion; however the corps has promised to make efforts to stabilize the area. The oldest layer is at the bottom, forming the beach and the first 6 to 8 feet. The Merchantville formation, as it is called, is dark gray and contains both a sandy silt and a silty, very fine sand.

The terms "sandy silt" and "silty sand" are applied to sedimentary materials according to the amounts of each substance they contain. The difference between sand and silt is the size of the individual particles. Sand is coarser than silt, which in turn is coarser than clay. The high amount of silt in this formation indicates that it was deposited at the bottom of the sea, not too far from shore. The basis for this conclusion lies in our understanding of how material from the land is deposited in the sea. Rivers running off mountains and high land in the interior carry pebbles, sand, silt, and clay to the sea. There, the vast body of the ocean slows the flow of the water. Any decrease in rate of flow decreases the stream's power to transport its burden of debris. No longer able to carry the heavier pieces, the stream deposits them at the edge of the sea, to be tossed back and forth by the waves and ground down into sand particles all roughly the same size—a beach. The finer material, which includes the silt, remains suspended in water until it reaches deeper waters, where the action of the waves no longer moves the water along the ocean floor (see **#7**). The depth at this point could be anywhere from 20 to 200 feet. Here, the silt drifts down to line the ocean floor. Such a process provided the raw material for the Merchantville formation.

The formation also contains mica, which indicates that the material originated in the Piedmont rocks to the northwest. These rocks were mostly schists and gneisses, which contain large amounts of mica. Another ingredient is a mineral called glauconite. It forms offshore in deeper, quieter waters of the continental shelf. Its origins are still unknown, although some evidence suggests that it may be formed out of fish and other animal feces in the water. Many mollusk fossils are found in this section of the bank, including the ammonite, which is shaped like a flat snail and is probably an ancestor of the snail (see **#23**). Also present are the burrows of benthic organisms, creatures which live on the sea bottom. The types of animals found and the abundance of glauconite also indicate that this formation was deposited offshore in calm waters.

Above the Merchantville is the Englishtown formation, a layer of rusty brown and orange sediments about 8 feet thick. Here the main ingredient is a fine sugary-textured sand, indicating that this deposit was laid down at the edge of the sea. As it lies above a layer that formed at the bottom of the sea, this sea must have been retreating. Another bit of evidence to support this conclusion is the great number of mud-shrimp burrows found in this layer: mud shrimp generally thrive in the intertidal zone of a beach. It is in this band that the bank swallows have made their homes. (The holes are more visible from the second stop.) Because they nest only in bluffs of this sort, bank swallows are quite uncommon. Digging straight into the cliff with their bills, the swallows push the dirt out with their feet and build a rude nest of grasses at the end of a short tunnel. They are considered colonial nesters, for their holes are often less than a foot apart. These nests, which are safe from predators, provide ready access to the food supply of flying insects. An advantage of colonial living is that the birds help one another find food: if a swallow darts after an insect without success, it will often follow another swallow, which may have a better location. The birds catch their prey by flying along with their mouths wide open.

The next formation is the Marshalltown, a solid wedge of dark greenish-gray material about 6 to 8 feet thick. It is very fine silty sand rich with mollusk fossils and glauconite. Like the Merchantville formation, it was probably formed at the bottom of a bay. The sea had advanced again when this formation was deposited.

The youngest layer, the Mount Laurel formation, is reddish-orange and sandy. At most it is only 2 feet thick and has been weathered away in many places. Its deposition parallels that of the Englishtown formation.

Remarks: *Fossil collecting is allowed, but only a few are found along the beach. Do not climb onto the bank. The material is loose and collapses easily. There is fishing in the canal. As it is open to the Delaware and Chesapeake bays, you do not need a license. Nearby is a small private fossil museum, located on Cox's Neck Rd., the second right north of the bridge. For further information on fossil collecting in Delaware contact the Delaware Geological Survey, University of Delaware, Newark, Del. 19711. Camping is available north of the canal at Lum's State Park near Kirkwood.*

37.
Armstrong Heronry

Directions: **New Castle County, Del., a few miles from Odessa. Contact Delaware Wildlands, 5th and Main Sts., Odessa, Del. 19730, (302) 834-1332, for specific directions and permission.**

Ownership: **Delaware Wildlands, Inc.**

In among a fine mature forest of tall trees, mixed oaks, beech, and hickory are some two hundred nests, which make up the largest great-blue heronry in Delaware and one of the most important on the Atlantic Coast. As you walk through the trees, you will see the nests—scraggly collections of branches about 100 feet above you. While great blues are often found in colonies with other herons (see **#28**), they frequently nest exclusively with each other, as they are doing here. The birds of this colony have an excellent fishing ground in the marshes just to the east, and many of them may stay in the vicinity during the winter. The great blue heron can live in both freshwater and saltwater environments and is a year-round resident over much of its range. This helps explain its wide distribution over most of the United States and Canada. As you walk in the woods, you will see that under the nesting trees, the undergrowth is sparse and stunted. This is due to the high alkalinity of the heron droppings (see **#33**).

Remarks: *Visits to the area are rarely scheduled during the height of the breeding season from April to July, but just before and right after this period some herons will be in the nesting area. Nearest camping is at Lum's Pond State Park along the Chesapeake and Delaware Canal near Kirkwood.*

38.
Blackbird
Creek

Directions: **New Castle County, Del. From Wilmington take U.S. 13 south to Odessa, about 21 miles. Turn east (left) at the light onto Route 299; go 1.5 miles. Turn south (right) onto Route 9 and go 4.3 miles to Taylor's Bridge. Park by the side of the road. Before canoeing the creek, check with Delaware Wildlands, Inc., 5th and Main Sts., Odessa, Del. 19730, (302) 834-1332.**

Ownership: **Delaware Wildlands, Inc.**

Blackbird Creek threads its way through tortuous meanders and oxbows to the Delaware Bay. Freshwater marshes of lush wild rice and arrow arum line the upper reaches of the creek, while along the bay, brackish water limits plant life to salt-marsh cordgrass and a few other salt-marsh plants. Waterfowl and marshbirds nest in the covering grasses; the clean waters of the creek abound in fish. Together with Appoquinimink Creek just to the north, this site is the only marsh area of any significant size in Delaware that has escaped development, pollution, drainage, or ditching.

The best way to see the marshes is by canoe. Below Taylor's Bridge are brackish marshes. Here the salinity of the creek varies from season to season. When summer droughts reduce freshwater runoff from the high ground, the tide sweeps more salt up the creeks. After the snowmelt and the spring rains, the creek is full of fresh water, and salinity may be near zero. Even the occasional brackishness of the water on the lower reaches of the creek, though, is enough to discourage freshwater species. Below Taylor's Bridge, salt-marsh cordgrass dominates the creek edge, while back from the intertidal zone, big cordgrass is the conspicuous plant. Salt-marsh cordgrass grows in the intertidal zone wherever salt appears in the water, but big cordgrass is a plant of the brackish marsh (see **#21**). The higher areas of the marsh support such species as marsh mallow, marsh elder, groundsel bush, and switch grass. The tall stands of big cordgrass hide most of the high marsh from view. In a number of places, especially at landing points, phragmites has grown up and is causing concern that it may take over much of the marsh. Upstream from Taylor's Bridge, the rising tide will take you into freshwater marshes. In addition to wild rice and arrow arum, one finds smart-weeds, wild millet, cattails, and Olney three-square (see **#94** and **#34**).

All up and down the coast, small streams such as this one play a vital part in the life cycles of many species of fish. Some species spend their entire lives in these waters, while others come to spawn or to feed during certain seasons or certain phases of their life cycle. These streams are rich in food—tiny crustaceans, fish, and plankton, the microscopic plant and animal life that is the basic foodstuff of both fresh and salt water. The shallow waters provide a haven from predators, and the warmth required by eggs and young fish.

The American eel is one remarkable species that spends part of its life here. The adults travel to the Sargasso Sea east of the West Indies to spawn once, and then they die. The first stage of the eel is a transparent, leaf-shaped little creature called a leptocephalus, which looks nothing like the adult. Drifting north with the Gulf Stream, thousands of these tiny creatures reach the Atlantic shore by winter. By spring they have become elvers, which look like very small eels. Only the females make their way upstream into freshwater creeks

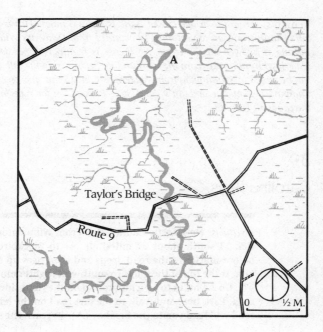

and ponds. There they grow for several years into yellowish adults. Eventually, in the late summer or fall, they turn silver, and migrate downstream to join the males and begin the long journey together to the Sargasso Sea. The gut atrophies at this time, and the eels do not eat during the trek.

Other species found in Blackbird Creek, the white perch and weakfish for example, migrate into the shallow creeks to spawn in the warm months and move out into the bays or the ocean in winter.

Several species of catfish are also found here. They may not migrate out of the creek at all. Catfish are an old family, which dates back 10 to 20 million years to the Miocene epoch. Among many species of catfish, the male plays an active role in protecting the young. This is unusual among fish, which generally simply drop their eggs and forget about them; survival of the species is insured by the vast number of eggs each female produces.

Downstream at **A** is a hummock known as Red Bank. Standing about 10 feet above the marsh, it supports a completely different habitat. Upland forest of post and Spanish oak about 40 feet tall forms the canopy. The shrub layer of bayberry, highbush blueberry, and blackberry often shows signs of heavy browsing by deer. The hummock provides a wide view of the marsh.

Remarks: *From the bridge to Red Bank is about 3 miles. This is private land, and permission to visit must be obtained from Delaware Wildlands. Fishing is allowed on the creek. No license is required. Some deer and waterfowl hunting occurs in the surrounding fields during the fall. Canoes can be rented in Wilmington from Wilderness Canoe Trips, Inc. (see #40). Camping is available at Lum's Pond State Park. Look for signs north of the canal on U.S. 13.*

39.
Carolina Bays

Directions: **New Castle County, Del. From Wilmington, take U.S. 13 south about 27 miles, almost to Blackbird. Just before Blackbird the road drops and then rises up a steep hill. At the top of the hill turn southwest (right) onto Route 471. Go 2.4 miles to a picnic ground on the right side of the road. Park here and walk to the dirt road on the left. This road will lead you to the first bay (A). To reach the second**

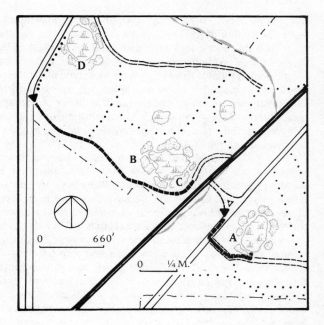

bay (**B**) continue southwest on Route 471 to the first cross-roads, 0.6 mile, and turn northwest (right) on Route 47. Follow this road 3.4 miles to Route 476, and turn south (left). Go 0.6 mile and park at the side of the road. A dirt road on the left leads into the bay. This tract has a number of Carolina Bays in addition to the one discussed here.

Ownership: **Blackbird State Forest, Delaware Forest Service.**

These two ponds, ringed by trees and covered with buttonbush, seem ordinary enough, but they belong to a chain of mysterious oval depressions found all along the Coastal Plain. They are called Carolina Bays because they are particularly well developed in the Carolinas. Each depression lies on a roughly northwest-to-southeast axis and is surrounded by a rim of slightly higher ground. The regularity of their shape and their alignment suggests a common origin. Scientists have offered a number of theories to explain the bays, some of them quite intriguing, if improbable. One explanation is that stranded pods of whales or schools of fish thrashed out these areas, but this does not satisfactorily account for the great number and wide distribution of the bays nor for their alignment. Another supposition is that a vast shower of meteors once struck the plain; this seems unikely too, especially as no trace of these meteors has been found. More probable theories include some type of wind erosion in the severe climate that attended the Ice Age (see **Introduction**), subsidence, the action of underground aquifers, or perhaps some combination of these. Movements beneath the earth's surface may also have played a part. Scientists may never be able to agree on the origins of the Carolina Bays.

The two located in Blackbird State Forest stand in the midst of upland woods. Surface water collects in them, and there is some standing water in them all year round. Other bays are only seasonal ponds, drying out in summer. Because they tend to be wet, soggy places, bays have become islands of undisturbed vegetation in the midst of highly developed agricultural lands.

The first bay (**A**) is a small one. Leaving your car at the picnic ground, walk up the road a few yards and turn left onto a forest-service road. The road soon forks; go left and almost immediately turn left again onto a small track that leads a few yards to the bay. In spring the area is very wet and it is difficult to approach the water's edge. The rich woods around the pond are typical of second-growth forest on the Coastal Plain. Assorted oaks and hickories dominate the canopy, along with red maple, sweetgum, blackgum, some sweetbay and tuliptree. Dogwood is an abundant understory species. Closer to the water, where the ground is flooded seasonally, the principal species become swamp white oak, willow oaks—some of very good size—sweetgum, blackgum, and red maple. Swamp cottonwood, another wetland tree, is also present. In this area dogwood is replaced in the understory by numerous wetland shrubs, including sweet pepperbush, maple-leaf viburnum, and highbush and lowbush blueberry.

In the middle of the pond the water is about 4 feet deep. Here buttonbush covers much of the surface. This shrub develops round fruits (hence its name), which stay on the branches into the winter, providing a source of food for waterfowl, especially wood duck. The buttonbush is ringed by persimmon trees, a southern species that never grows very tall. Its fruit is a favorite for larger animals.

The second Carolina Bay is larger. It is also more accessible throughout the year, as the surrounding land is higher. Walk along the logging road for about 5 minutes and the bay will appear on your left. There has been considerable logging in the area which impairs the beauty of this pond. A vast willow oak stands at the water's edge (**C**).

Remarks: *Camping at Lum's Pond State Park west of U.S. 13 on the Chesapeake and Delaware Canal. You can hike along the several miles of forest-service roads. Another bay (D) sits right on the road leading to the Van Dyke tract.*

40.
Woodland Beach Wildlife Area

Directions: **Kent County, Del. From Wilmington, drive south on U.S. 13 about 21 miles to Odessa. Turn left onto Route 299 and go 1.5 miles to Route 9. Continue south on Route 9 for about 10 miles until it crosses the Smyrna River at Fleming's Landing, which marks the northern boundary of the area. The Tower (A) is about 1 mile south of Route 82 on Route 9, visible on the left. Parking is provided near the tower. The Tidal Flats (B) can be reached by boat only.**

Ownership: **Delaware Division of Fish and Wildlife, and numerous private owners.**

The eastward view from the watchtower is an unbroken vista of tidal marsh, jewel-green in May, tawny gold in September. Hidden within it, clapper and king rails are nesting, and armies of shorebirds scour the mudflats. Occasionally a bald eagle, a northern harrier, or an osprey glides across the horizon. To the right, a series of farm ponds attracts migrating shorebirds, dabbling ducks, whistling swans, and geese. In spring and summer, cattle egrets, great blue herons, snowy egrets, and other wading birds come to feed here. More Canada geese are seen here than anywhere else in the state. Adjoining the broad marshes of Bombay Hook, the Woodland Beach area provides salt marsh, freshwater marsh, and woodland habitats for a variety of wildlife.

A number of tidal creeks meander throughout the salt marsh. At low tide, large areas of mudflats emerge, offering excellent feeding grounds for migrating shorebirds in May and again from July to October (see **#21** and **#42**). A wealth of invertebrate life attracts other animals, including raccoons and an occasional otter. Canoeing

Inset: Whistling swan

early in the morning is best for seeing animal life, and low tide is the best time for bird-watching. Throughout the marsh, stands of phragmites dwarf the other marsh plants. Approximately 50 percent of the marsh is dominated by it. Once this alien has a foothold in an area, often in disturbed soil, it competes aggressively with native species (see **#31**). A phragmites-control program is presently underway, which appears to be successful in stemming the invasion, allowing other marsh grasses—especially salt-meadow cordgrass, salt grass, salt-marsh cordgrass, and big cordgrass—to reclaim the marsh. In contrast to phragmites, these species are important as sources of food for wildlife.

With a boat you can weave in and out of the tidal creeks and visit the mud flats (**B**). This is a haven for migrating shorebirds in May and again from July through September (see **#41** and **#42**). Out in the deeper waters of Taylor's Gut, visible from the tower, diving ducks gather, particularly in fall and early spring. Canvasback, redhead, ruddy duck, and ring-necked duck are among the species you may find.

In 1957 Taylor's Gut was impounded by a sluice, which created a freshwater marsh across Route 9 from the salt marsh (**C**). The sluice is designed for one-way flow of water, preventing the brackish waters of the salt marsh from entering the impoundment. The creation of the freshwater marsh now enables migratory waterfowl, particularly Canada geese, to breed here. Although these birds winter in brackish waters, they require a freshwater habitat for nesting. Black duck and mallard also nest in the area.

The creation of the Taylor's Gut impoundment has produced an interesting development: because the salt marshes of the gut now merge into the freshwater marshes of the impoundment, the king rail, a freshwater species, and the clapper rail, which nests in salt marsh, have interbred to produce a hybrid form, which is fertile. This is very unusual—most crosses, like the mule, are infertile. (see **#67** on rails.)

A variety of reptiles and amphibians inhabit the marsh and woodlands. Black rat and northern water snakes are common. Found only in fresh water are spring peepers, cricket and chorus frogs, and several other species of frogs. Because their skins are porous, most frogs cannot stand salt water. They quickly lose their body fluids if exposed to it (see **#21**). Woodland Beach is the northernmost breeding ground for the green treefrog, one of the few frogs occasionally found in brackish water.

Remarks: *The best times to visit the area are in the spring and fall; avoid the summer, when the area is plagued with biting flies and mosquitoes. There are three public boat ramps, two into the inland waters and one into the bay. Permits must be obtained from the Division of Fish and Wildlife, P.O. Box 1401, Dover, Del. 19901. This is a major hunting area. Other activities include fishing and crabbing. A public fishing pier is located near Woodland Beach on Route 6. Crab restaurants were once common in the area. One of the few remaining is just off Route 9 in Leipsic. Arrowheads from the Lenape tribe can be found on the beach south of town. You can camp at Lum's Pond State Park along the C&D Canal west of U.S. 13. Canoes can be rented from Wilderness Canoe Trips, Inc., located on Route 202 just north of the intersection with Route 141 north of Wilmington, (302) 654-2227. They will ferry canoes to and from the area. There are no boat rentals nearby.*

41.

Bombay Hook
National Wildlife Refuge

Directions: **Kent County, Del. From Wilmington, head south on U.S. 13 about 33 miles to Smyrna. At the third traffic light turn east (left) on Route 12 for 4.7 miles. Turn south (right) on Route 9 and go 0.5 mile. Turn east (left) on Route 85 and go 2.4 miles to the visitors' center.**

Ownership: **U.S. Fish and Wildlife Service.**

Undisturbed salt marsh threaded with tidal creeks, several freshwater impoundments stocked with food plants, and patches of lowland forest draw a great parade of birds through Bombay Hook in the course of a year. In the fall and winter as many as 50,000 Canada geese and 40,000 greater snow geese may use the refuge at one time, shuttling back and forth between the safety of the marsh and impoundments and the grain fields inland where they feed on the waste corn (see **Chesapeake Bay**). Flocks of snow geese feed out in the marsh (see **#98**), and thousands of dabbling ducks gather in the impoundments and the marsh. Heavy hunting in the surrounding fields and marsh drives the birds to seek sanctuary here in fall and winter. Winter is also the time to see the pair of bald eagles that nests each year on Parson's Point (**A**). Although the eagles have only had four successful broods in the past 20 years or so, the birds continue to come back to the point and probably will continue to do so as long as their habitat needs are met. They can be seen regularly until about April. Shorebirds are plentiful here, stopping on their northern (May) and southern (July–September) migrations; the refuge staff has recorded thirty-four species. The best time to see them is at low tide, when they collect on the mudflats. This is also an excellent place to observe spring migrations of thrushes, warblers, and vireos. In the breeding season prothonotary and Kentucky warblers, blue grosbeaks, and Acadian and willow flycatchers nest in the wet woods and thickets surrounding the pools and marshes.

A dirt road runs along the Shearness dike that separates the salt marshes on the east from the freshwater impoundments on the west. Salt-marsh cordgrass, salt-meadow cordgrass, and big cordgrass (see **#21**) predominate in the salt marsh, with groundsel and marsh elder marking the higher elevations. The marsh and impoundments are

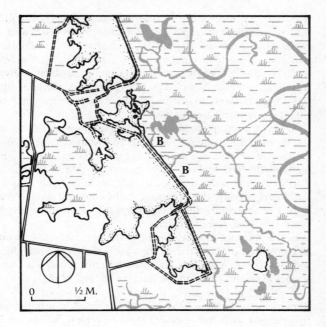

always full of Canada geese in the fall and winter, but the snow-goose population fluctuates dramatically, perhaps because of changes in the food supply. In some years, the snow geese collect at Black-water NWR (see **#64**) on the Chesapeake Bay side of the peninsula. In others, Bombay Hook is the main stopping ground for these birds on their way south to Back Bay and Currituck Sound, where they spend the coldest months.

The Delaware Bay is an extremely important flyway for shore birds moving north and south. At low tide the mudflats to the east of the dike (**B**) are exposed, and here in the spring, late summer, and fall you may see turnstones, avocets, as many as ten species of sandpipers, phalaropes, or perhaps a golden plover. The mudflats are like a rich pudding stuffed with mollusks, crustaceans, insect larvae, marine worms, and the seeds of marshplants—all of which the birds can extract with their long pointed bills. With bills that vary in shape and length, different species can feed on different layers and ingredients. Watch for ruffs, birds whose breeding plumage (male) is a splendid mane of black, red, or white feathers. The black birds and those with markings are dominant males. On the breeding grounds these males fight fierce battles to protect territory and to attract fe-male birds. The lesser males are usually white with colored markings. This variation is highly unusual. The female is a drab brown bird, bearing little resemblance to the male. She is called a reeve. The ruff is a European species once only accidental to the Atlantic Coast; it is now being seen regularly though still in small numbers (see **#42**). Hudsonian godwits and, more rarely, marbled godwits pass through the refuge. Marbled godwits were once plentiful along the East Coast, but were so heavily hunted in the late nineteenth century that their numbers are still low.

In May the best place to view the migrations of shorebirds is along the shore of the Delaware Bay from Port Mahon south to Slaughter Beach. Go south along Route 9 to Little Creek, 7.4 miles,and turn east toward Port Mahon. Drive out to the end of the road. Here, during the high tides that come with the full or new moon in the latter part of May, the horseshoe crabs come up to lay their eggs. Waves of shorebirds time their arrival in the Delaware Bay for this event (see **#26,** Reed's Beach).

In the summer months the king, clapper, and Virginia rails and the soras nest in the marshes, though they are extremely difficult to see (see **#67**). American and least bitterns, glossy ibis, and nine species of herons frequent the tidal creeks. (see **#28**).

Remarks: *Summer can be very buggy. An excellent way to explore the refuge is in a small boat or canoe. There are three nature trails and three observation towers. The center provides a variety of programs. For further information contact Bombay Hook National Wildlife Reserve, R.D. 1, Box 147, Smyrna, Del. 19977, (302) 653-9345. During hunting season, parts of the refuge are closed off. Nearest public campground at Blackbird State Park, 20 miles northwest. The refuge is open dawn to dusk all year round. A spotting scope is a must for scanning the ponds.*

42.
Little Creek
Wildlife Area

Directions: **Kent County, Del. From Wilmington, drive south on U.S. 13 about 46 miles to Dover, then go east on Route 8 about 3.5 miles. Turn south (right) onto Route 9 and go 2.7 miles to Route 349. Turn east (left) and go 1.5 miles to the entrance, which is on the left. Follow the winding,**

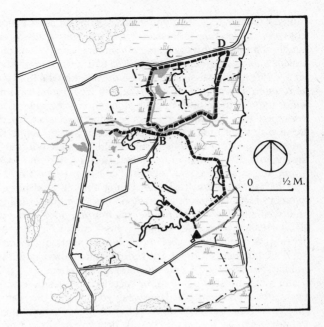

very rough dirt road 0.4 mile to the parking area. Walk along the dike east from point **A**.

Ownership: **Delaware Division of Fish and Wildlife.**

At Little Creek two broad and shallow impoundments of fresh water are separated from the surrounding salt marsh by earthen dikes. It doesn't look like much, but from spring through fall it becomes a hot spot for a spectacular variety and volume of migrating shorebirds; nesting terns, rails, and bitterns; and a population of herons and egrets, which hunt but do not nest there. The two impoundments are the key attraction, especially in late summer when the eastern one dries to a mucky plain, dotted with small pools and clumps of marsh grasses. This is an ideal feeding ground for many species of migrating shorebirds that eat mosquito larvae, plant seeds and leaves, small mollusks, worms, algae, aquatic insects, and crustaceans. Because these freshwater flats are set amidst the salt marshes, the long-billed dowitcher, a freshwater species, is found together with its saltwater relative, the short-billed dowitcher.

In May, a number of shorebirds fly northward through the central

United States, rather than along the Atlantic Coast. Inland, away from the moderating influence of the sea, spring advances more rapidly than along the coast, and burgeoning populations of insects provide an abundant supply of food. The birds follow a route bounded on one side by the Mississippi and on the other by the Rocky Mountains, often lingering for several weeks to feed. In fall, on the other hand, some of these birds migrate along the coast. Now the climate is tempered by the summer warm sea, and insects and marine life are at a peak of production. The American avocet, white-rumped sandpiper, pectoral sandpiper, stilt sandpiper, and Wilson's phalarope follow this circular route. Other species follow the coast each spring, stopping to feed on horseshoe crab eggs (see **#26**).

In late summer and early fall, young birds, the offspring of the summer's breeding season, generally do not leave the nesting grounds until well after the adult birds. Setting out unguided, some wander off course, and some lose their way; this accounts for some unusual sightings at Little Creek. For example, the migratory route of the Baird's sandpiper is through the central United States in both spring and fall, but every year some juveniles are seen here.

Still other unusual sightings, or "accidentals," result from changing weather conditions. The Hudsonian godwit, the American golden plover, and the northern phalarope migrate south over the ocean and are blown back onto the coast by heavy winds or storms. While migrating over the ocean, the birds do not feed, apparently traveling south from Hudson Bay to South America nonstop at altitudes of 10,000 to 20,000 feet!

Other unusual migrants seen regularly at Little Creek include the rare curlew sandpiper, an Asiatic species which roams widely,and the ruff, a Eurasian bird seen in small numbers in both spring and fall. The ruff is named for the flamboyant breeding plumes of the male (see **#41**).

Two species which nest in the area are at the northern limit of their range. The black-necked stilt began to nest at Little Creek in the early 1970s. South of Delaware the closest known nesting grounds are in North Carolina. Most of the population is centered around freshwater wetlands in the western plains and Central and South America. The stilt is apparently working its way northward along the coast, perhaps in response to the earth's slowly warming climate. The gull-billed tern is a southern species that was once common as far north as New Jersey. Because their eggs were considered a delicacy and their feathers prized by the fashion industry, this and other terns were nearly wiped out by the beginning of the century. The gull-billed tern now nests only in scattered locations along the coast.

Remarks: *This area is heavily used in hunting season, so Sunday is the best day for a visit. Other excellent vantage points are the tower (**B**) on the headquarters entrance road, a pullover along Port Mahon Rd. (**C**) (best in the afternoon), and 1 mile farther, a footbridge to the dike (**D**) (best light in the morning). In spring, willets nest along the path. If a bird is flushed, look for its well-disguised nest of grasses and brown-spotted eggs. A spotting scope is essential here. For further information contact the Division of Fish and Wildlife, P.O. Box 1401, Dover, Del. 19901, (302) 736-4431.*

43.

Norman G. Wilder
Wildlife Area

Directions: **Kent County, Del. From Wilmington go south on U.S. 13 about 45 miles to the junction with U.S. 113 in Dover. Continue on U.S. 13 for 3.5 miles; turn west (right) onto Route 10. At 0.8 mile, Route 10 jogs sharply left. Keep on Route 10 and go 4.5 miles from the jog to Route 246. Turn south and drive 2 miles. Turn right onto the dirt road and park. The tallest oaks stand to the south of the road.**

Ownership: **Delaware Division of Fish and Wildlife.**

There are very few places on Delaware's Coastal Plain where one may see white oaks standing 100 feet tall against the sky. Throughout the region most of the mature forest of oaks and hickories has been cut down. Other canopy species here include large chestnut and willow oaks growing on the slightly higher ground where soils are better drained and drier. The principal understory species is American holly. Underneath the white oaks, red maple trees are reaching up. The future of this woodland is in doubt due to heavy infestations of gypsy moth, which are moving southward in Delaware. Oaks are the favorite food of these insects. Below the trees, the shrubs are varied and abundant, including highbush blueberry, swamp azalea, southern arrowwood, deerberry, and strawberry bush (not related to the small plant that produces the berries). In spring and summer the undergrowth becomes nearly impenetrable as Jap-

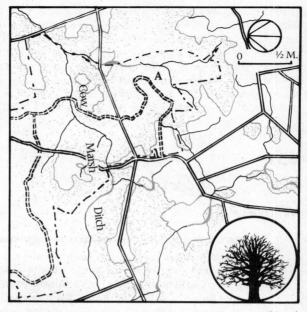

Inset: White oak

anese honeysuckle and greenbrier entangle themselves in the shrubs. The only easy time to walk through the stand is in winter and early spring when the vegetation has died back.

Across Route 246, a fifteen-minute walk will bring you to a lush stand of club moss (**A**), one of the most extensive in Delaware, according to the Delaware Nature Education Society. Four species of club moss are abundant: crowfoot club moss, ground cedar, ground pine, and running club moss. *Lycopodium X haberii* (a rare hybrid with no common name) can also be found. Club mosses are miniature relics of the forests that covered much of the earth 350 million years ago, forests which eventually became coalfields, such as those of Pennsylvania and West Virginia.

Remarks: *The stand of white oaks is on a tract of about 25 acres. There are no trails, but in winter the woods are open enough to wander at will. The road through the woods is good for birding during the spring migrations. Camping at Killen Pond southeast of Felton. A short shotgun season on deer is generally scheduled in November. For further information contact the Division of Fish and Wildlife, P.O. Box 1401, Dover, Del. 19901, (302) 736-4431.*

44.

Prime Hook
National Wildlife Refuge

Directions: **Sussex County, Del. From Wilmington, take U.S. 13 to Dover, about 45 miles. Take U.S. 113 south 17.5 miles to the junction just north of Milford. Take Route 1 and 14 south 13.6 miles to Broadkill Beach Rd. (Route 16). Turn east and go 1.2 miles to the refuge entrance.**

Ownership: **U.S. Fish and Wildlife Service.**

A perfect site for a spring canoe trip, Prime Hook Creek winds through red-maple swamp out into brackish marshes of cattail and phrag-mites and on into the salt-marsh grasses that line the Delaware Bay (see **#64** and **#21**). This is one of the few places where you can see seaside alder, a shrub with glossy leaves and small, red fruits that look like miniature pinecones. It grows only along the banks of coastal streams in Delaware and Maryland and on the Red River of Oklahoma. Botanists are as yet unable to explain this odd dispersal. Typical wetland shrubs like blueberry and sweet pepperbush line the banks of the stream as it runs through the swamp, making an ideal habitat for prothonotary warblers. A variety of warblers, thrushes, flycatchers, and other migratory landbirds can be found in spring along with great blue and green herons and otters. Muskrat lodges are scattered through the cattail marshes farther downstream (see **#64**). Several species of dabbling ducks nest here in the marshes; black duck and mallard are most common, but gadwall and blue-winged teal may also breed on the refuge.

The road that continues on past the refuge entrance leads to Broadkill Beach. It runs by open creeks and brackish and salt marsh, a good place to find black rails calling on spring nights (see **#65**) (**A**). In the less saline stretches of the marsh (**B**) look for the uncommon short-billed marsh wren or sedge wren. There is good birding for shorebirds along the beach in late May and in late summer and early fall.

Remarks: Open from sunrise to sunset. Canoeing is best in spring before the bugs come out and the weather turns hot. Maps of the refuge are available from the refuge manager: Prime Hook National Wildlife Refuge,

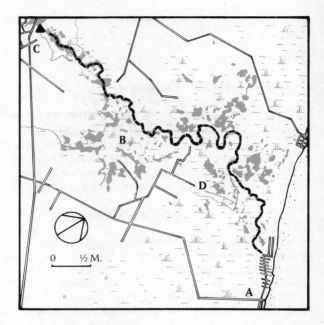

*R. D.1, Box 195, Milton, Del. 19968, (302) 684-8419. Access to the creek is from Route 1 at the junction with Route 5 (**C**). A private canoe-rental business is located right there. Canoes may be taken out (and launched) at (**D**), the refuge headquarters, after a good daylong trip. There is camping at Cape Henlopen State Park to the south, from April to November. Other activities: good fishing for largemouth bass, pickerel, and white perch in the creek (license required).*

45.
Beach Plum
Island

Directions: Sussex County, Del. From Wilmington, go south on U.S. 13 about 45 miles to Dover. Take U.S. 113 south 17.5 miles to the junction north of Milford. Take Route 1 and 14 southeast 13.6 miles to Broadkill Beach Rd. (Route

16). Turn east and go 3.9 miles. Turn south in Broadkill and drive along the road, about 1.8 miles. Beyond this point, the road deteriorates. From here it is a half-hour walk south along the beach.

Ownership: Commissioners of the Town of Lewes, trustees.

Like a miniature version of the barrier islands along the Atlantic Coast, Beach Plum Island lies at the western shore of the Delaware Bay. A narrow strip of active beach, a small dune, typical barrier-beach vegetation, and a tidal marsh at the inland edge: all the pieces are there, but compressed on a strip of land barely 1000 feet across at its widest point. It is the only such island on the western shore of the bay. To the north are thousands of acres of marshland; to the south is the point of Cape Henlopen and then the sea. The source of the island was the sand swept in around the cape by the longshore currents (see **#25**). Since the early 1900s, no new sand has been added to the island. Although most of the sand drops out at the spit, some is brought into the bay and washed ashore.

The outer barrier islands are battered by the full strength of the Atlantic Ocean; the inner waters of the bay are more protected, and Beach Plum Island is not subjected to the vast breaking waves of autumn and winter storms. Even so, the killing salt spray that prunes and restricts vegetation along the coast is also a factor here.

Remarks: *The best seasons to visit are spring and fall. The nearest camping is at Cape Henlopen State Park. Canoeing on nearby Prime Hook Creek.*

46.
Cape Henlopen
State Park

Directions: Sussex County, Del. From Wilmington, take U.S. 13 south to Dover, about 45 miles. In Dover watch for signs above the road that read "Delaware Beaches" and follow U.S. 113 as it splits off to the east from U.S. 13. Go 18 miles to the junction just north of Milford. Take Route 1 and 14 southeast about 20 miles; look for signs to the Cape May

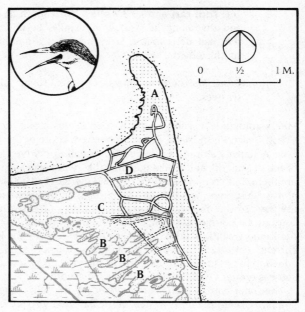

Inset: Common tern

Ferry. Follow U.S. 9 east to the end of the road, 2.8 miles, and turn south (right). The tollgate for the park is 1.2 miles straight ahead.

Ownership: **Delaware Division of Parks and Recreation.**

Cape Henlopen is a sandy thumb of land jutting into the mouth of the Delaware Bay and separating it from the Atlantic. It has existed for thousands of years in one form or another, and the signs of its transformations are scattered across it. There is the "walking" or great dune, which moves southward 5 to 14 feet per year; the coastal dune parallel to the shore, which is one of the highest along the entire Atlantic Coast; and marking the shape of earlier capes are the fingers of pine forest that lie on the salt marshes to the west.

To reach the spit at the end of the cape (**A**) drive past the toll-booth to the end of the road and turn left. Continue on to the parking area overlooking the spit. Looking northward, you can see that this is a simple spit, extending in a straight line into the mouth of the bay. This profile of the cape is new. Two hundred years ago, there was no spit at all, but a curving promontory that looked much like Cape Henry (see **#88**) today. Fifteen hundred years ago, the cape ended in a cockscomb of sharply arching spits, like Sandy Hook but more acute (see **#1**). Like all sandy coastal features, the cape changes continually in response to rising sea level, vegetative cover, ocean currents, and storms (see **Introduction**).

Sand from the Atlantic beach is continually swept northward by the longshore currents, which in Delaware move from south to north, and by the tidal currents, which push into the bay. Currently the cape is wearing away at the rate of about 10 feet each year (see **#25**). This process began in the period following the retreat of the last ice sheet, when the whole topography of the present coastline began to emerge. Over time, as sea level rose and waves further eroded the Atlantic shore, the entire cape gradually migrated north and west in stages, each stage accompanied by a series of spits. Traces of earlier spits now show up clearly on the topographic maps of the area (**B**). They survive as ridges of high ground running out into the salt marshes to the west. These old spits are difficult to spot from the ground; many of them are off limits, lying on military property. Furthermore, the walking dune described below (**C**) is gradually burying these relics as it moves southward. The wooded land visible to the south of the dune marks the positions of the ancient spits.

Eventually, the simple spit now visible at the cape may also curve to the west and is, in fact, already beginning to do so. Left to itself, it will one day enclose part of the inner bay, creating a shallow lagoon linked with the sea by a narrow channel. Gradually, salt marsh will replace the open water. Then the cape will look as it did two hundred years ago, a rounded point of land at the entrance to the bay. The salt marshes visible to the west of the walking dune (**C**) may have formed in just this way.

The spit has been a breeding ground for terns, black skimmers, and piping plovers for many years; the bird population has shifted as the shoreline has changed and human interference has increased. Storm tides destroyed the nesting area of the least terns at the foot of the dunes on the ocean side, and, for a time, the terns decreased rapidly. Now they are increasing again, because they have found alternative nesting sites in the dunes themselves. Black skimmers have been driven away almost entirely, probably because more people and dogs use the area; the skimmer is extremely sensitive to disturbance. There are still many common terns and piping plovers using the area. The nesting grounds are roped off to protect the birds from human traffic. You can walk down along the beach, but stay near the tide line. In spring and fall the bay side of the cape is an excellent place to see great flocks of migrating shorebirds. Hawks and songbird migrations are also very good in autumn, as this is the first landfall once the birds have left Cape May (see **Cape May**).

To reach the walking dune (**C**), drive back toward the tollbooth and turn left just beyond it toward the campgrounds. Go 0.4 mile from the turn and make a right. Park in the campground parking lot and walk east by the old tower. You are now on top of the walking dune, a mysterious ridge of sand lying about half a mile from the bay shore and perpendicular to the Atlantic Ocean. Scientists speculate that it was created in the wake of the deforestation of the cape in the nineteenth century when the harbor breakwaters were built. The dune is still moving, covering woods and buildings in its path.

Although it is far from the sea, you will notice as you walk over the dune that many of the species associated with seaside dunes are growing here too, including American beach grass, beach heather, broom sedge, and switch grass. These plants are able to survive in the very hot, very dry conditions of the dune. Salt spray is not a factor here so far from the ocean, and eventually other vegetation will take over. The first woody plants will include pitch pine, Virginia pine, poison ivy, and bayberry. These will provide organic litter, shade, and therefore more moisture, so that other species such as oaks and red maples can sprout and grow. If left to itself, the dune will probably become a forested and stable ridge, no longer a dune at all.

Numerous species of insects have also adapted to life here. Among them are wolf spiders, tiger beetles, digging wasps, ant lions, and locusts. These insects also inhabit the ocean dunes (see **#55**). They have developed an assortment of survival strategies. Some, like the ant lion and the wolf spider, burrow into the sand to escape the very high surface temperatures. The ant lion, which is a larval stage of an insect similar to a damsel fly, spends its time at the bottom of a funnel-shaped depression. When it hatches out of the egg, the small ant lion immediately begins to dig into the sand, abdomen first. Its hindparts are pointed and covered with forward-pointing bristles which help it to burrow. As sand strikes the insect's head an automatic reflex causes the ant lion to toss its head, scattering sand in every direction. All the while the insect slowly revolves. The ant lion emerges from the egg with this instinctive pattern of behavior. Once it has built its trap, the ant lion sits buried at the bottom of it with only its pincer jaws exposed. When ants stumble upon the trap, they either fall directly to the bottom or partway down the sides of the funnel. This dislodges sand onto the ant lion's head. Again it tosses its head instinctively, and a shower of sand strikes the ant, or a small landslide occurs, sending the prey down to the pincers of the ant lion. Once the ant lion has a grip on its prey, it injects digestive juices into the body. The soft internal organs of the ant are liquified and sucked out, and the empty husk of the ant's body is thrown out of the trap. Because digestion occurs within the body of the ant and not within the body of the ant lion, there are no waste products for the insect to dispose of. It can continue to sit at the bottom of its lair indefinitely.

Winged insects such as the locust and the digging wasp can survive in the dunes by flying to cool themselves. All of the insects found here have thick layers of hair on their bodies, often light-colored, to help insulate them and to reflect the heat. Mammals of various sorts, including rabbits, mice, and foxes also forage on the dunes by night, when the intense heat has abated.

Later stages of succession in the dune forest can be seen on the Pinelands Nature Trail, which begins at **D**. (A trail guide is available at the nature center just up the road on the left.) The highlights of the trail include several small cranberry bogs where the water table is so close to the surface that these wet-loving plants are able to flourish in the seemingly dry and barren sandy soil. Insect-eating sundews also grow in these low spots (see **#89**). The first part of the trail runs through forest recently disturbed by fire, where vines and undergrowth are thick, but in the middle section the trail passes pine woods that escaped burning. Ground cover is sparse in the shade of these trees. Eventually, this type of woodland will cover the walking dune.

Remarks: *The Pinelands Nature Trail is a 2-mile circuit of easy walking. The best times to visit are spring and fall. Biting flies are fierce in the summer, especially away from the ocean breeze, and mosquitoes can be bothersome from spring through fall. Poison ivy is abundant in the woods. Camping is available. Other activities include surf and bay fishing, and swimming. For further information contact Cape Henlopen State Park, Lewes, Del. 19958, (302) 645-8983.*

47.

Savage's Ditch
Osprey Colony

Directions: **Sussex County, Del. From Wilmington, drive south on U.S. 13 about 45 miles to Dover. There take U.S. 113 south about 18 miles to Milford. In Milford take Route**

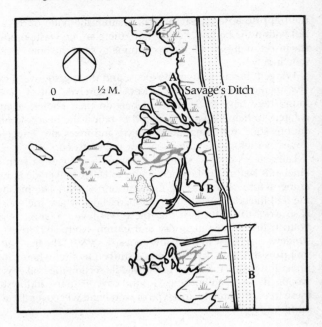

1 and 14 southeast 28 miles to Savage's Ditch just north of the Indian River Inlet (A). By the small green-and-white sign, turn right into the parking area. Walk 300 yards to the edge of the bay. In summer, parking is by permit only.

Ownership: **Private, and Delaware Division of Parks and Recreation.**

North of the Indian River Inlet on the marsh-covered mudbanks of a tidal delta is the largest osprey colony in Delaware. With at least ten active nests in 1983, it is one of the most important along the Atlantic shore. Because of the flat terrain, you can observe the birds from the bay shore without disturbing them.

Ospreys are birds of prey unlike any others. They are bound to the water, living entirely on fish. Even during migration they closely follow the rivers and seacoast. Soaring overhead an osprey is mostly white underneath with a characteristic crook in the wings and a dark streak through its eyes. Its tail is banded with black and white. The feathers are tightly packed and act as a buffer when the bird makes its spectacular dives into the sea. The osprey often strikes the water with such force that it completely disappears beneath the surface, only to reemerge grasping a fish in its talons. Its nostrils close on impact. The feet are well equipped to handle slippery fish; the soles are studded with prickly nubbins, and the outer toe can move from front to back, allowing the bird to get a firmer grasp of its prey. An osprey can carry a heavy fish by aligning the fish with its body, thereby reducing wind resistance.

Ospreys were once common all along the Atlantic Coast, but have dwindled, mainly as a result of pesticide pollution and destruction of habitat (see **#32**). Before human settlements clogged the shore, ospreys used trees, particularly dead snags, as nesting places. Now they appear to favor man-made structures such as duck blinds, buoys, special nesting platforms, power-line towers, and other unlikely places. They build their nests out of sticks, rubbish, seaweed—virtually anything at hand. Year after year they will return to the same site and add to the existing structure until its bulk rivals that of an eagle's nest—as much as a ton of material.

The delta surrounding the Indian River Inlet formed as sands swept in by tides and sediments from streams feeding into the bay settled at the mouth of the inlet. The incoming tide passes through the inlet and curves around the two spits of land. The friction created as the water moves along the land slows the current and some of the suspended sediments drop out (see **#25**).

Remarks: *Ospreys return to the nesting site in March and April; the main period of breeding and feeding the young occurs from May to July. The female sits on the eggs while the male hunts, providing food for both of them. North and south of the inlet are several protected stretches of beach where colonies of least terns and black skimmers nest (see #30). These are marked with signs (B). Common terns nest on small islands in the bay. In the winter the Rehoboth and Indian River bays are full of waterfowl, and the stone jetties that edge the inlet attract common eiders, grebes, oldsquaws, loons, and purple sandpipers. Other activities include fishing and crabbing in the bay. Equipment for rent in Rehoboth and Bethany Beach. Party-boat charters sail from the Indian River Inlet boat basin. There is swimming at nearby beaches. Camping at Cape Henlopen State Park.*

48.
Broad Creek

―――――――――――――――――――――――――――――――――――――――

Directions: Sussex County, Del. From Wilmington take U.S. 13 south to the outskirts of Laurel, about 90 miles. Turn west (right) on U.S. 9 and go 0.7 mile to the intersection of several roads. Go straight across the intersection toward Woodland Ferry and continue west on Route 78. Go about 2.6 miles to Route 493 and turn south (left). Drive 0.9 mile into Bethel. If you are canoeing or boating, you can put in at the Broad Creek Bridge in Bethel. To reach the takeout point at Phillips Landing (**A**), keep driving south on Route 493 about 1 mile to Portsville. Drive through Portsville on Route 496 about 2 miles to the end. (These route numbers are posted on small black-and-white signs.)

Ownership: Large parts of both banks of Broad Creek are part of the Nanticoke Wildlife Area under the Delaware Division of Fish and Wildlife. The rest is privately owned.

Early on a September morning the golden stands of wild rice at the mouth of Broad Creek (**A**) are full of red-winged blackbirds gorging on the newly ripened grain. The arrow arum and pickerelweed which grow along the quiet waters are still green and the darker shapes of cedars and pines mark the skyline. This stream and the Nanticoke into which it flows are special. The American white-cedar which lines the banks has vanished rapidly from the rest of the state, where it has been heavily timbered for its valuable wood. Once cut, this tree rarely comes back on Delaware's Coastal Plain (though they do in the Pine Barrens of New Jersey); other more aggressive species replace it. Loblolly pine reaches its northern limit here, and nowhere else in Delaware is there a finer stand of wild rice, a plant especially sensitive to pollution (see **#94**).

The best way to enjoy the creek is to canoe it or use a small powerboat. Although far from the Chesapeake Bay, this freshwater stream is still tidal. You can ride the tide down from the bridge in Bethel to Phillips Landing at the mouth of the creek. Much of the land bordering Broad Creek has been farmed in the recent past, and the woods are in various stages of succession (see **Introduction**). In addition to loblolly and American white-cedar, pond pine, and Virginia pine are common evergreens in the canopy. Along the lower banks blackgum, red maple, and sweetgum are also prominent. Over

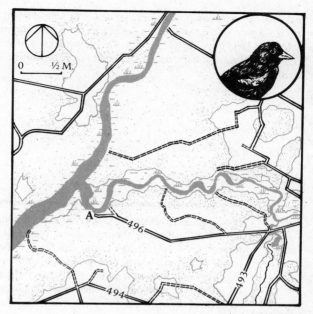

Inset: Red-winged blackbird

time they will tend to replace the less shade-tolerant conifers. Back from the edge of the creek, especially on the sandy bluffs to the south, a variety of oaks—including white, chestnut, Spanish, post, and blackjack—appear. Throughout the area the common shrubs are mountain laurel, bayberry, huckleberry, and blueberry, which grow well on the sandy, acid soils (see **Introduction**). American holly is common in the understory, while in the lower, wetter areas sweetbay magnolia is also found. Its white sweet-scented blossoms are in full bloom along the creek in June.

Unlike most of the waterways in Delaware, the Nanticoke and its tributaries empty into the Chesapeake Bay, which lies farther south. As a result, the spring runs of shad traveling upstream to spawn occur a month earlier in these waters than in the rivers and creeks which drain into the Delaware. Other anadromous fish (those that migrate from the sea up rivers to breed) such as striped bass, alewives, and blueback herring also use the Nanticoke.

Remarks: *From the bridge in Bethel to Phillips Landing is about 5 miles. If planning a summer outing, go early in the morning, as both the Nanticoke and Broad Creek are heavily used by power boats and water skiers particularly on weekends. Activities include fishing for white perch, yellow perch, largemouth bass, and pickerel—with a proper license. Nearest camping is at Trap Pond State Park to the east. Canoes are for rent in Wilmington (see #40). There are many trails winding through the Nanticoke Wildlife Area.*

49.
Trap Pond State Park

Directions: Sussex County, Del. From Wilmington go south on U.S. 13 to Laurel, about 90 miles. Turn east (left) on Route 24 and go 4.5 miles to the sign for Trap Pond State Park. Turn south (right) and go 0.8 mile to Cypress Point Rd. Turn east (left) and go 0.3 mile. Turn right and drive 0.7 mile to the parking area. The nature trail begins on the left side of the lot.

Ownership: **Delaware Division of Parks and Recreation.**

This trail winds through second-growth woods in many stages of succession, from scrubby Virginia pines to mixed oaks, from baldcypress to gums and red maples. The pond itself, like so many in Delaware, is an old millpond built about 1790. Originally, these lowlands were covered with baldcypress and white-cedar swamp forests, all of which were logged for their valuable timber. The land was also cleared for farms, so the forest you see here is a young one.

The trail begins in the woods of mixed pines (loblolly and Virginia) and oaks (including white, willow, basket, and black). Along the trail an assortment of other oaks will be found, among them post, scarlet, Spanish, and northern red oaks. Scattered sprouts of American chestnut also occur in these upland areas, but because of the blight that attacks them, they will not grow very tall.

At post 7 a spur of the trail leads down to the pond edge. In the light along the banks, a thick growth of blueberry and sweet pepperbush has grown up. Back under the shade of the trees the undergrowth is much sparser. Swamp rose blooms at the water's edge in spring. A little farther out in the shallows is a band of emergent vegetation, including bayonet rush, pickerelweed, and spatterdock.

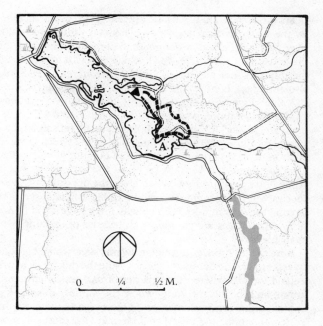

These plants grow with their roots in the pond bottom and their flowering parts above the surface. Look for bladderwort floating on the surface of the water. This species of plant is not rooted at all, but is supported by tiny air pockets on a network of rootlike hairs. These bladders also obtain nutrients for the plant by engulfing small insects (see **#17**).

Beneath the litter of leaves and needles along the trail, sandy soil is occasionally laid bare. This is evidence of the marine origins of the Coastal Plain. Such soils have developed from deposits of sediments laid down at the edge of the sea or along the ocean floor (see **Introduction**). While wetland species such as baldcypress grow along the edge of the lake and out into the water, upland species such as black oak appear on shore just a few feet from the water's edge. This rapid transition is due to the sandy soils surrounding the lake, which do not hold water well.

Farther down the trail at post 9, look for young hickories. Along much of the Coastal Plain, foresters consider oaks and hickories to be the main climax species. Woodlands will go through a series of successive stages until they reach a somewhat steady state, the climax. Then a windstorm, a plague of gypsy moths, or a logging crew clears the woods and begins the process of succession all over again. By the water, swamp azalea, an evergreen shrub which blooms in May, and hazel alder are abundant in the understory. Together with the sphagnum moss (see **#15**) which covers much of the ground these species indicate that conditions here are wet. Persimmons are also abundant, but they are also found on dry upland sites.

A fine grove of wax myrtle about 20 feet tall is clustered at post 11. By the seashore, wax myrtle is a shrub (see **#55**). Here conditions are gentler, for there is ample moisture, no salt, and a greater supply of nutrients. This illustrates that plants which grow in harsh environments do not necessarily do so because these conditions are ideal for them, but because they can tolerate such environments, while other plants cannot. When given the opportunity, these hardy species will flourish dramatically in kinder habitats (see **#21**). Just beyond the wax myrtles is an equally impressive stand of American holly. These trees are growing well because of the ample moisture available here.

Now the trail moves through a swamp area where blackgum and sweetgum are the dominant species. Note the difference between the upland woods, where many species of oak and other trees can be found, and the swamp zone, where the number of species is more limited. There is a verdant cover of ferns over the wet ground: New York, cinnamon, and netted chain fern are the most common.

On Cypress Point (**A**) you can look out across the water at the cypress swamp. This is the northernmost stand of any size that is open to the public (see **#53**). There is a large beech tree on the point. Beech trees are not terribly common in the Coastal Plain woods of Delaware. On the western shore of the Chesapeake they are an increasingly important part of the canopy (see **#79**).

Moving away from the water, the trail passes through drier woodland once more. Mountain laurel and pink azalea, species found in well-drained, somewhat acid forests, begin to appear. The mountain laurel blooms in June, the pink azalea in April. A stand of young Virginia pine indicates where an opening in the forest has recently occurred. Along with redcedar, Virginia pine is the common pioneer tree species throughout most of Delaware's Coastal Plain. In this region and to the south, loblolly pine is another pioneer. This means that when cleared land is allowed to revert to forest or some natural opening in the canopy is created, Virginia pine and redcedar are the first trees to take hold. Being intolerant of shade, they are soon replaced by deciduous species. Across the road the path continues through upland woods of oaks and red maples and loblolly plantations back to the parking area. The forest here is full of food for wildlife. Various species of vines, including greenbrier, poison ivy, and Virginia creeper, all produce fruits. The blackgum and sweet-gum, the oaks, the hickories, persimmon, dogwood, and redcedar all have fruits or nuts that birds and animals relish.

The pileated woodpecker, brown-headed nuthatch, yellow-throated warbler, and summer tanager are nesting species here. The Delmarva Ornithological Society notes that fields in and around the park are often breeding grounds for vesper sparrows. These birds do not follow a pattern of returning to the same nesting site year after year, so you must be willing to spend some time to find them.

Remarks: *Walking is easy. Part of the trail is accessible to wheelchairs. The entire circuit is 1 mile long. There are also a number of unmarked trails in the park property. Camping is permitted at the park from April through October. The best sites are #137 and #139, which sit on a small point of land out in the lake. The park is beautiful all year long. Activities include boating and canoeing (rentals are available), swimming, and fishing (a license is required). A canoe trail leads from the lake up into the cypress swamp. For further information write Trap Pond State Park, Route 2, Box 331, Laurel, Del., 19956; (302) 875-5153.*

50.
Trussum Pond

Directions: **Sussex County, Del. From Wilmington, go south on U.S. 13 about 90 miles to Laurel. Continue south on U.S. 13 past the intersection with Route 24; go about 1 mile and turn east (left) at the sign for Hearns Crossroad. On Route 70 go east 2.4 miles, then bear left on Route 72. About 0.5 mile further on, Route 72 crosses the dam at the north end of Trussum Pond. There is a public parking and picnic area on the far side of the bridge on the right.**

Ownership: **Delaware Wildlands, Inc.**

In spring the surface of Trussum Pond is crowded with white fragrant water lilies and, in their midst, majestic baldcypress trees, hundreds of years old. This is a small place of great beauty. The trees that stand out in the water were there before the dam was built about 100 years ago. At its deepest, the water is no more than 4 feet, but that is enough to ensure that this stand will not be able to reproduce

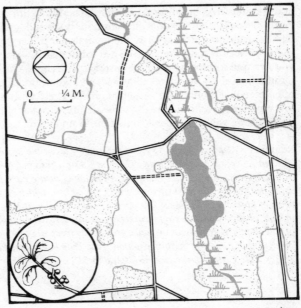

Inset: Bayberry

itself. Baldcypress seedlings need damp soil in which to sprout (see **#73**). As you look out across the water, you can see pockets of vegetation around the bases of some trees or on the stumps of cypress that have died. Windblown soil and decaying organic matter collect in hollows and crannies, providing nurseries for a variety of shrubs. Among them are hazel alder, inkberry, red chokeberry, maleberry, sweet pepperbush, and bayberry (see **#100**). Water lilies have special stems which help to keep the plant supplied with oxygen. As the bottom muck of any pond is very poor in oxygen, the upper part of the plant must procure it. The upper surfaces of the floating leaves are covered with small openings or stomata which absorb air. After blooming the water lily retracts its stem to release the seeds under water. Protected in a small sac, the seeds drift to a new location and take root.

Walk back across the dam and turn down the small path which leads to the banks of James Branch. Here there are some fine large cypress (**A**). These trees may be able to reproduce themselves, for the seedlings will have a chance to take root. The knobby cones projecting from the cypress roots are called "knees." The two major theories as to their function are that they help to bring oxygen to the submerged roots of the tree and that they help support the tree in soft swamp soils. Without oxygen the tree cannot maintain the chemical reactions which power the life processes of the plant (see **#73** and **#96**). Other swamp trees, including sweetgum and red maple, are also found here. American holly is abundant in the understory, and holly seedlings also form much of the groundcover. It is an adaptable species, able to flourish in both the very wet conditions here and the dry conditions of the back-dune forests (see **#1**). Sweetbay magnolia is another common understory tree. The variety of trees and shrubs is limited in swampy environments. Many cannot survive the frequent flooding, which cuts off oxygen supplies. Some of the shrubs that are able to grow under these conditions include southern arrowwood and strawberry bush.

Remarks: *Arrangements can be made to canoe down the James Branch to Records Pond in Laurel. En route there are impressive stands of white-cedar and large baldcypress. One of these, a truly massive tree, has been bored to determine its age, which proved to be an astonishing 540 years. Contact Delaware Wildlands, 5th and Main Sts., Odessa, Del. 19730, (302) 378-2736. Canoe rentals are available in Wilmington (see **#40**). Boating and fishing (with a license) are also allowed. The best season is March when the water is high. Birding is similar to Trap Pond State Park (**#49**). See that entry for activities and camping. Poison ivy is a flourishing ground cover along the branch. In summer biting insects are fierce.*

51.
Great Cypress Swamp

Directions: **Sussex County, Del. The area straddles Route 54 in southern Delaware a few miles west of Selbyville. The swamp belongs to the Delaware Wildlands and permission to explore it must be obtained. The local representative will direct visitors to trails and birding spots. Contact Delaware Wildlands, Inc., 5th and Main Sts., Odessa, Del. 19730, (302) 834-1332.**

Ownership: **Delaware Wildlands, Inc.**

Burnt, logged, drained, and farmed many times over, this tract of lowland is a crazy quilt of gums, maples, oaks, pines, and baldcypress. Nowhere else in Delaware is there such a stand of forested land, though the 11,000 acres now remaining are just a shadow of the 50,000 acres of baldcypress and Atlantic white-cedar swamp which once stood here. This is the northernmost colony of baldcypress along the Atlantic Coast, an outlier of the southern forests (see #73). Swainson's Warbler, a bird whose primary breeding range is far to the south, still nests here in small numbers.

A great fire raged over the forest in 1930, burning unchecked for eight months. The great danger in a swamp fire is that the thick layer of peat—the partially decomposed plant material that lies below the ground—will ignite. The fire can then smolder and break out from time to time as a tree burns from the roots upwards. This usually does not happen, for normally the peat is saturated by the swamp water. But in the fire of 1930, the 6-to-8-inch peat layer in the Great Cypress Swamp probably caught fire, destroying much of the forest.

Very little cypress still remains, but there are scattered pockets of tall trees that are over 180 years old. Sweetgum, blackgum, red maple, pond and loblolly pines, and swamp cottonwood are more important in the canopy now. Water, basket, and swamp white oak are also found in the wetter locations. On patches of higher ground scattered through the area, American beech, loblolly pine, and Spanish and white oak share the canopy. In the understory American holly, swamp magnolia, young oaks, and young maples dominate, while mountain laurel, clammy or swamp azalea, various species of blueberry, and wax myrtle are also common.

In the hope of catching sight of a Swainson's warbler, birders collect each spring along the roads of the swamp and in the neighboring Pocomoke swamp. Until recently the favorite ploy to attract a warbler was to pay a tape of its song; however, this practice was banned after it became clear that the birds were disappearing from the region.

The male warbler sings in order to establish breeding territory. Hearing the tape, a male Swainson's thinks he is being challenged by a rival and is drawn to the sound to confront this rival. If the tape were a real bird, some resolution would occur, and one of the birds would eventually retreat. As the tape continues to play, regardless of the bird's presence, the warbler becomes very agitated. If tapes are played too often, the male becomes so distressed that it will leave. The Swainson's warbler is very secretive, living in dense wet undergrowth. Although rarely seen without the use of a tape, the bird's five-note song is very distinctive. The first two notes slur downwards, the second two are low and the last one high.

Other birds of interest here include a nesting bald eagle, red-headed and pileated woodpeckers, summer and scarlet tanagers, blue grosbeaks, wood ducks, and yellow-throated and worm-eating warblers. Carpenter frogs are plentiful, their loud call sounding like a hammer striking wood (see **#100**). The red-bellied water snake is at the northern limit of its range here. A beautiful snake with a rich brown back and deep coppery belly, it hunts for fish, frogs, salamanders, and crayfish. Both the carpenter frog and the red-bellied water snake are Coastal Plain species.

Remarks: *Copperheads are regularly encountered in small numbers. Spring is particularly good for birds and flowering shrubs. Summers are hot and buggy. The most accessible birding area is along Route 418 (look for small white highway maintenance signs) south of Route 54 about 5 miles west of Selbyville. This road is heavily used on spring weekends by birding groups from all over the Northeast.*

52.
Assawoman
Wildlife Area

Directions: **Sussex County, Del. From Wilmington, drive south on U.S. 13 to Dover (about 45 miles). There, take U.S. 113 about 50 miles southeast to Dagsboro and turn east (left) on Route 26. Go 12 miles to Bethany Beach; turn south (right) on Kent Ave., just before U.S. 1. Go 1.4 miles and bear left. Go 2.0 miles and bear left. Go 1.2 miles and turn left. Go another 1.1 miles and turn left again. Proceed 0.6 mile and look for the sign to the Wildlife Area. The route is easy to follow because it is well marked with signs to Camp Barnes, which lies just beyond the Wildlife Area.**

Ownership: **Delaware Division of Fish and Wildlife.**

Sheltered behind a barrier beach lies the Little Assawoman Bay, bordered by the marshes and freshwater ponds of the Assawoman Wildlife Area. In late fall and winter great numbers of waterfowl come in to rest and feed, but May, when the marshes are bright green, and herons and egrets stalk the shallow ponds, is especially

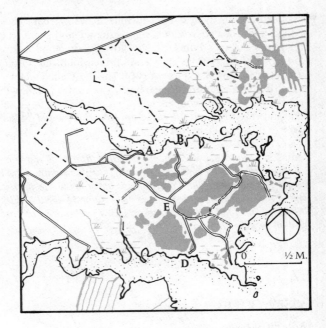

fine. Many species of warblers, flycatchers, and other landbirds pass through the loblolly woods and bayberry thickets, while shorebirds feed on the tidal mudbanks and in the marshes. Part of the broken chain of barrier beaches and tidal marsh that hugs the coast, Assawoman Wildlife Area is an important stopover for birds migrating northward.

There are four landing areas accessible by car (**A, B, C, D**), which provide views of Miller Creek and Dirickson Creek. These are good vantage points from which to scan for waterfowl. The observation tower (**E**) provides an excellent view of some of the impoundments. These ponds were created in the 1950s to bring back the water level of the marshes, which had been drained during the 1930s and 1940s for mosquito control. This procedure was common at that time, for there was little understanding of the importance of the salt marshes to the coastal ecosystem (see **#21** and **Chesapeake Bay**).

Since the ponds were created, natural vegetation has moved in without any help from the Division of Fish and Wildlife. Submerged plants include wigeon grass and sago pondweed. The principal emergent species are millet, smartweed, cattail, and phragmites. Ponds are by definition shallow bodies of water. Vegetation grows through-out because ample light reaches the bottom. Depending on the tem-

perature in the pond and the amount of animal and plant life growing in it, levels of oxygen can vary tremendously. Aquatic species
must be able to withstand these fluctuations. Land plants draw in
oxygen from the ground in order to carry out the conversion of
stored energy to usable energy. Aquatic plants must draw it in from
the surrounding water, because the bottom muck of the pond has
virtually none. Like all green plants, aquatics also manufacture oxygen during photosynthesis, using sunlight and carbon dioxide to
store energy in the form of starch. Submerged plants like wigeon
grass are limp when you pull them up. Supported by the water, they
do not require the stiff cell walls of terrestrial species. Their flexible
fronds also provide a home for all sorts of tiny animal life.

Remarks: *During the fall and winter, the area is used for duck hunting
except on Sundays. A short shotgun season on deer is generally scheduled
during November. It is open from dawn to dusk. Activities include fishing
for bluefish and flounder in Indian River and Rehoboth Bay, charter-boat
fishing from Ocean City, Maryland, and swimming at nearby Delaware
Seashore State Park. Biting insects are a problem from the middle of May
to the first frost. Camping is available at Trap Pond State Park west of U.S.
113 on Route 24 (see **#49**). For further information contact the Division
of Fish and Wildlife, P.O. Box 1401, Dover, Del. 19901; (301) 736-4431.*

53.
Nassawango
Creek

Directions: **Worcester County, Md. From Washington, D.C.,
take U.S. 50 east across the Chesapeake Bay Bridge and
south to Salisbury, about 120 miles. From Salisbury take
Route 12 southeast (toward Snow Hill) 15.5 miles to Red
House Rd. Turn west (right) and go 1.2 miles to the bridge.
Park by the road.**

Ownership: **The Nature Conservancy.**

In spring the banks of Nassawango Creek are a rich, dense green,
shot with yellow-crimson trumpet flowers of the crossvine, fine white
tendrils of the fringe tree, and huge, redolent blossoms of the
sweetbay magnolia. Eighteen species of warblers nest in the area,

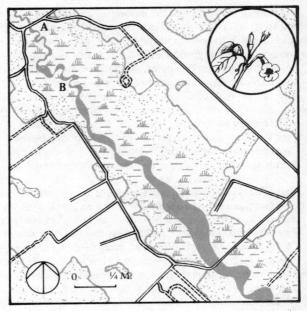

Inset: Crossvine

including various southern wetland warblers: prothonotary, Kentucky, and perhaps the rare Swainson's. River otters are abundant.

At Red House Rd. bridge (**A**) the Nassawango is a narrow, freshwater tidal creek. When the tide rises in the Chesapeake Bay, its current is stronger than that of the Nassawango and the Pocomoke into which the Nassawango flows. The waters of creek and river back up, rising 1.5 to 2 feet daily. The Pocomoke River system is an outpost of the southern hardwood swamps that line the rivers south of the James. It is the only such southern swamp on the Eastern Shore (see **#95**). Blackgum, baldcypress, and water oak dominate the canopy, mingling with willow oak, swamp red maple, and hickories. The wetland understory species include southern species like sweetbay, persimmon, and horse sugar. Common alder, southern arrowwood, swamp azalea and pink azalea, fetterbush, highbush blueberry, and sweet pepperbush are the common shrubs along the banks of the stream. Take note of the size of the small cones on the alders. Farther downstream a different species with noticeably larger cones will appear. Scientists do not yet understand why the Pocomoke is a southern system while the Wicomico just to the west is not. Many thousands of years ago, baldcypress forests did grow as far north as Baltimore, and then vanished in subsequent glacial ages. This swamp may be a remnant of those forests.

Downstream the creek changes from fresh to brackish water. About halfway between the Red House Rd. bridge and the Nassawango Rd. bridge, seaside alder begins to replace common alder, its fresh-water counterpart. (see #44). The mature cones of the alders near Red House Rd. are small, from about ⅜ to ⅝ inch long. The small dangling red and yellow male flowers bloom in early spring. (The female flowers are the cones.) The seaside alder blooms in late summer or early autumn and develops larger cones, from ⅝ to ⅞ inch long. The cones of both species last throughout the year.

Crossvine, a climbing plant common in this part of the Nassawango and uncommon elsewhere on the Delmarva Peninsula, is extremely sensitive to salt. It is abundant on the trees along Red House Rd. There it winds around the trunks and branches of trees which stand on slightly higher ground, for it will not grow with its roots in saturated soil. Crossvine vanishes to the north of Red House Rd. because it apparently needs minute quantities of salt. Although the Nassawango is fresh here, every so often serious droughts strike the area. As the flow of the creek falls off sharply, the high tides bring salt water much farther upstream, enough to keep the cross-vine growing here.

All along the length of the creek are muddy shallows where wild rice, spatterdock, golden club, blue flag, and submerged pondweeds grow. This is typical of slow-moving Coastal Plain streams, which descend very gradually to the sea over the flat terrain (see **Introduction**). The incoming tides counteract erosion by carrying sediments back upstream and redepositing them. In May the wild rice is just coming up, ripening in late summer and early fall. Once abundant all over the East Coast in fresh and brackish marshes, wild rice has lost much of its habitat owing to pollution and siltation. Wild rice is an emergent, which means that it grows with its roots in water and its stem and flowers above water. Small changes in water depth will favor different species; agriculture and deveopment around the Chesapeake and elsewhere have drastically increased the sediments being deposited along the waterways, with the result that wild rice has been replaced in many places with other plants.

Like many other coastal streams, the Nassawango is spring-fed. Water from snowfall, rain, and even dew percolates down through the soil until it reaches a layer of compacted minerals and clay called the hardpan. This layer is waterproof, forcing the water to flow horizontally until it finds a way out to the surface once more as a spring. Since there is little agricultural activity or development in the

area, the Nassawango watershed is not polluted and the water quality of the stream itself is very high. This is one reason for the thriving
population of river otters.

The otters are most often seen in early spring just after the kits
have been born. River otters have sinuous, lithe bodies well suited
to aquatic life. Their undercoat of fur is oily and is covered with a
rich brown coat of heavy guard hairs. This insulates them against
cold. The ear and nose openings close whenever the animal dives
underwater. Otters stay active all year long, fishing under the ice in
northern habitats. Though they are primarily nocturnal, they do
hunt and play during daylight hours. Their prey includes fish, crayfish, frogs, birds, and reptiles. Otters are playful, apparently joyous
animals. They tumble and chase each other, slither down mud slides,
and play with rocks. The best time and place to see them is early on
an April morning from the Furnace Rd. bridge, just north of Red
House Rd.

At **B**, where the stream loops in a sharp S curve, a large baldcypress, many hundreds of years old, stands on the west bank (see
#73). The cypress is covered with a small plant called resurrection
fern. Like many lichens and mosses, it turns brown and withered in
dry weather, appearing quite dead. When rains come, however, it
quickly grows green again. Rare this far north, it is most commonly
found on old live oaks in southern forests of the Coastal Plain.
Clinging to the rough bark of this cypress for support only, the fern
is an epiphyte, a plant which draws moisture and nutrients from the
atmosphere (see **#88**).

Below this point the creek widens, and the banks are often higher
and drier than upstream. Groves of loblolly pine appear on these
patches of high ground with American holly and dogwood in the
understory and huckleberries, mountain laurel, teaberry, and check-
erberry replacing the wetland shrubs. Pink lady's slippers are common in May.

Although this is an excellent place to see nesting warblers, very
few migratory birds of any sort pass through the central peninsula.
They follow the barrier islands and the Atlantic coastline and the fall
line where the Piedmont meets the Coastal Plain. As food is plentiful
throughout the region, the birds are probably following the routes
which provide the best landmarks. The coastline is a clear geograph-
ical feature.

The eighteen species of warblers which do nest here avoid excessive competition with each other by using the great variety of habitats which lie side by side and one above the other. The prothonotary
warbler, for example, lives right by the water's edge, eating the
larvae of aquatic insects as well as caterpillars, spiders, and beetles,

and it builds its nest 5 to 10 feet off the ground in the trunk of a dead tree. The Louisiana waterthrush also lives right by the water-side, but it nests just above the waterline in the crevices of roots or in the bank. It feeds on the ground, eating dragonflies, craneflies, mollusks, and snails. The low shrubs of swampy woods are the favored home of the hooded warbler. Its nest is usually about 15 feet off the ground and it hunts insects on the wing like a flycatcher. Another ground-dwelling species is the ovenbird. It prefers slightly drier and more mature woods with little undergrowth. The bird gets its name from the shape of its nest, a small "oven" of grasses and needles on the forest floor.

Some unusual species of birds have been identified along the creek. Brown creepers, birds which generally breed in the Appala-chians and the north, are frequent nesters in the cypress trees. Creep-ers like peeling flaky bark; they make their nests underneath loos-ened sections of bark, right against the trunk of the tree. Cooper's hawks, an uncommon species, and wild turkeys are also found here.

Remarks: *Autumn is also a beautiful time on the creek. In September the wild rice, a delicate, feathery plant, is still in bloom, along with swamp rose mallow and mistletoe. Summer can be very hot in the glare off the water, though the bugs are usually not too bothersome. Beware of strong winds, which can make paddling a real effort. A canoe trip from Red House Rd. bridge to Nassawango Rd. bridge and back takes 4 to 5 hours, including a stop for lunch. Canoes may be rented at Shad's Landing State Park but cannot be taken out of the park. Canoes are also for rent from Barry Laws in Snow Hill on Route 12 by the bridge over the Pocomoke. Camping at Shad's Landing State Park and Milburn Landing along the Pocomoke; the latter is quieter and less heavily used. There is good fishing on the lower Nassawango and the Pocomoke. No license required, as these are tidal streams. Hiking may be open in other parts of the preserve. For further information contact the Nature Conservancy, 1800 N. Kent St., Arlington, Va., 22209, (703) 841-5300.*

54.
The Continental
Shelf

Directions: Organized daylong excursions venture onto the
waters over the continental shelf from Cape May, N.J., and
Ocean City, Md. For further information contact Cape May
Observatory, New Jersey Audubon, P.O. Box 3, 707 E. Lake
Dr., Cape May Point, N.J. 08212, (609) 884-2736; or Ron
Naveen, P.O. Box 9423, Washington, D.C., 20016, (301) 854-
6262. You can also organize your own trip by gathering
together a group of friends and chartering a fishing boat
at any marina along the coast. It would be helpful to speak
with one of the contacts given above before setting out.

The Atlantic Coastal Plain does not end at the sea's edge. Sloping
gently beneath the ocean, it continues out many miles before dropping steeply down to the abyssal plain which lies on the surface of
the oceanic crust. This flat skirt of land is the continental shelf; the
steep slope at its margin is the continental slope (see **Introduction**). The waters over these regions are rich in marine life and are
feeding grounds for many species of oceangoing or pelagic birds.
These birds spend most of their lives at sea, coming in to land only
to breed or when blown off course during a storm. Their names
seem as exotic as their life-style: the northern fulmar, Manx's shear-
water, south polar skua, Wilson's storm-petrel, pomarine jaeger, red
phalarope, and Atlantic puffin, to name a few. With these flocks of
birds are other forms of marine life. Depending on the time of year,
humpback, sperm, minke, and other whales swim these waters along
with various species of porpoise and dolphin. The only way to see
this wealth of life is to venture out 50 to 80 miles from the Mid-
Atlantic coast.

The richness of life on the waters of the shelf is partly due to deep
canyons and cliffs which cleave the surface of the continental slope.
The origins of these rifts are puzzling. Because they are so deep the
water at the bottom is very cold and full of nitrates, phosphates, and
other nutrients. Cold deep waters contain more oxygen, nitrogen,
and mineral salts such as potassium chloride and sodium chloride
because of the circulation of the oceans. As water evaporates from
the surface of northern seas, a denser, heavier mixture of seawater is

left behind, which sinks and flows toward the equator. The store of nutrients is not depleted as long as the water remains in the deeps, for the microscopic plants which convert these nutrients to growing tissue need the energy of the sun and stay near the surface. Circulation in the ocean brings this nutrient-laden cold water up from the depths, especially in spring after the turbulent storms of winter. Fed by these nutrients and powered by the sun's energy, an explosion of microscopic plant and animal life, plankton, takes place. Plankton is the basic stuff of the oceanic food chain. The small fish and tiny crustaceans which feed on the plankton are in turn eaten by larger fish, whales, birds, and other creatures.

A number of pelagic birds are associated with the Gulf Stream, a current that brings warm water and warmwater species of fish up from the tropics. Many pelagic species nest on islands in the Caribbean and the South Atlantic. After the nesting season is over, they follow the current into the North Atlantic. Like other surface ocean currents, the Gulf Stream is driven by the prevailing winds, by the circulation of water from the equator to the poles, and by the spinning of the earth. The northeast trade winds blow steadily westward just north of the equator, powering the current. Just as air over the equator is warmed and rises, so does the ocean (see #7). The ocean is actually higher at the equator than at the poles, creating a slight slope and a flow from the equator to the poles. In the Arctic and Antarctic, cold dense water sinks and flows very slowly over hundreds or even thousands of years toward the equator. The spinning of the earth causes the circular movement of winds across the surface of the globe. In the same way the waters also arc as they move across the earth. As the Gulf Stream moves toward the American continent it strikes the Yucatán Peninsula and the waters of the Gulf of Mexico and is deflected north and east, shooting through the passage between Florida and Cuba. Running northeast along the Atlantic Coast, the Gulf Stream eventually heads across the ocean toward Ireland. The Gulf Stream has a major moderating effect on the winter climate along the Atlantic Coast (see **Introduction**).

Most of the pelagic bird species look quite similar. They tend to be dark, gull-like, and have long pointed wings. Because they depend on fish and other marine life for food, they spend much of their life in the air, patrolling the surface of the ocean. They have had to develop methods of flight which are not too tiring, and ways of coping with their salty environments. All of these birds are colonial nesters. There is little space on the small rocky islands, cliff-faces, and tundra meadows near their ocean fishing grounds. Colonial nesting allows them to use every scrap of it. Another advantage is that among a number of species the birds which breed first are protected in the middle of the flock. The colony also stimulates breeding activity because the birds imitate each other.

One family of pelagic birds is the tubenoses. It is made up of birds which all have a long horny tube lying along the top of their bill. This covers the open nostril and may provide some protection against salt spray. These tubes also contain small air sacs, which apparently aid the bird in determining changes in air pressure. This information may help the bird to soar, for areas of low pressure mean rising air (see #7). The tubenoses and other pelagic species use both flapping and soaring flight and vary their flying to fit particular conditions. In winter, the North Atlantic is often warmer than the atmosphere. This means that the air just above the ocean's surface is warmed and will rise. If the day is still, birds will rise upwards in a circular pattern, following the outline of the rising column of air. If a good wind is blowing, from about 15 to 25 mph, the columns of air no longer rise upwards but blow along the surface of the sea in parallel lines. These thermals account for the clusters of gulls seen far out to sea during the winter.

Pelagic birds can also soar in the absence of thermals, a trick that gulls are unable to manage. When a steady strong wind blows over the ocean, the wind travels at different speeds close to the water and high above it. This happens because friction slows the wind moving over the water. If a bird descends with the wind and then turns quickly into the wind as it encounters the slow-moving wind near the water, the momentum will carry the bird upwards again. Think of running down into a ravine and up the other side. The speed you pick up as you run down will send you up the rising slope. As the bird rises, it moves back into the stronger winds which give it more lift so that it can regain its original height. This is called dynamic soaring, and the most expert at it are the albatrosses. They are rarely seen off the Atlantic Coast, for the best winds for this kind of flight are found elsewhere.

The flight of Wilson's storm-petrels, also members of the tubenose family, is swallowlike. Skimming over the waves, they fly into the wind. As they fly they often slap the waves with their feet to push off and give themselves additional lift. Storm-petrels are apparently named after Saint Peter, who also walked on water. Shearwaters too are named for their flying technique. Gliding just above the ocean surface, they seem to slice the waves with their wings.

Most pelagic birds are capable of wandering greater distances when not breeding and no longer tied to their nests. Landbirds that breed in northern edges of our hemisphere must cope with drastically different conditions in summer and winter. Most do so by departing before the really cold weather sets in. In contrast changes of temperature over the ocean are much smaller and food supplies much less affected by changing seasons (see **Introduction**). As pelagic birds move over the oceans to feed, they accomplish tremendous flights at great speeds and are able to navigate with extraordinary accuracy. They can find the same small island on which they breed year after year.

Another family of birds that makes its way south into our waters during the winter are the alcids. Puffins, murres, auks, razorbills, and dovekies are all members of this group. Like the penguins of the Antarctic they are diving birds of the colder waters, able to swim skillfully underwater using their short pointed wings. The alcids are not related to penguins, although when standing upright they look very similar; their plumage is black and white, their shape short and stocky. Unlike the penguins, alcids can fly, beating their wings in a rapid blur. At rest on the water, these birds resemble neckless ducks with pointed bills of various shapes and sizes. The most startling you are likely to see is the Atlantic puffin, whose large, crescent-shaped bill is dull yellow in winter and orange in summer.

On a spring trip you may see huge gatherings of red and northern phalaropes. These are the most oceanic shorebirds, spending the winter at sea and the summer on their breeding grounds in the Arctic tundra. Small, neat waterbirds about the size of a robin, phalaropes have very dense feathers on breast and abdomen, which trap so much air that they are very buoyant and ride high on the water. Their breeding plumage is beautiful, a combination of rich rust, black, gray, and white. Unlike most other species, it is the female that is more brightly colored. She is also more aggressive than the male and defends the nesting territory while the male incubates the eggs.

Like the plants of a salt marsh, pelagic birds must manage to draw in the water they require from seawater, which contains toxic levels of salt. The kidneys of birds are even less efficient than human ones in removing unwanted salt from the body, yet the birds are able to drink seawater, which would quickly kill a human being. They are equipped with a special salt gland, which is situated close to the nostrils. When too much salt collects in a bird's bloodstream, within minutes the gland begins to remove salt and excretes it in a fluid through the nostrils. The bird then shakes its head to rid itself of the salty liquid.

During the colder months of the year you are likely to see whales. Most of the whales in the world are filter feeders. Their main source of food appears to be small schooling fish. These whales, the humpback and the fin whale among them, are equipped with a network of fringed cartilage called baleen on the sides of their mouth. The whales swim with their mouths open and then expel the excess

water through the sides of their mouth through the baleen. A few
species such as the sperm whale are toothed. Their diet is confined
to squid. These whales have also been hunted for their sweet-scented
oily wax, spermaceti, which is contained in a reservoir in the head.
The function of this substance is still unknown.

Remarks: *Pelagic trips go out at all times of year. February and March
can be particularly interesting, with a wide variety of species, though the
weather is chancy and often bitterly cold. An ocean trip generally lasts all
day from very early in the morning till dark. Arrangements must be made
in advance, as trips are very popular and limited in number. Even in
summer take warm clothes and, of course, be prepared for seasickness. Eat
plain crackers and take your favorite pharmaceutical preparation. Binoculars are useful, but scopes are not needed.*

55.
Assateague
Island

Directions: **Worcester County, Md. From Washington, D.C.,
go east on U.S. 50 across the Chesapeake Bay Bridge, south
to Salisbury, and east toward Ocean City to Route 611,
about 150 miles. Turn south on Route 611; go 9 miles to
Assateague. This route leads to the Maryland state park
section and the national seashore. To reach the Chincoteague National Wildlife Refuge, the southern third of the
island, see next entry.**

Ownership: **Assateague Island State Park is administered
by the Maryland Park Service; Assateague Island National
Seashore is administered by the National Park Service; and
the Chincoteague National Wildlife Refuge (see #56) is
administered by the U.S. Fish and Wildlife Service.**

A narrow buttonhook of land, nearly 30 miles long, Assateague
displays all the volatile beauty of a barrier island: windblown dunes,
tidal marshes, ephemeral pools, old inlets, new inlets, washover flats,
the endlessly changing beach. It invites exploration.

Assateague was part of a long peninsula until 1933, when a storm broke through at the Ocean City Inlet (see **#25**). Over the years hunting clubs and vacation homes sprang up on the northern end of the island. Then, in 1962, a great storm virtually destroyed all development. Preservation of the island as a wild seashore followed.

This island is one stop on the grand highway of migration known as the Atlantic flyway. By late July the southward migration has already started, led by the shorebirds moving south from the Arctic (see **#42** and **#22**). Behind them come thousands of landbirds: thrushes, vireos, warblers, flycatchers. Every few days the scrubby thickets and woodlands fill with huge flocks seeking shelter and food. November is the peak of the southward movement of ducks, geese, and swans heading toward their wintering grounds in Back Bay, the Chesapeake, and North Carolina.

The Open Beach

From the parking area of the state park (**A**) walk northward along the beach. To the south the beach is often disturbed by heavy foot traffic and rutted by off-road vehicles. The island environment is made up of a series of zones which run from the ocean's edge on the east to the marshy shore of the bay on the west. The open beach lies before you, from the wet sand of the foreshore to the line of the dunes. In the sunshine, the sand glitters. The sparkle is from tiny pieces of quartz which make up 90 percent of the sand along the Mid-Atlantic coast. The other main ingredient is feldspar. Under a hand lens you can also see dark red grains, which are garnets. In some places black patterns streak the sand like remnants of an oil slick. These are dark grains of ilmenite and magnetite, heavier minerals than quartz and feldspar. The lighter-weight grains are blown away leaving this dark residue. The composition of these coarse sands is a clue to their origins. Quartz, feldspar, and garnet are all common in the igneous and metamorphic rocks of the Piedmont and the Ridge and Valley Province to the west (see **Introduction**). To the south, in Florida and the Caribbean, the beaches are very different, a blinding white due to fragments of coral and shell.

The rolling and tumbling of the ocean can wear down grains of sand to a certain size and no smaller. At 0.07 millimeters in diameter, about the size of a pinhead, abrasion ceases because each grain is surrounded by a thin film of water. Made up of billions of movable grains separated by tiny cushions of air and water, a beach is able to absorb and dissipate the power of crashing surf, where a rock cliff or a concrete wall cannot.

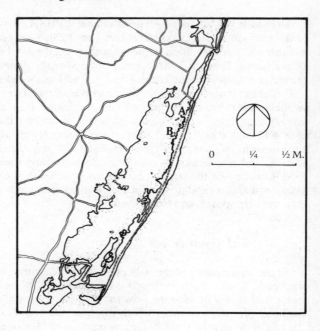

As you walk in the shallows out toward the breaking waves, you may suddenly step down into a trough of coarse sand. The waves move the finer sand up onto the beach or out into deeper water; the heavier material sinks to the bottom. Walk up to the face of the dunes. Here you find the finest sand of all, light enough to be moved by only a slight breeze.

Where the waves move back and forth across the sands, no plants can grow, but a few tiny animals flourish. Right in the turbulence of the surf zone, you can find the coquina, a small clam, which may be red, yellow, brown, or purple. As each wave crashes down, the clam is dislodged. Quickly the coquina burrows down into the sand and extends tiny feathery appendages into the retreating backwash. These delicate antennae strain the water for microscopic bits of plant and animal life carried in by the waves. Coquina make excellent soup. Mole crabs, light-colored crustaceans half an inch to an inch long, also live in the surf. They too are scavengers and feed in the same way. They dig into the sand only to be uprooted by the next wave. Sandpipers hunt in this zone. As each wave slides back, they race along its edge trying to catch the small crustaceans before they disappear into the sand.

In the shallow water just beyond the surf, lady crabs and hermit crabs hunt for organic debris. Hermit crabs are not true crabs. Their abdomens are soft and elongated, with little hooklike appendages. Finding an empty snail, perhaps a moon shell or a whelk, the crab inserts its abdomen inside the shell. Should it outgrow one home, the hermit crab will easily move into a new shell. It is virtually impossible to extract this small crustacean without harming it.

Where the sand is wetted by each wave, numerous small holes prick the surface of the beach. These are caused not by animals but by air escaping from between the grains of sand. If the tide is going out, you may notice a tracery of intersecting curving lines along the high-water mark. As the backwash of each wave retreats, it leaves behind a tiny driftline of sand and bits of debris. Another curiosity are the intersecting V's in wet sand formed as the backwash runs back down the beach. For some reason this pattern seems to arise on beaches of intermediate steepness. At times the water creates a drainage pattern like a miniature river, complete with tiny branches, larger tributaries and a main stream. This may be due to water trapped in the sands which slowly finds its way out.

The face of the beach slopes from the water's edge back to a crest and then levels off toward the dunes. This crest and the flat area behind it are called the berm. It can be almost imperceptible or striking, especially in winter (see **#7**). It forms at the high-water mark of the daily tides. Sometimes the beach develops a miniature escarpment that runs parallel to the shore line. This occurs when the waves of the rising tide approach the shore at a sharp angle so that they bite into the face of the beach.

The zone between the berm and the dunes is the *drift line*. Only storm waves reach this far up the beach. Here the sand is littered with seaweed, driftwood, seashells, neat black egg cases, old sand buckets, pieces of smooth glass, and other bits of trash.

Seaweeds are primitive plants of very simple construction. Classi-fied chiefly by color, most of those found on the open beach are red and brown algae. These ropy strings of rotting algae often contain significant amounts of important nutrients and provide food, shelter, and moisture to a few other hardy plants. Sea rocket, which produces great numbers of seeds, is sometimes found sprouting in the drift line. Sea rocket has fat succulent leaves which store water. Its lav-ender flowers bloom in midsummer. Young leaves are supposed to taste of horseradish. Its numerous seed pods are distributed along the shore by the tides. Rhizomes of American beach grass are also washed ashore and take root. Less frequently you may find other species like saltwort and, rarely, seabeach amaranth. Saltwort is cov-ered with very fine hairs, which help reduce water loss. Seabeach amaranth hugs the ground, conserving moisture both in and under its fleshy leaves. If there is a long period without storms, the vegetation in the drift line grows tall enough to trap windblown sand, and new dunes begin. Behind each solid object a small wind shadow of sand forms, an incipient dune. With the next hard blow, however, the young dune and the anchoring plants may be destroyed.

Among the interesting litter are small, puffy black "maiden's purses" with four wispy tails. These are the empty egg cases of skates, flat round fish which flap their way through the water by means of their specialized pectoral fins. The two longer tendrils on the egg case supply the eggs with oxygen and food from the water. The shorter ones remove wastes. The egg cases of whelks also end up in the drift line. These look like a string of creamy, translucent beads. Each bead holds many eggs. As the first tiny whelks hatch, they feed on the remaining eggs. Delicate whitish sand collars hold the eggs of moon shells. These become very fragile when dry.

The driftline is the best place to look for unbroken shells. Once cast up by the storm, they are safe from the roiling surf. Whelks, coquinas, moon shells, blue mussels, bay scallops, and surf clams are common finds along much of the Atlantic Coast (see **#23** on mollusks and snails). Occasionally there are the shells of lady crabs marked like a leopard skin with purple clusters.

Two crustaceans are abundant in this part of the beach. In and around the bits of driftwood and seaweed live beach fleas or hoppers. When disturbed, they give a sharp flick of their abdomen and tail, leaping tremendous heights for their size. The debris along the drift line shades the sand beneath it and keeps the sand moist. This is essential to the beach fleas because, like other crustaceans, they breathe through gills, which must be moist to function properly. Ghost crabs are common from Virginia southwards. Like beach fleas they are scavengers, scuttling down to the water to search for food and to wet their gills. These pale creatures are abroad mostly at night. Find a small hole about an inch in diameter and a trail of dashes leading into it. Wait patiently and one will probably emerge. Their burrows may be up to 4 feet deep, reaching down to cool, moist sand. By tunneling deep, ghost crabs can live in the arid area behind the first line of dunes, but they must return to the sea occasionally to wet their gills.

From south of the North Beach campground to the Maryland-Virginia line, vehicles are allowed on the beach. The constant traffic can have a devastating effect on crustaceans. It also drives away birds such as terns, black skimmers, and piping plovers which nest on the upper edges of the beach. Nesting colonies do occur along the northern tip of the island. The open beach north of the state park is also a gathering place for shorebirds during spring migrations in May and autumn migrations from July to October (see **#56**).

The Dunes

Along much of the island the dunes have been stabilized by snow fencing. The storm of 1962 destroyed the natural dunes, and it was decided that an artificial dune should be maintained along the state park, the national seashore facilities, and the refuge. The dune is low and covered with American beach grass, much of it planted. North of the state park and south of the parking areas, the dunes are allowed to come and go. Both artificial and natural dunes rely on beach grass to anchor the sand. Once beach grass is established it contributes to building up the height of the dune. If the wind blows between 9 and 12 miles an hour, it will pick up sand and move it. The wind slows as it blows through the leaves of the grasses, dropping some of its load of sand. Beach grass actually grows more vigorously if it is continually buried in new sand. It simply continues to grow upwards. Although beach grass does produce seeds, it regenerates primarily from specialized underground stems called rhizomes. The rhizomes are rather fat and fleshy because of the large amounts of food stored in them. The stems run horizontally; new roots grow down from them and new shoots grow up.

The conditions on the front of the dune are very harsh. There is no protection from salt spray and fierce winds. Summer temperatures on the surface of the sand are scorching. Fresh water is in short supply. Although the upper layers of sand often contain large amounts of nutrients like potassium and calcium deposited there by the salt spray, soil conditions vary enormously. Rhizomes are a much surer method of reproduction than seeds in such an environment. Even if chopped into tiny pieces and scattered, a bit of rhizome can become a new plant.

Rhizomes are characteristic of the more advanced group of plants called the monocots, which includes grasses, orchids, lilies, and many aquatic plants. As plants have evolved, they have become simpler. Flowers of this group have fewer parts; the veins in the leaves are parallel instead of branched and leaves are generally larger and fewer in number.

American beach grass is a terrestrial plant that has moved back to the seacoast. It is able to withstand the hot, salty environment because of the special design of its leaves. The plant is made up of long, narrow leaves joined at the base. The inner side of each leaf is lined with minute ridges and hollows which run the length of the blade. In the hollows are the small openings through which green plants take in carbon dioxide for photosynthesis and expel oxygen (see #56). On very hot days, the leaf curls tightly around the stem and the ridges clamp together. This seals off the openings from the air, reducing moisture loss. The ridges are so close together that salt particles from the salt spray are caught on them and cannot reach the openings. The next rain washes the salt away. A waxy coating on the leaves also prevents water loss, and the leaves' flexibility keeps them from breaking in high winds. The long roots reach many feet down to the water table.

From New England south to Virginia, American beach grass is the most successful plant on the dunes, but other plants are occasionally found there. In addition to sea rocket and saltwort, there is seaside goldenrod, a taller plant that blooms throughout the summer. Its leaves are fatter, carrying more water than those of inland varieties. Look for the small flat rosette of leaves of seaside spurge. Hugging the ground, the leaves trap moisture beneath them which is absorbed by the plant. Originally introduced from Asia as a cultivated plant, dusty miller bears small yellow flowers here in May. Farther north it blooms in July and August. Its grayish leaves matted with furry white hairs provide a defense against loss of moisture. These plants become more numerous on the back side of the dune where they are sheltered from the salt spray.

The severe conditions on the dune restrict animal residents to a variety of insects (see **#46**). Many creatures pass through the dunes, especially on summer nights when the sands are cool. Foxes, rabbits, raccoons, wild ponies, and deer leave their tracks in the sands.

The dunes are more sensitive to human influence than the beach. Infrequent trampling of dune grasses may be enough to kill them. Once that happens, the sands are no longer anchored and a blowout or opening through the dune can occur. The wind blows most strongly at the top of the dune, carrying sand away. As sand disappears, the beach grass cannot resprout. The hole tends to get bigger and bigger. For this reason, stay off the dune as much as possible.

In some places the dune disappears altogether, and a broad flat area called an overwash occurs. Perhaps the dune has been destroyed or for some reason never formed here. Storm tides sweep sand into the lagoon at these points. The new sands can help to build the salt marsh and counteract rising sea level. If the new layer is not too thick, salt-meadow cordgrass can grow right up through it. Overwash zones also provide a passage for storm waters, reducing their force and protecting the shoreline. South of the parking areas, old overwashes can be seen at the Fox Hill Levels (**B**).

The Back Dunes

Behind the primary dune, the habitat is very different from the windswept sands of the open beach. As you walk on the self-guiding nature trails or explore on your own, you will observe a clear transition from the dune to the bay. Plantlife becomes more lush and more varied. The bare loose sand of the primary dune turns gradually into sandy earth. Shrubs and trees grow taller. Then as you walk out toward the salt marsh fringing the bay, the trees give way to shrubs, the shrubs to marsh grasses.

These changes are related to the decreasing impact of salt spray as you move inland and the increasing influence of the brackish tides as you approach the bay. As windborne salts diminish, plants can grow that are more susceptible to the drying effects of salt (see **#21** and **#31**). The greater abundance and variety of plants divert nutrients and water away from American beach grass, which in turn becomes scarcer the farther inland you go. With richer plantlife comes more organic material to decompose into humus. Humus enriches the soil in two ways: it releases nutrients into the soil and it holds the grains of sand together so that they can hold more moisture. Under the shrubs and the trees, the ground begins to look like soil. On the bay side, vegetation again thins out, where the occasional very high tide is enough to kill off most species.

In the lee of the primary dune a number of other plants join American beach grass. Panic grasses and broom sedges are as important as beach grass in some places. Although not as tolerant of salt, they are able to grow in very poor soil. Seaside goldenrod, dusty miller, sea rocket, and seaside evening primrose are common but not as widespread. Often a second line of dunes lies behind the primary dune. Like the face of the primary dune, the seaward side of this secondary dune is more exposed to salt spray and wind than the back of the dunes or the low ground between them. Vegetation on it is sparse.

One of the most important plants of the back dunes is beach heather, or poverty grass. It grows in dense, dark green mats which act as sand traps. Beach heather often helps to build small dunelets. It blooms golden yellow in May.

Although somewhat protected, back-dune vegetation must also be able to withstand the drying effects of salt spray. The spray is mostly sodium chloride, which is not particularly useful to plants, but it also contains smaller amounts of very important nutrients such as magnesium, calcium, and potassium. The spray lands on the leaves of the back-dune plants and dries there, leaving a residue of mineral salts. With the next rain, the salts are washed into the soil where the nutrients can be absorbed by the roots.

Farther back toward the bay, shrubs such as wax myrtle, bayberry, poison ivy, and marsh elder begin to appear. Bayberry is a northerly plant, wax myrtle southern. Both are members of the same family and both are important in building up the soil of this zone. These plants carry special bacteria in nodules on their roots. The bacteria transform inorganic nitrogen, which plants cannot use, into an organic form which the host plants absorb and pass on into the soil (see #31).

The shrub zone gives way to taller trees: black cherry, redcedar, American holly, loblolly, red maple, and Spanish and water oaks. Loblolly is the dominant species throughout most of the woodlands (see #56). Many of the pines have a curious shape. None of them is very tall, and the lower branches sweep down to the ground. Farther inland, loblolly pines grow high and straight, losing their lower branches as they grow. If the branches of the trees here reach up too high, though, they become exposed to the salt spray and die. All of the trees are stunted and will never reach the heights of similar woodlands along the inner coast.

Lichens also play a part in building up the soil. In the wooded areas of the island you may find the small red-topped British soldier and a spiky variety known as old-man's-beard, which grows on trees, living or dead. Lichens are really two plants, an alga and a fungus, which live and grow together. Scientists still do not agree on the nature of this relationship. The fungus, the part that we see, clearly draws food from the alga. It is also possible that the fungus provides a source of moisture to the alga during drought. The red cap of the British soldier produces the fruits of the fungus. This lichen is brightest in early spring.

Fungi, which include mushrooms, toadstools, and puffballs, are not able to produce their own food like green plants. They must draw sustenance from other plants, either living or dead. The forms which we recognize as fungi are only a small part of the plant, which is made up of many long threadlike cells which run underground. The toadstool or the mushroom is merely the plant's fruit-producing appendage.

A number of mammals, large and small, move about through the several zones described above. Eastern cottontails are very common in the early morning and again in the evening. White-tailed deer and sika deer are abundant. The sika deer, related to the elk, is a small Japanese species, which was introduced in the 1920s. The plentiful shrubs offer good browsing for the deer. Wild ponies also wander into the woods, thickets, and out onto the marsh grasses (see **#56**). Raccoons and red foxes are common, while the Virginia opossum is uncommon but more and more frequently sighted. Smaller creatures include the white-footed mouse and the least shrew. Shrews are intriguing. They are mammals and are therefore warm-blooded. This means that they must keep their body at a stable temperature in order for their metabolism to work properly. Being small, shrews have a large surface area relative to their volume. To stay warm their metabolism must operate at a frantic rate, and their heart must beat hundreds of times per minute. They eat their own weight in food each day and can starve to death in a matter of hours. Shrews tend to be omnivorous and are fearless hunters. Larger mammals do not have to eat so much to maintain their body temperature. Since volume increases much faster than surface area, they have a built in heat-storage system in their own bulk.

Remarks: *Assateague Island is glorious at any time of year. Summer is a little less glorious due to biting greenhead flies, salt-marsh mosquitoes, and summer crowds. On the beach, however, there is usually a breeze to keep the bugs inland. If you are willing to walk, the many miles of beach offer refuge from too many people. The mosquitoes are fierce from about the middle of May to the first frost in October. Always arm yourself with repellent. Ticks arrive with the first warm weather. Check yourself over after a walk. To remove imbedded ticks try one of these methods: apply a few drops of rubbing alcohol, some Vaseline, or some lighter fluid, or use a hot needle. Hold the end of the needle with a scrap of cloth or tissue. Heat the point with a match and touch the tick, not yourself. Never pull them out; that will leave the head in you, which may lead to a bad infection. At the northern end of the island there are drive-in camp sites available on a first come, first serve basis in both the state park and the national seashore. Camping is available all year in the state park; some sites may be reserved for a week at a time during the height of the summer season. Make your reservations early. For reservations and further information on the state park write the State Park Superintendent, Assateague Island State Park, Route 2, Box 293, Berlin, Md. 21811, (301) 641-2120. The national seashore has some sites for tents only as well as several canoe-in and hike-in sites scattered along the island. The backcountry sites are popular, and are reserved well in advance. For reservations and information contact the Superintendent, Assateague Island National Seashore, Route 2, Box 294, Berlin, Md. 21811, (301) 641-1441. Although the canoe-in sites are open from April through October, backpacking campsites are open all year long. Canoe rentals are available in the area (see **#53**). Collecting shells is allowed in moderation. There is good crabbing in the bay with a line or trap; equipment is available at local stores. In the warmer months, fish for*

*black drum, channel bass, weakfish, white perch, croaker, and other fish
in the surf. No license required. Clamming is best off the bay shore along
the Maryland section of the national seashore. Visitors' centers at both the
national seashore and the state park offer a variety of information and
nature programs. There are no poisonous snakes on Assateague.*

56.
Chincoteague
National Wildlife Refuge

Directions: Accomac County, Va. From Washington, D.C.,
go east on U.S. 50 across the Chesapeake Bay Bridge and
south to Salisbury, Md., about 120 miles. Take U.S.13 south
37 miles to Route 175 in Virginia. Turn east (left) and go
10 miles across the causeway to the town of Chincoteague,
stopping to scan the marshes and waterways en route.
Turn north (left) on Main St. and then east (right) on Mad-
dux Rd., following signs to the refuge. The refuge covers
the southern third of Assateague Island.

Ownership: U.S. Fish and Wildlife Service.

Moving from the deep shade of an old oak forest to the open, shell-
scattered beaches, from the marshy impoundments full of black duck
and mallard to the mudflats where shorebirds prod and poke for
marine life, even the casual observer will see a splendid array of
birdlife. Two hundred and sixty species have been recorded at the
refuge. Twelve miles of wild beach stretch from here north to the
Maryland line, protected from the off-road vehicles which tear up
the sand along the national seashore further north.

As you cross the causeway, look for wading birds out in the salt
marsh on either side. Throughout the spring and summer, they fly
in from their roosts on the mainland and on islands in the bay to
feed in the marshes. Nine species of egrets and herons are common
here, as is the glossy ibis. All but the great blue heron nest in the
area (see **#28**).

After the causeway the road turns right abruptly. The visitors'
center is on the left and just beyond it is the entrance to the wildlife
drive that circles Snow Goose Pool. This impoundment varies from

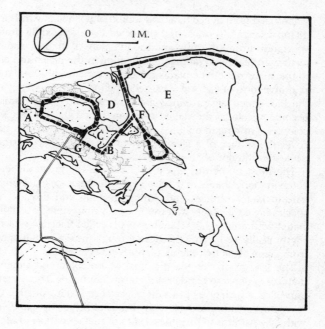

fresh to slightly brackish water. Around its edge are phragmites and cattails, and in summer such flowering plants as crimson-eyed mallow add color to the marshy shore. The pool attracts snow geese, whistling swans, dabbling ducks, and some Canada geese during fall and winter. In spring and summer, belted kingfishers and tree swallows are common. This is the southernmost breeding area for tree swallows. Barn swallows also nest here.

From the northern corner of the pool (**A**), a footpath leads northwards past several smaller freshwater pools. These pools form in small hollows behind the dunes where the water table is very close to the surface. Rainwater collects in these hollows and is unable to drain away; during summer droughts, some of the ponds disappear, except those that have been dammed to increase habitat for migratory waterfowl. Although the sea may be only a few hundred feet away, these ponds tend to stay fresh on the surface because of the different densities of fresh water and salt water at the same temperature. As fresh water is lighter than salt water, rainwater filtering down to the water table through the sands will sit in a layer on top of the salty or brackish water below.

Protected from agricultural and industrial pollutants which threaten inland lakes and ponds, and protected by surrounding dunes and vegetation from salt spray and the full glare of the sun, these pools teem with plant and animal life. Floating in the water and attached to the stems of aquatic plants are many varieties of algae, the most primitive form of life. Algae existed 2 billion years ago. They include the blue-green algae, which are tiny one-celled organisms. They become visible to the naked eye only when they collect in huge colonies. Thriving in polluted waters full of organic matter, they can cover the surface of a farm pond with a smelly green scum. Such explosions do not occur on these pools.

The most numerous group of algae are the green algae, which come in many shapes and sizes. Some are single-celled, some aggregate in large colonies, and others are long and thready. Certain species have the ability to move about, a characteristic usually associated with animal life. They have tails called flagellae which move rhythmically, propelling the algae through the water. It is apparently from green algae that higher plants have evolved.

The last group are the diatoms. Microscopic and single-celled, diatoms are encased in delicate translucent boxes. These shells contain silica, which gives them their special crystalline quality. Under a microscope, diatoms exhibit many beautiful geometric shapes, marked with lacy patterns of fine lines. Diatoms make up most of the plankton found in the sea (see #54). Together these various forms of algae are a basic source of food for aquatic animal life, from one-celled protozoa to tiny crustaceans, snails and other mollusks, worms, and small fish.

There are many species of submerged plants such as water milfoil and water purslane. Submerged plants are rooted in the shallow bottom, drawing in oxygen from the water rather than through their roots. The muck on the bottom is poor in dissolved oxygen because circulation is poor in the water-saturated soil. Submerged plants are characterized by many feathery leaves. The feathery leaves improve the plant's ability to absorb enough sunlight to power photosynthesis. Photosynthesis is the conversion of water and carbon dioxide to food and oxygen in the presence of light. This chemical reaction is found only in green plants, which contain the pigment chlorophyll. Green plants are unique among living things in being able to create food out of inorganic materials. Some species of submerged plants can absorb enough sunlight for photosynthesis even 15 to 20 feet below the surface.

Reproduction under water is difficult for more complex forms of plantlife. These species have developed flowers which produce male cells, pollen, and female eggs. On land the flowering plants rely on wind and insects to carry the pollen from one flower to the eggs of another. Pollen is not very waterproof. To solve this problem, submerged plants send up shoots to the surface of the water so that the flowers will be in the air. Fertilization then takes place in the usual fashion. Once the seed is formed with its tough impermeable coating, it will float away and eventually drift to the bottom to germinate.

Around the edges of the ponds are emergent species like three-square, cattails, water pennywort, sedges, and spike rush. They are called emergent because a large part of the plant stands above the water line. Many emergent species have strong stems with leaves layered around an inner hollow core. This construction helps them to withstand strong winds and waves, although on these small ponds waves are insignificant. Emergent species pass oxygen down through the stem to the roots (see #50). All these plants are a source of food for waterfowl.

An intriguing puzzle is the thriving populations of frogs which live in and around some of the pools. With their porous skins, amphibians are vulnerable to salt water, and yet somehow they have crossed the wide bay between the barrier island and the mainland. Bullfrogs were apparently introduced to the island.

Around the rim of Snow Goose Pool is a woods of loblolly pines with an understory of holly, redbay, red maple, sweetgum, wax myrtle, and winged sumac. Various species of blueberry are common in the shrub layer. Cut over and farmed until the 1930s, this woodland is in the early stages of forest succession (see **Introduction**). Loblollies reach their peak at 75 to 100 years old. After that they become more vulnerable to disease. By the lighthouse and on the Pony Trail you can see much later stages in forest succession. The pine warbler nests in the loblollies along with the summer tanager, chuck-will's-widow, brown-headed nuthatch, and other woodland species. In many parts of the refuge you can see fish crows and common crows. Fish crows are found only along the coastline and are virtually indistinguishable from the common crows. Only the call is different. The fish crow has a shorter and more nasal croak.

Return to the main road and continue on toward the beach. The road makes another abrupt turn to the left. Just beyond on the right is an extensive marshy area covered with salt hay and dotted with loblolly hummocks (**B**). This is a good place to see the Chincoteague ponies and Sika deer. A romantic account of their origin makes them the descendants of Spanish horses from a galleon shipwrecked offshore. They may instead have sprung from horses brought over by early settlers in the area. The cattle egret is commonly seen in among the wild ponies and deer, eating grasshoppers and other insects which fly up as the horses move through the grass. Originating in Africa, the cattle egret moved west to South America and then northward. By exploiting an ecological niche that other American species had not discovered, these bird have been very successful.

On the other side of the road are two shallow impoundments, Black Duck Marsh (**C**) and Swan Cove (**D**). From fall to spring, dabbling ducks and diving ducks are abundant. During the height of the migrations in October through December and again in March and April, the most common species are American black duck, common pintail, and American wigeon. Others include mallard, green-winged and blue-winged teal, gadwall, northern shoveler, wood duck, hooded merganser, pied-billed grebe, and ruddy duck. Many also nest here, including black duck, mallard, blue-winged teal, wood duck, and gadwall (see **#64** and **#66**). Herons and egrets come to feed here in the summer months. On rare occasions white ibis have been reported here, far north of their accustomed range from southern North Carolina to northern South America.

Across the road from Swan Cove is Tom's Cove (**E**), which is open to the sea. The sandy hook of land that partially encloses it took shape as sands were carried by the longshore current southward and into the inlet (see **#25**). The spit is young, only about 100 years old. In the cove extensive mudflats are bared at low tide, bringing great numbers of migrant shorebirds in April and May and again from late July to October (see **#42** and **#26**). During the autumn flights several species are occasionally found at Chincoteague which are even rarer during the spring migration. These birds migrate northward through the Mississippi River valley. They include Baird's sandpiper, white-rumped sandpiper, stilt sandpiper, and the Hudsonian and marbled godwits. More common are the greater and lesser yellowlegs, and short-billed dowitcher, dunlin, ruddy turnstone, pectoral, spotted, semipalmated, least, and western sandpipers. In the marshy areas common snipe and willets, which also nest here, are common. Brant collect in the cove each fall and winter to feed on the green algae sea lettuce.

At the beach parking area go south toward the end of the hook. Between the cove and the dunes piping plovers nest in early summer above the high-tide line (see **#30**).

Remarks: *The wildlife trail is 3.5 miles long. Until 3:00 p.m. each day it is open only to bicyclists and walkers. From 3:00 p.m. to dusk it is open to cars. Bicycles are an excellent way to get around the refuge, especially in summer when traffic can be heavy and parking limited. Bikes can be rented at the Refuge Motor Inn just across the causeway and at other shops in Chincoteague.*

The Pony Trail

The pony trail (**F**) winds through a system of old dunes now covered with pines and mixed deciduous trees. This woodland and the one along the old lighthouse trail (**G**) represent a rare habitat on Assateague. Elsewhere the forests are too young or too near the ocean to have developed to this stage of succession.

Loblolly pines and deciduous species such as red maple, water oak, southern red or Spanish oak, and white oak grow on the drier dune ridges. Black cherry is abundant in the understory along with sassafras. Wax myrtle, shadbush, and dwarf sumac are common shrubs. Where the sun can break through the canopy, greenbrier and poison ivy grow rapaciously. In sunny damp hollows there are thickets of willows. This forest is older than that by Snow Goose Pool, for oaks are later in the sequence of succession than pines (see **Introduction**). On these coastal islands, mixed oaks and loblolly pines apparently make up the climax forest. Hickories and beeches, important climax species in mainland Coastal Plain forests, do not grow here.

The woods and thickets are full of warblers, thrushes, and other landbirds, especially during autumn migrations from August through September. In spring most of these birds migrate northwards along inland routes (see **#53**). The vines and shrubs all provide berries, which the birds feed on. Nesting species include the brown-headed nuthatch, eastern wood pewee, eastern phoebe, house wren, Carolina wren, white-eyed and red-eyed vireos, black-and-white warbler, common yellowthroat, yellow-breasted chat, and summer tanager. These woods have a greater mixture of habitats than the stand of pines north of the Snow Goose Pool, which in turn brings a greater variety of birds here.

The Delmarva fox squirrel, a rare and endangered species, was introduced to the refuge in 1968 and is flourishing. It is a large, light-gray animal which bounds along the ground when startled instead of heading for the nearest tree like other squirrels. Open understories of mature woods such as these are its preferred habitat (see **#64**).

57.

Virginia Coastal Reserve

Directions: **Northampton County, Va. From Washington, D.C., head east on U.S. 50 across the bridge at Annapolis and south to Salisbury, Md., about 120 miles. Pick up U.S. 13 and continue south about 57 miles to Nassawadox, Va. Turn east (left) on Route 606 at the blinking light in Nassawadox. Go 0.3 mile and turn east (right) on Route 608. Brownsville, the headquarters for the reserve, is at the end of the road. There is a parking area near the dock.**

Ownership: **The Nature Conservancy.**

From Assateague Island south to the tip of Cape Charles, all of the outer coastline of the Delmarva Peninsula is protected by a network of islands, lagoons, and marshes. All or part of thirteen of these islands are now owned and protected by the Nature Conservancy, while another five are under the jurisdiction of state or federal agencies. Encompassing 35,000 acres of salt, brackish, and freshwater marshes, open dunes, beach, wax-myrtle scrub, and old dune forest, this is the largest stretch of undeveloped barrier islands along the entire Atlantic shoreline.

Once these islands were dotted with summer homes, hotels, hunting lodges, and coast guard stations. Now they are quiet and undisturbed, their beaches providing nesting grounds for thousands of gulls, terns, plovers, and black skimmers. The nesting birds are more numerous here than anywhere else along the coast because of the refuge these isolated islands provide.

The only way to explore these islands is by boat, and while you may organize your own expedition, the best way to see them is by scheduling a tour through the office at Brownsville. Daylong trips include stops at several of the islands, depending on the interests of the group and the time of year.

The islands of this chain have the same origin as Assateague to the north (see **#55**). Like Assateague and the barrier islands all along the coast, they are moving westward as sea level gradually rises. This continual westward creep has been a main factor in the survival of the islands as natural areas. During the nineteenth and twentieth

Inset: Laughing gull

centuries, various attempts were made to settle the islands and to turn them into summer resorts or hunt clubs. Time after time hurricanes and winter storms buffeted the coast and the rising sea rolled over the towns and hotels. The chain of islands is also moving southward, the result of the southward flow of the longshore current (see **#25**).

Because of different patterns of currents and wave action at different parts of the coastline, the islands here are following three distinct patterns of migration. The northern group of Wallops, Assawoman, Metompkin, and Cedar is moving west evenly, maintaining a parallel line to the shore. The islands of Parramore, Hog, Cobb, and Wreck, which compose the middle group, are each rotating. This is especially clear if you look at the first three on the map. The northern end of each is jutting out into the ocean while the southern end has swung in toward the land. This swing is the result of sand being deposited at the northeastern tip of these islands and eroding away at the southern tip. The southernmost islands are Myrtle, Ship Shoal, Smith, and Fisherman Island. Fisherman Island is relatively recent and continues to grow (see **#58**). The others are disappearing.

Lying midway along the Atlantic shore, the barrier islands are in a transition zone for northern and southern species. The live oak is found only on Smith Island and not further north. Sea oats, which replaces American beach grass as the primary dune cover farther south, is scattered among the beach grass on Hog and Smith islands, and is found only as far north as Assateague. Revel Island supports the northernmost stand of yaupon, a species of holly which grows in the thickets behind the dunes. Maritime ground cherry is also found at its northern limit in these islands, growing on the dunes.

Birdlife is spectacular throughout the year. In May and again from July to October, migrations of shorebirds are outstanding. At the height of the nesting season in June, beaches fill with colonies of American oystercatchers, black skimmers, and common, royal, gull-billed, Sandwich, Caspian, and least terns. In among them are Wilson's and piping plovers. Willets claim the grassy edge of the beach. In the marshes Forster's terns and clapper rails nest among the cordgrasses. Large colonies of herring and laughing gulls also collect on the islands. Here, these birds can find protection, for there are few predators, although raccoons pose a threat on some of the islands. (For nesting of terns and plovers see **#30**.)

In addition to raccoons, muskrats, deer, and rice rats are found on most of the islands. Less numerous are mink, red fox, river otter, and eastern cottontail rabbit. These species probably established themselves on the islands by swimming the channel. Smaller animals, such as moles, shrews, and mice, are scarce or absent, because the water barrier was too great. Some animal populations, such as the house mouse and Norway rat, are reminders of former settlement. Marine mammals are seen offshore and regularly wash up on the beaches. Several species of porpoise as well as pilot, fin, goose-beaked, and short-finned pilot whales have been recorded.

Remarks: *These islands are owned by the Nature Conservancy. To visit them you must obtain permission from the local office (see below). The best times to visit the islands are in the spring, summer, and fall. Winter weather is very unpredictable and cold. The open boat used by the Conservancy staff holds six people, and you may either sign up as an individual or as a group. As of spring 1983, the cost of the boat is $120 per day. Sunscreen, bug spray, extra clothing, sneakers or rubber boots, lunch, and water are indispensable. For information and reservations call or write: The Nature Conservancy, Virginia Coast Reserve, Brownsville, Nassawadox, Va. 23413, (804) 442-3049 Camping at private campgrounds in Chincoteague, at Lone Pine Campground on Route 695 west of Temperanceville, and at Seashore State Park in Virginia Beach.*

58.

Fisherman Island
National Wildlife Refuge

Directions: **Northampton County, Va. Fisherman Island is open to bona fide environmental groups by appointment only, and only outside of the breeding season, which is roughly April through September. To join a regularly scheduled group, write or call the Back Bay NWR office, Pembroke Office Park, Pembroke Building #2, Suite 218, Virginia Beach, Va. 23462, (804) 490-0505. Fisherman Island lies under the northern end of the Chesapeake Bay Bridge and Tunnel ($9 toll), which joins the tip of the Delmarva Peninsula to the Virginia mainland. A locked gate and regular patrols prevent unauthorized access.**

Ownership: **U.S. Fish and Wildlife Service.**

Fisherman Island is little more than a low-lying, scrub-covered mound of sand in the mouth of Chesapeake Bay, part of the chain of barrier islands that hugs the coast. It is a haven for birds at all times of the year. By the end of March, 1982, ten pairs of ospreys had refurbished existing nests or established new ones on the derelict piers and towers of the abandoned naval station. Each pair usually produces two eggs, rarely three. Once in serious decline, due to a combination of pesticide poisoning and loss of nesting sites, populations of ospreys are once more increasing and are thriving in the Chesapeake Bay region (see **#32**). The birds live almost entirely on fish. Diving powerfully into the water, often submerged up to their wingtips, they grasp the fish with their feet and spring up again into the air. They pause in midair to dry their wings and to align the fish so that its head is facing forward, which reduces wind resistance. Weighing only 2.5 to 4 pounds themselves, ospreys have been observed carrying fish as large as 4 pounds (see **#47**).

Early spring is also a time to see American oystercatchers as they begin to arrive at their nesting grounds (see **#21**). They cluster along the beaches, more visible now than later, when they scatter to establish their nests. Bonaparte's gull, an uncommon species that winters along the Atlantic Coast, is most often sighted here on its spring trek to the north. Double-crested cormorants convene in great numbers, using the island and the waters around it as a resting place during migration.

One of the highlights of a visit at any time of year is the pair of peregrine falcons which has made the island its home. Peregrine falcons have not bred naturally along the eastern seaboard for many years (see **#32**). An extensive program is now under way to reintroduce the falcon as a nesting species in scattered sites along the coast. Hatched in a laboratory at the Cornell Laboratory of Ornithology, the young birds are placed in "hacking" boxes, boxes which are open on one side and fixed on top of a pole. The birds are fed until they can fly. Feeding is gradually tapered off as the birds learn to hunt on their own. The peregrine is fiercely loyal to an established nest site, and it is hoped that once some of these introduced birds mate, a new breeding population will begin. In 1982 the first successful natural breeding took place on Assateague Island. Three young were born. Although peregrines, which are swift and strong fliers, can migrate for thousands of miles, the pair on Fisherman Island does not: all winter long they can feed on the flocks of waterfowl and the many sparrows that collect here. Peregrines are able to spot a bird in the air from several thousand feet away and dive on it with speeds approaching 100 to 200 mph, knocking it out of the sky with a heavy blow from their feet (see **#32**).

Lying at the bottom of the Delmarva Peninsula, a long funnel very much like Cape May, Fisherman Island is an excellent vantage point for the autumn hawk migrations. In addition to the endangered peregrine, great numbers of broad-winged, sharp-shinned, and Cooper's hawks, northern harriers, and kestrels are seen. Less common species include merlins and bald eagles (see **Cape May**). In winter the sheltered waters on the north side of the island are visited by Canada, snow, and brant geese as well as many dabbling and some diving ducks (see **#64**).

During the late spring and summer the island is closed due to the great numbers of shorebirds, gulls, and terns that lay their eggs along the beaches and the herons and egrets that roost in the scrubby trees in the interior of the island.

Fisherman Island owes its existence to the ocean currents that sweep into the bay around the end of the Delmarva Peninsula, bringing sands down from the beaches to the north (see **#25**). Sand is continually being deposited and removed with each tide and each storm. The vegetation is similar to the primary dune and back-dune habitats of Virginia's barrier islands: beach grass and seaside goldenrod flourish by the beach and wax myrtle predominates further back from the water. The position of the island along the coastal flyway and its isolation from human disturbance are what make it such an excellent refuge for birds.

Remarks: *Fisherman Island is well worth the effort it takes to arrange a trip. Regular visits to the refuge are made by the Maryland Ornithological Society, Cylburn Mansion, 4915 Greenspring Ave., Baltimore, Md. 21209, and the Virginia Society of Ornithologists, Mrs. John L. Dalmas, Treas., 520 Rainbow Forest Dr., Lynchburg, Va. 24502. There is camping at Seashore State Park in Virginia Beach.*

Nearby Places of Interest

Islands of the Chesapeake Bay Bridge and Tunnel: **En route from Fisherman Island to Norfolk.**

Four rocky man-made islands mark the tunnel exits and entrances of the Chesapeake Bay Bridge and Tunnel. An astonishing array of birds congregate on and around them, especially in fall and winter. During migrations the islands become way stations on the arduous flight across the wide mouth of the Chesapeake Bay. On the grassy strips of the three northern islands, shorebirds, vireos, rails, bitterns, warblers, and virtually every other migrant can be seen side by side. In summer the terns and gulls from nearby Fisherman Island roost on these islands, and occasionally pelagic birds like the Wilson's storm petrel are blown in from the sea. Porpoises are often seen in the channel, and a white seal has spent the last three summers on the rocks of the northernmost island. Winter brings sea ducks from the Arctic, including harlequin, eider, and oldsquaw, as well as loons, diving ducks of all sorts, and many gulls, including rarer species such as lesser black-backed, glaucous, and Iceland gulls.

The southernmost island has a restaurant and a fishing pier from which eleven species of fish, including sea trout, bonito, channel bass, bluefish, and black sea bass, can be caught. It is the least interesting island for birds. For permission to visit the northern three islands, write in advance to Mr. James K. Brookshire, Jr., Deputy Director and Chief Engineer, Chesapeake Bay Bridge and Tunnel, District P.O. Box 111, Cape Charles, Va. 23310, (804) 331-2960. He will send you a letter granting you permission, which must be presented at the toll plaza as you go out to the islands. Without this permission, you will be ticketed by the police.

The Chesapeake Bay

In late fall when the marshes of the Chesapeake are gold and rust, muted green and brown, an extraordinary event occurs. Millions of waterfowl—snow geese, Canada geese, whistling swans, bay ducks, and marsh ducks—converge on the bay, flying in wispy lines above the marsh, bursting from the ponds, or gathering offshore in huge fleets.

The bay lies along the Atlantic flyway, one of four migratory highroads that lead from breeding grounds in the Arctic and the northern plains to wintering grounds in the southern United States, the Caribbean, and Central and South America. The Atlantic flyway is shaped like a vast funnel that stretches from Alaska in the west to the Hudson Bay in the east, narrows at the Chesapeake, and continues south along the coast to the Carribean and South America. Twenty-five percent of the millions of birds on the Atlantic flyway winter here. For thousands of years, waterfowl have followed the course of the bay's tributaries, arriving here where abundant food and protected waters provide a way station on the journey south or a safe winter home.

Lying at the mouth of the Susquehanna River, the Chesapeake is the largest estuary in North America. An estuary is a protected basin at the mouth of a river where fresh water and salt water converge and mingle. It forms when a rising sea level drowns the lower portion of a river valley or other coastal embayment. Like the zone of change at the forest edge or the brushy border of a field, an estuary is a unique habitat, different both from the river and from the sea. One of its most notable characteristics is frequent fluctuation and change. Daily tides that flood the bay, fluctuations in salinity, (see **#21**), changes in temperature of as much as 10°F within a few feet, and changes in oxygen content and in amounts of sediment create a severe environment which relatively few species can withstand. Those that can, whether plants or animals, are well rewarded, however, for the estuary is a nutrient trap that supports millions of microscopic plants and animals in every cubic foot of water. These in turn feed small fish, mollusks, and crustaceans. At the top of the food chain are the larger predators: fish, birds, and mammals. This wealth of life exists because rivers carry tons of topsoil into the bay each day, the marshes provide a continuing supply of decaying vegetation, and the sea sweeps in twice daily, bringing in mineral salts and preventing nutrients from leaving the system.

The present-day Chesapeake Bay is the latest in a series of bays formed during the interglacial periods of the Ice Age (see **Introduction**). As each ice sheet began to retreat, some of the meltwater fed into the Susquehanna River, and with each interglacial period the river wore deeper and deeper into its channel, carving a long, narrow path to the sea. With the melting of the ice sheet the sea level began to rise until, toward the end of the interglacial period, the sea drowned the lower reaches of the Susquehanna, creating a vast body of water. Then, as the next ice sheet advanced, the sea again retreated. This cycle has been repeated several times over the last 2 million years. Today about 200 miles of the Susquehanna River valley lies buried beneath the bay. The many bluffs along the western side of the bay, like those at Calvert Cliffs (see **#75**) are characteristic of estuaries. They are the remnants of the high ground that once overlooked the river valley. Most of the rivers that now flow into the Chesapeake were once tributaries of the Susquehanna: these include the Patuxent, the Potomac, the Rapahannock, the York, the James, the Pocomoke, the Chester, the Choptank, and the Nanticoke. They are the source of fresh water which, combined with salt water, produces the estuarine environment. The long narrow shape of the bay and the depth of the river channel in its midst produce both a vertical and horizontal circulation of seawater and fresh water. This circulation distributes nutrients, oxygen, and plants and animals throughout the estuary. As the fresh water flows south, beneath it a heavier layer of salt water pushes north. The salinity of the upper layer ranges from near zero at the Susquehanna Flats in the north to 25 or 28 percent at the mouth of the bay. The lower layer varies from 2 or 3 percent salt at the upper reaches of the bay to about 34 percent salt (the salinity of seawater) at Hampton Roads.

Salinities also fluctuate seasonally in the bay. In summer and early fall when the rivers are low, the tide pushes saltwater far up the bay to Turkey Point. Later in the autumn, rains sweep the sea southward again to the vicinity of Tolchester. In winter and spring, a similar cycle occurs as the fresh water is first tied up in ice and snow and then released in the spring thaw. Certain species, the blue crab for example, use different parts of the estuary during different stages in their life cycle. The first larval stage of the crab needs a high degree of salinity to survive. Following the summer mating season, the female crabs move southward toward the mouth of the bay. They spend the winter in the deep mud and in the next summer bring forth the young. As the young molt and become more crablike, they begin to move northward toward the less salty waters. A reverse cycle is followed by the anadromous fish like the shad and the striped bass. These species spend their adult life in the sea and come into the fresh water of the upper bay to spawn.

As the seasons change there is vertical mixing of the bay waters, which is equally important to life in the estuary. All summer long the upper layers of the bay are warmed in the sun and the growth of microscopic plants explodes. Through photosynthesis, the tiny green plants add oxygen to the water, in turn creating a perfect environment for all manner of animal life. Deeper layers become depleted of oxygen as the summer progresses. One factor is that there is less mixing of bay waters, as the warmer surface waters sit on top of denser, cooler waters below. Another factor is that the huge populations of plant and animal life drift downwards as they die and are decomposed by oxygen-consuming bacteria. Finally, all the water in the bay rises in temperature during the hot months, and water holds less oxygen as it become warmer.

With the cold weather the upper waters cool more rapidly than the oxygen-poor water in the depths of the channel. As they cool, the waters become denser and heavier; they begin to flow downwards while the warmer water rises from below. The layers mingle, and oxygen is restored to the depleted waters. Nutrients are also redistributed. The surface waters carry with them the abundance of microorganisms that flourished all summer. As the waters sink, blue crabs and several species of fish also descend to feast on the bounty and to spend the winter in the depths of the channel. Here they will stay warmer, insulated from the cold winter above. With the spring the cycle reverses. Now the waters at the surface of the bay are full of oxygen and begin to warm in the spring sun. Plankton and algae begin to grow, attracting the fish and crabs back to the surface.

All along the Eastern Shore and lining the lower reaches of each tributary are hundreds of miles of marsh—fresh, brackish, and salt.

These marshes are veritable assembly lines of production with an output of 5 to 10 tons of organic material per acre per year. This rivals the richest, most heavily fertilized grainlands (see **#21**). As the marsh plants die, they are broken down by bacteria. The microscopic bits of plant material together with the bacteria form a rich source of food called detritus (see **#23**). Detritus feeds a variety of animal life including young fish, clams, oysters, jellyfish, and crabs. The waste products of these creatures return nitrogen, phosphorus, and other nutrients to the marsh. On dry land, nutrients percolate deep into the soil or are washed away. In the marsh they are brought back with the next high tide (see **#21**).

Just as the marshes provide food, their dense vegetation also provides shelter for many birds and animals. Ducks, bitterns, rails, marsh wrens, and herons nest or winter in and around the marshes, along with such mammals as muskrat, mink, and river otter. Above the wetlands glide bald eagles and ospreys, endangered species which have made a comeback in the bay region (see **#47** and **#64**).

The fruitful croplands that surround the Chesapeake Bay also draw waterfowl, which feed on the waste grain in the fields. Due to mechanical harvesting, this residue amounts to as much as 5 percent of each crop. In fact the abundance of available food all winter has caused the birds to change their migratory patterns. Huge populations of Canada geese and lesser numbers of snow geese and ducks now winter in the bay region instead of moving farther south.

For many species of waterfowl, crop residues have replaced the submerged aquatic vegetation which once was a major part of their diet in the bay. Shoals covered with eelgrass and wild celery filled many parts of the bay until the 1930s. Now most of this vegetation has vanished for reasons which no one can adequately explain. One theory is that loads of sediment dumped into the bay by the rivers and streams have increased so much due to agriculture and development that submerged plants are starved for sunlight. Another possibility is that the use of fertilizers in the area has overloaded the bay with nutrients. As a result, explosive growths of microscopic plant and animal life, plankton and algae, have occurred, depriving other plants of light. Yet another possibility is that low levels of pesticides and herbicides are killing off the submerged vegetation.

Ten years ago the marshes were also in great danger. Development in the area stripped away the vegetation which holds moisture in the land and run-off increased enormously. The sea was gradually rising, and the land was sinking. The marshes were being drowned. Now, the marshes have apparently stabilized. Run-off has decreased markedly, and new marsh is forming to keep pace with rising sea levels.

Remarks: *Many of the areas described below are accessible by foot, but one of the best ways to see the more than 4000 square miles is by small boat or canoe, so that you can prowl the inlets and tidal channels. One warning: the bay is a large body of water, and the winds can whip up rough water very quickly.*

The best times to see waterfowl are in November and December and again in March and early April, when the migrations peak. Later in the spring there are migrating shorebirds, breeding herons and egrets, and other marsh birds. Summers can be very hot and buggy, especially in the marshes, but there is usually a breeze on the bay. With the first of the warm weather, ticks and chiggers begin to appear; come armed with bug repellent (for tick removal, see #55).

An excellent source for boat trips and information about the bay is the Chesapeake Bay Foundation, 162 Prince Georges St., Annapolis, Md., 21401, (301) 268-8816.

59.
Elk Neck
State Park

Directions: **Cecil County, Md. From Washington, D.C., drive north on I-95 to Exit 8, about 40 miles north of Baltimore. Drive south on Route 272 for 10.8 miles, through the town of North East and into the park. The visitors' center is on the right. The entrance to the Red Trail (A) is 0.2 mile further down the road on the right, just off the road to Mauldin Mountain and North East Beach. A second trail head is further up this road. Continue for 2.4 miles to the parking area for Turkey Point and the start of the Blue Trail.**

Ownership: **State of Maryland.**

Though this snaggletooth spit of land is a part of the Coastal Plain, the high sandy bluffs and rolling hills of Elk Neck are forested with the oaks and mountain laurel more common in the Piedmont. Just to the north of the park, Virginia pine dominates the woodlands. Then, quite suddenly, the topography changes. There are wooded hills crowned with chestnut oak and moist ravines where tall sycamores grow side by side with tuliptrees and American beeches.

The Red Trail winds through some of the oldest forest in the park. By counting the rings on trees removed from the area, park managers estimate that the largest specimens still standing range from 150 to 200 years old. On the higher ground are such species as chestnut oak and mountain laurel, which are generally found on the dry acidic soils of ridgetops in the Piedmont. White and northern red oak are also abundant. Although the terrain in these woods is gently rolling, the sandy soils do not hold moisture well. The chestnut oaks dominate the canopy here, because they have adapted to these highly drained soils. American holly is the dominant species in the understory, along with young red maple and hackberry. Shadbush or serviceberry is also present, its white flowers making it especially prominent in early spring. While sunlight can reach the forest floor before the leaves fill out the canopy, the ground is carpeted with birdsfoot violets and other spring flowers. These are known as ephemerals because the plants bloom and put forth seed before the trees have fully come into leaf. The plants die completely by full summer. The great majority of summer flowers are found along the forest edge—in old fields, by the open banks of streams and ponds, where sunlight can penetrate the canopy.

After a few hundred yards the trail descends slightly into a hollow where the moister conditions produce the right environment for beech, tuliptree, and even a scattering of eastern hemlock. Hemlock is rare on the Coastal Plain, where it is generally too hot and dry for this northern species. Here the understory is primarily tuliptree and American beech saplings.

Because Elk Neck is a peninsula jutting into the northern end of Chesapeake Bay, it is an important stopping point for migratory birds moving south in late summer and autumn along the Atlantic flyway (see **Introduction**). In these woods, look for migratory warblers, vireos, flycatchers, and other small landbirds as well as woodland birds of prey such as broad-winged hawks, Cooper's hawks, and sharp-shinned hawks. Some of the warblers which are found in upland woods are the black-and-white, the black-throated blue, and the black-throated green, the bay breasted, and the magnolia warblers and the American redstart.

As you continue south to Turkey Point, you approach a very different habitat. The trail to the point first follows along the top of the bluff about 50 feet above the Northeast River. The sandy deposits uncovered below your feet date back to the Cretaceous period, about 65 to 145 million years ago. Geologists cannot agree on the origins of these materials. Some say the sediments are principally marine; others that the sediments were deposited by streams. Loose and unconsolidated, these sediments were easily eroded away by the Elk River to the east and the Northeast River to the west during the retreat

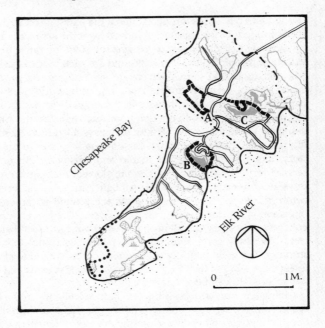

of the last glacier 15,000 to 20,000 years ago, when these streams were raging torrents carrying the meltwaters from the ice sheet which lay to the north. The two rivers once joined the Susquehanna somewhere not far to the south of Turkey Point.

The woods at Turkey Point are young, largely made up of black cherry and black locust. This area was farmland only 50 years ago. Near the edge of the bluff where strong winds come buffeting in from the bay, many of the trees have been uprooted, a sharp contrast to the older woods along the Red Trail where signs of disturbance are minor. Thick mantles of vines have taken advantage of the open canopy and many of the trees are being choked in greenbrier and poison ivy.

Farther along, the trail runs out into open fields maintained by the park staff. Broom sedge covers the ground; it is generally the first pioneer species to grow in old fields. The brushy edges of these fields also offer excellent birding during the fall migrations. Species which may be found in this type of habitat include the Cape May, blue-winged, Nashville, chestnut-sided, prairie, and Connecticut warblers and the common yellowthroat. September to mid-October is the height of the fall warbler migration and peak season for the smaller hawks, such as sharp-shinned and Cooper's, which hunt the smaller birds. Later in the season larger birds of prey like red-tailed and red-shouldered hawks and turkey vultures will soar above the open fields looking for rodents and snakes (see **Cape May** for more on hawk migrations).

*Remarks: A fresh-to-brackish marsh is encircled by the Black Trail (***B***) and a fresh water impoundment is located off the Green Trail (***C***). Both these bodies of water attract waterfowl in fall and spring. The Red Trail and the Blue Trail are easy walking, each about 2 miles long. Fishing boats are for rent on the way to Turkey Point. Salinity this far up the bay depends on the amount of rainfall and the runoff into the Susquehanna River. In some years bluefish can be caught in the vicinity. Jellyfish, which require a certain amount of salinity, do not come north of the Gunpowder River. Other activities include swimming at North East Beach and hiking in Elk Neck State Forest just to the north. There is camping at both the park and at the state forest. For further information contact the Park Superintendent, Elk Neck State Park, 4395 Turkey Point Road, North East, Md. 21901; (301) 287-5333.*

60.
Eastern Neck
National Wildlife Refuge

Directions: **Kent County, Md. From Washington, D.C., take U.S. 50 east to Annapolis and across the bridge to Queenstown, about 55 miles. Take U.S. 301 northeast about 5 miles. Go north on Route 213 for 19 miles, then west (left) on Route 291 for 0.7 mile. Turn right (west) onto Route 20 and go 13 miles to Rock Hall. At the first traffic light turn south (left) onto Route 445 and drive 8 miles to the refuge entrance.**

Ownership: **U.S. Fish and Wildlife Service.**

The surrounding water and diversity of habitats of this marsh-edged island attract an unusually wide variety of birds and mammals. In winter the mudflats on the north side of the island are covered with whistling swans, geese, and ducks. In June, dozens of mute swans come into Calfpasture Cove to molt their old flight feathers so new ones can grow. Hawks, songbirds, and ducks pass over the refuge in large numbers as they migrate, especially during the fall. This is also one of the few places where one can see the endangered Delmarva fox squirrel.

The bridge at the entrance of the refuge is an excellent place from which to see hawk migrations in the fall (see **Cape May**). From here you can also watch waterfowl collecting on the mudflats. Whistling swans come from nesting grounds in the arctic tundra, flying almost nonstop across Canada. Most of the swans on the Atlantic flyway spend the winter in the Chesapeake Bay. At one time the swans ate a mixture of water plants—wild celery, wigeon grass, and eelgrass—and mollusks. Today much of this vegetation has disappeared from the bay (see **Chesapeake Bay**), and the swans have turned to feeding in farm fields with snow and Canada geese. They gather on the water to rest in the middle of the day. The lonesome, resonant call of the whistling swan is created by air being forced through its long, convoluted windpipes.

There is an observation tower 0.7 mile from the entrance. Park on the right (**A**). A boardwalk leads out across the marsh to a hummock of loblolly pines. From the boardwalk, you can see distinct

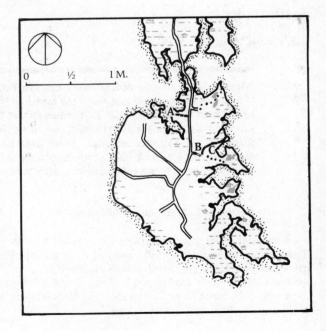

colonies of marsh plants, which reflect minute changes in elevation according to their ability to tolerate salt in the water. At the lowest level, tolerating the greatest degree of salt are patches of salt-meadow cordgrass, salt grass, salt-marsh cordgrass, and fleabane (see **#21**).

Stands of black needlerush, swamp rose mallow, and Olney three-square bulrush indicate slightly higher ground, for these species are less tolerant of salt. Along the landward edge of the marsh, ground-sel and marsh elder are abundant. The highest ground of all is the hummock with its covering of loblolly pines and holly. Loblolly pines, which are at the northern limit of their range, are able to grow much farther north on the Delmarva Peninsula than on the Western Shore, perhaps because the climate here is tempered by the bay. Loblolly can grow in a greater diversity of conditions than other southern pines, tolerating both sandy and wet sites.

From the observation tower, you can look out at the mud shoals where waterfowl gather in fall and winter and at the cove where mute swans come in June. Birds must replace their worn and broken feathers at least once a year, for fully developed feathers are dead and cannot mend themselves. Swans replace all the flight feathers on their wings once a year in the summer. During this period of 45 to 50 days they are unable to fly and are somewhat vulnerable to predators. The open water of the cove probably offers some protection. Only nonbreeding swans come to the cove in June. Breeding birds stay with their young and will not molt until later in the summer when the eggs have hatched. The female molts first and then the male, so that one bird is always able to guard the young. Mute swans, which were imported from Europe, may now pose a threat to native species; fierce and aggressive, they try to protect about 4 to 10 acres of territory around the nest. The swans are "mute" because their straight windpipes limit their vocabulary to weak hissing yelps.

Duck End Trail (**B**) leads off the road to Bogle's Wharf Rd., which is 1.2 miles from the entrance. The path passes along a ridge forested with loblolly, oaks, hickories, and sweetgum. To the left is a view over an extensive marsh of Olney three-square bulrush and cattail (see **#64**). These species indicate fresher water in this marsh. Bayberry and wax myrtle bushes line the edge of the marsh. The island has a large deer population, which in the past has overgrazed the wooded areas of the refuge, leaving few young trees.

Farther along the trail is a field that has been kept open by mowing (**C**). This is a favorite spot for nesting woodcocks. On spring evenings the males perform spectacular mating flights to attract the attention of the females. The birds spiral up into the sky, the wind making a strange whistling sound in the outer tips of their wings. At the top of their flight, perhaps 300 feet high, they hang for a moment, singing. Then they swoop back to earth and utter a series of "peent" calls for the female. Woodcock are related to sandpipers. Like them they hunt for food in the ground. They are found in wet meadows and boggy areas where they dig for earthworms. The tips of their bills have become prehensile—that is, woodcocks can open just the tips and grasp a worm. This special adaptation makes working in the heavy soils much easier.

Here, where field and woodland meet, is an excellent spot for spring warblers. The convergence of two habitats, an ecotone, is always richer than either habitat by itself. Not only are species of plant and animal life associated with each habitat found here, but also some species particular to the ecotone alone. The verdant shrubs and vines that grow at the edge of the field provide good cover and food for the birds.

At the end of the trail is a beach littered with shells. Archaeologists have established that this was the shell midden of a native American encampment.

Go 0.3 mile down the main road to the self-guiding nature trail leading through a mature hardwood forest. The Delmarva fox squirrel can be found here (see **#64**).

Remarks: *Much of the refuge is closed to the public, but you may take a boat all around it; a boat ramp lies at the end of Bogle's Wharf Road. There is a public crabbing and fishing area at the entrance of the refuge. For further information contact Eastern Neck National Wildlife Reserve, Route 2, Box 225, Rock Hall, Md. 21661, (301) 639-7415.*

61.
The Wye Oak

Directions: **Talbot County, Md. From Washington, D.C., take U.S. 50 across the Bay Bridge to Route 662, about 61 miles. Turn south on Route 662 and go 1 mile. The tree is on the left side of the road.**

Ownership: **Maryland Forest Service.**

The Wye Oak is a vast and beautiful white oak tree, reputed to be the finest specimen in the country. It is over 400 years old, which makes it one of the oldest as well. The wide-arching canopy of branches, which stretches 165 feet from one side to the other, indicates that the tree has stood on cleared land for most of its life. In a forest, it would become narrower and taller as it competed with surrounding trees for light.

62.
Wye Island
Natural Resources Area

Directions: **Queen Anne's County, Md. From Washington, D.C., take U.S. 50 east across the Bay Bridge at Annapolis to the junction where U.S. 301 branches off, about 55 miles. Continue on U.S. 50 another 3 miles east to the sign for the Aspen-Wye Institute. Turn south (right) and go 7.3 miles across the wooden bridge to the Nature Trail parking on the right. On the far side of the bridge the blacktop road becomes a dirt road.**

Ownership: **Maryland Forest Service.**

This grove of majestic straight-trunked oaks, loblolly pines, sweetgums, young beeches, and maples is one of the few places on the entire Eastern Shore where any mature forest still exists. Surrounded by farmland on every side, this copse of 250-year-old trees has somehow survived. A stand of swamp chestnut oaks and loblolly pines is not typical of the woodlands on the peninsula and reflects the poorly drained soils that lie beneath. In the understory are many young beeches and maples; because of their tolerance of shade and because they seem to secrete a substance toxic to other species, the beeches may eventually dominate the stand if it is left undisturbed. Dogwood, American holly, black haw, and persimmon are common in the understory as well. The herb layer and shrub layer are sparse, as one would expect in a mature woodland. There is one short trail through the woods, which takes about ten minutes to walk.

Remarks: *Poison ivy is abundant. Nearest camping is at Tuckahoe State Park.*

63.

Tuckahoe
State Park

Directions: **Queen Anne's and Caroline counties, Md. From Washington, D.C., go east on U.S. 50 across the Bay Bridge about 55 miles to the junction where U.S. 301 branches off. Stay on U.S. 50 and go about 7 miles further. Turn east (left) on Route 404 and go 7.2 miles. Turn north (left) onto Route 480. Go 0.1 mile and turn left again onto Eveland Rd. Go 3.8 miles to Crouse Mill Rd. Jog right then left onto Cherry Lane. Go 0.7 mile and turn left into the meadow. At the crossroads turn right to reach the parking area for the overcup oak (A) and left into the picnic area to reach the swamp trailhead (B).**

Ownership: **Maryland Park Service.**

At the edge of a wooded swamp, dwarfing the young second-growth woods around it, is the largest overcup oak tree in the United States. It is 118 feet tall, almost 12 feet in diameter, and 220 years old. Because the rich soils of the Delmarva Peninsula have been prized for farming, few trees of any significant age remain (see **#62**). The land here is soggy and frequently flooded, making it poor farmland. This may partially account for the tree's survival. Overcup oaks can withstand longer periods of flooding than other oaks (see **#95**), although the seedlings do need dry land to sprout. There are some younger overcup oaks growing around the great tree but they are still too young to produce acorns. On slightly higher and better drained soils in the vicinity you can find basket and white oak and pawpaw. Young red maples are common in the understory here. Red maple may be the most numerous tree in the region; it is shade-tolerant and can sprout beneath a heavy canopy and it grows well in both wet and well-drained soils.

From the southern end of the meadow at the picnic ground, a trail winds along the fringe of the swamp to Crouse Mill Lake. Tuliptree, white oak, southern red oak, and both mockernut and pignut hickories are common in the canopy. This forest type is typical of the Eastern Shore, where oak-hickory is the general climax forest (see **Introduction**). Oaks are moderately tolerant of shade, which means

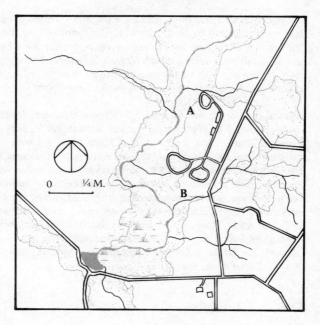

that the seedlings grow best where light strikes the forest floor. It seems surprising then that an oak forest can reproduce itself. One factor may be that oaks are long-lived, producing many acorns which are widely scattered by squirrels. These characteristics improve the chances that young seedlings will sprout where an opening in the canopy has occurred. River birch is common in the understory along the edges of the swamp.

Tuliptrees tend to be early in forest succession (see **Introduction**), for they are intolerant of shade. Although they grow best in rich moist soils, tuliptree seedlings cannot withstand flooding. The seeds can remain viable for several years, ready to sprout when a combination of full sun and moist soil is available.

The colonists who first came to Virginia found giant tuliptrees growing in the primeval forests. The great trunks of soft, lightweight wood were fashioned into canoes and lumber for furniture. The colonists found it such an excellent wood that they sent live young tuliptrees back to Europe to be planted. A fast-growing species, it continues to be a principal commercial hardwood. Today it is also used for musical instruments, toys, and pulp, as well as for furniture.

Swamp azalea and pink azalea are common shrubs. Swamp azalea, which blooms in June, grows in the moist soil by the edge of the swamp along with jewelweed, sweet pepperbush, and southern arrowwood. Pink azalea, which blooms in April and May, grows on drier soil along with maple-leaf viburnum, hobblebush, spicebush, common elder, shadbush, and red-panicle dogwood.

Remarks: *A canoe trail leads from the Crouse Mill Dam about 5.5 miles down to Route 404. There are four launch areas within the park property. From the dam down to area 4 south of Route 404 is 5.5 miles. A map is available from the park office. Vegetation along the stream is typical of freshwater tidal rivers (see #53, #69, and #72), with abundant stands of arrow arum, arrowhead, and pickerelweed. The creek is especially lovely below Hillsboro, where it runs through quiet, undisturbed woodland. Canoes cannot be rented locally, but there are several outlets in Washington, D.C. (see #92). Camping is available within the park. The lake above the dam offers fishing (license required) and boating. No gasoline engines allowed. For further information contact Tuckahoe State Park, Route 1, Box 23, Queen Anne, Md. 21657.*

64.
Blackwater National Wildlife Refuge

Directions: **Dorchester County, Md. From Washington, D.C., take U.S. 50 to Annapolis, over the Chesapeake Bay Bridge, and south to Cambridge, about 85 miles in all. Take Route 16 southwest for 7.5 miles. Turn south onto Route 335 and go 3.8 miles. Entrance to refuge is on the left on Key Wallace Rd. The visitors' center is 1 mile on the right and the Wildlife Drive, also on the right, begins 1.7 miles from the center.**

Ownership: **U.S. Fish and Wildlife Service.**

Blackwater is a maze of marshland, field, and forest, stretching for miles to a distant horizon. It is well protected and full of wildlife. Across the skyline stand islands of loblolly pine where bald eagles nest every year. The freshwater impoundments and brackish marshes teem with geese and dabbling ducks in the fall and winter. Diamondback terrapins wander along the impoundment dikes in early summer looking for a place to lay their eggs. In the woods along the Wildlife Drive, rare Delmarva fox squirrels are frequently seen.

The refuge lies on the banks of the Blackwater River, which empties out of swamps to the north. As the sea level rises and as the runoff from newly cultivated fields increases, areas of marsh are being drowned. New marsh is forming upstream, though, as river-borne silt is deposited (see **Chesapeake Bay**). However, the water is rising faster than the marsh can rebuild; in the last 50 years, 2000 acres of marsh have vanished. Muskrats, nutrias, snow geese, and Canada geese have aggravated the situation by feeding too heavily in certain areas.

The Wildlife Drive takes you through that section of the refuge open to the public. At **A** a short walk leads through a mature stand of loblolly pine and holly. In these woods you may see the brown-headed nuthatch, which is near the northern limit of its range. The

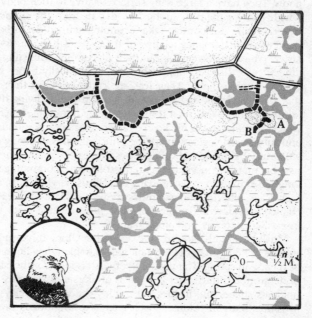

Inset: Bald eagle

bird travels up and down tree trunks looking for insects. It has been known to hold a piece of bark in its beak, using it as a tool to pry off other bits of bark in its search for bugs. This is very unusual; only a handful of the world's birds have been observed using a foreign object as a tool.

At the end of the trail is a short boardwalk that leads out into a marsh of cattail and Olney three-square bulrush along the banks of the Little Blackwater River. These are primarily freshwater marsh plants. It is an excellent habitat for dabbling ducks, which feed on the seeds, leaves, and stems of aquatic plants as well as on crustaceans and mollusks that live in the mucky bottom. Species of dabbling duck you can expect to see are green-winged and blue-winged teal in early autumn, black duck, mallard, gadwall, pintail, and wigeon from midfall onwards. They are called dabbling ducks because they feed on the surface of the water, dipping their heads under to forage for food, in contrast to diving ducks, which often immerse themselves completely in order to feed on the bottom in deeper waters. Dabbling ducks are well adapted to small ponds and marsh pools. They have a large wing surface relative to their body weight, which enables them to spring into the air from the surface of the water. Diving ducks must take a running start to get airborne, for their wings are smaller relative to their size. Diving ducks also fly faster, which makes landing in tight places more difficult. Another difference is that dabbling ducks are anatomically better suited to grazing in grain fields. Their legs are in the center of their body so that they can walk easily on land, while those of diving ducks are located farther back. As a result the diving duck is a skilled underwater swimmer and a mediocre walker. Crustaceans, mollusks, fish, and submerged vegetation are the principal foods of diving ducks.

During the spring and summer nesting season, many other species use this marsh. Among them are least bitterns, common gallinules, long-billed marsh wrens, redwing blackbirds, Virginia rails, and king rails. Rails, bitterns, and gallinules are very difficult to see. Your best chance is at dawn. The diets of these birds include plant material, insects, crustaceans, and amphibians.

Muskrats are also found here, using the Olney three-square bulrush as building material for their lodges, which they build or refurbish early in spring. The peat of the marsh is ideal for the canals and underground tunnels they construct; unlike sandy bottoms, the peat holds its shape, and it does not muddy the water as clay soils do. Muskrats settle in colonies. Each litter of young builds close to the parent lodge, until the area becomes overpopulated and the marsh denuded. Then the colony disperses, in search of new territory. King rails are often found near colonies of muskrats; they use the muskrat canals as pathways and hunt for crayfish in the ponds created by the muskrats as they pull up the bulrushes and cattails for food.

Continue driving on this road to an observation tower (**B**). From it you can look out over the marsh to the isolated hummocks of tall, straight loblolly pines. Although loblolly is an early succession species, these hummocks may never be covered with climax vegetation. Severe storms set back the process of succession, and the small size of the hummocks allows abundant sunlight, necessary for regeneration, to reach the pine seedlings (see **Introduction**). The shape and location of these trees makes them prime nesting sites for bald eagles, which are extraordinarily sensitive to disturbance of any kind. For instance, a motorboat repeatedly passing nearby can cause the birds to abandon a nest forever. Blackwater is the foremost breeding ground for bald eagles on the bay—as many as six to eight pairs have been sighted in and around the refuge. The birds begin nesting as early as December. They use the same nests over and over adding to it each year it is used. Some nests reach gigantic proportions, weighing as much as 2 tons. Throughout the nesting season until the young birds are ready to fly in the summer, the adult birds are very active hunting for themselves or for their young. To kill live prey, the eagles strangle it with their talons and puncture vital organs. Their diet includes fish, waterfowl, and carrion. They often perch on dead trees that stand at the edge of the marsh, trees that have been drowned by rising water levels.

Until recently bald eagles were fast disappearing from the East Coast of America for several reasons. Their nesting habitats were being rapidly destroyed. Their reproductive cycle was being interrupted by high amounts of DDT in their food, which weakened the shells of their eggs, causing them to break. Even today people still hunt them illegally. Now, however, this downward spiral seems to have ceased. Since the banning of DDT in 1972, there has been a dramatic increase in nesting. Habitat is now better protected and hunting laws are more strictly enforced.

In winter a few golden eagles hunt the marshes, taking healthy birds in addition to wounded and sick birds to supplement their diet of large rodents and small mammals.

Further along the drive at **C** is a short trail through a mature stand of loblolly, white oak, red oak, hickories, and sweetgum. This is the ideal habitat for the endangered Delmarva fox squirrel, a big, light silver-gray animal. The undergrowth is sparse in a mature forest, and the squirrels spend most of the time on the ground hunting for seeds and nuts, rather than in the trees like the common gray squirrel. The Delmarva fox squirrel was once found from southeastern Pennsylvania down to Northampton County, Va. Unfortunately, this habitat has been nearly destroyed, reduced to remnants in four counties in Maryland.

During the fall and winter, the open water of the refuge is usually covered with Canada geese. About 60,000 use the refuge in November during the peak season. The birds make heavy use of nearby cornfields, flying out to feed early in the morning and again in late afternoon. Their characteristic V-shaped flight pattern serves at least two purposes. As each bird flies, a rising column of air is created behind and to the side of the wing. Each goose flies a little to the outside of the one in front (relative to the axis of the V) and is able to exploit this updraft, thus using less energy to fly. It has been estimated that formation flight enables geese to fly as much as 70 percent farther than they would be able to manage alone. Some ornithologists also believe that the formation permits the birds to pool observations of landmarks and so allows them to steer a more accurate course.

From the refuge office continue driving east on Key Wallace Rd. for one mile. Turn right at the T junction on Shorter's Wharf Rd. This will take you out into the midst of the marsh, through stands of cattail and three-square bulrush to saltier areas where wide flats of salt-meadow cordgrass grow. Sharp-tailed and seaside sparrows, black duck and blue-winged teal, the tiny, very secretive black rail, and clapper rail nest in the salt-meadow cordgrass (see **#65**). The road is public, so you can come here at night in spring and early summer to listen for the rails calling. From here you are likely to see eagles, marsh hawks, and ospreys, and perhaps an otter running across the road.

Remarks: *From roughly April 1 to October 1 you are permitted to take a boat along the Blackwater River. There is a boat landing at Shorter's Wharf. Fishing is allowed during this period but is not good. Allow a half day to enjoy the refuge fully. It is open daily from dawn to dusk all year round. The visitors' center is open daily from 7:30 a.m. to 4:00 p.m. from September through May but is closed on weekends from June through August; (301) 228-2677. Biking is permitted on a section of the Wildlife Drive. No walking except on the two trails mentioned above.*

65.
Elliott Island
Marshes

Directions: **Dorchester County, Md. From Washington, D.C., take U.S. 50 east to Annapolis, across the Bay Bridge, south to Cambridge, and east to Vienna, about 100 miles. At the blinking light in Vienna, take a right, then left onto Race St. Go 0.2 mile and turn right again onto Elliott Island Rd. Follow it 14.1 miles to the bridge across the Pokata Creek. On the far side is a sign for Fishing Bay Wildlife Management Area.**

Ownership: **Part private; part Maryland Wildlife Administration.**

The road to Elliott leads across a vast plain of high marsh, which is bright, sharp green in May. Acre upon acre of salt grass and salt-meadow cordgrass stretch to the horizon, interrupted by loblolly hummocks and stands of taller marsh grasses. Along the tidal guts are lush stands of big cordgrass (see **#21**). In the heart of these salt meadows is one of the best-known spots for hearing the elusive black rail, a tiny bird about the size of a sparrow.

Black rails are so secretive and difficult to see that very little is known about their habits. It is evident that they nest here, though, for on clear, calm, warm nights from about May to early July they call to each other across the marshes. From a couple of hours after sunset to a couple of hours before dawn the males utter odd mechanical cries described as "kiki-krr" or "kick-ee-doo." The most reliable place to hear them is just south of the Pokata Creek. Avoid the use of taped calls. The decline of black rails in the area is probably due to overuse of tapes (as with Swainson's warbler, see **#51**; for rails, see **#67**).

In May, when leaves are well out on the trees further inland, the marsh is just turning green. The late spring here is a reminder of the tempering effect of the ocean, slower to warm up in the spring and slower to cool off in the fall (see **Introduction**).

The freshwater marshes to the north of Savannah Lake, 3.5 miles north of the bridge, are occasionally visited by nesting sedge wrens. This species is disappearing all along the coast. Ornithologists are at a loss to explain their decline. Henslow's sparrow is another species that is generally declining. It is seen regularly in this area alongside and just to the east of Savannah Lake, in scrubby fields adjacent to two farms. From Pokata Creek bridge go back on Elliott Island Rd. 5 miles and stop. The bird can be seen from the road if present.

66.
Dames Quarter
Marsh

Directions: **Somerset County, Md. From Washington, D.C. take U.S. 50 east across the Bay Bridge at Annapolis and go south then east to Salisbury, about 115 miles in all. Take U.S. 13 south 14 miles to Princess Anne. Turn west (right) onto Route 363; go 9 miles to Deal Island WMA sign. Turn left and drive 1 mile to parking area (A). To reach the other side of the impoundment, continue on Route 363 to the Dames Quarter Post Office, about 2 miles, and turn left on Riley Roberts Rd. Drive out along the dike to the parking area (B).**

Ownership: **Deal Island Wildlife Management Area, Maryland Wildlife Administration.**

In a spring mist, five great blue herons line up in a row, bodies poised, waiting to strike. A crowd of glossy ibis settle in to feed, and a blue-winged teal feeds in the marshy impoundment a few feet from shore. This is a wild and remote stretch of marsh in the northwestern corner of Somerset County. Because of its seclusion and the man-made pools and big ditches, it is rich in birds, both in numbers and variety.

The first entrance (**A**) leads to the less-traveled part of the area. From the parking area you can walk the dike for about 8 miles around to the western side (**B**), where people gather to go crabbing.

All of this marsh was once almost exclusively black needlerush, a tough spiky grass that does not provide much food for wildlife. Along the eastern shore of Chesapeake Bay, black needlerush is a

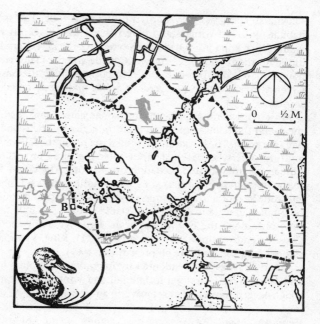

Inset: Blue-winged teal

major component of marshes as far north as Eastern Neck NWR. On the western shore its range is much farther to the south. This is because salinities along the Eastern Shore are much higher. The tides push more strongly along the Eastern Shore due to something called the Coriolis effect. It is created by the spinning of the earth (see **#7**). By digging canals and making a large 64-acre impoundment in the middle of the management area, the Maryland Wildlife Administration has created a far more diverse habitat. These pools and canals bring changes in salinity and in water level which favor other marsh species, most of which provide a better source of food for birdlife than needlerush. These species include extensive stands of salt-marsh bulrush, salt grass, and salt-meadow grass. All of these species flourish in the high marsh, growing above the high-tide line on soggy, poorly drained ground (see **#21**).

In the surrounding areas where black needlerush is still the main species, the greatest activity occurs along the tidal guts, the natural pathways carved through the marsh by the tide. The banks of these guts are slightly elevated and better drained than the surrounding marsh. Groundsel and marsh elder grow on top of the banks, while salt-marsh cordgrass grows down in the tidal zone. This is nesting habitat for green-winged and blue-winged teal, black ducks, gadwalls, coots, and long-billed marsh wrens. Gadwalls generally breed in the northern pothole country of Canada and the plains states and have only recently begun to breed in pockets along the East Coast. Green-winged teal nest all across Canada and rarely breed this far south.

Most of the herons and egrets that congregate along the impoundment and the pools come from their rookeries on the islands in the bay (see **#28**). These islands are visited mainly in the fall for hunting and are otherwise deserted. They offer the birds protection from human disturbance and predation by raccoons. The grassy tussocks in the impoundment are used by many nesting ducks. (The American coot is another uncommon nester this far east and south.) The boat-tailed grackle is common at Dames Quarter; a little farther to the north along the bay it disappears. Its range along the Atlantic Coast extends up into New Jersey (see **#21**). King, Virginia, black, clapper, and sora rails are all present (see **#67**).

These marshes are frequented by migrating shorebirds in spring and fall and by waterfowl in late fall and winter. Bald eagles and rough-legged hawks often soar overhead in winter.

Remarks: *In fall and winter the area is hunted, so it is best to come on a Sunday. An excellent way to explore is by canoe or flatboat, but rentals are not available. You can put in your boat at either end of the dike. From the western dike there is excellent crabbing. The best walking is along the dikes.*

67.
Irish Grove
Sanctuary

Directions: **Somerset County, Md. From Washington, D.C., take U.S. 50 across the Bay Bridge at Annapolis and go south, then east to Salisbury, about 115 miles in all. Take U.S. 13 south 19.7 miles. Bear south (right) on Route 413 (U.S. 13 swings east) and go 7.7 miles to Marion. Turn southeast (left) on Route 357 and go 2 miles to a T junction. Turn left on St. Paul's Rd. and go 0.2 mile to the**

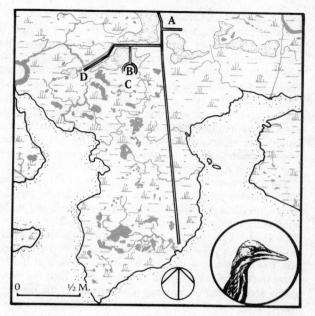

Inset: American bittern

church. Turn right and go 0.9 mile; turn right onto Rumbly Point Rd. After 0.6 mile there is a Y junction; bear right and go another 0.5 mile to the sanctuary, on the right.

Ownership: **Maryland Ornithological Society.**

Woodland, scrub, old fields, and cultivated land surround this old farm, lying on the brink of the Chesapeake Bay marshes. On a spring night you may go to sleep listening to the call of a chuck-will's-widow from the woods and a clapper rail clacking from the brackish marsh to the south. With trails that lead right out into the marsh, this sanctuary provides excellent access to the breeding grounds of rails, bitterns, ducks, and other marshbirds as well as to habitats used by other species.

Birding is particularly interesting in the winter, for the Delmarva Peninsula lies at the intersection of winter ranges of various species. Some migrants from the north winter all across the southern United States; some winter in a narrow band along the Atlantic coastline from Cape Cod southward, while others move from their freshwater breeding grounds to the salt and brackish marshes of the coast. The year-round ranges of many different species also overlap at the peninsula. For many species there is middle ground between the northern breeding range and the southern wintering range where the birds are found all year round. Some of these permanent residents are limited to the Mid-Atlantic coasts; others, like the house wren, are at the northern edge or, like the savannah sparrow, at the southern edge of their nonmigratory territory. While Irish Grove is neither unique nor especially beautiful, the diversity and accessibility of its various habitats provide outstanding opportunities to observe a broad cross-section of the birdlife of the peninsula.

On a given day in December the plowed fields just north of the farm (**A**) are patrolled by snipe and water pipits. Pipits are birds which breed in the Arctic tundra and in the western mountains at high elevations. Snipe winter as far north as Cape Cod and nest in New England and across Canada. These birds hunt for seeds together with killdeer, a year-round resident throughout the southern half of the United States. Red-tailed hawks, kestrels, and black vultures hunt over the fields all year; in winter their diets are primarily rodents and smaller birds. Look for sparrows in the brushy edges of these fields. The swamp sparrow and the savannah sparrow are birds with broad winter and summer ranges and narrow year-round territories. They share the hedges with several other species, living on the seeds of grasses and other plants.

Out in the marshes, along Rumbly Point Rd., most of the grasses die away in winter leaving only the spiky shoots of the black needle-rush and the sturdy plumes of big cordgrass (see **#66**). The only evergreen marsh shrub is wax myrtle, which grows on the high ground bordering the marsh. The yellowthroat, a warbler that is a permanent resident along the coast as far north as Long Island, and the long-billed marsh wren, found in local colonies as far north as Cape Cod, both skulk in the wax myrtle. Like many birds, they are secretive in winter, a dramatic contrast to their showy behavior during the breeding season. The shrubby borders of the marsh also host sharp-tailed and seaside sparrows, permanent residents along much of the coast. The seaside sparrow is never far from salt or brackish marshes, inhabiting the tall grasses and shrubs along the channel banks. Its long toes help it negotiate the muck. Like the marsh wren and yellowthroat, it is also secretive in winter. Because of the rapid development of the Atlantic Coast, this species is steadily losing its nesting habitat. The sharp-tailed sparrow, which inhabits both freshwater and salt marshes, has not been so threatened.

The small marsh pools are full of many species of dabbling duck in winter (see **#64**), and at the water's edge great blue herons are common. Other herons, like the snowy and great egrets, are occasionally sighted. Although Irish Grove is within the range of the little blue heron, Louisiana heron, and black-crowned night heron, they are seen more rarely. The American bittern, another member of the heron family, is a resident species along the Atlantic Coast from North Carolina to Cape Cod. It is very difficult to spot even in winter because of its protective coloring and behavior. Marked with buff and white striping on the underside of its throat, the bird stands motionless with its bill pointing straight up. The markings blend perfectly with the tawny marsh grasses. On warm spring nights the bird gives a distinctive call, best described as like the sound of an old steam-powered pump. The expansion and contraction of the bittern's unique esophagus produces this peculiar noise. Other wintering birds seen over the marsh include short-eared owls, which are most often seen at dusk and dawn, and rough-legged hawks, which migrate from the Arctic. The greater and lesser yellowlegs are at the northern edge of their wintering range here.

One permanent resident of the marsh is invisible in winter. The fiddler crab, a cold-blooded creature (see **#100**), buries itself in the mud and hibernates during the cold weather. From spring to fall the crabs are very active and can be seen at low tide scuttling back to their holes in the mud of the tidal ditches. Specially adapted to life in the marsh, they are one of the few creatures which spend their entire life there. They have both lungs and gills so that they can breath under water at high tide and in the air at low tide. During the breeding season the females produce thousands of eggs which are scattered widely over the marsh by the tides. Many of the eggs are eaten by predators, but there are so many of them that the species will find its way into any suitable habitat over the length and breadth of the marsh.

At the end of Rumbly Point Rd. is Pocomoke Sound. Out on the water diving ducks such as goldeneye, canvasback, and bufflehead feed in the cold season (see **#64**). To the east, across the mouth of Marumsco Creek, are some tall loblolly pines, a favorite resting place for bald eagles.

Walk along the path to the west of the house and turn south toward Round Pond (**B**). Here you might see a merlin, a hawk that breeds by the streams and lakes of Canada and which winters from the lower peninsula southward (see **Cape May**). Its diet is smaller birds of wetlands and woods. Occasionally a green heron is spotted by the pond. The winter range of this bird is generally from North

Carolina south. The Lincoln's sparrow, a secretive and uncommon bird of certain habits, now and then winters in the brushy areas near the pond.

Beyond the pond is an observation platform (**C**) that looks out over the marsh. Dotted across the plain are hummocks of higher land covered with loblolly pines and a thick undergrowth of bayberry, catbrier, and poison ivy, which in summer is virtually impenetrable. Great horned owls nest on these hummocks, while short-eared owls and barn owls use them for roosting. In invasion years, when food is scarce to the north, purple finches, house finches, evening grosbeaks, pine siskins, and white-winged and red crossbills feed out on the hummocks and can be sighted as they fly out across the marsh. Much of what is now marsh was farmland 200 to 300 years ago, and the hummocks were often the sites of farmhouses. Many of them still contain the remnants of family graveyards. The rising sea subsequently drowned the farmland and it became marsh (see **Chesapeake Bay**).

From the tower a short walk leads back to the house. This is a good place to hear rails and, if you are lucky, to see them. The Virginia rail and the sora are freshwater species during the breeding season. During the fall they migrate from the north and from the marshes inland to the brackish marshes where the water stays open. These brackish marshes are also a meeting ground for the clapper and the king rails, which are permanent residents here. The clapper rail is generally associated with salt marshes and the king rail with brackish marshes, but where they overlap they interbreed. This leads ornithologists to believe that they are members of the same species which have adapted themselves to different habitats. Rails are well suited to their life in the marsh. Their long spidery feet support them on the marsh ooze, and their narrow build enables them to move through the dense growth easily. Rails are most readily identified by their distinctive calls, which range from the wooden clacking of the clapper rail to the piglike grunts of the Virginia rail. These calls are most often uttered from dusk until just before dawn in the breeding season and serve both to declare territory and to help the birds find each other. Rails can sometimes be startled into short flight by loud clapping or by a stone tossed into the marsh. In spring and early summer, Rumbly Point Rd. is a good location to listen for the tiny elusive black rail (see **#65**).

Remarks: Rubber boots or waders are recommended for prowling the marsh. Low tide is the best time. Be aware that the ground under the fine salt-meadow cordgrass is soggy but firm, but the taller salt-marsh cordgrass indicates treacherous footing. In winter, when the grasses have withered, you will be better able to see where you are going. Two paths lead out across the marsh, one from the end of the canal (**D**) and one heading south from the observation platform (**C**). The latter is marked with tall stakes. The marshes farther out along the road are posted. For permission to stay at the house write to the Maryland Ornithological Society (see below). Camping is available at the sanctuary by permission only and at Shad's Landing State Park near Pocomoke City. Summer is buggy with several species of ticks, mosquitoes, and biting flies. Bring bug spray in spring and fall too. Other activities include charter fishing out of Crisfield (where you can also get excellent shellfish) and canoeing on the Pocomoke River (see **#53**). For further information contact the Maryland Ornithological Society Sanctuary Chairman, Cylburn Mansion, 4915 Greenspring Ave., Baltimore, Md. 21209.

68.

Michael Marsh

Directions: **Accomack County, Va. From Washington, D.C., drive east on U.S. 50, crossing the Bay Bridge at Annapolis and continuing south to Salisbury, Md., about 115 miles in all. Turn onto U.S. 13 going south and drive about 40 miles to Temperanceville, Va. Turn west (right) onto Route 695 and go 8.5 miles passing through the town of Grotons. Turn south (left) onto Route 698 and drive to the end. From here you can launch your canoe or boat into Messongo Creek. Another landing is located on Cattail Creek south of Poulson. To reach Poulson go south from Grotons on Route 701 to the end. Turn east (left) on Route 692 and then right on Route 688 to Poulson. Take the second dirt road on the right.**

Ownership: **Virginia Commission of Game and Inland Fisheries.**

Every fall, thousands of black ducks settle in Michael (pronounced "McKeel") Marsh and the other wetlands edging the Chesapeake Bay's Eastern Shore. Ranging from saline to brackish, these marshes are apparently better suited to black ducks than to their close relatives, the mallards, which prefer brackish to freshwater marshes. Where these two species of dabbling duck mingle they often interbreed, producing fertile hybrids. Although black ducks appear to be very numerous, they are gradually decreasing over much of their range because mallards are encroaching on their breeding grounds. These lie primarily from New England north into Canada to the shores of Hudson Bay. By March, before the flat meadows of low marsh here have turned green again, most of the ducks at Michael Marsh have flown north. A few remain to nest and raise their young.

Large, wily, and tasty to eat, the black duck has always been a favorite among hunters. The bird is somber colored, with a blackish body and lighter brown head. Its wings, outstretched in flight, are lined with white; on top of each wing is a striking patch or scapular of deep purple. The tip of a duck's bill is tough while the sides are soft and very sensitive, so the black duck can sift out seed and other food from the water. Black ducks are especially agile, able to leap 8 to 10 feet straight into the air and take off flying (see **#64**).

By August, male and female black ducks have already formed an attachment that will keep them together through the winter. Once

0   ½ M.

A

B

Inset: Black duck

the female has begun to incubate the eggs, however, the male departs, leaving her to raise the young. This is the general rule among dabbling ducks. As these birds often nest on open ground, having only one bird at the nest makes the site less conspicuous and therefore less vulnerable to predators. Another common trait of many ground-nesting birds is their subtle coloring. All female dabbling ducks are streaky browns, which enables them to blend into the background of marsh grasses. They will sit motionless on the nest until an intruder is nearly on top of them. The eggs of dabbling ducks, on the other hand, are whitish and very conspicuous. When the female leaves the nest for any reason, she covers them with dark downy feathers plucked from her breast. Some other ground-nesting species such as plovers and terns have eggs that blend into the nesting ground. To protect their eggs, these birds fly away from the nest when approached and often attack the intruder (see **#30**).

Black needlerush, salt-marsh bulrush, and salt-meadow cordgrass are the principal species in the Michael Marsh and provide ideal nesting materials for black ducks. They build their nests on small hummocks in the marsh but also nest in trees, on stumps, under bushes, or in abandoned nests of other birds.

Black ducks vary their diet considerably according to the season. In summer they eat pond weeds, wild celery, eelgrass, aquatic insects, amphibians, worms, snails, and seeds. With the coming of autumn, berries, grain, acorns, and beechnuts become important; during the winter, snails, mussels, periwinkles, and crustaceans are the staple of their diet. The birds tend to rest on the open water during the day and fly into the marshes, woods, and fields to feed at night.

All species of dabbling ducks lay large clutches of eggs. Although the young are feathered when they hatch out and are soon able to swim, they cannot fly for several weeks. This makes them very vulnerable to predators during the first few weeks of life. Large clutches ensure that enough young will survive to maintain the population. Another protective mechanism is that the female will not begin to incubate the eggs until all are laid. As a result, all the young will hatch out and be ready to take to the water at the same time, about two days after hatching. The sight of a female followed by a string of ducklings is familiar to many of us. The babies instinctively imitate everything the mother does because of a bond that is established soon after birth. This bond forms between the ducklings and the first large object they see. This is usually their mother, but the babies can also attach themselves to human beings and even boats. The urge to make this bond exists for a short period of time; once it is established nothing breaks it.

Many other species of duck are also found here in smaller numbers through the fall and winter. Dabbling ducks include pintail, wigeon, and green- and blue-winged teal. Diving ducks gather on the open waters of Messongo Creek, among them canvasback, redhead, oldsquaw, goldeneye, bufflehead, and merganser (see **#64**).

In March the waters of the marsh become a major stopping area for pied-billed and horned grebes migrating northward. Although grebes look like small ducks, the two species are not related. In fact, grebes have no known close relatives. Although migratory, they are not strong fliers, but they are highly skillful swimmers, moving under water with speed and agility as they hunt insects and small fish. Their lobed toes are shaped like small flippers, similar to those of coots and phalaropes, both of which are masterful swimmers. The lobes are open on the back stroke and, as the foot is drawn forward, fold to reduce water resistance. Grebes can dive about 20 feet and stay submerged an average of 30 seconds. The pied-billed grebe has a startling method of self-defense. When frightened, it forces the air from its body and feathers and sinks slowly under the water so that only its head is exposed. Then it may retreat to a clump of sedges or reeds and hide there. Other species of grebe will also do this from time to time. The breeding plumage of the horned grebe is striking: a bright chestnut neck, dark face and golden ear tufts, and red eyes. The pied-billed grebe is small and brown with a black stripe around its bill and a black chin.

In late spring and summer the marshes are visited by a variety of wading birds, including glossy ibis, great blue and Louisiana herons, and egrets (see **#28**).

*Remarks: Michael Marsh is a refuge and no hunting is allowed. Just to the north, however, is Saxis Wildlife Management Area, an extensive area of marsh that is hunted. Sundays are the best time to visit during hunting season. The only way to explore Michael Marsh is by boat. From the landing at the end of Route 698 you can spend half a day canoing up into Messongo Creek. If you have a motorboat, you can move around to the south side and travel up Cattail Creek. A hummock of loblolly and red-cedar and wax myrtle lies at the head of Cattail Creek (**B**). Winds can be very strong at all times of year, making boating tricky on the open waters. Nearest camping is at Tall Pines Campground on Route 695 near Sanford.*

69.

Gunpowder Delta Marsh

Directions: **Baltimore and Harford counties, Md. Take Route 40 about 8 miles northeast from the junction with I-695. At the traffic light by the Joppatowne Shopping Plaza turn right on Joppa Farms Rd. Drive 1.5 miles and turn right on to Kearny Rd. The Gunpowder Cove Marina is just down the road on the right (A).**

Ownership: **The surrounding land is partly private, partly state land. No permission is needed to canoe the waterways.**

The river called the Gunpowder Falls flows from its headwaters near the Pennsylvania border across the Piedmont, then tumbles over a series of rapids at the fall line before reaching the Gunpowder River. Just upstream from the Gunpowder River, Little Gunpowder Falls flows into Gunpowder Falls. Below this confluence (**B**), a delta covered by an extensive marsh has formed. This freshwater marsh is virtually undisturbed, although sand and gravel are quarried nearby. It is inaccessible by foot, but a journey by canoe is well worth your while to view the lush marsh vegetation and wonderful range of birdlife.

Great expanses of cattails, rising high over the canoeists' heads, form a seemingly impenetrable jungle. Other marsh plants such as wild rice, various smartweeds, and rice cutgrass are interspersed with the cattails. Arrow arum, pickerelweed, and river bulrush, all of which require more frequent flooding, grow in the many tidal guts that penetrate the marsh. Some of these guts provide canoe access deeper into the marsh during times of high water. The marsh supports a large and varied bird population. It is a suitable habitat for wetland birds, such as rails, snipes, and green and blue great herons. Mallards, black ducks, and other dabbling ducks, whistling swans, and Canada geese are among the migratory waterfowl that often set down in the marsh. Bobolinks congregate here during the fall to feed on wild rice, and the elusive soras, common gallinules, and least bitterns may breed in the marsh. Red-winged blackbirds and

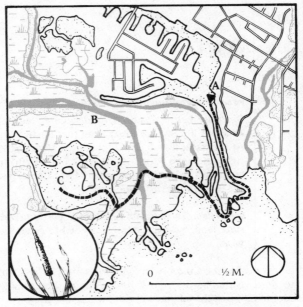

Inset: Cattail

long-billed marsh wrens make their nests in the sturdy cattails (for more on marsh birds see **#28, #64, #67, #72**). The waters of the Gunpowder Delta Marsh serve as a spawning ground for the fish of Chesapeake Bay. Finally, the marsh acts as a filter, catching sediments and many pollutants and preventing them from entering the bay.

Standing tall on the floodplain beyond the marsh's edge are deciduous trees, primarily green ash and sycamores. American kestrels, wood ducks, and screech owls nest in the trees. Several species of woodpeckers also reside in this forest. With its understory of Japanese honeysuckle, red willow, and common elder, this habitat is an important wintering ground for wildlife. An early morning paddler may catch a glimpse of the deer, raccoons, or muskrats that often leave their tracks in the muddy banks. The value of the floodplain forest, like that of the marsh, reaches beyond food and shelter: by trapping debris and sediments washing off the surrounding land, the forest helps buffer the marsh from the detriments of development.

Between the marsh and the forest lies a transitional shrub swamp such as that around the perimeter of Day's Cove (**C**). It is composed of marsh plants and hardier floodplain species in addition to wetland shrubs. Green ash form a thin canopy over black willow, common elder, red maple, smooth alder, and swamp rose. Arrow arum, smartweeds, cattails, sedges, and grasses mark the wetter sections. The scattered dead trees, standing as solitary sentinels, were most likely killed by flooding. The swamp is another vital wildlife habitat. Muskrats and waterfowl come here to feed. Other animals, particularly songbirds, such as white-throated sparrows, Carolina chickadees, and tufted titmice, take refuge here in winter to scrounge for seeds.

Although the Gunpowder Delta Marsh has so far escaped the degrading influences of development, the activities of man have had a significant effect. When the surrounding land was first settled in 1650, much of it was cleared for farming. Up until that time, the rising sea had eroded the seaward edges of the marsh while new marsh was forming along the protected landward side(see **Chesapeake Bay**). The removal of the vegetative cover together with poor farming practices caused an enormous influx of sediment into the marsh. Although sea level continued to rise, the process of marsh development was altered. A thick layer of sand and silt buried the preexisting marsh. Shrubs and trees grew out over what had been marsh, while new marshlands emerged farther downstream, filling in protected open water. After the Civil War, some of the land was allowed to revert to forest. The amount of sediment entering the wetlands thus decreased, but the marsh continued to build seaward. Between 1848 and 1939, 413 acres of emergent land were created. The trend still continues today, though to a lesser degree.

Remarks: *The boat-launching fee at the Gunpowder Cove Marina is $3 on weekdays and $4 on weekends. Call (301) 679-5454 for more boating information. Stay close to shore while traveling across the open water of the Gunpowder River, which can get very rough. The best route to take is marked on the map. Plan to spend at least half a day exploring the marsh. Canoe rentals are available in Washington (see #92) and outside Baltimore at Springriver Corp., 6434 Baltimore National Pike, Baltimore, Md. 21228, (301) 788-3377.*

70.
Baltimore Sewage-Treatment Plant

Directions: **From Baltimore get onto I-695 (the Beltway) and go to exit 38. Turn east onto Eastern Ave. (Route 150) and go 0.7 mile. The entrance is on the right.**

Ownership: **City of Baltimore.**

Although it is difficult to consider this a natural area, the sewage-treatment facility offers excellent birding, especially during the fall shorebird migration and in the winter. Sunday, when the garbage trucks are out of the way, is the only day to visit. Drive in and turn left at the first opportunity. This will take you past filtration tanks on the right and out to the banks of a tidal creek where there is a small planting of pines and a parking area. At low tide the creek is transformed into broad mudflats where you may see a wide variety of shorebirds, including ruffs in July and American avocets in August. On the other side of the parking area are rain pools and landfill areas where ducks and sandpipers can be seen. In winter and spring the landfill areas are excellent for gulls. Twelve species have been identified here.

71.
Sandy Point State Park

Directions: **Ann Arundel County, Md. From Washington, D.C., take Route 50 east. About 6 miles past the Severn River Bridge at Annapolis, take the last exit before the Chesapeake Bay Bridge. Following signs, go left across the overpass and into the park.**

Ownership: **Maryland Park Service.**

Jutting into Chesapeake Bay, Sandy Point State Park's many habitats attract a great variety of birds, providing some of the best birding opportunities on Maryland's Western Shore. Nearly every bird found in Maryland has been recorded at Sandy Point State Park. Two factors are largely responsible for the sometimes outstanding concentrations of birds. Sand moved by currents (see **#25**) has built Sandy Point out into the bay at its narrowest section, where birds are attracted by both the relatively short (4-mile) east-west span of the bay and by the point's prominence as they follow the bay's land-water boundaries north and south during migration. Secondly, the 679-acre park includes a surprising variety of habitats, partly as a result of human influence: in addition to beach and open water, we find Mezick Pond (**A**), which was dredged for boating, and mudflats (**B, C**), which sometimes form behind the spoils piles. The scattered woodlands (**D**) are made up of oaks, hickories, Virginia pines, and redcedars. The largest trees are in the mature woodlands surrounding the group camping area (**E**). Fresh and brackish marshes (**F**), fields of shrubby multiflora rose, grassy stretches, and bare parking lots complete the array of environments.

Mallards, black ducks, oldsquaws, canvasbacks, and Canada geese

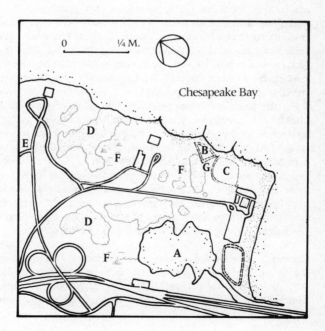

flock to the bay and pond in late fall. Their numbers and date of arrival vary greatly and may depend on weather conditions in the north. The waterfowl arrive anywhere from mid-October to January. Many remain through winter and leave in early spring, while others linger until May.

Shorebirds, including plovers, sandpipers, great blue and green herons, and common egrets, visit the park in spring and fall. Pools that occur on the beaches, grassy areas, and parking lots during rainy weather provide the best shorebird conditions. Mudflats may also form behind the spoils from Mezick Pond. These areas, fringed by phragmites, once attracted many shorebirds, but are now usually dry and unexciting. Areas **B** and **C** are under consideration for possible reconversion into a sanctuary for shorebirds. An observation platform on the dike between them (**G**) offers a good view of the spoils flats and the open water of the bay. The most favorable circumstances for sighting shorebirds occur during stormy weather when winds blow out of the southeast in spring and the northeast in fall.

Fall hawk migrations can be spectacular, with as many as 4000 broadwings passing overhead in one day. These showings are sporadic, often occurring when the migrants must reestablish their southwestward course after being blown off course by northwesterly winds. They fly across the bay from the east, parallel to the Chesapeake Bay Bridge, then circle to gain altitude before resuming their journeys to Texas, Mexico, or South America. The exact route that these birds follow is not fully understood. In spring, large flights of kestrels, sharpshins, ospreys, and other raptors can be observed following the western edge of the bay on their way north to their breeding grounds (see **Cape May**).

For the past four years, peregrine falcons have wintered on the Chesapeake Bay Bridge, feasting on the hordes of pigeons that dwell beneath it. This year (1983) the falcons are attempting to nest here for the first time. They can be observed in or from the park.

In May, the woods can be full of warblers. The only species not found here are those of the Piedmont environments to the west and those, like the prothonotary, that live in stream valleys, a habitat not found here. Among the less common but regularly seen songbirds are snow buntings and Lapland longspurs, most often seen on the beaches or parking lots in November and December.

Remarks: *Open for day use year round; to encounter the greatest number of birds and least number of people, visit between Labor Day and Memorial Day. An entrance fee is charged, except on Mondays and sometimes in winter. Other facilities and activities include picnicking and swimming;*

boat launches and rentals of row, motor, and paddle boats; fishing and crabbing; and naturalist activities. Nearby is the wooded Corcoran Environmental Study Area. Contact the park for more information: Sandy Point State Park, 800 Revell Highway, Annapolis, Md. 21401, (301) 757-1841 or 974-1249.

72.
Jug Bay
Natural Area

Directions: **Prince Georges County, Md. From Washington, D.C., take Route 4 (Pennsylvania Ave.) south; go 7.9 miles beyond I-95 (Capital Beltway). Take U.S. 301 south 1.8 miles, turn left onto Croom Station Rd., and continue 1.7 miles to the end. Turn left onto Croom Rd., drive 1.5 miles to Croom Airport Rd. and turn left. Follow the road as it bears to the right. The park entrance will be on the left after 2 miles. Drive approximately 1.7 miles down the park entrance road to the parking area by the red barn that is the park headquarters.**

Ownership: **Maryland–National Capital Park and Planning Commission; Department of Parks and Recreation, Prince Georges County, Md.**

The Patuxent River rises in central Maryland, flows halfway between Baltimore and Washington, D.C., in its middle reaches, then cuts through southern Maryland on its way to the Chesapeake Bay. Some 50 miles above the mouth of the river, the narrow river channel suddenly broadens into Jug Bay, which is 2 miles long and 0.5 mile across at its widest, then narrows again before gradually opening into Chesapeake Bay. The freshwater and brackish marshes along the river between Jug Bay and Benedict serve as a year-round haven for an enormous number of local and migratory birds. Within the Jug Bay Natural Area, part of the Patuxent River Park, numerous habitats create a zone of great diversity. There are upland woods typical of the nearby Piedmont, fields, hardwood swamps, and vast tidal marshes bordering the river and tributary creeks. Each habitat houses its own assortment of plants and wildlife.

0   2000'

An extensive system of trails and approximately half a mile of boardwalks leads through the woodlands and swamps and along the edge of the marsh. The hardwood trees are a second-growth forest composed mostly of red maple, sweetgum, sycamore, and tuliptree. Nearly all the trees were logged some 50 or 60 years ago. Those that were too inaccessible were spared and are now noticeably larger than the rest. Mountain laurel, viburnum, and small holly trees, along with twelve species of ferns, form a thick undergrowth. From spring through fall, the woods are full of blossoming wildflowers. Skunk cabbage first appears in February and is exeedingly prevalent in moist places. Round-lobed hepatica and trailing arbutus flower in April, followed by pink lady's slipper and mayapple. During summer, in more open places, the uplands boast trumpet creeper and Virginia dayflower, while the wetter areas are aglow with cardinal flowers, crimson-eyed rose mallow, and New York ironweed.

This is one of the finest places in the Chesapeake Bay area for bird-watching year round. Great numbers of birds flock here, attracted by the varied habitats, abundant food sources, and the moderate climate. Of the 374 birds on the Maryland state list, nearly 250 species have been recorded here, over 80 of them nesting. The tidal wetlands are a major attraction, drawing hundreds of thousands of birds throughout the year. In fall, migrating ducks, herons, and other waterbirds come to feed, as do many southbound landbirds. Spring migration time is equally busy. In early spring the waterfowl move north to breed, while later in the season local warblers and other songbirds return to the area to nest. Other birds pass through en route to more northern breeding grounds. Hawks are seen heading north; ospreys return for the summer. Bald eagles are occasionally sighted; two active nests are located downstream. Canada geese by the tens of thousands, along with snow geese, whistling swans, and 20 species of ducks, winter in the vicinity of Jug Bay (see **Introduction** and **#64**). A large rookery of great blue herons is located in the riverside swamp, which also provides homes and breeding roosts for nearly 30 species of cavity-nesting birds (see **#37**).

Jug Bay marks the boundary of the brackish water of the Chesapeake Bay and the fresh water of the Patuxent River. The tides bring salt water upstream as far as Jug Bay, but the tidal influence is evident even above that point. The force of the tides sweeping in from the Chesapeake Bay slows the flow of the river, backing up the waters. Downstream, the water steadily becomes saltier until, some 25 miles away at Benedict, the water is as saline as the bay itself (see **Chesapeake Bay**). Although the water is often slightly brackish here, freshwater marsh plants predominate. Jug Bay has one of the most extensive wild-rice marshes in the Chesapeake Bay drainage system. Spatterdock, pickerelweed, cattail, and arrow arum grow abundantly among the dominant wild rice, providing food for waterfowl and other wildlife. As salinity increases downstream, saltwater plants begin to outnumber the freshwater ones, and big cordgrass replaces the wild rice.

The appearance of the marsh in Jug Bay Natural Area and the life within it change dramatically with the seasons. In winter, the view from shore to shore across the bay is unobstructed, and the area is cloaked in brown. Summer brings a dense green curtain of growth so tall and luxuriant that, as one approaches the marsh along the boardwalk, the open water cannot even be seen. In September, the feathery inflorescence of the 8- to 9-foot-tall wild-rice plants gives the marsh a golden tone. The seeds, which ripen in early fall, are a primary food source for many birds. Hundreds of thousands of redwinged blackbirds, separated by sex into wintering male and female flocks, may come in search of food by early September. Along with migrating bobolinks, the blackbirds often eat the ripening seeds before other birds have the chance. Sora and king rails may jump up to retrieve whatever seeds are left on bent-over plants. Because the seeds of wild rice fall off the stalk very easily, some of the grain falls to the ground to become prime food for migratory ducks. The fall migrants continue their journeys south in October, about the time that northern waterfowl arrive here to settle down for the winter.

Nonseasonal changes are also taking place in this marsh and in most of the country's marshes. Sedimentation from nearby gravel operations, both active and abandoned, and from erosion caused by development is filling in the river and the bay. The grasses trap the sediment by slowing the flow of water, which causes the particles to settle. Wild rice is being replaced by the less desirable phragmites, a major stand of which extends more than halfway across the bay from the far shores at its southern end. A highly adaptable plant, phragmites grows abundantly on fill but is a poor source of wildlife food. The firm hold of its tightly interwoven roots crowds out all other plants. The extent to which the bay has filled in is striking and disturbing when one considers that, during the nineteenth century, 100-ton sailing ships and 250-ton tobacco steamers routinely plied the waters of the Patuxent River. Today, Jug Bay averages only 2 to 3 feet deep.

Life abounds in a marsh. Here, as in all ecosystems, many food chains exist. Small fish feed on minute organisms and, in turn, are eaten by larger fish or birds. Muskrats chew on cattails. A snapping turtle may dine on an unlucky duckling which once ate plants or insect larvae. The larvae fed upon microscopic organisms which fed upon algae. Certain bacteria and fungus complete the cycle by decomposing dead plant and animal material into its component nutrients, which are then available for use. Thus, an intricate and delicately balanced web of life is established. The amount of living matter formed—the productivity—in a marsh is higher than that of any other ecosystem. At the foundation of this extensive food web, feeding the consumers, are the green plants and algae—the primary producers. Through the process of photosynthesis, these plants use sunlight to convert carbon dioxide and water into the sugars that are the fuels for all life processes. Plants also require oxygen to convert these sugars into energy. Unable to create their own sugars, the rest of the living world must eat the plants, or other animals that have eaten the plants, in order to survive.

When pollutants wind up in the water, they are introduced into the food chain. Millions of gallons of waste effluents from various treatment plants are pumped into the Patuxent River daily. By trapping the pollutants in the marsh, the high sediment load that is choking the river compounds the problem. Varying amounts of the chemicals accumulate in fish, frogs, and other water dwellers. Animals near the bottom of the food chain may collect only small amounts of the pollutant. As they are eaten, and the animals that eat them get eaten in turn, the chemicals are concentrated within the consumers' bodies until lethal levels are reached. The bald eagle, osprey, and peregrine falcon were once decimated by DDT and other chlorinated hydrocarbons in this way (see **#58, #64**). Those birds are now returning to this area, but could be threatened again by other pollutants. These pollutants remain within the ecosystem because each flood tide returns the polluted, ocean-bound water and redistributes it across the marsh. Another source of pollution is the excessive nutrients supplied by sewage effluents. In such large amounts, these nutrients stimulate explosive growth of algae, which depletes the available oxygen. In extreme cases all oxygen-dependent plants and animals will die, leaving the marsh virtually devoid of life (see **Chesapeake Bay**).

Destruction of any marsh also destroys a natural flood-control system. Floodwater rolls easily across the marsh, while the grasses slow its velocity and dissipate its energy. Excess water overflows onto the marsh's floodplain where it is, in effect, put into storage. Gradually some of the excess water will flow into the creeks when their water levels have dropped sufficiently. The rest of it will percolate slowly into the ground to replenish the groundwater supply.

Remarks: *Because Jug Bay Natural Area is managed primarily to protect the river and wildlife, a permit is required for all uses. Due to this policy no detailed site map is included. Visitors are asked to make advance reservations for orientation to the area. The park office is open Tuesday to Saturday, 8:00 to 4:30. RR Box 3380, Upper Marlboro, Md. 20772, (301) 627-6074. The annual fee for residents of Prince Georges and Montgomery counties is $5. Nonresidents must pay $5 a day from Memorial Day through Labor Day; admission is free during the rest of the year. Permits, however, are required year round. Other activities include hiking, horseback riding, primitive camping, fishing, hunting, and boating. The flatwater canoeing here is excellent for beginners, families, and marsh explorers throughout the year. You can launch your own canoe or rent one from the park (by reservation). The park staff can suggest where to canoe and will tell where canoe-camping is permitted. Interpretative activities highlight living history, natural history, and the river, and the Duvall tool museum exhibits antique tools. As many as 30,000 Canada geese winter at the nearby Merkle Wildlife Management Area, and are often seen throughout the area. Adjacent to Patuxent River Park just south of Jug Bay, Merkle is accessible by canoe from Jug Bay and by road. Visitation is limited in order not to disturb the birds. Check with the Maryland Wildlife Administration at (301) 372-8128 for more information.*

73.

Battle Creek
Cypress Swamp

Directions: **Calvert County, Md. From Washington, D.C., take Route 4 (Pennsylvania Ave.) east. From the intersection with I-95 (Capital Beltway), continue east then south on Route 4 about 33 miles. Turn west (right) onto Route 506 and follow signs to the Nature Center.**

Ownership: **The Nature Conservancy; managed by Calvert County.**

Hidden away in a small, steep-sided ravine is a stand of baldcypress trees, perhaps the northernmost stand of real significance in North America (see **#51**). The tall, shaggy trees, some of them 100 feet high, are one of the oldest known species, one that has especially adapted to life in the swamp. A quarter-mile boardwalk winds through the area.

The present cypress swamp had its beginnings around 10,000 years ago, after the last glacier departed and the climate grew warmer (see **Introduction**). As the seas rose, sediments began to accumulate in Battle Creek, creating swampy flats suitable for baldcypress growth. The stream valley opens to the south and lies between two bodies of water, the Chesapeake to the east and the Patuxent River to the west. The southern exposure and the moderating effect of the two bodies of water may create a slightly warmer microclimate in the Battle Creek valley, which has favored baldcypress. It is thought that at one time this cypress swamp was the northern finger of an extensive southern cypress forest.

The boundaries of this stand of baldcypress are sharply drawn. To the south where the creek opens out into tidal marsh on its way to the Patuxent, cypress occur sporadically along the banks where sedimentation created areas of higher elevation. To the north and on the slopes of the ravine where the soil is drier, the cypress disappears, unable to compete with other species of trees, which are able to grow here. You will notice a dramatic change in vegetation as you walk the path from the edge of the escarpment down into the swamp. In just a matter of a few feet the hillside forest of white and red oaks, hickory, Virginia pine, tuliptree, mountain laurel, and American holly gives way to the wetland where cypress mixes with red maple, blackgum, and ash, with a shrub layer of southern arrowwood and spicebush.

Cypress trees are adapted to swamp life in several ways. The trunks of the trees widen out at the base, giving greater support on the soft wet ground. The roots spread through the surface of the soil, erupting now and again into the characteristic knees. These protrusions apparently occur only where water levels fluctuate; they do not occur on trees that are permanently flooded or those planted on dry land. Scientists are still researching the function of these growths. It has been theorized that the knees provide additional stability to the tree and that they play a role in its respiration. The heartwood of the cypress is a soft but durable and resinous material which repels insects and rot. This helps the trees survive in the difficult conditions of the swamp. If left to itself, a baldcypress can live for a thousand years. The tree's decay-resistant wood also makes it a prized construction material, and consequently little is left of the extensive cypress swamps that once covered the southeastern United States. Most of this stand has been cut over within the last 70 years; the oldest specimen is 450 years old, but it is not visible from the boardwalk.

The baldcypress must be long-lived in order to reproduce, for it has developed a very hit-or-miss method of propagation. The tree does not produce seeds every year. And being unable to sprout in water, the seeds, if they are to develop, must fall on a hummock or else drought conditions must exist. However, the seeds can remain viable for as long as 30 months. The hummock must remain moist but not flooded for 3 to 5 years for the sprout to become a thriving seedling. This means that rainfall in the region must be less than average during those years.

Battle Creek Cypress Swamp is flooded only after heavy storms during the spring and summer. At other times there may be no standing water in the swamp or at most only a few inches. However, the soil remains soggy and mucky all year. Here and there are small spring-fed pools, the perfect spawning ground for salamanders. Eight varieties have been found in the swamp: northern dusky, four-toed, marbled, red-backed, northern red, northern spotted, northern two-lined, and red-spotted newt. In early spring the egg masses can often be seen floating in the water of these pools.

The periodic standing water of the swamp makes an ideal breeding ground for insects as well, which in turn attract migratory warblers. Several species which nest here such as the Kentucky and the northern parula warblers are southern birds. The hooded warbler, which nests as far north as central New York, is associated with cypress-gum swamps in the southeastern United States. Other nesting warblers include the prothonotary and the yellow-breasted chat.

Remarks: *The area is worth visiting in all seasons, though it is buggy in summer. A nature center contains exhibits on the natural and cultural history of the area; open Tuesday through Saturday 10:00 to 5:00, Sunday 1:00 to 5:00; closed Mondays, Thanksgiving Day, Christmas Day, New Year's Day.*

74.
Zekiah Swamp

Directions: **Charles County, Md. From Washington, D.C., take Route 5 south. From the intersection with I-95 (Capital Beltway), continue south on Route 5, which becomes U.S. 301, for about 30 miles to Route 234. Turn left and go 1 mile to Allens Fresh, where the road crosses Zekiah Swamp. Pull off the road to park.**

Ownership: **Private and Maryland Department of Natural Resources.**

A jungle of luxuriant greenery shades the many braided stream channels that lace across some 18 miles of southern Maryland farmland. Zekiah Swamp, averaging half a mile in width, is one of the largest freshwater swamps remaining in the state. As the water flows from its narrow headwaters (see Nearby Places of Interest) to the mouth of the swamp (**A**), then continues into the Wicomico River to the Potomac, it passes through several different habitats, which support an abundance of wildlife. Mammals (deer, beaver, raccoon, and mink), turtles (mud and box, and diamondback terrapins), and several species of snakes live in or frequently visit the swamp. Some songbirds pause here to feed and rest before continuing their northward migrations in spring; others remain to breed here. Bald eagles sometimes soar overhead with the more common osprey and various hawks.

The bottomland woods that cover the length of Zekiah Swamp

are composed primarily of sweetgum and red maple, as well as pin oak, sycamore, green ash, tuliptree and river birch. The area has been logged sporadically in the past, so the trees range in size from 18 inches in diameter down to small saplings. Some dense thickets of spicebush, sweet pepperbush, and arrowwood grow beneath them.

Many different birds take advantage of the food and shelter offered by Zekiah Swamp. A great variety of warblers, vireos, and other songbirds migrate through; some, including parula and Kentucky warblers and white-eyed vireos, stay to breed. Pileated and red-bellied woodpeckers, wood ducks, red-shouldered hawks, and barred owls also nest here. Quite a few birds, such as catbirds and hermit thrushes, are winter residents. Brown thrashers and eastern phoebes, which are near the northern limits of their wintering ranges, are also found (see **#67**).

At Allens Fresh (**A**), the two main streams filtering through Zekiah Swamp merge, the channel widens, and the tangled swamp gives way to unobstructed marshland. Loblolly and Virginia pines and southern red oak grow in this area. Because the land is slightly higher and the gravelly soils are well-drained, these and other up-

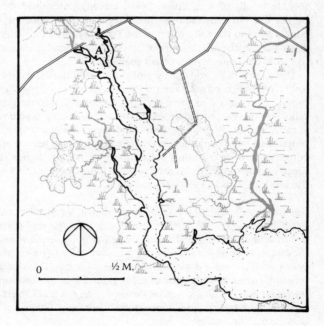

land species, such as American holly and pignut hickory, are able to survive. Similar patches of drier ground with its attendant vegetation occur irregularly throughout the swamp.

The fresh water first encounters the tidal influences of Chesapeake Bay just below the bridge and becomes slightly brackish. The salinity here varies, depending on tidal and seasonal changes, precipitation, and wind conditions (see **#72**). Further downstream, the Wicomico River becomes increasingly brackish. Meadows of tall marsh plants mark the transition from Zekiah Swamp to the Wicomico River. The marsh is rich with life supported by the influx of nutrients that comes with each tide (see **Chesapeake Bay**). From spring to fall, grasses and sedges like big cordgrass, wild rice, Olney three-square, cattails, and river bulrush ripple in breezes that blow across the flat terrain. Among them are the lovely pink flowers of the swamp rose mallow. Red-winged blackbirds, least bitterns, and long-billed marsh wrens nest here. Both freshwater species such as arrow arum and picker-elweed, and saltwater plants such as salt-marsh water hemp, can thrive in the slightly brackish water. The lush marsh extends a couple of miles along Allens Fresh Run to the Wicomico River. As is characteristic of river valleys on the western shore of the Chesapeake Bay, low hills of agricultural fields, loblolly pines, and woodland border the Wicomico and narrow fringes of marsh dot the water's edge. Closer to the salty water of the Potomac, the freshwater marsh gives way to the black needlerush, salt-marsh cordgrass, and salt-meadow cordgrass typical of salt marshes.

The many bays and coves along the sinuous shorelines of the lower Wicomico provide shelter for waterfowl wintering on the Potomac. They also feed there on sago pondweed, wigeon grass, and other submerged vegetation. Migrating and wintering waterfowl may venture up the Wicomico. Blue- and green-winged teal, mallards, pintails, shovelers, and hooded mergansers have all been seen. Large congregations of common snipe occur in winter. Egrets, herons, soras, and the secretive Virginia rails are found in the marshes during the breeding season (see **#28** and **#67**).

Remarks: *Allens Fresh provides a lovely view of the marshes and Allens Fresh Run to the south. Fishing and boating are the only things to do besides bird-watching. Small boats can be put in on the northeast side of the bridge, where a dirt road leads to the water. Allens Fresh Run and the Wicomico River make a pleasant flatwater canoe trip. Zekiah Swamp is privately owned and not open to public explorations. Immediately before the bridge over Zekiah Swamp, on the north side, is a small parcel of state-owned land. A path leads between the abandoned cabins for a short distance into the swamp.*

The central section of the swamp can be observed only where Routes 5 and 6 cross it. At these points, the water runs in uncharacteristically well-defined channels. Within a very short distance, these channels disperse into the braided system that washes through the swamp. At the Route 5 crossing, water backed up by the highway bridge created a sizable impoundment. Several types of smartweed, lizard's tail, arrow arum, both species of tearthumb, and other freshwater marsh plants have colonized the open water. Willow and alder shrubs are now invading; eventually red maples and other bottomland trees will grow here again. Swamp cottonwoods grow on both sides of the road here, in one of only two or three locations in the state. The trees are few and scattered and may be hard to spot; look for their large, distinctive leaves. Both Routes 5 and 6 intersect Route 301 north of Route 234. Each road crosses Zekiah Swamp about 5 miles east of Route 301.

Nearby Places of Interest

Cedarville Natural Resources Management Area: **From Route 301, about 11 miles south of I-95, turn left onto Cedarville Rd. After 2.3 miles turn right onto Bee Oak Rd. The ranger station is on the right in 1 mile. Continue another 0.5 mile past it, then turn right onto Forest Rd. and go 1.4 miles. Park on the left just before the pond.**

At Cedarville, a number of springs and small creeks, together with the drainage from the pond, form the headwaters of Zekiah Swamp. The man-made pond, created in the 1950s, is slowly filling in. Alders are now crowding out the pitcher plants, sundews, nodding ladies' tresses, and other bog plants that grow sparingly along its northern edge. The first half mile of the green-blazed Swamp Trail leads along the headwaters of Zekiah Swamp, from the pond. The thick forest bordering the small stream contrasts sharply with the scene at Allens Fresh. This section is worth exploring if you pay a visit to Cedarville Natural Resources Management Area. It is a multiuse area managed for recreation, forestry, and wildlife. One can hike, horseback ride, fish, camp, picnic, hunt, and visit the warmwater fish hatchery. Naturalist activities and an orienteering course are also available. For more information contact Cedarville NRMA, Route 4, Box 106 A, Brandywine, Md. 20613, (301) 888-1622.

75.
Calvert Cliffs
State Park

Directions: **From Washington, D.C., take Route 4 (Pennsylvania Ave.) east. From the intersection with I-95 (Capital Beltway) continue on Route 4 east, then south, about 45 miles. The park is on the east side of the road. Follow the red trail 2 miles out to the beach and the cliffs (A).**

Ownership: **Maryland Park Service.**

A line of sandy and clayey cliffs forms the western shore of the Chesapeake Bay for 30 miles from Drum Point to Fairhaven. These cliffs contain a wealth of fossils—shells, shark teeth, the vertebrae of whales and porpoises, and miscellaneous bones—constituting one of the most detailed records known of life as it existed 15 million years ago. On the beach at the park, fossils litter the sand, and you may keep whatever you collect. (No digging is allowed in the cliffs.)

Twelve to seventeen million years ago a shallow sea full of marine life covered the entire area. As mollusks, fish, and other creatures died they drifted down into the sand and silt on the sea floor and became embedded there. Millions of years of deaths and burials accumulated and preserved in the strata of Calvert Cliffs. These strata, signifying varying compositions of sands and clays, reflect the conditions that existed when the strata formed. If you stand on the beach and look northward you can see these different layers as varicolored bands in the face of the cliff. At the park only the Choptank formation has many fossils. Look for its yellow sandy layers at the foot of the bluff.

Over a period of millions of years the bottom of the sea was lifted up by forces within the earth to become high land. During the glacial age that began 1 to 2 million years ago, sea level dropped as tons of water became trapped as ice. The young Susquehanna River cut a channel through these layers of sedimentary rock. The river deepened and extended its valley southward toward the retreating sea. As the glaciers melted, sea level rose and flooded the lower reaches of the river, forming Chesapeake Bay. Calvert Cliffs are the eroded uplands of this ancient river valley, today the edge of the western shore of Chesapeake Bay.

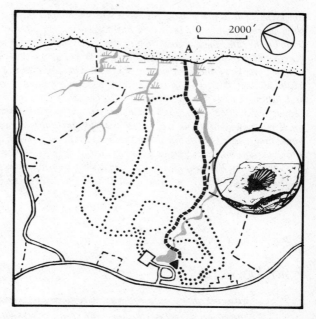

Inset: Chesapecten nefrens fossil

The cliffs are very unstable, easily eroded, and subject to landslide. Fossil-bearing material is continually being swept into the bay and washed back onto the beaches. There are three types of fossils, all of which are found here: (1) A shell, bone, or plant may leave an imprint in soft mud or silt that eventually hardens, retaining the imprint of the organism, long after the organism has disintegrated. (2) The animal or plant itself may be preserved in the surrounding material. (3) It may be chemically altered into a harder, more durable substance.

Over 600 species are fossilized in the cliffs. What they are, where they are found and in what condition tells a great deal about what life was like in this ancient sea and nearby. The multitude of immature porpoise and whale bones indicates that this area may have been used as a breeding ground. Many of the bones show signs of attack by sharks, and scores of shark teeth have in fact been found. The sharks may have been drawn here by the presence of vulnerable young mammals. Other fish bones uncovered reveal the early existence of such species as cod, sturgeon, saltwater catfish, swordfish, ocean sunfish, and mackerel.

Remarks: *The 2-mile walk to the beach passes through a mature forest of pines, beeches, oaks, and holly trees and takes about 45 minutes. Do not climb on the cliffs; there is great danger from landslides. Another site along the cliffs where you can collect fossils for a fee is at Matoka Cottages in St. Leonard, north of the park just off Route 4. The day rate is $1.50 for adults. Cottages for rent. Activities include boating, swimming, crabbing, and fishing. For information contact Matoka Cottages, L.E. Smith, St. Leonard, Md. 20685, (301) 586-0269. Just south of the park is an excellent small museum with displays of fossils and geologic history as well as an interesting selection of reading material. From the park, go south on Route 4 to the bridge and turn left just before it; the Calvert Marine Museum is a few yards down the road on the left. For further information contact the museum at P.O. Box 97, Solomons, Md. 20688 (301) 326-3719.*

76.
Point Lookout

Directions: **St. Mary's County, Md. From Washington, D.C. take Route 4 (Pennsylvania Ave.) east and south; follow Route 4 about 60 miles to the end, crossing the Patuxent River. At Route 235 turn south (left) and drive another 23 miles to the end of the road. Park by the small naval installation (A). From here you can view the bay and the mouth of the Potomac; there is no walking trail here. (Although Route 5 looks more direct on the map, it takes much longer due to traffic lights. Route 4 also takes you past Battle Creek Cypress Swamp and Calvert Cliffs State Park; see #73 and #75). To reach the campground, backtrack about 2 miles and turn left. After the entrance booth, bear left for Green's Point and good views of a sheltered bay.**

Ownership: **Maryland Park Service.**

This low windswept peninsula is bordered on one side by the murky, silt-laden waters of the Potomac and on the other by the wide reach of the Chesapeake Bay. A broken canopy of loblolly pines rises above the flat marshes and sandy strips of beach. Tapering to the southeast, the peninsula is a natural trap for migratory birds moving south, especially in westerly or northwesterly winds. Though much less well known as a birding spit than Cape May or Cape Charles, Point Lookout is an outstanding area from fall to spring.

At the very end of the peninsula by the parking area, you can stand in one place and look for diving ducks in the bay; then walk a few steps and scan the broad mouth of the Potomac. Waterfowl are especially abundant from fall to spring. Large groups of whistling swans, Canada geese, and all sorts of diving ducks spend the winter here. Oldsquaws, all three species of scoter (see **#20**), red-breasted mergansers, both greater and lesser scaups, horned grebes by the hundreds, buffleheads, and canvasbacks are all common. From the end of the point a series of wooden pilings juts out into the Potomac. Double-crested cormorants and gulls perch here. Cormorants are excellent divers and swimmers and are adept at fishing, but unlike most water birds their feathers are not heavily oiled. After a time they become waterlogged; the characteristic pose of the cormorant— sitting with wings outstretched—serves to dry out their plumage. Bald eagles nest just to the north near the town of Ridge and

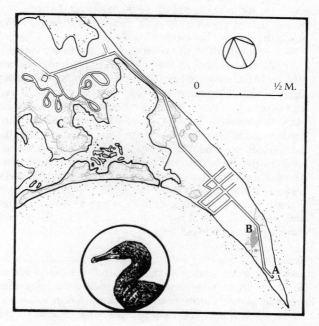

0 _____ ½ M.

Inset: Double-crested cormorant

often can be seen patrolling the marshes and the shallow bays that line the Potomac River to the west (see **#64**).

Driving back toward the campground, stop at the shallow tidal ponds (**B**) to the west of the road. Herons and egrets like to fish here. Look also for the boat-tailed grackle. Point Lookout is the only known nesting area for this species on the western shore of Maryland. The low marshy land and loblolly forest of the point are very like the coastal habitats the grackle inhabits on the Eastern Shore. To the north of Point Lookout sandy bluffs and hardwood forests dominate the shore. The brown-headed nuthatch, another Eastern Shore species scarce west of the bay, lives in the loblolly groves (see **#64**).

Great clusters of migrating songbirds are often caught at the point, especially after a spell of cold weather moving out of the north. Thrushes, warblers, flycatchers, and vireos throng the shrubs and the woodlands. The berries of poison ivy, greenbrier, and bayberry offer a good supply of food. As might be expected, hawk flights are also excellent in the autumn (see **Cape May** for information on hawk flights). Look for the hawks out in the open, soaring overhead or beating across the Potomac, and in the woods where they rest up and hunt for food. Just north of the point on the west is a picnic area. A network of informal trails meanders through the woodland just to the north of the picnic ground.

Two miles north of the point turn west into the camping area. Bear left toward Green's Point. There is an osprey platform right offshore in the sheltered bay. The ospreys begin to nest early, returning in April from southern wintering grounds (see **#47**). Geese and ducks take shelter here in the colder months. The surrounding brackish marsh is similar to those all along the Eastern Shore, with black needlerush, salt-meadow cordgrass and salt grass, groundsel, and marsh elder (see **#60**). Further back from the water a few redcedars stand in the open sun, and behind them are clumps of loblolly. Another woodland trail of about one mile begins near the visitors' center near the camping area (**C**).

North of the park are open fields where in winter you may find birds of the plains and open tundra such as rough-legged hawks, water pipits, and horned larks (see **#67**).

Remarks: *Several other interesting birding spots are nearby. North of the park turn right on Scotland Beach Rd. and take the first left on Rodo Beach Rd. Take the second left and drive to a tidal pond where marsh and shorebirds gather. Further north along Route 5 turn left onto Cornfield Harbor Rd. and drive about a mile to the bridge. In spring and summer rails and seaside sparrows rustle in the marsh grasses. In winter redhead* *and canvasback flock on the creek. St. George Island is famous as a collecting point for great cormorants each winter from December to March. These birds are rare here. To reach the island drive northwest on Route 5 to Callaway, about 20 miles north of the point. Take Route 249 south all the way to the end, about 15 miles. The birds sit on pilings out in the channel of the Potomac; a spotting scope is needed to see them properly. Camping is available at the park all year round for trailers; tent camping begins in April. Other activities in the area include saltwater fishing (charters run from the park), boating, and canoeing. Boat rentals are available from spring to fall. Swimming beaches are open in summer. For further information contact Point Lookout State Park, P.O. Box 48, Scotland. Md. 20687, (301) 872-5688 or (301) 475-8016.*

77.
Westmoreland
State Park

Directions: **Westmoreland County, Va. From Washington, D.C., take Route 5 south about 15 miles to U.S. 301. Go south on U.S. 301 about 40 miles to Route 3. Turn east (left) and go about 19 miles to Route 347. Turn left into the park and go 1 mile to the contact station. Stop here and then continue 0.7 mile to a parking area on the right near the concession stand.**

Ownership: **Virginia Division of State Parks.**

Any outdoor enthusiast, with or without specialized interests in rocks, plants, or birds, will be rewarded by a trip to Westmoreland State Park. Heavily wooded land cut by deep ravines covers most of the park, extending right to the brink of cliffs that loom 150 feet above the Potomac River. The woods are interrupted by a marsh stretching in a wide, wet swath to the broad Potomac, where a small beach links the marsh to the cliffs.

Begin your walk with a detour to the edge of Horsehead Cliffs (**A**) to peer down at the river and scan the lay of the land. Then head down the road past the information center to Big Meadow Interpretive Trail and follow it through the woods. The mixed hardwood forest contains oak, tuliptree, American beech, and red and silver

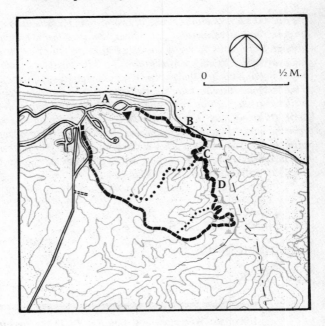

maple trees. Flowering dogwood, spicebush, rhododendron, and mountain laurel decorate the understory with their colorful blossoms, as do a good assortment of spring wildflowers, including three species of orchids. In certain areas, pines, which were planted, dominate.

A left turn at the trail junction will lead you to the small beach (**B**). Depending on the time of year, this is an excellent place to look for waterfowl on the river, ospreys soaring overhead, and songbirds in the woods behind you. Examine the cliffs closely and see how the coursing river rapidly erodes them. Do not walk under the cliff ledges, though; they are very unstable.

The clays, sands, and silts exposed in the many different-colored layers of Horsehead Cliffs date back 5 to 15 million years. At that time a shallow sea extended north and west to what is now the fall line (see **Introduction**), and a subtropical climate prevailed, much like that of northern Florida today. The cliffs formed from sediments that settled to this sea floor. Embedded in them are great numbers of fossils, ranging from tiny marine organisms to remains of the 35-foot-long ancestors of today's baleen whales. Sharks, porpoises, sea cows, and crocodiles also inhabited the sea. Other fossils, though rarely found, indicate that land was close by. An occasional small horse, mastodon, or rhinoceros drowned, drifted out to the sea, and was buried in the accumulating sediments (see **#75**).

Sea level then was higher than it is today. As the climate began to cool some 2 million years ago, great amounts of water became locked in the expanding polar ice caps at the expense of the sea. Sea level dropped lower than the present one; rivers carved deeper and longer valleys. Once the glaciers began to melt about 20,000 years ago, swollen rivers raced to meet the rising sea as it flooded their lower reaches. All this rushing water accelerated erosion and widened the once narrow Potomac River valley. Erosion continues to alter the shape of the land. Horsehead Cliffs are retreating at a rate of about one foot per year as winds, rising out of the northeast and northwest, drive waves destructively against the soft sands and clays, undercutting all that lies above.

Return to the trail junction and bear left on the boardwalk that leads to the marsh observation tower (**C**). Continue on Turkey Neck Trail along the length of Big Meadow (**D**). The marsh seems particularly well named in early spring when the thick, bright green cover of common cattail shoots belies its wetness. The impression of a grassy field is marred only by croaking frogs and their constant splashings. Other freshwater marsh plants here include arrow arum, arrowhead, and pickerelweed. Marsh mallow, jewelweed, and jack-in-the-pulpit add their flowers to the edges of the marsh. Many birds frequent the marsh to feed on the vegetation, search for prey, or peck for insects in the dead trees.

The marsh is very new with respect to geological time. At some time more than 50 years ago, beavers dammed the outlet of this stream. Water spread out behind the dam and eventually filled with enough sediments for the marsh plants to take root (see **#92**). The dam is no longer there, but a constant flow of fresh water from the spring-fed stream maintains the water level. The beach sand deposited by the river currents helps impede the flow of water and prevents the brackish river water from intruding.

The trail proceeds into the woods and loops back to the parking area.

Over a hundred species of birds have been recorded in the numerous habitats of Westmoreland State Park. Among them are diving ducks, such as scaups, canvasbacks, goldeneyes, and buffleheads, which return each fall to winter on the river. Whistling swans, horned grebes, common loons, and Canada geese are also winter residents. Springtime brings horned grebes and common loons followed by migrating warblers, vireos, and other songbirds. In summer, the park receives many visitors, so although a number of species nest here, birding is not at its best. Wild turkeys are permanent residents; osprey rest in the area and are frequently seen (see **#47**). A lucky birder may spot one of the bald eagles, which are present year round. There are now about ten active bald-eagle nests in Westmoreland County (see **#64**).

Remarks: The trail is easy walking on rolling terrain. Allow two hours. Open year-round. A 50¢ parking fee is charged from Memorial Day through Labor Day. Activities include cabin and tent camping, swimming in the pool, naturalist activities, fishing, hiking, and picnicking. There is a boat launch, and paddle boats and rowboats can be rented. Digging in the cliffs and collecting fossils are not allowed. For more information about facilities and seasonal restrictions contact the park at Route 1, Box 53-H, Montross, Va. 22520, (804) 493-8821.

78.
Dragon Run
Swamp

Directions: **Middlesex and Gloucester counties, Va. From Richmond head east about 25 miles on I-64 to Exit 52. Take Route 33 east 19.3 miles. Turn north (left) on U.S. 17; go 1.6 miles to the bridge over the Dragon Run. There is a small public parking area and boat launch to the right of the road beyond the bridge. Allow 4 to 6 hours to paddle downstream to Cypress Shores Campgrounds. To reach the campgrounds by car, go back to the junction of Routes 33 and 198 and U.S. 17; turn left on Route 198. Drive 4.9 miles and turn left into the campgrounds (A).**

Ownership: **The lands bordering the stream are private; do not get out of your canoe.**

The Dragon Run is one of many small streams winding through the Coastal Plain to the Chesapeake. Along the upper reaches it is narrow and clear, shaded by tall trees and edged by thickets of alder and mountain laurel. Downstream it emerges into the broad brown tidal waters of the Piankatank River, and the bottomland forest gives way to marshes of cattail, big cordgrass, and wild rice.

Early spring is an ideal time to canoe this waterway, for water levels are high, making passage over the windfalls easier, the mosquitoes are not biting, and warblers are still easily visible among the shrubs and thickets. Baldcypress, blackgum, sweetgum, and red maple are the principal species along the wooded banks. As early as March, the red maples flower, turning the tops of the trees a misty red. The flowers have lain fully formed within the buds of the tree all winter long. They are released only after being subjected to the winter's cold and the subsequent warming of spring. Both the heat and cold are necessary for flowering to occur. Native species of temperate climates do not do well in tropical climates partly because they require a period of cold; the coming of spring then acts as a signal for the species to put forth new growth.

Another blossom of early spring is the serviceberry or shadbush. The white flowers of this shrub appear when the shad are making

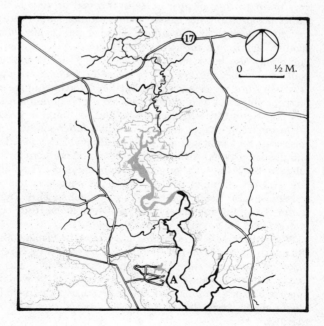

their run up the coastal stream in order to spawn (see #38). The alders along the banks are easily distinguished even before the leaves have come out, for the branches are tipped with tiny cones, which are the female parts of the plant. The male pollen-producing flowers are small delicate wisps of red and yellow. Because the alder has separate cones and flowers, it is a more primitive species than the shadbush, which has male and female parts combined into one flower. Look for brightly colored prothonotary warblers in the low branches of the alder. They arrive from their wintering grounds in April (see #53). Overhead in the treetops look for other insect eaters like the blue-gray gnatcatcher.

Along the riverbank a number of the trees are ringed with the small neat holes of the yellow-bellied sapsucker, a woodpecker that feeds on the nutrient-rich liquids found just under the bark of the tree. This is a wintering ground for the species. Pileated woodpeckers, perhaps the largest American woodpecker still in existence, are common. Look for their oblong or oval holes.

Along the banks, turtles bask in the spring sun, perched one on top of another. A large turtle seen here may be a red-bellied turtle or a species of cooter, though Florida and river cooters are at the very northern edge of their range in this part of Virginia. Smaller turtles are probably the eastern painted turtle. Turtles can be extremely difficult to identify from a distance and equally difficult to capture, sliding into the water well before they are within reach. There may also be water snakes here, which like to bask on the banks and in the branches of shrubs near the water. You may spot a brown or a northern water snake, but don't worry about the poisonous cottonmouth. The northernmost colony of cottonmouth is in the Newport News City Park (see #84) south of the York River. (See #100 on water snakes and turtles.) Two other southern aquatic species are the rainbow snake, with its elegant black and red stripes, and the eastern mud snake, which reaches the northern limits of its range in this vicinity. The primary foods of these species are amphibians and eels. Though not considered an aquatic snake, eastern kingsnakes also frequent the banks of coastal streams. They bask during the spring and fall and are good swimmers. Turtle eggs and water snakes are among their favorite foods.

Where the stream broadens out to become the Piankatank River, the marsh species take over. Because of the tempering effect of the water on the temperature, the marsh stays brown long after shrubs and flowers are blooming in the woods (see #65). The wild rice first appears in April, coming into flower in August. The male flowers bloom about a week before the female flowers. (See #94 on tidal marshes.)

Remarks: *The upper portion of the trip will take 3 to 4 hours depending on your inclination to drift. It is about the same distance from the marshes down to Cypress Shores Campgrounds, where you can take out the boat. Check the tide charts and try to reach the Piankatank with the outgoing tide. You may encounter a stiff headwind once you emerge from the shelter of the trees. Canoe rentals are available in Richmond at Alpine Outfitters, 11010 Midlothian Pike, Richmond, Va.; (804) 794-4172; Blue Ridge Mountain Sports, (804) 740-2887; and Arrow Rent-alls, 2367 Staples Mills Rd., Richmond, Va.; (804) 359-2408. Call Cypress Shores Campgrounds, (804) 693-3792, ahead of time to let them know you want to land at their dock. Other activities include swimming at the campgrounds and fishing for bluegills, rockfish, perch, pike, and sunfish.*

79.
York River
State Park

Directions: **James City County, Va. From Richmond go southeast on I-64 to Exit 54B for Croaker, about 40 miles. Follow Route 607 north 1.2 miles. Turn east (right) on Route 606 and drive 1.5 miles to the entrance to the park on the left. Drive to the visitors' center and park. To reach Croaker Boat Landing continue straight on Route 607 past Route 606 about 3 miles to Route 605. Turn right at the sign to the landing.**

Ownership: **Virginia Division of Parks.**

Steep-plunging ravines, ridges topped with chestnut oak and mountain laurel, and forests with large, splendid trees make York River State Park seem more like the uplands of the Piedmont than part of the flat Coastal Plain. It is an undeveloped area offering hikes on rough trails, canoeing on tidal creeks, and a place to observe songbird migrations in spring and fall.

The soft Coastal Plain sediments, which form the bluffs over the York River and the undulating topography were deposited at the bottom of shallow seas, which stretched far inland, during the late Miocene epoch, 8 to 9 million years ago, and the early Pliocene, 3.5

to 5 million years ago. The flat terrace below the visitors' center was deposited by the ancient York River during the late Pleistocene, several hundred thousand years ago. There followed many cycles of falling and rising sea level (see **Introduction**). During periods of falling sea level, the ocean retreated far to the east and the streams running across the Coastal Plain wore their way down into the soft sediments. Tributaries to the larger rivers also bit deeper and deeper into the plain. As sea level rose again, covering this area once more, sediments accumulated in the ravines and on the river bottom, only to be flushed away when the seas withdrew and the streams again flowed in their channels. Although the bluffs exposed along the York River (**A**) are underlain by fossil-bearing formations, none is visible here due to the leaching away of the calcium in the fossils by acidic groundwater (see **#83**).

The Taskinas Creek Trail begins at the parking lot and passes through open ground scattered with loblolly and Virginia pine. These trees are the first woody plants to move into a cleared area. Now the trail moves into mature upland forest with large well-spaced trees, a sign that this forest has probably been undisturbed for some time.

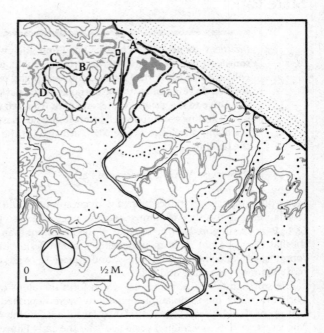

White, northern red, Spanish, black, and chestnut oak grow on the
tops of the ridges together with beeches, tuliptrees, sycamore, and
hickories. Mountain laurel and huckleberry are among the principal
shrubs, but in the shade of the canopy, the forest is quite open and
the shrub layer is thin. The understory is primarily flowering dogwood and American holly. Chestnut oak, mountain laurel, and
huckleberry are not common on the Coastal Plain, being plants of
dry upland soils. The prominence of beeches in the canopy is another indication that this is an older stand; these slow-growing trees
belong to the later successional stage of the forest (see **Introduction**). At one time it was thought that beeches grew only on steep
north-facing slopes in the Coastal Plain; this view is changing as
second-growth stands on old farmlands are allowed to age, rather
than being cut. From recent surveys it is apparent that beech is
becoming a dominant species in mature forests on the Coastal Plain.
This is nicely illustrated at York River State Park.

From the trail there is a good overlook onto Taskinas Creek (**B**),
which meanders from salt marsh at its mouth to freshwater marsh
at its head. Tidal creeks often form meandering patterns; there is no
satisfactory explanation for this. At the border of the creek a boardwalk goes out across the marshes to a hummock (**C**). Salt-marsh
cordgrass marks the intertidal zone, while the high marsh is covered
with salt-meadow cordgrass and big cordgrass (see **#21**). The creek
is still brackish here.

Now the trail turns back toward the high ground. At **D** there is a
fallen tuliptree covered with resurrection fern. This fern is more
common farther south, where it regularly grows on live oaks (see
#53). Its name springs from its ability to wilt during dry weather
and spring back to life with the rain.

The park staff is in the midst of laying out trails on a number of
old logging roads, which are indicated on the map. From most of
these you can strike off into the ravines. One interesting route is into
the upper section of Taskinas Creek. Walk back toward the entrance
to the park. Just before the metal gate there is a field to the west
(right) of the road. Cross the field going west, and once in the woods
on the far side, drop down into the ravine to the north (right). This
ravine will lead you down into the wooded swamp that lies above a
beaver dam at the head of the creek. Vegetation in the ravines is
very different from that of the ridges. Runoff from the hillsides collects; conditions become wetter and wetter as you approach the
swamp. In the upper portion of the ravine look for ferns such as
broad beech, lady, Christmas, and rattlesnake. By the swamp, cinnamon, royal, and marsh fern are common. Lowland trees such as

red maple, sweetgum, and ash replace the oaks of the ridges; in the understory you will find pawpaw and eastern hophornbeam. Spring wildflowers are abundant, ranging from spring beauty, violets, round-lobed hepatica, and wood sorrel in the drier portions to golden club and marsh marigold by the border of the swamp. At the swamp edge turn north (right) and follow the upland edge of the swamp around to the beaver dam, a scramble of 15 minutes through holly and mountain laurel. Then turn east again and scramble back up the ridge and out to the road. The swamp trees are primarily red maple, blackgum, and sweetgum. In spring and summer watch for wood ducks, which nest in the dead trees here. In fall and winter, dabbling ducks also find shelter in the swamp.

Birding along the York River is excellent in winter, for large flocks of diving ducks gather there. Canvasback, goldeneye, ruddy duck, and bufflehead are among the species regularly observed. The up-land woods fill with thrushes, vireos, and warblers during spring and fall migrations. Birds of prey seen around the park include turkey vultures, black vultures, red-shouldered hawks, red-tailed hawks, marsh hawks, and during the summer ospreys along the river. Bald eagles are also sighted regularly.

The best way to see Taskinas Creek is by canoe. Put in at the visitors' center or at Croaker Landing and paddle down the York about 1.5 miles to the creek. Remember that both the York River and the creek are tidal. You can travel up the creek as far as the beaver dam, a good daylong expedition. At the mouth of the creek, you will find salt-marsh cordgrass along the water's edge and on the higher ground extensive patches of salt-meadow cordgrass. Other brackish marsh species such as big cordgrass, salt-marsh bulrush, and Olney three-square are scattered through the marsh. As you move upstream, narrow-leaved cattail and buttonbush, which are less tolerant of salt, begin to grow along the upland border of the marsh where freshwater runoff from the uplands dilutes the brackish water of the creek. Closer to the beaver dam, freshwater marsh species take over. Arrow arum and pickerelweed dominate, followed by cattail and lesser amounts of wild rice, smartweed, and marsh hibiscus (see #94). Long-billed marsh wrens nest in the salt-marsh grasses; sedge wrens are sometimes seen in the fresher marshes during migration and in winter. The transition from brackish water to fresh makes this a good habitat for several rail species, including clapper rail and sora (see #67).

Remarks: *Spring, fall, and winter are the most interesting seasons. Nearest camping is at private campgrounds along Route 607 just outside of Croaker, along I-64, and on Route 31 near Jamestown, and at the New-*

port News City Park (see #84). Canoes can be rented in Richmond at Alpine Outfitters, (804) 794-4172; Blue Ridge Mountains Sports, (804) 740-2887; Arrow Rent-alls, (804) 359-2408 (for addresses see #78). Guided canoe trips are run by park personnel on weekends, no canoe needed. Fishing without license in the York River. Walking can be strenuous on old logging roads and moderately hilly along Taskinas Creek. The Taskinas Creek Trail is about 2 miles long. Further information: York River State Park, Route 4, Box 329F, Williamsburg, Va. 23185, (804) 564-9057.

80.
Jamestown
Island

Directions: James City County, Va. From Richmond, take I-64 southeast to Williamsburg, about 50 miles. Take Exit 57A for the Colonial Parkway to Jamestown. Go 3.6 miles on Route 199 and turn south (left) on the Colonial Parkway. Go 7 miles to the entrance. There is an admission charge of $2. Drive to the visitors' center and park, or follow the paved road in a circuit around the island.

Ownership: Virginia Division of Parks and National Park Service.

The site of the first successful colony in North America is now a quiet preserve of upland ridges forested with pine and oak interspersed with fresh and brackish marshes. It is easy to imagine this island as the colonists first saw it, the trees tall and mighty. Under the canopy little could grow in the melancholy half-light, and the colonists remarked on how open the woods were. They chose Jamestown for their settlement primarily because it was cut off from the mainland and they could defend it. Its topography of ridge and swale extended out into the river, providing a better landing for boats than most of the marshy shoreline of the James.

The island consists of a series of roughly parallel ridges running east to west, two larger ones and several small curving fingers at the southeastern tip. Present-day Jamestown Island is the severely eroded remnant of a descending sequence of beach ridges or point bars.

These were deposited along the inside curve of a meander in the James during the last interglacial period 70,000 to 80,000 years ago (see **Introduction**). The ice sheet had retreated temporarily to the north and the sea was 10 to 20 feet higher than it is today. The James was already an old river, meandering in great curves across the Coastal Plain. Sediments carried by a meandering river tend to be deposited on the inside of a curve, in a beach called a point bar. Why a river begins to meander is a mystery. Once it does however, the flow of the river increases the swing of each curve. This happens because water flowing on the outside of the curve moves more rapidly and therefore has greater cutting power. On the inside of the curve, the current slows, sediments are deposited, and the point bar builds outward. Meanders tend to be associated with older streams. The beach follows the contour of the curve and is slightly higher on the upstream end. That is because the current is slowed most dramatically when it first strikes the curve and therefore drops more of its load of sediment at that point.

As the last ice sheet began to creep south, sea level started to drop again. Over many thousands of years, the sea retreated eastward and the river cut down further into the Coastal Plain. At each stage

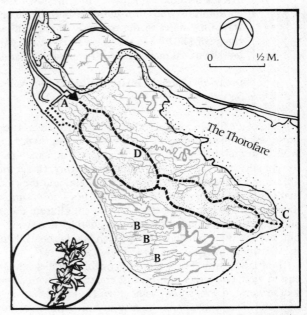

Inset: Pickerelweed

another point bar formed lower than the old one and outside it, so that over time a procession of stepped curved terraces developed along the meanders of the James. Once more, the climate warmed and the ice sheet faded north. Gradually the sea rose and reclaimed much of the river, impeding the flow of the James so that the river spread out along its banks and flooded the lowlands. Between the beach ridges, marshland and tidal creeks developed, augmented by runoff from the ridges. This sequence of events explains a number of "islands" along the James, including Hog Island (see **#82**) and Ragged Island. They are really extensions of the shoreline and not islands at all.

The shape of Jamestown Island has been drastically modified by erosion. From 1607 to 1907, 1800 feet of the western shore have vanished. That is why only the tips of the outer beach ridges remain. Park your car at the visitors' center and go to the site of Newtown (**A**), the first settlement. From there a path leads to the western beach. Follow this for about 1.5 miles to the area known as Goose Hill. You will have to ford Passmore Creek en route. You can walk inland along the ancient beach ridges (**B**) and look down into the low-lying swamps, which are now extensions of the Passmore Creek marsh.

Jamestown Island lies at the very limit of saltwater intrusion. In winter and spring when streams are filled by rain and melted snow, the river is fresh. In summer and fall or after a period of drought, the water becomes brackish; this has led to an interesting mix of freshwater and brackish species. From the ridges (**B**), you can see wild rice, arrow arum, pickerelweed, smartweed, and other freshwater plants. Where Passmore Creek enters the James, big cordgrass is the dominant species. This gradation occurs because in the upper reaches of the creek, the runoff from the higher ground dilutes the slight amount of salt in the water enough for freshwater species to grow (see **#21**).

The park-service road around the island offers several views of the brackish marshes. Stop at Black Point at the eastern tip of the island (**C**). Parking is allowed for short periods of time. A trail leads out to the point. An extensive stand of big cordgrass edges the creek and the river. Where the road passes through the Pitch and Tar Swamp (**D**), the freshwater portion lies to the south of the road. Cattail, common threesquare sedge, arrow arum, and pickerelweed are the main species. To the north of the road, big cordgrass lines the shores of Kingsmill Creek.

The upland forests have been left to themselves for about 50 years. In places loblolly pine still dominates the canopy. Elsewhere a mixture of oaks has become more conspicuous. American holly and persimmon are common understory species.

The river, the marshes, and the upland forest provide a variety of bird habitats. Great numbers of canvasbacks, greater scaups, common goldeneyes, ruddy ducks, and Canada geese collect on the river in fall and winter. Smaller flocks of redheads, ducks that have become rarer and rarer along the East Coast, are regular visitors. In the marshes look for nesting clapper rails and long-billed marsh wrens. Winter residents of the upland woods include brown-headed nuthatches, ruby-crowned and golden-crowned kinglets, and white-throated sparrows. Six species of woodpecker nest in the uplands: yellow-shafted flicker, red-headed, red-bellied, pileated, hairy, and downy. Look for the yellow-breasted chat and the Louisiana waterthrush at the edges of the wooded swamp (**E**). The pine warbler is common throughout the island during breeding season. During the autumn migrations, numerous species of songbirds occasionally congregate on the island before crossing over the river.

Remarks: *There is an active tick population from the first warm weather in March or April to the first frosts in October (see #55). Mosquitoes are abundant. The water in Passmore Creek is about 2 feet deep and 3 to 4 feet wide. Canoeing is not permitted in the creeks of the island, but you may walk anywhere. Activities: The Jamestown and Williamsburg area is excellent for bicycling. Nearest rentals are in Williamsburg, Norfolk, or Richmond. Birding is excellent along the Colonial Parkway. Newport News City Park is close by and offers riding, fishing, golf, hiking, boating as well as camping. There are private campgrounds along Route 31. For further information contact Jamestown Visitor Center, (804) 229-1733.*

81.
Chippokes Plantation
State Park

Directions: **Surry County, Va. From Richmond, take I-64 southeast about 50 miles to Williamsburg. Take Exit 57A for the Colonial Parkway south to Jamestown. Go 3.6 miles on Route 199 and turn south (left) on the Colonial Parkway. Go 7 miles to the park entrance. Turn west (right) just before the toll booth and go 0.2 mile to Route 31. Turn south (left) and drive straight on to the ferry (frequent service, $1). On the far side, drive 4.2 miles (still on Route**

31) into Surry. Turn east (left) on Route 10 and go 1.7 miles. Turn north (left) onto Route 634 and drive 3.6 miles to the park entrance. There is an entrance fee of $1.

Ownership: **Virginia Division of Parks.**

The beach below the old Chippokes Plantation is littered with shells, large gray scallops, pinkish clams, and many others. Many of them are still whole and in perfect condition, making it still harder to fathom that these shells are the fossils of animals that lived in the sea 3.5 to 9 million years ago. Equally awesome and considerably larger are the 400-year-old trees hidden away in a pocket ravine on the park property.

The trail to the beach leads from the mansion through a stand of mature second-growth forest. White oaks, red oaks, American beech, hickories, and tuliptrees predominate. The abundance of young beeches in the understory suggests that this species may become more important as the stand ages (see **#79**). There are unusually large American hollies in the understory, which may be due to an old superstition common among loggers in the area that cutting a holly brings bad luck. Persimmon, pawpaw, and mulberry are also present in the understory. At the bottom of the ravine is a small stand of young baldcypress mixed with ash and sweetgum. Baldcypress once grew extensively in these ravines, but was thoroughly logged. (For discussion of formation of ravines see **#79**.)

The fossil-bearing cliffs at Chippokes are made up of two formations, the older Eastover (St. Mary's) formation and the younger Yorktown above it. The Eastover was laid down in the late Miocene, 8 to 9 million years ago; the Yorktown was deposited during the early Pliocene, approximately 3.5 to 5 million years ago. During these periods a shallow sea covered this portion of Virginia. Although the Eastover contains more iron, both are medium-gray to reddish-brown to tan in color, and it is difficult to tell one from the other. They are commonly differentiated on the basis of the fossilized shells they contain. A large, squarish clamshell *(Isognomon maxillata),* which is shiny and pinkish, with many pearly layers, is characteristic of the Eastover formation. The presence of *Pecten clintonius,* a reddish-brown scallop with a thin shell, identifies the Yorktown.

Remarks: The walk to the beach is an easy twenty minutes. Collecting shells is not permitted here; you may gather them at Rice's Memorial Fossil Pit (see **#83** *for directions). Camping is available at Newport News City Park and at private campgrounds on Routes 5 and 31. Birding at Hog Island (see* **#82***) and along the James. Hiking and bike trails in the park. A variety of activities is available at Newport News City Park (see* **#84***).*

82.
Hog Island Wildlife
Management Area

Directions: **Surry County, Va. From Richmond, take I-64 southeast to Williamsburg to Exit 57A for the Colonial Parkway and Jamestown. Go 3.6 miles on Route 199 and turn south (left) on the Colonial Parkway. Go 7 miles and turn right on Route 359 past Jamestown Festival Park just before the entrance to Jamestown Island. Go 0.3 mile to Route 31, turn south (left), and drive straight on to the car ferry (frequent service, $1). On the south side drive 4.2 miles on Route 31 to Surry and turn east (left) on Route 10. Drive 4.9 miles to Bacons Castle and go left on Route 617. Drive 1.3 miles to Route 650 and go left again. Drive 6.4 miles to the entrance to Hog Island, past the VEPCO sign. Open 8:00 a.m. to sunset.**

Ownership: **Virginia Commission of Game and Inland Fisheries.**

Hog Island is not an island at all but a peninsula of pine-covered ridges and marshy sloughs, formed in the same manner as Jamestown Island across the river (see **#80**). Here, the pockets of tidal lowland have been sealed off to create a series of shallow impoundments in order to attract migratory waterfowl. Battalions of ducks and geese pass through here in fall and winter. In late summer, when the water of the impoundments has been drawn off for crops, shorebirds flock to the mudflats to feed.

Hog Island sits slightly downstream from Jamestown, and its vegetation reflects the higher salinities here. There are no freshwater marshes of cattails and arrow arum. Instead, looking west from the entrance road at **A**, you will see stands of big cordgrass ringed by a fringe of salt-marsh cordgrass. There are also patches of salt-meadow cordgrass and salt-marsh bulrush. Around the impoundments, (**B**) crops are planted to provide additional food for waterfowl, but there is a scattering of big cordgrass as well. This indicates that these were once tidal wetlands.

The several dirt roads at this preserve are laid out on the old beach ridges, built up by dredging and filling operations. Hog Island has

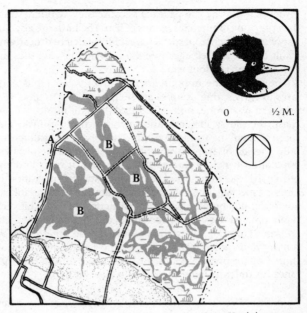

Inset: Hooded merganser

been subject to severe erosion, especially along the western edge, but the ridge-and-swale topography is clear. Stands of loblolly pine line the drier soil of the ridges. Loblolly is the common pioneer species of tree on the coast, which indicates that these woods are younger than the forest at Jamestown, where oaks are numerous and sometimes dominate the canopy (see **Introduction**).

An unusual event occurs in the late spring. Schools of carp find their way into the impoundments through pipes which carry overflow into the James. The shallow, warm water is a favorite spawning ground, and thousands of them roil the water, turning and flashing as they break the surface. After laying up to 2 million eggs each, the fish go back to the river. Carp destroy the eggs and nests of other fish by stirring up the mud as they feed along the bottom.

In late fall and winter look for ring-necked duck, common and hooded mergansers, and other diving ducks clustering in the river. Dabbling ducks use the impoundments and the marshes (see **#64**). The roads provide good views over both the marshes and the river. Snow geese are occasional transients, and for the last several winters a white pelican—a western bird only rarely seen along the East Coast—has visited the area. The species is declining over its range.

Fishermen destroy the pelicans because they wrongly suppose that they prey on commercial species of fish. The birds are also vulnerable to pollutants such as pesticides and chlorinated hydrocarbons, which result in thin-shelled eggs (see **#64**). Many nesting sites have been destroyed by development.

The flats by the impoundments attract water pipits and horned larks in early spring. Rarities are seen from time to time, such as the northern phalarope, normally found in small numbers closer to the coast, the glossy ibis, and the fulvous whistling-duck, a southern species extending its range north. The fulvous whistling-duck is the only species of waterfowl which breeds in all hemispheres, each population widely separated from the next. It nests in dense stands of marsh vegetation. The late summer and fall migration of shore-birds is especially interesting, because both coastal and inland species are found side by side. The lesser (American) golden plover, and the semipalmated, western, white-rumped, stilt, and pectoral sandpipers are most common along the mudflats of the outer coast, while the solitary and spotted sandpipers are most frequently seen along the shores of freshwater ponds farther inland. Birding in the upland pines is similar to Jamestown Island (see **#80**).

Remarks: *There is no fishing in this area because of Kepone contamination. A number of private campgrounds lie along Route 31 on the way to Williamsburg. Activities include hiking at Chippokes Plantation State Park (**#81**) and Jamestown Island (**#80**). Newport News City Park (**#84**) offers a number of activities, as well as camping.*

83.
Cornwallis Cave

Directions: **Yorktown, Va. From Richmond take I-64 south-east about 50 miles to Exit 57B for Route 199 and the Colonial Parkway and Yorktown. Drive 2.1 miles to the parkway and turn east (right). Follow the parkway east about 7 miles to signs for the Yorktown Victory Center. Turn east (left) onto Route 238; continue into Yorktown. Drive under Coleman Bridge and drive 3 blocks to Read St. Turn right and go one block to Main St., turn left and go one block to Comte de Grasse St., turn left again and go one**

block. Turn left on Water St. The parking area for the cave is half a block further on the left.

Ownership: **National Park Service.**

A soft reddish-brown stone called coquina, composed of sand-sized, broken fossil shells, and cemented by calcium carbonate, is exposed at Cornwallis Cave. From the angle of the deposits and the condition of the shells, scientists have worked out the conditions under which this formation was created. Look at the front of the cave and you will see that the material lies in parallel layers that tilt downwards to the northwest. Such a tilt usually signifies that beds of sediment, which were originally horizontal, were subsequently lifted up and tilted by movements within the earth. This is not the case here, and the proof is intriguing. Over the right-hand top corner of the entrance to the cave you may be able to make out the imprint of a long, vertical burrow. (The burrow now stands out in shallow relief, because after it was formed, it was filled in with other sedimentary material, which has eroded more slowly than the surrounding stone.) This burrow was made by a fairy shrimp at the same time as the deposits. If the deposits had been laid down horizontally and then tilted, the burrow would be at an angle too. Here is how the event unfolded. Marine invertebrates, mostly an assortment of mollusks, lived in the shallow waters on an offshore shoal 3 to 4 million years ago. At that time the sea was much higher than its present level and all the Coastal Plain was under water. As the creatures died and disintegrated, their shells were broken up by the action of the surf pounding on the sandbar. The debris was swept across the bar into the quieter, deeper waters on its shoreward side. The bits and pieces of shell and sand settled onto the sloping face of the bar, eventually forming the thick layer of sedimentary deposits exposed at Cornwallis Cave. Sea levels went up and down a great many times during the next several million years. When sea level was lower, the York River carved its way through the deposits, creating the bluff in which the cave is located. The cave itself is man-made.

The red color of the coquina comes from iron oxide. As rainwater falls through the air it picks up molecules of carbon dioxide, and weak carbonic acid begins to form. Then as the water percolates down into the soil, it becomes more acidic as it absorbs more carbon dioxide from decaying organic matter. The acid groundwater dissolves iron from younger deposits on top of the bluffs and carries it downward into the coquina. The acid then dissolves some of the calcium carbonate contained in the shell fragments, which in turn neutralizes some of the acid. As a result some of the iron precipitates, becoming a solid again. Wherever the iron is exposed to air it oxidizes, the same process that creates rust on iron nails left in a damp place. The calcium-rich groundwater descends farther through the formation. As the water evaporates, the calcium carbonate is redeposited as a hard mineral, calcite. Together the iron oxide and the calcite act as weak binders for the sandy sediments. Notice that the material inside the cave where water cannot seep through so readily is much softer and more crumbly than the outer face of the bluff, which carries most of the runoff from the top of the cliffs.

Remarks: *Absolutely no collecting is allowed. If you wish to gather fossils, go to Rice's Memorial Fossil Pit, located in Hampton. Drive southeast on I-64 and take the Mercury Blvd. exit (Route 258) going east. Drive 2.6 miles to Sinclair traffic circle, go three-quarters of the way around it, and head north on N. King St. (Route 278). At the first light turn east (right) onto Fox Hill Rd. (Route 169). After 1.6 miles go northeast (left) onto Harris Creek Rd. The fossil pit is 0.7 miles up the road on the left. It is privately owned, and you must call ahead at least a week in advance to make arrangements. Over 175 species of marine fossils have been found here. Tel. (804) 851-3080.*

84.
Newport News
City Park

Directions: **Newport News, Va. From Richmond, drive southeast on I-64 about 74 miles. Exit onto Route 105 going east and at the first intersection turn north (left) onto Jefferson Ave. Go 0.2 mile to the park entrance on the right. The interpretive center is 0.9 mile down the road on the right. Park here and pick up maps and further information.**

Ownership: **City of Newport News, Department of Parks and Recreation.**

Partially within the Newport News city limits is an 8300-acre park, which is intriguing at any time of year. Surrounded by military installations and urban development, it is a refuge for wildlife, and a variety of orchids, a rich and diverse forest. In summer, cottonmouths bask on fallen logs and along the shores of the swamp at the head of Lee Hall Reservoir. The thick mat of swamp vegetation is pricked with the colors of pink swamp rose, purple swamp loosestrife, and white swamp rose mallow. Under the thick canopy of pines, oaks, and hickories, shrubs are thick and verdant, providing nesting sites for many species of warblers. In winter, the forest looks empty, stark except for the dark, glossy green of hollies. The reservoir becomes a haven for whistling swans, Canada geese, and many sorts of dabbling and diving duck. The swamp trees are bare but misted light green with lichen.

The park is situated on the flat Coastal Plain, underlain by clays, sands, and silts, and drainage here is very poor (see **Introduction**). Much of the park is swampland and is under water in the wet winter season. The soggy conditions have helped protect the area from development; as a result, such sensitive and unusual species as bobcat and river otter are able to live here. The wettest and most impenetrable part of the park is between the Lee Hall Reservoir and the Harwood's Mill Reservoir (**A**). It is in this area that bobcat have been sighted. A system of trails is being completed there, but has not yet been mapped.

There is a well-marked self-guiding nature trail, 6.5 miles long,

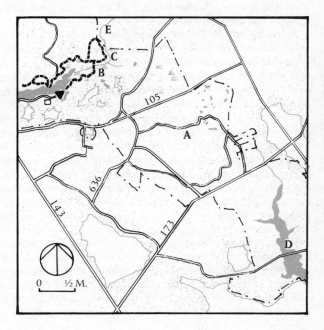

which begins by the Interpretive Center and leads through second-growth upland forest, lowland forest, and swamp. The swamp bridge (**B**) provides an excellent view into the swamp. Because this is a reservoir, the water level in the swamp fluctuates enormously. In winter most of the swamp is under water; in summer only the middle area is flooded. White ash and red maple dominate the canopy at the wet edges of the swamp. Farther out in the water, smaller trees and shrubs like red-osier dogwood, hazel alder, and buttonbush predominate. Black willow, a species which tends to follow the dogwood and the alder in succession, is becoming prominent in the swamp. It grows taller along the edges of the swamp, where conditions are less harsh (see **#95**). Willow oak, which also grows here, is found both in the successional swamp forest and in the climax forest. In winter, the only green in the swamp is the lichen that grows on the trunks of trees and shrubs down to the high-water mark; lichens thrive in wet conditions but cannot survive if flooded. Great clumps of mistletoe stand out in the bare tops of the trees (see **#100**). In spring and summer, growth explodes in the swamp. The deep, open water is hidden beneath a mat of smartweed, swamp loosestrife, beggartick sunflower, and arrow arum, all providing food for the wood ducks that nest in seclusion in the trees. To the northeast of the swamp bridge lies one of the largest great blue heron rookeries in the southeast (**C**) (see **#37**).

This park has the northernmost colony of the poisonous eastern cottonmouth; the snakes winter in underground nests on the high ground close to the swamp. As the weather warms, the snakes begin to make their way to the water and are often seen crossing paths near the bridge. When they bask motionless in the summer sun, their camouflage can make them almost invisible (see **#100**). Until this population was discovered, it was thought that the cottonmouth came no farther north than the James River. Other water snakes you may see are the red-bellied, the northern, and the brown, none of which are poisonous. Twenty-four species of snake have been sighted here, but most are shy and well concealed by their camouflage, and it is unlikely that you will see them. Northern copperheads dwell in the northern wooded sections of the park, and the canebrake rattlesnake, an endangered species, is fairly common in the lowlands above Harwood's Mill Reservoir (**D**); both are poisonous.

The abundance of shallow water, small pools, and streams makes this an ideal habitat for many amphibians and turtles. Twenty-eight species of salamanders, frogs, and toads have been identified. They are most active during the breeding season, from mid-March to mid-April. On warm, wet early spring nights the salamanders make their way to small pools in the forest to deposit their egg masses, which are clearly visible in the water.

Turtles are also abundant, particularly in the swamp. Several varieties of cooters and sliders—large turtles that are difficult to tell apart—lie on a log or bank and absorb the sun's heat. Many even lie on top of one another. These species are very shy and will disappear as soon as you are in sight. The red-eared turtle, once a common pet, is well to the east of its usual range, having been established here by the releasing of pets. The red-eared is one of the few which can easily be identified, as it usually has a conspicuous patch of red where its ear ought to be. The species is thriving in the slow, muddy waters of the swamp. Other species of turtles like the stinkpot, mud, and spotted turtles are not so shy and can be approached more easily (see **#100**).

Back along the edges of the swamp and in low spots throughout the woods are stands of climax lowland forest (see **Introduction**). Red maple, white and green ash, sycamore, water and willow oaks, and swamp chestnut oaks form the canopy. The shrub layer is sparse, dominated by blueberries and wax myrtle. Even on the low relief of the Coastal Plain there are upland areas where pines and oaks and hickories dominate the canopy. Some of the high ground was artificially created during the Civil War, when this whole area was fortified for the Peninsula Campaign. Old earthworks appear all along the nature trail. These upland stands are in transition. Large old loblolly and Virginia pine are surrounded by white oak, southern red or Spanish oak, post oak, and others. Just below them and now reaching the canopy are several species of hickory—mockernut, pignut, and bitternut. The climax forest here will probably be oak-hickory for the oaks are reproducing. An example of the climax woods can be seen at the bridge over Beaver Dam Creek (**E**). This tall stand of oaks and hickories was left to grow because it was inaccessible. Scattered here and there are remnants of the pioneer species, redcedar and black cherry, which first moved into the open fields. There are many other, less abundant species: clusters of beech, American elm, slippery elm, sugar maple, red mulberry, and others. The understory is filled with American holly and a scattering of common smaller trees, including dogwood, hornbeam, sourwood, redbay, persimmon, pawpaw, and sassafras. The shrub layer is dominated by many species of blueberry and huckleberry throughout the forest, along with spicebushes and beautyberry. The exuberant growth in these woods reflects the clement conditions: a warm climate, abundant moisture, and a slightly acidic soil. Compare this site with the New Jersey Pine Barrens or with hemlock forests to the north.

The woods show their richness in spring, when dozens of flowers bloom in them. Bloodroot blossoms early, sometimes in February. A little later one can see the flowers of pink lady's slipper, showy orchis, two-flowered solomon's seal, spiderwort, mayapple, and many others scattered throughout the woods. Displays of spring flowers are common in rich deciduous woods: blooming occurs when the trees are just beginning to leaf, and ample sunlight can reach the forest floor. In summer there are a variety of orchids. Look for cranefly orchid, nodding ladies' tresses, downy rattlesnake plantain, and the yellow or orange fringed orchis throughout the woods in both moist and drier sites. In the winter, the dark-green leaves of the rattlesnake plantain, delicately striped with white, stand out against the dead leaves on the forest floor, along with the smaller spotted wintergreen and brighter patches of Christmas fern.

The park lies between two large rivers on the Atlantic flyway. Throughout the year, it offers ample food in the midst of a developed area, and the elbow-shaped Lee Hall Reservoir provides protection from the winds. These factors make the park a fine refuge for birds. Nearly two hundred species have been recorded. Warbler flights are outstanding in the spring; about 20 species breed here while another 14 pass through the area en route to northern nesting grounds. Winter birding offers a great variety of waterfowl, including flocks of whistling swans, common loons, horned and pied-billed grebes, and a large assortment of both diving and dabbling ducks (see **#64**). Calm water can always be found on the reservoir, despite shifting winds—in winter when the winds are often from the northeast, the eastern arm is still; when the wind swings to the northwest or west, the southern arm remains calm.

Remarks: *There are a great many activities. With a license you can fish in the reservoir for largemouth bass, bluegill, chain pickerel, northern pike, white and yellow perch, and others. Boats and canoes are available for rent and a totally aquatic self-guiding canoe trail is under construction at the Lee Hall Reservoir. There is a bike trail with rental bikes available, and about 50 miles of hiking trails on easy terrain. A sensory nature trail specifically designed for the sight-handicapped begins and ends at the Interpretive Center. There are two golf courses. Camping is also available, year round. For further information contact Newport News City Park, 13564 Jefferson Ave., Newport News, Va. 23603, (804) 877-5211. Nature Center: (804) 877-7411.*

85.

Northend Point
Natural Preserve

Directions: City of Hampton, Va. From Richmond take I-64 about 70 miles southeast to the exit for Mercury Blvd. (Route 258) north. Go 2.3 miles and turn north (left) onto Fox Hill Rd. (Route 169). Drive 2.9 miles and bear left onto Beach Rd. Continue on 2.7 miles and make a left on the State Park Dr. Park by the entrance gate. Walk 0.5 mile to the beach. From here to the end of the point is about 2 miles.

Ownership: Virginia Division of Parks.

Like a crooked finger, Northend Point curves around to the west away from the Chesapeake Bay. At low tide, dilapidated bits of marsh peat are uncovered in the shallow water by the shore. There are old stumps of trees as well, evidence of the continuing retreat of the Atlantic shoreline over the last 15,000 years or so. Birding is good along the bay side and in the marshes to the west of the spit.

The point is a remnant of a barrier island system which formed within the Chesapeake Bay from tons of material which had been eroded off the mainland. These islands acted in the same way as the coastal barrier islands, retreating westward as the level of the sea and the bay rose. (see **Introduction** and **#55**). South of Northend Point at Grandview, there is no sign of this barrier system. It has been incorporated into the beach of the mainland. Only at the northern and southern ends of this beach do traces of the barriers remain as spits. The spit at Northend is migrating rapidly westward, about 10 feet per year. This is in part because of rising sea level, but more as a result of attempts to stabilize the beaches to the south by the construction of groins (stone piers) and seawalls. This has choked off the supply of sand which was once carried north by the longshore current and deposited along the spit (see **#25**).

The traces of marsh and forest may well be thousands of years old. The tree stumps are remnants of an upland forest that stood in back of the active shoreline. As sea level mounted, the forest drowned and became marsh sheltered behind the barrier islands. The sea

257

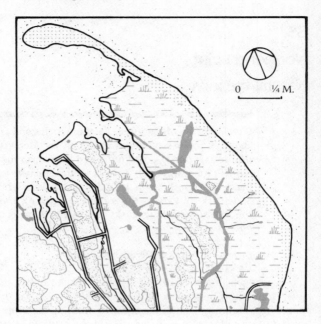

continued to rise, sweeping the sandy barrier before it until both the old forest and the marsh were buried in sand. Now the line of the beach has migrated far enough to the west to uncover these fragments of an earlier time.

With the bay to the east and the marsh to the west, and two miles of relatively undisturbed beach, Northend Point provides refuge for a variety of birds. There is a large nesting colony of least tern here in the summer. Scattered among them are usually several pairs of piping plovers. Both of these species have very vulnerable nests; be especially careful at this time of year (see **#30**). Common gallinules, which are uncommon in Virginia, nest in the marshes. Most varieties of dabbling and diving duck can be seen here in fall and winter. Brant, a species of goose more common along the Atlantic shore, is often seen here. Other more unusual winter visitors include snow buntings, pipits, and fox sparrows. Spring, late summer, and early fall bring shorebirds in numbers along the beach and in the marsh.

Remarks: *Camping at Newport News City Park, which also offers a wide variety of activities, including many miles of hiking trails (see* **#84**).

86.

Ragged Island
Wildlife Management Area

Directions: **Isle of Wight County, Va. From Richmond take I-64 southeast to Hampton, about 70 miles. Take the exit for U.S. 258 (Mercury Blvd.) and U.S. 17 going south over the James River Bridge. Just 0.3 miles beyond the south end of the bridge, turn left into a dirt parking area marked with a sign for Ragged Island Wildlife Management Area.**

Ownership: **Virginia Commission of Game and Inland Fisheries.**

Downriver from the span of the James River Bridge, Ragged Island lies in a curving sequence of narrow, wooded strips of land and tidal creeks. Like Hog Island and Jamestown farther upstream, the island is made up of a series of stepped beach ridges, formed as the James meandered through the Coastal Plain 70,000 to 80,000 years ago (see **#80**). At Ragged Island the arching shape of the inner curve of the meander is still visible, for erosion has not been as severe here as at Jamestown. The downstream sections of the ridges have disappeared, drowned by the rising sea.

A rough trail leads from the parking lot (**A**) eastward along one of the old beach ridges. In winter, when the area is dry, you can walk just about to the end, about 2 miles. The island is forested with loblolly and a mixture of red maple, sweetgum, and various oaks. Holly is the prominent understory species and wax myrtle the common shrub. Numerous vines of greenbrier and poison ivy make the undergrowth impenetrable in places. All of the islands along the James have been cut over so many times that the usual process of succession has been disrupted and is rather confused. Loblolly pines are the pioneer species. Generally, they are followed by oaks and red maples, but it is still too early to tell what the climax forest will be. These woods are inhabited by white-tailed deer, raccoons, red foxes, and gray squirrels.

The Virginia Ornithological Society has not yet finished compiling information about birds at Ragged Island, but the woodland species should be those found on Hog Island (**#82**) and Jamestown Island (**#80**), since the habitats are similar.

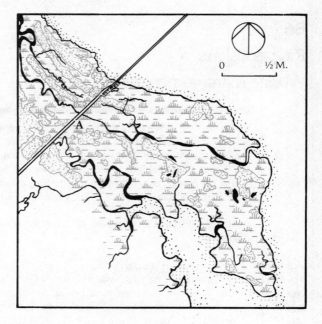

From the ridge trail, smaller paths lead out onto the marsh along Cooper Creek. These are salt marshes, for the island lies close to the mouth of the James and the Chesapeake Bay. Salt-marsh cordgrass lines the creek, while higher in the marsh above the intertidal zone, black needlerush is the dominant species. Smaller stands of salt-meadow cordgrass and salt grass also occur (see **#21** for the devlopment of salt marsh). Black needlerush remains erect throughout the winter, because it contains substantial amounts of cellulose, more than other marsh grasses, which collapse in late winter. Because of its durability, needlerush resists erosion well. It serves as valuable cover for waterfowl and marsh birds but provides little food. Muskrats, which are common at Jamestown, are not found here because conditions are too salty. The marshes are full of dabbling ducks in the fall. The island is heavily hunted, so visit only on Sundays during the season from mid-November to the first week in January. In spring look for clapper and king rails and herons and egrets.

Remarks: *Warm weather is tick-and-mosquito season. No fishing due to Kepone contamination. Camping and many activities at Newport News City Park. (see* **#84***).*

87.

Craney Island

Directions: **From Richmond take I-64 southeast about 95 miles to Norfolk. Take I-264 southwest about 9 miles. On U.S. 17 go 3 miles west to Cedar Lane and turn north (right). Look for a large nursery on the right at the corner. There is a sign for Craney Island. Go 1.8 miles to River Shore Rd. and turn left. Go 0.9 mile and turn right onto Hedgerow Lane. At the fork, bear left into the facility. Craney Island is open on weekdays, 8:00 a.m. to 4:00 p.m. Sign in at the office when you enter. Follow the dirt road that circles the impoundment, stopping often to scan the shallow water and mud flats.**

Ownership: **U.S. Army Corps of Engineers.**

The flats at Craney Island are man-made, but they have become a collecting point for migrating shorebirds and waterfowl that is famous among Virginia birders. According to the Virginia Ornithological Society, this is the best place in the state to see American avocets (see #22). Several species of shorebirds uncommon to the Atlantic Coast are regular visitors during migration. They include Wilson's phalarope, the stilt sandpiper (seen mostly in late summer and fall), and the white-rumped sandpiper. Wilson's phalarope is the most terrestrial of the phalaropes. While sitting on shallow water, the bird spins in rapid circles to stir up food from the bottom. Least tern and piping plover nest here (see #30). In winter, great numbers of waterfowl settle in, and Lapland longspur, snow bunting, glaucous gull, purple sandpiper, and short-eared owl are regular visitors.

Remarks: *May and July through September are peak months for shorebirds.*

88.
Seashore
State Park

Directions: **Virginia Beach, Va. From Richmond, take I-64 southeast toward Norfolk. About 90 miles from Richmond the road crosses the Hampton Roads Bridge and Tunnel. At the southern end take U.S. 60 east 16.5 miles to Seashore State Park. Turn right and park at the visitors' center.**

Ownership: **Virginia Division of Parks.**

Pockets of cypress swamp shrouded in Spanish moss, open beach and dunes, a towering ancient dune, salt marsh, and old dune forest lie side by side on the tip of Cape Henry. Bird and animal life are as varied as the habitats. To the north the Chesapeake Bay forms a formidable barrier, and some species of plants and animals apparently reach their northern boundary at the cape. Throughout the year this is a place of great beauty in the midst of dense development.

During the time of the last glacier, the present shape of Cape Henry began to develop. Over thousands of years, ocean currents carrying sand northward along the coast deposited their burden at the tip of the cape (see **#25**). Winds sweeping in from the sea built up lines of dunes, which migrated inland as the cape grew out into the bay. Land plants gradually grew out over the bare sand (see **#7**). Swamps and marshes formed in the damp hollows behind the dunes. The vegetation of the cape has been logged, grazed, and burned so often since the colonists arrived 300 years ago that the stages of succession are extremely tangled. The coastline continues to evolve even today as sand is swept by the tides and the longshore current (see **#25**) off the ocean beach (**A**) and deposited on the bay side (**B**).

Just behind the visitors' center is a network of trails, all of which lead through the old dunes habitat. Walking along the Bald Cypress Nature Trail (**C**), you pass through small swamp pools held between the old dunes. Created by the high water table, the swamp ponds are a breeding ground for many species of amphibians and a home for a variety of reptiles. This is one of the northernmost coastal locations for the poisonous eastern cottonmouth. The northern and

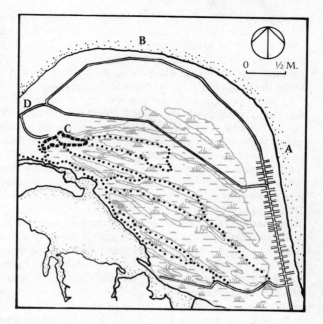

the red-bellied water snake are seen regularly. Chicken turtles were abundant in the park during the 1960s and 1970s but have now almost disappeared. As the nearest population of chicken turtles is 75 miles farther south at Mattamuskeet, N.C., their presence, however limited, at Cape Henry is surprising. Someone may have released several turtles here, which multiplied and flourished for a time before dwindling off. Many of the amphibians here have acquired a protective coloring that is darker than normal to match the dark tannin-rich waters of the swamp. (The same species found in a spring-fed clear pond would be considerably lighter.) Being so dependent on water for their life cycle, these creatures are very sensitive to changes in rainfall. During periods of drought such as that of 1980 and 1981, the numbers of amphibians decline dramatically. Then, as rainfall picks up, as it did in the winter of 1981/82, the amphibians quickly come back.

The vegetation of the swamp is similar to that of cypress swamps farther north (see **#73**) with one obvious difference—the gray-green trailers of Spanish moss, here at its northern limit. The moss is not a moss at all but an epiphyte, a plant that draws nutrients and water from the surrounding air. The tree is merely a resting place for the plant, not a source of food. The plant does, however, obtain some nutrients from rainwater, which picks up organic materials as it trickles down the trunk. Scientists do not fully understand how the plant is able to absorb nutrients from the air, but it is clear that air pollution interferes with this process. As a result, Spanish moss is vanishing from many of its former habitats.

In and around the swamp you can expect to see many birds, especially during the spring and fall migrations. Pileated woodpeckers are common and wetland warblers such as the hooded, Kentucky, prothonotary, yellow-breasted chat, and Louisiana waterthrush can be found in spring and fall.

On the ridges that cross the swamps the vegetation is very different. Varying mixtures of loblolly pine, Virginia pine, pignut hickory, white, post, and southern red oak reflect varying successional stages. The trees grow most vigorously along the base of the slopes, where more moisture is available. In the understory look for American holly, sweetbay, and osmanthus or devilwood—a southern evergreen which is also at its northern limit here. In spring and summer the ridges are thick with flowering shrubs, vines, and herbs. This is botanically the richest habitat of the area because it has the kindest conditions. There is no salt to contend with and no oxygen-poor water.

Across the northeastern boundary of the park runs the Great Dune, in some places as high as 50 feet. From post-colonial times until quite recently, it was nearly bare of vegetation. Although scientists are not sure why, islands of vegetation appeared and now cover most of the dune. Wax myrtle, bluejack oak, and other southern species dominate these islands. A similar dune exists along the outer banks of North Carolina. Both dunes probably formed in the same manner as the other dunes on the cape, but for some reason they became both higher and steeper. Precisely how these escarpments were formed, though, remains a mystery.

Opposite the entrance to the park is a road to the beach and the campgrounds (**D**). In summer, access to the beach is limited to overnight campers. Here the transition from open beach to back-dune forest parallels that of the barrier beaches to the north (see **#7**). On this southern beach, however, sea oats are more important than American beach grass in holding and building the dunes. Southern trees such as live oak, bluejack oak, and persimmon are more numerous than black cherry, which is a dominant species farther north. Bayberry is replaced by wax myrtle as the most common shrub. This is an excellent place to see the fall hawk migrations: raptors follow the seacoast of the Delmarva Peninsula, cross the Chesapeake Bay, and fly right over Cape Henry. Porpoises and dolphins out in the bay are frequently visible from the shore. Four species show up in these waters: Atlantic bottlenose dolphin, longbeak dolphin, common dolphin, Atlantic harbor porpoise. Large sea turtles occasionally wash up, dead, along the shore. During the summer, they feed far up the bay and with the return of colder weather make their way south again toward warmer southern waters.

Remarks: *Walking is easy. Changes in elevation are minor. The more than 22 miles of trails are open all year round from 8:00 a.m. to dusk. Poisonous snakes are present but rarely encountered. Summer can be hot and buggy, and the traffic to and from the beaches is heavy. Camping facilities are available from spring through fall. For more information contact Seashore State Park, 2500 Shore Drive, Virginia Beach, Va., 23451, (804) 481-2131, or the visitors' center, (804) 481-4836. Boats can be launched in spring, summer, and fall from a pier reached by driving further south on U.S. 60 to 64th St. and turning right. There is fishing in Broad Bay, no license required. From Memorial Day weekend to Labor Day weekend a parking fee is charged. Bicycles are allowed along the main trail and on the paved roads in the park.*

89.
Suitland Bog

Directions: **Prince Georges County, Md. Located off Suitland Rd., about 1 mile west of the Capital Beltway. See Remarks.**

Ownership: **Maryland–National Capital Parks and Planning Commission, and Prince Georges County Department of Parks and Recreation.**

Some thirty bogs once dotted the area around Washington, D.C. Due to urban expansion over the past 75 years, only the tiny quarter-acre Suitland Bog remains. Here one can find carnivorous pitcher plants, which were introduced in the 1930s, and sundews, as well as other plants unusual for this area, including bog club moss, dwarf huckleberry, swamp azalea, and swamp magnolias. Over 225 species have been identified in and around the bog. A boardwalk has been built to protect these plants from trampling feet.

Carnivorous plants trap and digest insects to obtain nitrogen lacking in the soil. The pitcher plant's wide tubular leaves open upward and collect rainwater. Nectar glands along the rim and the red markings of the leaves attract insects. Downward-pointing bristles lining the mouths of the pitcherlike leaves prevent the unsuspecting insects which have fallen into this pitfall trap from escaping. The insects drown in a solution of rainwater and plant-secreted enzymes, which digest them.

A unique environment exists within these "pitchers." Here, the pitcher-plant mosquito, a nonbiting variety, thrives on the nutrients provided by the decomposing insects. Biologists believe that this mosquito survives by producing a substance that counteracts the digestive enzymes of the pitcher plant. Sharing this habitat are two other insects: a species of midge and a species of mite. In winter, the evergreen leaves of the perennial pitcher plant persist. The water in the pitchers often freezes solid, apparently causing no harm to the plants or to the inhabiting insects, which spend the winter in an inactive larval or pupal stage.

Two varieties of sundews are found here: the thread-leaved and the intermediate- or spatulate-leaved. These plants use a different method of capture—the flypaper trap. Red, gland-tipped, hairlike tentacles cover the leaves, exuding sticky droplets of fluid that gleam like dewdrops (hence the name). Small insects thus attracted find themselves stuck. Nearby tentacles curve around the prey, helping to secure it. As with the pitcher plant, digestive enzymes break down the insects into amino acids which are absorbed by the plant.

Water-tolerant trees and shrubs, such as alder and red maple, are gradually encroaching on the bog. Eventually their shade would probably cause the sphagnum mat and other specialized bog plants to die out. Because of this, they are selectively cleared to help slow the process of forest encroachment. Siltation resulting from nearby development has smothered much of the original bog; sediments from an unused sand and gravel pit and from the nearby housing development have filled in much of the western portion of the bog. The sedimentation problem is now under control. Though much reduced, Suitland Bog persists and is likely to do so as long as it receives an adequate supply of water. The Maryland–National Capital Parks and Planning Commission owns 20 acres of land surrounding and including the bog, so the immediate area will remain undeveloped. This buffer zone should allow the continued infiltration of rainwater to the water table, which is necessary to prolong the life of the bog.

Remarks: *In order to visit the Suitland Bog, you must make an appointment with the Clearwater Nature Center, 11000 Thrift Rd., Clinton, Md. 20735, (301) 297-4573. The best time to go is in late spring when the plants are in bloom.*

90.

Huntley Meadows Park

Directions: **Fairfax County, Va. Take the Capital Beltway to Exit A for U.S. 1. Go south for 3.5 miles. Turn right at the light onto Lockheed Blvd. Take the third turn to the left at Harrison Lane, where the park entrance is located.**

Ownership: **Fairfax County Park Authority.**

Huntley Meadows Park is a large, 1262-acre natural area of wetlands and woodlands in suburban Washington, D.C. Beginning in March, frogs sing in loud chorus for about six weeks. Marsh plants bloom in mid-June, creating a carpet of pink and white. In September, the park's meadows are vibrant with acres of yellow tickseed sunflowers, which are unusually abundant here. A trail and boardwalk lead into the marsh, crossing indistinct boundaries between two types of hardwood forests and a hardwood swamp. An observation tower in the marsh provides a good vantage point for the entire area.

An immature forest, dominated by red maple and Virginia pine, covers the northern section of the park. Farther along, the trail swings through the southern portion of the park where the forest is older, composed mostly of oaks (white, red, willow, and pin, among others). The sparseness of the understory, characterized by highbush blueberries and a few wildflowers, may be due to the dampness and poor soil. The northern forest was cleared for farming as recently as the 1940s, but this section, some 25 feet lower and wetter, was not as suitable for farming and has not been cut for the past 100 years. The boardwalk circles through the wetlands, passing into hardwood swamp en route to the marsh. Red maples, sweetgums, and black willows grow in the swamp, while the marsh is dominated by swamp rose, buttonbush, and cattails.

Huntley Meadows Park lies in what was once a meander of the Potomac River, which now flows 3 miles to the east. (See **#80** for more on stream meanders.) This area is flatter and lower than the land to the north and west. Beneath the surface are marine clays, whose particles pack down easily into an impermeable hardpan through which little water seeps. These factors lead to standing water and the creation of marshes and swamps. The water level has been rising in recent years due to the activities of resident beavers (see **#92**). At the time of this writing, four beaver lodges were located near the observation tower, with six additional ones elsewhere in the park. Drainage from nearby subdivisions also adds to the water level.

The bird population is quite varied. Permanent residents, such as red-shouldered and red-tailed hawks, live in the woods along with great horned and barred owls. Over fifty species of birds nest here. These include a number of warblers, wood ducks, mallards, and woodcocks, whose flight displays begin in early spring (see #60). Large flights of warblers, thrushes, and vireos migrate through the area during springtime. Wading birds, such as green herons and sora rails, breed here. Some, like great blue herons are regular visitors to the marsh, while snowy egrets are seen only occasionally.

Among the interesting inhabitants of Huntley Meadows are the many frogs and toads that, although difficult to see at times, make their presence known in springtime. The males fill the air with mating songs that declare their territories and attract females. Each of the ten species of frogs and toads found here has its own distinctive sound, ranging from the tiny 1-inch spring peeper's loud shrill whistle to the resounding croak of the 3-pound bullfrog. Air is pushed back and forth between the lungs and closed mouths, inflating the one or two vocal sacs that serve as resonating chambers that amplify the sound. Temperature and rainfall affect the volume of frog songs, some of which can be heard up to a mile away. Optimum temperatures are between 55° and 70° F, and increased rainfall seems to stimulate mating instincts. Primarily nocturnal creatures, frogs generally sing from dusk until midnight.

These amphibians begin their life in water, hatching from eggs into tadpoles. This stage may last several weeks or several years, after which they become land-based adults, exchanging their gills for lungs while retaining the ability to respire through their skin. Throughout the early stages of their life cycles, frogs and toads are highly vulnerable to predators. Because most of the young do not reach maturity, thousands of eggs are laid by each female to increase chances of survival. The American toad may lay up to 12,000 eggs at one time. A slippery gelatinous mass surrounds the eggs, and provides some protection. Tadpoles are nearly defenseless; they can only swim from danger. Those that survive into adulthood acquire camouflage coloring, blending into the soil, leaves, or dappled sunlight of their environments. Toads have special skin glands that secrete poisonous substances, another protective adaptation. These glands form the "warts" of toads, which, contrary to popular notion, are not transferable to humans. The secretions, however, are irritating to people as well as to predators. Skunks and some snakes can eat toads, after rolling the prey around until all the poison has been released. Frogs, though, are eaten by other animals, particularly birds and snakes. Frogs and toads react to danger by running away, or by playing dead, then leaping off at the first chance of escape. Some burrow into the soil, leaving only the hard tops of their heads exposed, or inflate themselves into fierce-looking objects too wide for swallowing. When annoyed or scared, they open their mouths wide and scream.

Frogs and toads are very sensitive to environment. All amphibians absorb both water and oxygen through their moist skins. Direct sunlight must be avoided; if the skin dries out, the animal will suffocate. They are cold-blooded animals; their circulation and respiration rates depend on the temperature, slowing as the air cools, increasing with rising temperatures. They survive the cold better than heat: temperatures over 105° F kill them, but below 50° F they merely crawl into burrows to sleep. In winter, these dormant creatures are often trapped in frozen mud or water. They can recover if their protoplasm doesn't freeze, even though their vital processes may have stopped. Never at an advantage either in water or on land, yet limited to the interface between these two habitats, it is no wonder that these animals have never dominated. Few fossils of amphibians have been found. Today amphibians are numerically outclassed: fish have eight times as many species, reptiles four, and birds ten.

Remarks: *The best time to listen to and look for frogs and toads is in April at dusk. An annual evening "frog romp" is led by park staff; contact the park for details. The park has 3 miles of trails and a visitors' center. Maps can be obtained from the park: 3701 Lockheed Blvd., Alexandria, Va. 22310, (703) 768-2525, 8:30 to 5:00 daily.*

91.

Dyke Marsh

Directions: **Fairfax County, Va. From Washington, D.C., take the George Washington Memorial Parkway south through Alexandria. Cross over Hunting Creek, just south of town, and continue less than a mile to the Belle Haven Picnic Area. Turn east (left) into the picnic area and park in the lot on the right. Walk south along the road toward the Belle Haven Marina to the dirt trail heading off to the right, marked by a sign: Dyke Marsh Wildlife Habitat.**

Ownership: **National Park Service.**

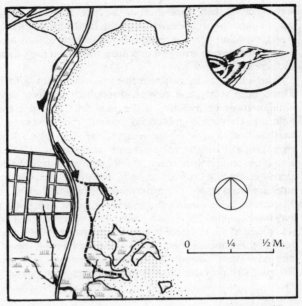

Inset: Least bittern

Dyke Marsh is one of the prime birding spots near Washington, D.C. A multitude of land and water birds inhabit or visit the marsh and its environs year round; over 250 species have been counted. The food and shelter offered by the river, marsh, swampy woodlands, and the ecotones where these habitats meet combine to attract this wealth of birdlife.

The trail passes alongside a stretch of swampy bottomland woods before emerging into the marsh. Willow oak, river birch, pumpkin ash, and scattered pines are among the trees able to tolerate the wet conditions (see **#95**). Tangles of wild grape and bittersweet vines dominate the understory.

Dyke Marsh is a freshwater marsh with a tidal range of 3 feet. In summer, it becomes a prairie of narrowleaf cattails, sturdy plants that have successfully competed against other common marsh species, such as sweetflag and spatterdock. Arrow arum, pickerelweed, and wild rice grow in the tidal guts. Wild rice was abundant along the Potomac prior to the 1920s, but died out because of poor water quality. Recent attempts at revegetation have been only moderately successful (see **#72**). Cattail, a hardier plant, quickly fills in vacancies. Phragmites, prevalent throughout the East Coast marshes, is also present. Both yellow and blue varieties of wild iris, tickseed sunflower, rose mallow, and Pennsylvania bittersweet color the marsh and its edges at different times from spring through fall.

This lush marsh was severely disturbed during the 1950s, when much of it was mined by a sand and gravel company. Earlier, the marsh was nearly 50 percent larger than its present 240 acres. The wetlands were restored by the National Park Service after the dredging in order to create this mini-wilderness. Isolated patches of red maple and river birch stand on islands of higher ground in the marsh. The road that leads out into the marsh was created by the dumping of subway construction diggings.

The muddy point at the road's end is drowned by each high tide. In the middle of the raised area are trees cut by beavers and a muskrat house of sticks. Over thirty species of reptiles and amphibians reside in the marsh, along with a handful of common, small mammals.

Birds abound, but the time of year, the time of day, and chance all influence which species you are likely to see. Less than 15 percent of the species found here are permanent residents. Many more winter here, and others breed or visit in summer, but the vast majority are those that stop briefly, on spring and fall migration flights. Among the birds that winter here are sparrows, several species of hawks, and a variety of waterfowl. Saw-whet owls, common red-polls, and black-capped chickadees at the wood's edge and short-eared owls hunting over the marsh are occasionally sighted. Common summer breeders include least bitterns and long-billed marsh wrens, as well as the resident black ducks and mallards. Less abundant are the green herons, Canada geese, and common gallinules that also breed in the marsh. King rails are rare and apparently no longer breed here, but Virginia rails are somewhat more common. During spring and fall, Dyke Marsh is inundated by all kinds of migrating birds— waterbirds, shorebirds, and landbirds. More than 30 species of warblers have been counted, along with numerous vireos, thrushes, and flycatchers.

These are but a sampling of the rich birdlife that the marsh harbors. The casual birder will enjoy glimpses of birds in flight and snatches of song, while the persistent visitor, armed with binoculars, may be rewarded by sightings of vagrant birds not usually seen at Dyke Marsh.

Remarks: *The trail is short, about 0.5 mile long. The above description concerns only the northern part of Dyke Marsh; another 80 to 100 acres of marsh lie farther south. That area can be explored by canoe or by bushwacking through the swampy woods. The southern woods and marsh are more accessible from the bike path that parallels the highway. About 0.8 mile south of the parking area, the bike path crosses Hog Island Gut, and the bridge there provides a wide view of the marsh. When frozen in winter, the marsh can be explored on foot from here. Another birding area is along the river, from the picnic area north to Hunting Creek, particularly at low tide. Keep watch for the many ducks, gulls, terns, herons, and other species that frequent the river and its shores, during fall, winter, and spring.*

Nearby Places of Interest

Any of the pulloffs along the highway should be profitable for viewing waterfowl in winter. Noteworthy among the many birding places along the Potomac River in suburban Virginia are:

Roaches Run: Accessible only from the southbound lane of the George Washington Memorial Parkway, a waterfowl sanctuary is located west of the highway, just north of National Airport. From fall until spring, dabbling ducks, black-crowned night herons, and a variety of gulls can be found on this tidal lagoon.

Four Mile Run: The mouth of this stream is where ruddy ducks, green-winged teal, horned grebes, and diving ducks might be observed. Located just south of National Airport, it is safest to park at the Washington Sailing Marina and walk north on the bike path along the cove to Four Mile Run.

92.

Mason Neck National Wildlife Refuge

Directions: Fairfax County, Va. From Washington, D.C., take I-95 south about 20 miles to Exit 55 for Lorton. Following signs for Gunston Hall and Pohick Bay Regional Park, turn

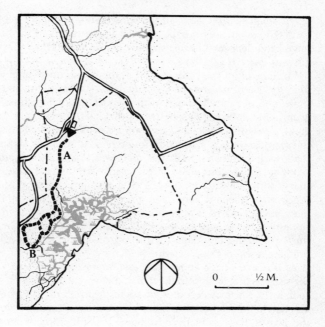

left onto Lorton Rd. (Route 642 east). After 0.9 mile, turn right onto Armistead Rd. (Route 748). After 0.1 mile turn right onto U.S. 1 going south. After 0.8 mile turn left onto Gunston Rd. (Route 242). After 3.5 miles, bear right on Route 600. Drive 0.7 mile and bear right again onto High Point Rd., marked with signs for the refuge. Drive 0.7 mile and park on the left.

Ownership: U.S. Fish and Wildlife Service.

In the Chesapeake Bay region, *neck* is the term for an irregular, truncated peninsula jutting out into the bay or one of its tributaries. Mason Neck, on the Potomac, is a quiet corner of woods and freshwater tidal marsh. Though it is only about 25 miles from the heart of Washington, D.C., the refuge harbors a nesting pair of bald eagles—in fact, it was established to protect them.

From the parking area a well-marked nature trail leads out to the Great Marsh (**A**) through a woodland of mixed oaks, hickories, and pines. The Great Marsh lies in a protected curl of the shoreline where seven small streams flow off the surrounding dry land. Sediments carried downstream from the uplands and carried in by the high tide have been deposited in this shallow pocket to form the marsh (see **Chesapeake Bay**).

Virtually all of the plants found in the marsh offer some form of food to waterfowl and marsh animals such as muskrat, star-nosed mole, and rice rat. Wild rice, with its graceful double plume, arrow arum, blue-flowered pickerelweed, two species of cattail, rice cut-grass, softstem bulrush, and several species of smartweed are among the many important food plants found here. In summer, swamp rose mallow and crimson-eyed rose mallow add splashes of pink and white to the intense green of the marsh; around the edges of the marsh look for cardinal flower, wild rose, and evening primrose. Black duck, mallard, blue- and green-winged teal, and other dab-bling ducks (see **#64**) migrating south are drawn into the marsh to rest and feed. Arriving on the winds of a cold front out of the north, they will stop a few days, then move on as the next front arrives bringing new flocks of waterfowl.

At **B** beavers have built a long and impressive dam across one of the streams that feeds into the marsh. Beavers are the largest aquatic rodents in North America, with bodies from 25 to 30 inches long. The flat, hairless tail adds another 9 to 10 inches. Through evolution, the beaver has gradually developed an extraordinary range and number of physiological features which enable it to survive. Its large lungs and large liver allow it to stay submerged for fifteen minutes without running out of oxygen. It is able to shut its lips behind its large incisor teeth so that it can gnaw under water. Its nose and ears are equipped with valves that automatically close as the animal submerges. The large webbed back feet are used for swimming and for spreading water-repellent oil on its fur, while the agile front feet are used like hands to pick up and hold stones and sticks and mud. The tail is particularly useful. In the water it works as a rudder. It is also a thermostat, helping the beaver regulate its body temperature. During the summer beavers build up stores of fat in the tail, which help it survive the winter. By slapping the tail on the water, beavers alert each other to danger.

While all species must adapt physiologically to their particular habitat, the beaver is noteworthy because it also takes part in creating its habitat. With its special skills and tools, the beaver works together with the other members of the colony to build a dam. The dam creates a pond, which will protect the den and the baby bea-vers, or kits, and provide a safe haven in winter. The pond must be deep enough not to freeze solid, so that the beavers can continue to move around in winter. Grass, sticks, and leaves are woven together and compacted with mud into a small dam, which begins to slow the current of the stream. To this are added sticks which are pushed into the mud on the downstream side of the dam and woven into an interlocking network. The sticks are wedged with stones and mud. The finished dam is fairly smooth on the upstream side, rough and tangled on the downstream side. The animals are continually repairing and adjusting their work. As water level rises, so does the dam. In winter, part of the dam may be lowered in order to insure an adequate air space under the ice. Eventually, as with all dams, sediments will accumulate in the impoundment behind the dam and the pond will become too shallow. The beaver colony will then move on to a new site. Beavers have been responsible for creating marshland and wet meadows all across America in just this way. The long dam you see here probably took several generations of beavers to complete.

Upstream of the dam is the beaver lodge, a thatchwork of branches, mud, and clay. The walls are 2 to 3 feet thick at the base. The top of the lodge is loosely woven to allow ventilation. On cold winter days, steam rises from the lodge like smoke from a cabin. The opening is below the water, which protects the young against predators and allows the animals to come and go in winter when the pond is frozen. The den is up above the water, and as water level rises, the beavers will scrape away at the ceiling and add new material to the floor.

The average size of a family is around six or seven individuals, including the adult pair, which mates for life, yearling offspring, and the new litter of kits. When the young beavers are two years old, they are driven out of the lodge. Because of their large size and strength and their well-protected lodges, beavers do not need to produce large litters in order to maintain their numbers.

Beavers eat sedges, rushes, roots, and particularly the tender bark of saplings. To feed themselves over the winter, the animals collect large supplies of saplings and cache them in the bottom of the pond near the entrance to the lodge. Canals are dug in the bottom for easy transport of logs and saplings. Although the colony becomes less active during the cold weather and spends a great deal of time huddling together for warmth, the animals do not hibernate. Beavers are basically nocturnal animals. Your best chance of seeing them is early in the morning. They will venture out during the day in the summer and occasionally in other seasons.

Red foxes, long-tailed weasels, minks, and short-tailed shrews are some of the other animals you may see in and around the marsh.

Remarks: *The refuge is open during daylight hours April through November; it closes from December through March to protect the eagles during the height of the breeding season. The Woodmarsh Trail is the only public path open in the refuge. It is 3 miles round trip, with two shortcuts. The walking is easy. Nearby activities at Pohick Bay Regional Park include boating on Pohick Bay and Accotink Creek and swimming. Sailboats and paddleboats can be rented. Although the refuge is closed to canoeists, both Pohick Bay and Accotink Creek are open and offer good views of marsh vegetation. Canoes for rent in Washington, D.C. at Hudson Trail Outfitters, 10560 Metropolitan Ave., Kensington, Md. 20895, (301) 949-2515, and 9683 Lee Highway, Va. 22030, (703) 591-2950; Springriver Corp., 5606 Randolph Rd., Rockville, Md. 20852, (301) 881-5696, and 2757 Summerfield Rd., Falls Church, Va. 22042, (703) 241-2818.*

Park naturalists conduct a number of programs. Mason Neck State Park south of the refuge will probably be open to the public in 1984. For further information contact Mason Neck National Wildlife Reserve, 9502 Richmond Highway, Suite A, Lorton, Va. 22079, (703) 339-5278.

93.
Presquile
National Wildlife Refuge

Directions: Chesterfield County, Va. From Richmond, take I-95 south for about 14 miles to Exit 6E. Go east on Route 10 for 6 miles to Route 827 (Allied Chemical Rd.). Turn left and proceed to the end of the road. Park by the ferry slip. You must call ahead to make arrangements for the ferry to meet you. Refuge manager: (804) 458-7541.

Ownership: **U.S. Fish and Wildlife Service.**

Presquile is a low floodplain circled by a broad, gentle curve of the James River. Just a few miles upstream from Hopewell, it is surprisingly remote and serene. Swamp forest and tidal marsh, which make up 80 percent of the refuge, provide a haven for thousands of ducks and geese during the fall migration. Upland forest and agricultural fields as well as wetlands attract numerous songbirds. Red-shoul-

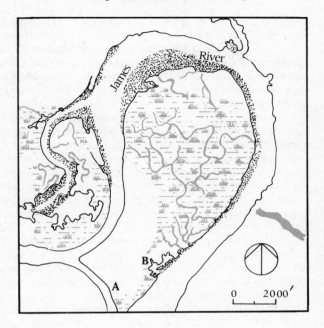

dered and red-tailed hawks and black and turkey vultures hunt in
the skies all year round.

Presquile was once a thumb of land jutting into a meander of the
river. In the 1930s a channel was dug through it to facilitate navigation. As you cross the channel by ferry, you can see a steep em-
bankment on either side of the river to the west. The cut has exposed
a thick layer of river-borne sediment, material that eroded from the
Piedmont Plateau to the west. Over many years the sediment was
deposited on the inner curve of the river meander (see **#80**). Over
time the river might have cut its own channel across the base of the
thumb. The entrances to the old channel would eventually silt in,
sealing it off from the rest of the river, thus creating an oxbow lake.
Bank swallows have colonized the wall of sediment. Because these
birds like to nest in sandy cliffs, they are an uncommon sight.

Although the James is not salty here, about 65 miles from the
Chesapeake Bay, it is tidal, flooding portions of the swamp and
marsh with each high tide (see **#72**). During spring tides (the particularly high tides that occur with the new and full moons) an even

greater area of the wetlands is inundated and, in heavy rains, the normally placid river becomes a torrent, submerging most of this land. As with all floodplain habitats, minor changes in elevation produce major changes in vegetation. The higher the ground, the less frequent the flooding, and the deeper the water table. The island thus owes both its existence and character to the shaping forces of the river.

The southern tip of the refuge where the nature trail begins (**A**) is covered with fill dredged from the channel—sandy, sterile material, containing few nutrients. The plant life now growing here is undergoing primary succession—that is, it is colonizing new territory, ground which has had no previous plant history. Most of the sites in this book contain examples of secondary succession in which one group of plants is being replaced with another (see **Introduction**). Primary succession is a much slower process, because there is no reservoir of nutrients to work with; the plants must create their own environment. As with secondary succession, each stage in the cycle enhances the environment by producing organic material, which enriches the soil as it decays. And each cycle changes the conditions; because of more shade, richer soil, and increased moisture, a new mixture of vegetation will replace the old.

On the highest and therefore driest portions, about 18 feet above sea level, black locust and redcedar dominate. Special bacteria live in nodes on the roots of the black locust. These bacteria can convert inorganic nitrogen to a form usable by the tree (see **#31**). This enables the tree to grow in very poor soil. Excess nitrogen is passed to the surrounding soil, thus enriching it. Clumps of rabbit tobacco and dog fennel, which are early succession species, grow around the edges of this area.

At lower elevations the soil is somewhat richer and more moist, allowing turkey oak and Spanish oak to grow. Down by the river, the wet soils have been fertilized by water-borne nutrients, and growth is rapid and abundant. Sycamore, cottonwood, red maple, and tuliptree form a dense canopy under which few other plants flourish. Patches of horsetail, one of the most ancient plant forms, are found on the fill. It can grow on the very sandy soil because these spots are close to the water table. Its sturdy form is supported by silica contained in the cell walls. Throughout, an abundance of fruit-bearing vines provide food for wildlife.

Along the nature trail there is an excellent view of the tidal marsh (**B**). Food plants are plentiful here: arrow arum, arrowhead, wild rice, common cattail, smartweed, bulrush, beggarticks, pickerelweed, and rice cutgrass. As a result, animal life is also plentiful. In the fall great numbers of ducks, especially mallard and pintail, feed here. In spring bobolinks pass through on their way to the grasslands of the north. During the breeding months the marsh is full of herons, egrets, and rails feeding on small fish, amphibians, crustaceans, and insects. Northern harriers, bald eagles, and snipe own the marsh in winter.

In early spring, when the geese and most of the ducks have headed north to their breeding grounds, the two creeks that traverse the swamp are open to canoeing. The trees here, having never been cut, offer an excellent example of an undisturbed, mature swamp forest. The species are few: blackgum and ash are most common; red maple is widespread too, though less abundant. Clustered in stands throughout the swamp are baldcypress and water tupelo, here at its northern limit. The shade in the swamp is heavy, and the only significant understory species is ironwood. Some flowering plants, notably lizard's tail and arrow arum, may be seen in the few spots where light strikes through the trees.

Along the edges of the creeks are small dikes of riverine sediments, which have accumulated there naturally. As floodwater strikes the trees of the swamp, it slows, dropping much of its load of silt. Because conditions on these banks are drier, different species are found here: overcup oak, willow oak, tag alder, wild plum, swamp dogwood. Wetland warblers are abundant in the swamp in spring and summer. The fruits and nuts of swamp trees are another source of food for ducks on migration.

Remarks: *Camping at Pocahontas State Park, west of I-95. An ''open house'' is scheduled in the fall and the spring during which there are scheduled activities and the whole refuge is open. Access is by water only, by refuge-operated ferry or private boat, both of which should be arranged ahead of time. Call the refuge manager to find out when the creeks are open to canoes. The refuge is close to a number of the James River plantations.*

94.

Gordon's Creek

Directions: **James City County, Va. From the junction of I-64 and I-95 in Richmond, take I-65 east to Laburnam Ave. Turn south and go 5 miles to Route 5. Turn southeast (left) and go about 30 miles to the bridge over the Chickahom-**

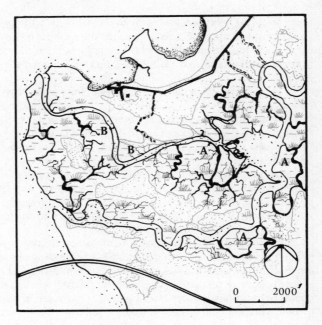

0   2000'

iny River. Turn left immediately after crossing the bridge
at the sign for the Holiday Travel Park. Canoe rentals are
arranged at the store. Park at the boat landing.

Ownership: Public waterway. The lands bordering the creek
are private property.

A canoe trip on Gordon's Creek will take you through freshwater
marshes bright green with pickerelweed and arrow arum in summer, golden with wild rice and beggarticks in fall. During the early
spring, flights of snipe leap and settle, and as the seeds of marsh
herbs and grasses ripen each fall, countless dabbling ducks collect to
feed. At the fringes of the marsh stand baldcypress, red maple and
blackgum where the marsh becomes wooded swamp.

Freshwater tidal wetlands such as these are the most productive
lands we have. On each acre of marsh several tons of food-producing
plants grow each year; unlike the marshes of the coast there is no
salt to limit the variety of species, so that diversity is added to abundance (see **#21** for discussion of salt marsh). This in turn brings a

more diverse and numerous animal population, including birds, fish, reptiles, and amphibians. As in the salt marsh, the action of the tides results in a recycling of nutrients. Each high tide brings a fertilizing substance called detritus, formed when microscopic animal life feeds on microscopic pieces of decaying vegetation. Detritus is also a source of food for crustaceans, mollusks, and other aquatic life, including many fish. Both freshwater and saltwater species are abundant including pickerel, largemouth bass, carp, catfish, white perch, shad, and striped bass. Unfortunately, the fish taken in Gordon's Creek should not be eaten due to Kepone pollution in the river.

Because of the greater diversity of species, seasonal changes are far more dramatic at Gordon's Creek than in the salt marsh. In late spring and summer the marsh waterways are dominated by blue-flowered pickerelweed and its companion plant arrow arum; swamp or marsh rose blooms white and pink in shallower water, and the round white balls of the buttonbush mark where the marsh changes to wooded swamp. In late summer and early fall higher portions of the marsh are full of ripening wild rice (**A**) whose seeds are prized by migrating green- and blue-winged teal, wood ducks, early mallards, pintails, and black ducks, as well as red-winged blackbirds, bobolinks, and sora rails. Beggarticks, one of the dominant species in the wetter areas, becomes conspicuous only in early fall when it blooms with gold-yellow flowers. By November, the pickerelweed and arrow arum have virtually disappeared without a trace, while the wild rice is denuded but still standing. The grasses have greater amounts of cellulose in their cell walls, which stiffens the plant and retards decay. Rice cutgrass, which grows at (**B**), flowers in the latter part of autumn, its greenish-yellow heads standing out in the dun marshes. Back toward the swamp, buttonbush, a woody shrub, also keeps its shape all winter. Instead of white fluffy flowers, small round brown seed cases appear. All of these plants and a number of other species produce seeds that are eaten by waterfowl or bear fruit at the time of the autumn migrations.

Remarks: *There is a fee for using the boat launch. To make a full circuit of Gordon's Island takes most of a day. The area is heavily hunted from blinds in the fall, so it is best to explore the marshes then on a Sunday. Camping is available at the Holiday Travel Park.*

95.
River Swamps of the
Nottoway and the Blackwater

Directions: **Isle of Wight, Sussex, and Southampton counties, Va. To reach the Blackwater River, go south from
Richmond on I-95 to Petersburg, about 23 miles. Then take
U.S. 460 southeast about 40 miles to Zuni. Turn west on
Route 614 and stop at the bridge (see Remarks, #96). To
reach the Nottoway River, continue south from Petersburg on I-95 about 12 miles to Route 35. Turn southeast
(left) and go about 26 miles to Route 653. Turn southwest
(right) and go about 2.5 miles to the bridge.**

The Nottoway and the Blackwater rivers flow gently along the
southern Coastal Plain, winding through flooded forests to the Chowan River. Here begin the vast, impenetrable wooded swamps of
the southern Coastal Plain, covering millions of acres. High water
and mucky soils have saved much of these forests from farming and
logging, and they are the least disturbed lands of the entire Coastal
Plain. The swamps and the lowland woods that rim them are enormously important. The peat and muck soils act as sponges to absorb
floodwaters, preventing erosion. They also filter impurities from the
water. The wealth of microorganisms and plantlife in the waters
feeds many species of fish, many of which raise their young in the
flooded woods. Reptiles, amphibians, birds, and mammals forage
and nest in the lowland woods and at the edge of the water. They
hunt fish in the swamp waters, forage for seeds and nuts, and eat
insects and each other (see **#97**).

As the glaciers moved back and forth across the northern United
States, the sea retreated and rose and retreated across the Coastal
Plain (see **Introduction**). When the sea lay far to the east, the
rivers of the southern Coastal Plain cut their valleys deeper into the
surface of the plain. Unlike the rivers to the north, however, these
waters were not fed by the runoff from the great ice sheets. They
moved more gently across the flat Coastal Plain, cutting valleys that
were shallow compared to the deep paths worn by the Susquehanna
and the Delaware. Then, as the sea rose again, the rivers were pushed
back, drowning the valleys and spreading out across the plain.

Another factor unites these swamps with those to the south. Average temperatures are warmer in this southeastern corner of Vir-

ginia than in the rest of the state. A number of southern species reach their northern limit here.

In the wettest portions of the swamp, along the edges of the river channel, water is standing or flowing most of the year. Two species of tree dominate the canopy: baldcypress and water tupelo. They flourish where other trees cannot grow because they have adapted to the oxygen-poor swamp muck. Although plants produce oxygen during photosynthesis (see **#56**), they must also draw in some oxygen to carry out respiration, the conversion of starch and sugar to energy. This energy is used by the plant for growth and reproduction. The roots of most plants must be able to draw in oxygen from the soil in order to live and grow. Respiration can occur without oxygen but as a result, toxic substances accumulate in the surrounding soil, killing the roots. Ironically, most plants die of dehydration when flooded, for the dead roots can no longer draw in moisture. The baldcypress and the water tupelo are able to survive flooding because of several mechanisms which are still not fully understood. Their network of small branching roots does not die off; in fact, new ones sprout under water. Oxygen is brought from other parts of the tree to the roots, the rate of respiration is regulated, and the roots can withstand the toxic substances which accumulate. As the land rises and grows drier, tree species have fewer of these adaptations and are thus less able to withstand flooding. Timing of high water is also important, for seedlings are far less tolerant of flooding than mature trees. If high water occurs in spring and early summer when seedlings should sprout, many trees will not grow.

Water tupelo is one of the most common trees in these river swamps. Each year it produces many fruits, each containing a seed. The fruits fall into the river or are devoured by small animals, and the seeds are disseminated, unharmed, in their feces. The seeds can lie underwater for months and remain viable, but to sprout they must be exposed to the air in full sunlight on a moist bed of earth or rotting wood (see **#100**). Water tupelo can still reproduce in flood conditions, however, because the stumps of old or damaged trees sprout very easily. Southeastern Virginia is the northern limit of this species. (For a discussion of baldcypress, see **#73**.)

As you move away from the river channel, water tupelo and baldcypress begin to thin out and share the canopy with other species which are a little less tolerant of flood conditions, such as water hickory and overcup oak. Here the soil is still inundated during a major part of the growing season. Both these species have seeds which remain ready to sprout after months underwater, but their seedlings are more vulnerable to flooding than cypress or water tupelo. Of all oak species, the overcup oak seedlings are the best able to withstand flooding. This tree's name comes from the scaly coat that encompasses the nut, which is prized by ducks and animals. Water hickory, which reaches its northern limit here, is the tallest of the hickories; its bitter fruits are also eaten by ducks and small animals. Both of these species usually sprout where an opening in the canopy has allowed light to reach the ground.

On higher ground around the edges of the swamps are hardwood forests of great variety. Here the soils may be flooded for only a month or two at the beginning of the growing season. Common species in this zone include red maple, green ash, laurel oak, willow oak, river birch, American elm, and hackberry. Hackberry is a northern species and laurel oak a southern tree, while green ash and red maple are found throughout the eastern United States. As one would expect, these trees are less tolerant of flooding than the swamp species.

Remarks: *The best way to see these swamps is by canoe. There is no whitewater on the Coastal Plain, so the only danger is taking the wrong fork in the stream. If you watch carefully for the drift of the current, you should eventually find your way. The best example of a river swamp is along the Blackwater (see Remarks, #96). A popular trip is to float the Nottoway from Route 653 to the bridge at Courtland, a distance of about 8 miles. This trip takes about 4 hours. You can generally put the canoe in at any of the bridges over these streams. Remember that distances can be very deceptive on a map and allow plenty of time. Take a friend and a topographic map of the area. Canoes are for rent in Richmond at Blue Ridge Mountain Sports and at Alpine Outfitters. Topographic maps are available from Virginia Reproduction and Supply Co., P.O. Box 1244, Richmond, Va. 23241.*

96.
Zuni Pine Barrens
Natural Area

Directions: **Access to this site is limited. For permission to visit, contact J. A. Minetree at Union Camp Corp., Franklin Woodlands, (804) 569-4276.**

Ownership: **Union Camp Corp., Franklin, Va.**

The Zuni Pine Barrens contains the northernmost remnant of the once extensive southern longleaf-pine–turkey-oak forest type. There are ecological similarities to the Pine Barrens of New Jersey, but species differences are striking.

Soon after leaving the gate, the sand road passes a stand of longleaf pines on the right with an understory of dogwood-sized turkey oaks and a knee-high layer of shrubs of the heath family (**A**). This site was the floor of a tidal estuary when its sands were deposited about 70,000 years ago, during the warm Sangamon interglacial period (see **Introduction**).

There are several special times to be in the barrens. On splendid fall days the understory blazes with the shimmering orange of turkey oak and scarlet-leaved shrubs. During overcast days in late winter the green mosses and lichens are bright against the wet black tree-trunks, and the damp sand is carpeted with emerald pyxie moss and the Christmas colors of teaberry. In April the pyxie moss glows pink with dainty flowers.

There were originally a few small savannah-like areas in the Zuni Pine Barrens. Look for one of these, a white sandflat now largely overgrown with shrubs, at the end of the first road to the right, near

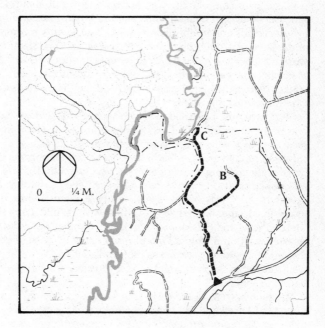

the center of the natural area (**B**). Dig a hole here and you may be surprised to find the water table just a few inches below the surface. Dig a bit more and the edges of the hole begin to melt like those of an excavation for a sand castle on the beach. Wetness in these soils, which farmers used to call quicksand, is caused by a high water table. The upper layer of sand overlies an impervious clay formation. With no way to drain, each rainfall simply fills the porous sands. Despite the abundance of moisture, the surface can dry out enough to support frequent fires, which keep out shrubs and allow savannah grasses and herbs to thrive. Look for pyxie moss and teaberry in openings among the shrubs. In fall, the rare October-flower blooms here at its only locality in Virginia, and 150 miles north of the next known location.

Continuing west along the road from the entrance, cross a small blackgum swamp to where the road forks. Take the right fork along a sand ridge paralleling the Blackwater River. On low bluffs along the Blackwater (**C**) you may find evergreen shiny-leaved galax in extensive communities, cool-climate relics which have persisted here during the 10,000 years since the end of the Wisconsin glacial period. Listen for great-horned, barred, and screech owls in the evening, and for the snort of deer along well-worn trails through the heath.

Existence of the barrens was not reported until about 45 years ago. The desultory botanical exploration of Virginia has been plagued by lost records and unfinished manuscripts. The only record of flora of the state was published over 200 years ago. The largest body of work has been compiled by M. L. Fernald, author of *Gray's Manual of Botany*, the standard field reference for the northeastern United States. The irrepressible Fernald described the discovery of the Zuni Pine Barrens in July 1936:

"Following the cart-road to which we were directed, we entered one of the botanical paradises of the summer. . . . The thin woods were carpeted with white sand, with a dense thicket of the usual shrubs of sandy woods, but wherever there was an opening exciting herbs were growing. *Carphephorus bellidifolius* abounded and on the more open sands *Euphorbia ipecachuanhae* [wild or Carolina ipecac] occurred. . . . I was happy to collect these plants, which seemed interesting to me; but, while I was thus wasting time, Long shouted 'Here's Pyxie' and Griscom replied 'Here's another *Liatris*-like thing' [blazing star]; and, before I could reach either of them, there came the report '*Seymeria cassioides* again.' And so it went. We had stumbled into what we had sought for four years, real unspoiled pine barren in Virginia."

The pine barrens of the eastern United States originally extended from New Jersey and southeastern Virginia, along the Coastal Plain, to Texas. The common denominators were deep sand soils and frequent fires, set by lightning and by Indians (see **Pine Barrens**). In the south, fire is the life's blood of savannah, pocosin, and sandhill vegetation, and is consequently significant for the wildlife which lives in these habitats. The endangered red-cockaded woodpecker, for example, nests only in mature pines. Contrary to the general opinion, fire does no harm to the trees, shrubs, herbs, and wildlife adapted to these regions. It keeps the vegetation from being overrun by those of later successional stages (see **Introduction**).

Fire leads to similarities of vegetation structure in northern and southern barrens. Both tend to have a very open canopy of fire-resistant pines. Nutrient-poor sandy soils and plenty of light favor a rich layer of shrubs of the heath family—mostly blueberries and huckleberries. Some of the rare herbs occur on bare patches of dry white sand, while savannah species thrive on sandflats which appear dry and burn frequently, but have a water table near the surface for much of the year. The splendid longleaf pine savannahs, with their hundreds of rare species, including most of our insectivorous plants and many magnificent orchids, are now one of the rarest communities in the east.

The Zuni Pine Barrens have in common with the New Jersey Pine Barrens the fire ecology and structural similarities mentioned above, and a shrub layer of many of the same blueberries and huckleberries. Here the similarities end. In New Jersey you can see miles of fire-blackened trunks of pitch pine sprouting masses of lush new needles. But there is no pitch pine on the southern Coastal Plain. It is replaced here by longleaf, with needles up to a foot and a half long.

Old longleaf pines resist fire with an absurdly thick bark, 2 to 3 inches deep. Often the trees do not even lose their needles in a fire which completely eliminates competitors. Young longleaf seedlings look for several years like a large tuft of grass a foot or two in diameter. During a fire the green needle mass is sacrificed to protect the central column, which has enough food reserves to produce a new bush of needles. This grows well in the clearing created by the fire. Turkey oak is a small tree with a different strategy—it resprouts from the ground after fire.

Longleaf pine is now gone from about 80 percent of its original range. Captain John Smith and later settlers imported boatloads of hogs from England. The animals rapidly became established in the wild, and reached a saturation population in the 1700s. By the time of the Revolution, it was found that there were around 20,000 hogs on open range in the woods in every county. The hogs devoured longleaf pine seedlings, which, unlike other pines, have a juicy, palatable stem in the "grass" stage.

Longleaf is the most resinous of southern pines and this quality contributed to its downfall. The wood resists rot, and for 200 years it was the most prized material for building construction. More significantly, during this time, tar, pitch, and turpentine distilled from this species were used for most things for which petroleum products served later. During the colonial period, small quantities of longleaf were used for sawtimber, and dead, resin-impregnated "lightwood" was collected and burned to make tar and pitch. Live trees were boxed for turpentine, a process which involved scarring the surface of the tree and cutting a large box in the base of the trunk to collect crude resin which was later distilled into turpentine. Introduction of the copper still into the woods in 1834 made this operation commercially profitable, and most of the longleaf pine in Virginia was destroyed in the next few years. Commercial success touched off a wave of destruction which spread south through the Carolinas, eventually to Texas, with the last of the virgin longleaf forests decimated by 1920. The average net profit for each tree, two to three centuries old, was 10 cents.

Trees that escaped the boxing operation were logged. Invention of steam power early in the nineteenth century led to portable sawmills and a proliferation of logging railroads into every stretch of woods by the 1870s. "Fence laws," requiring confinement of one's livestock, were passed in the late 1800s, and a few stands of longleaf reappeared during the years between removal of feral hogs from the woods and the beginning of modern fire suppression.

Fire control, established around 1920, largely spelled the end for this species and many of its associates in Virginia. Over much of its range, longleaf, the original forest dominant of the Coastal Plain, has been replaced by fire-intolerant species like loblolly pine. The last stands of longleaf, about 100 years old, have been cut in recent years, and at the Zuni Pine Barrens, you may see one of the only remnants of this important forest type in the northern 100 miles of its range.

Remarks: *There is canoeing on the Blackwater River. This pleasant stream winding through bottomland hardwood forest and swamps is at its best when there has been enough rain to ensure a flowing current. It is an unobstructed flatwater stream and requires no experience. There are large cypress in shallow water along the shore, and beaver, river otter and deer may be seen. At night an unearthly series of hoots and cackles from barred owls provides a most spectacular sound. Put in just west of Zuni where Route 614 crosses the river. Interesting places to stop and explore are steep bluffs on the west side covered with hickories and white oaks large enough to rival those of the virgin forest; low pine barrens on the east, and alluvial bottomland forest on either side. Take out at Route 630, 7.5 miles downstream, or continue. The region is sparsely populated; there are dry places to camp and the river is long enough for a journey of several days. Camping at private campground on U.S. 460, 0.5 mile east of I-95 and I-85.*

97.

Dismal Swamp
National Wildlife Refuge

Directions: Cities of Suffolk and Chesapeake, Va., and Gates, Camden, and Pasquotank counties, N.C. From Richmond, drive south on I-95 to Petersburg, about 23 miles. Take U.S. 460 southeast to Suffolk, about 60 miles. To reach the refuge office go south on U.S. 13 and Route 32 about 1.5 miles. The office is on the left. To reach the swamp from Suffolk turn east (left) on East Washington St. and go 0.6 mile. Turn south (right) on White Marsh Rd. and drive 0.6 mile; turn into Jericho Ditch Lane (A) and park by the gate. From here walk or bicycle along the dirt roads. To reach the boardwalk (B), continue south on White Marsh Rd. (Route 642) 4.5 miles to Washington Ditch Rd. Turn east (left) and drive 0.9 mile to the parking area. Drummond Lake can be reached by hiking along Washington Ditch Rd. for about 4.5 miles or by canoeing in from the east along the feeder ditch from U.S. 17.

Ownership: U.S. Fish and Wildlife Service.

This thick, impenetrable tangle of swamp forest has been a mystery since the colonists first arrived in Virginia. It lies on a plain that slopes gently from west to east. Geologically, the swamp is new. The deepest layer of peat is only about 9000 years old. Why and how the swamp formed here are questions that are still only partly answered. Lake Drummond, at its center, is one of only two natural lakes in the state of Virginia. Unlike most lakes, it is higher than the surrounding swamp, and scientists have yet to explain its origin.

The Dismal Swamp was once a vast lowland forest of huge bald-cypress, water tupelo, and Atlantic white-cedar. Geologists estimate that it once covered 2200 square miles of the Coastal Plain in Virginia and North Carolina. Since early colonial times, the swamp has been logged, ditched, diked, and burned until only 100,000 acres remain, bearing little resemblance to the primeval forest. The extensive disturbance has destroyed the stands of huge cypress and of white-cedar. Only the scattering of large cypress on the shores of Lake Drummond remains as a clue to the former grandeur of these

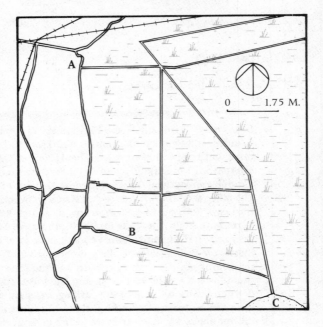

forests. Diversity, on the other hand, has increased. A great variety of trees, shrubs, and flowering plants can be found, including rarities like the dwarf trillium, log fern, and silky camellia. Habitat diversity has probably increased animal diversity as well. The Dismal Swamp is a haven for many wintering species of birds and for migratory warblers, thrushes, and other landbirds. Black bear and bobcat still prowl through the undergrowth, one of the few places they can be found east of the mountains. The shrubby woodlands are an excellent habitat for white-tailed deer, gray fox, and Eastern cottontail rabbit.

The western boundary of the swamp is a ridge of higher ground known as the Suffolk scarp. In places it is 60 feet high, while the swamp below slopes gradually from about 25 feet to less than 15 feet on its eastern edge. As you walk in along the Jericho Ditch Lane, look back toward White Marsh Rd. and you will see the change in altitude. The Suffolk scarp is an ancient beach ridge marking the shoreline of the ocean about 80,000 to 100,000 years ago near the end of the Pleistocene, the age of glaciers (see **Introduction**). Underlying the Suffolk scarp is a clayey formation compacted into an impermeable layer, made up of formations deposited at various times during the Pleistocene, when bays, estuaries, and the shallows of the ocean covered the region. Above it are younger formations largely made up of sand. Rainwater moves freely down through these materials and strikes the impervious material below, draining into the swamp.

After the Suffolk scarp came into existence, the most recent ice sheet, the Wisconsin, moved south. As the ocean retreated far to the east, streams such as the Cypress, the Corapeake, the Northwest, and the Pasquotank cut their way across the area toward the sea. With the glacier's retreat, the sea rose again, elevating the water table and slowing the flow of the rivers. Marshes and swamps developed along their banks. Then about 9000 years ago the rivers were blocked. One theory is that beavers dammed the streams. The waters flowed out across the surface of the land. As plant material drifted to the ground, it was covered by water and cut off from oxygen, drastically slowing decomposition. Peat, which is nothing more than partially decayed vegetation, began to accumulate. Once peat begins to form, the ecosystem tends to be self-perpetuating, due to the peculiar qualities of peat. It is spongy stuff full of pockets that can fill with water. Peat can absorb roughly ten times its weight in water and will stay wet even during long periods of dry weather. It was when the peat began to form that the swamp forests of baldcypress, blackgum, and Atlantic white-cedar arose. The Dismal Swamp still drains into the Northwest and Pasquotank Rivers, but there is no sign of these streams in the swamp itself. The old channels are buried under many feet of peat.

This history has been reconstructed partly through borings of the underlying geological formations and partly through examination of pollen contained in the peat. The peat is vital to the swamp's continued existence. Two centuries of ditching and draining have caused much of it to vanish, for once the peat is left dry and open to the air, it decomposes rapidly. Although these 100,000 acres are protected, the long-term future of the Dismal Swamp is still in doubt.

Because of its configuration the swamp is very different from the river swamps of the region (see **#95**). The area is generally flooded from December to sometime in May. From late spring to late fall, rainfall decreases somewhat and evaporation increases with longer daylight hours. Transpiration is also occurring. This is the process by which trees draw water up out of the ground and out through their leaves. Thus, the soil is damp but not inundated during much of the growing season, and many species can grow here. The greatest destruction of cypress occurred after World War II. Since then the most common tree has become red maple, growing well both on wet sites and on the hummocks. Blackgum is also abundant. Other species which grow on wetter ground include swamp chestnut oak, water oak, willow oak, sweetgum, water tupelo, and Carolina, green, and pumpkin ash. Common understory trees include redbay, sweetbay, and American holly. Wetland shrubs include inkberry, fetterbush, swamp azalea, poison sumac, and sweet pepperbush.

The boardwalk (**B**) begins on a slight hummock. The minute change in elevation produces a radical change in vegetation. On it you will find loblolly pine, American beech, and a variety of oaks. The oaks tend to hybridize with each other, making identification very difficult. Openings in the canopy give light to a host of vines. The refuge lists 21 species of vines, including greenbrier, rattan, poison ivy, Virginia creeper, crossvine, trumpet vine, and yellow jessamine. Ferns are also lush around the boardwalk: look for marsh, netted chain, Virginia chain, and sensitive ferns. In the primeval forest with its thick canopy, light-loving ferns and vines were not abundant. In wet open areas with plentiful light, switch cane, which looks like bamboo, often creates dense thickets. Once it is established, it completely shades the forest floor so that other species cannot grow.

The swamp flowers in spring as the swamp magnolia, sweetbay, swamp azalea, redbay, jessamine, and dwarf trillium come into bloom. Dwarf trillium, a Piedmont species found only on the hummocks, blooms for only a couple of weeks in March. Silky camellia is also found on the hummocks. The swamp is the northernmost edge of its range.

Spring is also the time for migrant songbirds. Very high populations of nesting prothonotary warblers have been recorded. A southern subspecies of the black-throated green warbler reaches the northern limit of its range here. Other nesting species include Swainson's warbler (see **#51**), red-eyed vireo, hooded warbler, ovenbird, pileated woodpecker, and barred owl. Jericho Ditch Lane and the boardwalk are good places to see woodland species.

The many ditches have created a separate habitat, where aquatic plants and amphibians thrive. Great blue herons, green herons, little blue herons, and black-crowned night herons hunt along the ditches and nest in the swamp.

Winter brings great flocks of American robins, gray catbirds, eastern phoebes, brown thrashers, and other landbirds to forage in the forest. The winters are mild in the swamp and the woods are rich with berries. One of the great spectacles is the vast host of red-winged blackbirds, common grackles, and other blackbirds which roost along the eastern border of the swamp. Driving south just before dusk on U.S. 17 to the Virginia–North Carolina line, you will see millions of birds gathering in to the trees from the neighboring fields. The birds have been coming here for at least 80 years.

Lake Drummond (**C**) is a round shallow lake at most only 6 feet deep. One theory of its origin holds that a severe fire burned away the underlying peat. There are no other signs of such a fire, but burnings are common in southern swamps. The lake is younger than the swamp—about 4000 years old. Surrounded by peat, the acidic waters of the lake are stained dark. This inhibits the growth of bacteria, and apparently of microscopic plant and animal life as well. There are many fish in the lake, but they are stunted. Waterfowl use the lake for resting only, as food plants are almost nonexistent. Around the edges of the lake are some fine old cypress trees hung with Spanish moss (see **#88**). Northern parula warblers nest in the moss. In spring wood ducks bring their young down to the edge of the lake.

The swamp is not quite warm enough for alligators. Winters are 2 degrees too cold, and there are 4 days of frost too many. The cottonmouth is found in the southern part of the swamp but not in the north. This is curious, as the northernmost station for the cottonmouth is well to the north at Newport News City Park. Other southern species which are at their northern limit here include the yellow-bellied pond slider, the southern cricket frog, and the squirrel treefrog. The Dismal Swamp short-tailed shrew is found here and nowhere else.

Remarks: *Like winter and spring, fall is beautiful here. In the damp conditions, fungi are spectacular. Summer is hot and insect-ridden. Ticks and mosquitoes abound after the middle of May (see #55). One of the best approaches to the swamp is to canoe into Lake Drummond along the Feeder Ditch from U.S. 17 about 14 miles south of Deep Creek. A private company at the ditch rents canoes and also runs tours into the lake. The Army Corps of Engineers maintains a small campground by the Feeder Ditch. Camping is first come, first served. There is no charge. Other private campgrounds are located along U.S. 17. Fishing—with a license—is allowed only in Lake Drummond. Black crappie, bluegills, and catfish are most commonly caught. Spring is the best season. A bicycle is an excellent way to explore the refuge. There are no rentals nearby. The refuge is open from sunrise to sunset all year long. For further information contact the Superintendant, Dismal Swamp National Wildlife Refuge, P.O. Box 349, Suffolk, Va., 23434, (804) 539-7479.*

98.
Back Bay National Wildlife Refuge and False Cape State Park

Directions: **From Richmond, take I-64 to Norfolk. Thirteen miles beyond the Hampton Road Bridge and Tunnel, turn southeast onto Indian River Rd. and continue about 15 miles to New Bridge Rd. Turn northeast (left) and go about 1.5 miles to Sandbridge Rd. Turn east (right). Go 4 miles and turn right on Sandpiper Rd. This leads directly into the refuge.**

Ownership: **U.S. Fish and Wildlife Service and Virginia Division of Parks.**

Sheltered from the ocean behind a narrow stretch of barrier beach, this is a refuge of brackish marsh, freshwater impoundments, islands, and open bay. From October to February, it is alive with waterfowl migrating through or wintering. On cold, clear December evenings thousands of snow geese erupt noisily from the ponds. They mill over the dark-green loblolly pines and live oaks and then settle onto the next impoundment to feed on the sedges, bulrushes, and grasses. They are one of 250 species of birds that pass through Back Bay Refuge. In late spring or early summer, if you are very lucky, you may see the wide track of a female loggerhead sea turtle along the ocean beach, which stretches 11 miles to the North Carolina border and beyond. The turtles spend their entire lives at sea except for the short time it takes the female to lay her eggs in the sand.

The bay and the beach are in a continual state of change, partly because of human interference and partly because of the unstable nature of barrier beach systems. Wind, waves, tides, and currents are constantly rearranging barrier islands. Dunes are made and destroyed; bays fill in or open out; peninsulas become islands, and islands become peninsulas (see **#55**).

The Back Bay area, which includes both the wildlife refuge and False Cape State Park, consists of a barrier beach, the bay, and marshes that formed in the shelter of the beach. The barrier beach began as a spit of sand deposited by ocean currents and wave action, a part of the new shoreline that developed as the last glacier melted and the seas rose rapidly, (see **Introduction**). Now it is a peninsula stretching 69 miles southward into North Carolina.

The refuge lies at the northern end of Back Bay. Upon entering you will see a great dune blocking your view of the ocean. This dune is largely man-made, built after a tremendous hurricane devastated the coast in the 1930s. For some time before the great storm, no dune existed along this stretch of the beach. All the area now covered by the freshwater impoundments (**A, B, C**) was a "washover flat": any big storm or very high tide sent the sea sweeping in across the barrier island, carrying a load of sand, which was left in the bay. The terrace of ground that lies between the dune and the bay is made up of these sandy deposits.

The freshwater impoundments were created after the refuge was established in 1938. Now vegetation typical of the landward side of dunes—wax myrtle, bayberry, live oak, loblolly pine—is growing up with the pond vegetation of willows, three-square bulrush, cordgrasses, needlerush, and other species.

At one time a dune system did exist along this area of the peninsula. At **D**, where the trail splits, is a stand of stunted loblolly pines older than the surrounding trees. This was once part of a dune forest,

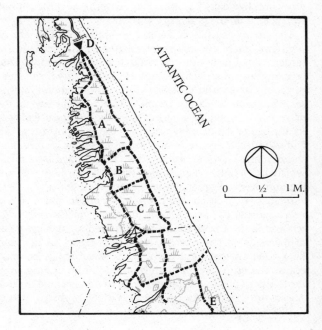

the rest of which has disappeared, killed off by one or more catastrophic storms years ago.

Thousands of greater snow geese gather in the impoundments each season, coming from northern breeding grounds above the Arctic Circle in Greenland and Ellesmere and Baffin islands. The birds arrive in November and December. Some will continue on to wintering grounds in North Carolina; some will winter on the refuge. They particularly like the three-square bulrush in the ponds; using the side of their bills, they pull up entire plants at a time, literally tearing the marsh out by the roots. A flock of geese can create holes in the marsh, known as "eatouts." In moderation this can be constructive, for it prevents the marsh from filling in entirely, allows new growth to occur, and provides open-water hunting areas for egrets and herons. Too many geese, however, can create a wasteland.

Since the melting of the last ice sheet, the sea has continued to rise over the Coastal Plain, pushing the coastline westward. Walking along the ocean at low tide, one sees half-submerged tree stumps in the shallow water, some 500 years old.

As you reach the False Cape section of the barrier beach, you enter an area in which a well-developed natural dune system has existed for many years (**E**). A mature forest dominated by loblolly pines and live oaks has grown up, covering a cluster of old dunes well back from the beach (see **#101**).

The ocean beaches at False Cape and Back Bay are near the northern limit of the nesting range of the endangered loggerhead sea turtle. From time to time the turtles will nest in the area. During the breeding season the female lays one, perhaps two, clutches of eggs of about 100 each in a shallow cup in the sand and returns to the sea. The young hatch in a couple of months and crawl for the safety of the water. Emerging at night, the young find the ocean by heading for the lighter sky over the water and the level horizon where ocean and sky meet. Because of intense development of the Atlantic seashore, many breeding beaches have been ruined by artificial light, which distracts the young turtles. Raccoons, furthermore, easily find the unprotected eggs and destroy many each year.

In the bay itself change has been dramatic and puzzling. Sixty years ago the bay was filled with diving ducks: ringneck, scaup, redhead, and canvasback. In the surrounding marshes great flocks of dabbling ducks—mallard, gadwall, wigeon, pintail, and black duck—fed on seeds and pond weeds, small mollusks, and crustaceans. The birds flew thousands of miles from nesting grounds on the northern plains, central and western Canada, and as far away as Alaska to winter on the open waters of the southern Atlantic bays.

During the morning and evening flights, the sky was dark with clouds of birds. Most spectacular of all were the huge flights of canvasback coming to settle in flotillas on the water, feasting on wild celery, their favorite food. Then came a period of steady decline, until twenty years ago few ducks of any sort could be seen in the bay. Today, dabbling ducks have reappeared in force but numbers of diving ducks are still way down.

A number of events, most of them related to human activity, have brought about these changes. The great breeding grounds of the United States and Canada have been drastically reduced, drained to increase farmland. Hunters killed thousands of birds a season, especially the canvasback, prized for its size and taste. In the heyday of wildfowling at the turn of the century, a day's shooting could easily have brought down hundreds of ducks. Countless other birds died or were sickened by the spent lead shot that littered the floor of the bay and the ponds. As agriculture increased in the region, heavy rains washed tons of earth from the plowed fields into the bay, which increased the turbidity of the water. By reducing the amount of light passing through the water, turbidity prevents the food plants from growing. Increasing levels of raw sewage and fluctuating salinity have also played a part.

In the 1960s a new development brought another change. Eurasian milfoil, a submerged water plant which is not native, made its way north into the bay. At about the same time turbidity in the water began to decrease, and salt water was pumped into the bay in a further effort to settle the sediments. Milfoil is an aggressive plant, apparently able to grow in less favorable conditions than the native species. Waterfowl will eat it although it is not as nutritious as the indigenous plants. Milfoil has undoubtedly played some part in bringing the dabbling ducks again to Back Bay.

Remarks: *Camping by permit at False Cape State Park, 6.1 miles' walk from parking area, and at Seashore State Park. For a permit write: Seashore State Park, 2500 Shore Dr., Virginia Beach, Va. 23451. Bicycling is an ideal way to see the refuge. Allow 2 to 3 hours to hike the 4-mile circuit. Carry water with you. Be prepared for mosquitoes, ticks, and other biting insects from spring to the first frost (see #55). Watch out for cottonmouths, which are poisonous and sometimes aggressive. This area is the northern limit of their range on the coast. (see #84). Canoes and boats small enough to be carried from the parking area can be launched on the bay. Canoe rentals are available from Blue Ridge Mountain Sports in Norfolk on U.S. 13 just south of U.S. 58. You may surf from the beach and fish from boats in the bay. No license is required. There are public boat launches on the western shore of the bay.*

For further information contact the refuge manager, Back Bay N.W.R., Pembroke Office Park, Pembroke Two Building, Suite 218, Virginia Beach, Va. 23462, (804) 490-0505.

99.
Mackay Island
National Wildlife Refuge

Directions: **City of Virginia Beach, Va., and Currituck County, N.C. From Richmond, drive south on I-64 to Norfolk. Ten miles beyond the Hampton Road Bridge and Tunnel, turn southeast on Route 165 and continue about 12 miles to Princess Anne Courthouse. At the T junction go east (left) on Route 149. After 14 miles bear right onto Route 615 at the traffic light and go south for 15 miles to the entrance. Most of the refuge is closed during the waterfowl season, from October 15 to March 15, but you can pull off along the causeway on Route 615 and look out over Back Bay and the marshes to the south. You may also launch a boat at Corey's Ditch at any time of year. From March 15 to October 15 the entire refuge is open to boating, walking, and bicycling.**

Ownership: **U.S. Fish and Wildlife Service.**

Mackay Island, a very different habitat from the Back Bay Refuge to the north, features 7055 acres of brackish marshes crisscrossed with canals, miles of which you can canoe, water levels permitting, in spring, summer, and early fall. In Barleys Bay hundreds of whistling swans arrive each fall and winter to feed on aquatic plants, and scores of other bird species seek out the shelter of the marsh.

During waterfowl season the refuge is closed to provide a haven for greater snow geese and other migrating birds. There is a parking area along the causeway at **A**, just beyond the sign for the refuge, from which you can look out over Barleys Bay to the north and across the marshes to the south. At the entrance to the refuge most of the marsh is covered with big cordgrass, a plant that grows on the

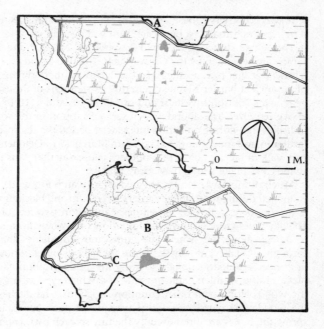

higher ground of brackish marshes. It is often found in disturbed areas, where ditching or diking has occurred. Because this plant stands erect all year it is an excellent cover for marshbirds. King rails hide in it, occasionally emerging to feed along the canals, (see **#67**), and flocks of red-winged blackbirds perch on the thick stems from early spring through the breeding season. Although long-billed marsh wrens are generally common in big-cordgrass areas, for some reason they have not nested here. Further to the east and south into the Great Marsh, patches of salt-marsh cordgrass, salt-meadow cord-grass, cattail, and phragmites are interspersed. Throughout are stretches of black needlerush, a sturdy plant which, once established, com-petes successfully with other plants, and eventually takes over. It is of little value to wildlife, and the refuge management has attempted to eradicate it, with little success. Great blue herons and great egrets are plentiful all year along the canals in the marsh, where they hunt for amphibians and fish. Traveling the wetlands by boat is an excellent way to observe these and other species of herons, egrets, bitterns, and rails that nest here each spring and summer.

The refuge stretches over two low islands, Mackay and Knotts, which are separated by the Great Marsh. The two islands are part of a low ridge that runs northeast across Back Bay, marking the outline of an ancient barrier island system that existed tens of thousands of years ago. The southwestern end of Mackay Island is 10 to 15 feet above sea level. The abundance of seashells found in the soil there indicates that during an earlier interglacial period the sea rose much farther inland than it does today. From March 15 to October 15 one can walk or bicycle across the southern causeway that joins the two islands and make a loop of Mackay Island.

Much of Mackay Island is covered with swamp forest (**B**), which is flooded during most of the winter. Sweetgum and blackgum dominate the lowest ground, sometimes standing in two feet of water. Loblolly pines grow on the small hummocks anywhere from 6 inches to 3 feet above the water. The gums and red maples that grow throughout will eventually shade out the loblolly pines, whose seedlings need abundant sunlight to grow. In spring prothonotary warblers, prairie warblers, and the red- and white-eyed vireos nest in the woods along with other common songbirds. The ditches along the woods and marsh are dotted with wood-duck boxes. In early spring the boxes are often used by the tiny screech owl. Later in the season when the owl's young are gone, a wood duck will frequently raise a brood of young in the same box.

At Bellows Bay (**C**) is a tree where ospreys have been nesting regularly. The first nest is right by the road. One season the young failed to hatch in this nest, so the female osprey built a second nest, called a "frustration nest," that same season. (This one lies to the left of the trail.) The male, however, took no part in this second nest and no courtship and mating took place.

Signs of fire are visible throughout the refuge. The management burns large areas annually to clear away underbrush and encourage tender new growth for wildlife to eat. Snow geese, particularly are attracted to recently burned marsh. Burning is always done in the winter when the damp weather makes it easier to control the fire.

Remarks: *From March 15 to October 15, the refuge is open daily from dawn to dusk for foot, bicycle, and boat traffic, and to fishing. The nearest canoe rentals are in Virginia Beach at Blue Ridge Mountain Sports just south of U.S. 58 on U.S. 13. Boats can be rented at Bayhaven Farms, on Route 615 a few miles north of the refuge entrance. Virginia fishing licenses are also for sale there. North Carolina fishing licenses may be purchased in the town of Bay Villa on Knotts Island. Be sure to be licensed for the proper state. Cars can be parked at the refuge office or along a mile-long stretch of road just beyond the office. There is a crude boat ramp along this road. Be on the lookout for poisonous cottonmouth snakes, which are sometimes seen on the roads. In spring and fall ticks, chiggers and mosquitoes appear, and greenhead flies are a nuisance in summer. For further information see #98.*

100.
Merchants Millpond
State Park

Directions: Gates County, N.C. From Richmond, Va., take I-95 south to Petersburg, about 23 miles. Exit onto U.S. 460; drive southeast about 60 miles. At Suffolk, turn south (left) onto Route 32 and go 17.4 miles to U.S. 158 west in Sunbury, N.C. Go west (right) 5 miles to a crossroads marked with a sign for the park. Turn south (left) and go 1.5 miles. The park office is on the left. Canoe rentals will remain at their present location but in 1984 a new park office will be located off U.S. 158 about 0.5 mile east of the crossroads, along with additional campsites.

Ownership: North Carolina Division of Parks and Recreation.

The millpond is a broad expanse of dark water reflecting huge trees, baldcypress, and water tupelo with massive swollen trunks. Spanish moss and resurrection fern cling to the trunks and branches. Scattered over the surface of the lake, old stumps have become islands of vegetation, pink with swamp rose in spring. In Lassiter swamp north of the pond, eastern cottonmouths sun on windfalls and carpenter frogs hammer noisily. Owls call; warblers nest in the moss. Cypress trees that were saplings at the time of the First Crusade about 900 years ago grow in the heart of the swamp. Dreamlike and phantasmagorical, this is a special place of great beauty.

Although the millpond is man-made, it has existed since 1811, and the vegetation has had a long time to adjust to the flooded conditions. The water tupelo or swamp tupelo is a southern Coastal Plain species adapted to living on soft, flooded soils. The wood of the trees is light and spongy, and the flared base of the trunk distributes its weight over a broad area. The strange burls and knobs in the tops of many of the tupelos are caused by American mistletoe, a parasite common throughout the southeastern United States. The mistletoe sends its roots into the tree and draws off nutrients from the living tissue. By surrounding the parasite with woody growth, the tree is apparently attempting to isolate the invaded area. If you look closely, you may be able to see strands of mistletoe emerging from these growths. The Spanish moss that hangs from every branch is not a parasite; it uses the tree only as a means of support (see **#88**). It is a favorite nesting material for parula, yellow-throated, and protho-notary warblers.

The many stumps are remnants of logging operations, which ended about 50 to 60 years ago. Carried by the wind, water, birds, or turtles the seeds of many terrestrial plants have been able to sprout and grow on these stumps, producing islands of vegetation that are richly varied in contrast to the uniform stand of tupelo and cypress. Trees such as red maple, loblolly pine, and swamp willow and shrubs like buttonbush, red chokeberry, fetterbush, sweet pepperbush, blue-berry, poison ivy, and wax myrtle are all commonly found. Royal

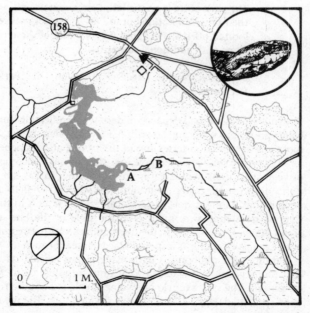

Inset: Cottonmouth

fern, false nettle, St. Johnswort, and water primrose are among the herbs competing for space on the stump hummocks. As more decaying plant material accumulates and the wood rots slowly away, and as the slow-moving current continues to deposit sediment around the stumps, these hummocks will gradually expand.

The millpond is quite shallow and carries a rich community of aquatic plants, a sign that a natural process of eutrophication is under way: as sediment is washed into the water from the surrounding upland, nutrients accumulate on the bottom and the lake fills in. First algae and then submerged plants flourish in the nutrient-rich shallows, returning nutrients as they grow and die. Later, emergent plants will appear; these are rooted beneath the water but have leaves and flowers that float on the surface or rise out of the water. Green mats of duckweed, fragrant water lily, water shield, spatter-dock, and plumes of parrot feather all grow in the shallower portions of the lake. As you canoe farther east and north toward the swamp, you must follow the deeper water of the channel, which is marked by an absence of vegetation.

Abundant plant material and clean water create a good habitat for fish, which include black crappie, chain pickerel, large mouth bass, and bluegill. Drawn by the food supply and the protected waters, many waterfowl remain throughout the winter. Dabbling ducks found here include wigeon, black duck, mallard, blue- and green-winged teal; common diving ducks are lesser scaup, ring-necked duck, and hooded merganser (see **#64**). Canvasback, redhead, and goldeneye are present in small numbers in winter. Wood ducks breed abundantly and can be seen all year long.

Toward the mouth of Lassiter swamp the millpond begins to narrow and the trees close in. A large beaver lodge is located at (**A**), and beyond it is a second one. By lining these two lodges up and following the line north you will come to the entrance to the main swamp channel. Beavers have only recently returned to the area (see **#92**). As you go up the stream through the swamp, the channel may be difficult to follow. Stop and watch the leaves and twigs floating on the surface. You will be able to detect the direction of the current even though it is often very slight.

Before the building of the dam most of the bottomland of the valley probably looked like this. Part of the tidewater section of the Coastal Plain, Lassiter swamp is only a few feet above sea level. It sits on an old seabed which in turn sits on an older seabed. The top layer of sediments is a recent development in geological history, dating back perhaps 2 million years. Beneath them lies a much thicker band of marine clays and sands, which dates back 6 to 8 million years. It is this thick band of impervious material that holds the water on the surface and accounts for the many swamps in the area. The uniform vegetation of the open pond gives way to a varied swamp forest with pumpkin ash, water ash, red maple, and swamp hickory sharing the canopy with water tupelo and baldcypress. These trees can grow in sodden but not continually flooded ground (see **#95**). As you make your way up the swamp channel, watch for some of the more unusual plants to be found here. Two small aquatic plants that flower in spring—a southern species of the bladderwort and featherfoil—float on the surface by means of air-filled sacs. Another floating plant, the yellow water crowfoot, a northern plant, reaches its southern limit in North Carolina. Along the branches of cypress look for log fern, a southern Coastal Plain species found almost exclusively in conjunction with cypress. It is much larger than resurrection fern, a species with a much greater range (see **#53**).

Few people make their way up into the swamp. Undisturbed, it is full of wildlife. Screech owls and barred owls as well as great horned owls nest in the woodlands. Minks and river otters are occasionally seen, and even bobcats have been sighted. Bobcats are shy of humans and require a large hunting territory. Their presence is therefore a good index of the remoteness of an area.

Reptiles and amphibians are especially abundant, for the swamp with its temperate climate and ample supply of water provides a perfect home. Great numbers of turtles bask on the old stumps and fallen logs. If approached, they quickly slide into the water. They are almost impossible to identify from any distance as the distinguishing markings on their shells can be very similar. The larger basking turtles (9 to 12 inches) include Florida and river cooters and red-bellied turtles. The spotted turtle, a much smaller species (about 4 inches) will continue to bask unconcerned if approached. Some species like the eastern mud turtle sun themselves in the water, lying half submerged in the shallows. The stinkpot, also known as the eastern musk turtle, is named for its noxious musk glands. It is able to climb trees up to 6 feet or so but spends most of its time patrolling the bottom of ponds and slow streams. There are also snapping turtles, so called because of their remarkably fierce behavior.

Sixteen species of snake live in and around the swamp. Most are secretive, preferring to hide under logs and stones. In addition to the cottonmouth, you are most likely to see one of the four species of nonpoisonous water snakes that are found in the swamp waters. Skillful swimmers and divers, water snakes hunt frogs, salamanders, crayfish, and fish. They look like cottonmouths and are often mistaken for them. Cottonmouths, however, are more lethargic and will stand their ground if cornered, opening their mouths wide and vibrating their tails. The white lining of the mouth gives them their name. Water snakes, on the other hand, are shyer and quickly retreat if approached. Although the water snake is not poisonous, it can bite hard if grabbed. The species you may encounter here are the brown water snake, a southern Coastal Plain species; the red-bellied water snake, a Coastal Plain species; the banded water snake, at its extreme northern limit; and the northern water snake, which is near its southern boundary.

Turtles and snakes bask in the sun in order to raise their body temperature. As cold-blooded animals, without fur or feathers to insulate them from their environment, they have nearly the same temperature as the air or water around them. This directly governs the rate of their metabolism—the ongoing train of chemical reactions which enable them to live, grow, and reproduce. The rate of every creature's metabolism increases as its temperature rises and decreases as its temperature falls (although if it rises or falls too far, the creature will die). Cold-blooded animals like snakes and turtles undergo drastic swings of temperature according to the weather. In winter they lie in a torpor, buried in the mud or hidden below ground so that they will not freeze. As spring comes and the water and the air warm, their metabolic rate increases and they become more active. Even so they don't have to feed very often, and their intake is about 10 percent of that required by mammals. Breeding, producing eggs, and delivering young require a great deal of activity, and because reptiles take in energy from the sun they spend much time basking during this period. Snakes also bask for long intervals prior to shedding their skins, which happens several times a year.

Amphibians are also plentiful. Several species of treefrogs and of true frogs are heard, especially in the spring. Amphibians require water for many of their life processes. Their eggs, having no shell, must stay in water to avoid drying out. Like fish, frogs rely on water as the medium for fertilization of eggs by sperm, and their skins, which are thin, dry out in the absence of moist, shady environments. Treefrogs are adapted to a climbing life, having long, agile legs and toes. At the ends of their toes are sticky pads which enable them to cling to precarious perches. Most species prefer brushy thickets and shrubs to trees. Their special equipment enables them to exploit a habitat out of reach of the terrestrial species. One species found here, the pine woods treefrog, is particularly associated with the cypress swamps and bordering forests of the southern Coastal Plain.

At **B** look for an iron post to your left. The giant cypresses are just beyond this marker. These are the oldest living trees you are likely to see in the Mid-Atlantic region.

Remarks: *Allow at least half a day to canoe up into the swamp. Canoes can be rented at the park at reasonable rates. There are primitive campsites available and several places along the trail where you can haul out your canoe. Wind tides can be strong and unreliable on the Chowan River so it is advisable to contact the park office before planning a trip. Out on the water the mosquitoes are seldom unbearable, but biting flies can be fierce in early summer. Be on the lookout for snags and submerged logs. If you get stuck, try to back off rather than rocking from side to side. In Lassiter swamp you should be prepared to get out and pull the canoe over fallen logs. There are 7 miles of hiking trails through bottomland and upland habitats, and primitive campsites for hikers too. All seasons have something to offer. Although overlooked by many visitors, the summer months are one of the best times to view the tremendous diversity of life associated with the millpond. Insects, reptiles, amphibians and many species of birds are especially abundant and visible this time of year. Be alert for poisonous copperheads in the drier areas. Ticks and chiggers may be bothersome in summer (see #55). Fishing licenses are available in neighboring towns. For information, contact Merchants Millpond State Park, Route 1, Box 141-A, Gatesville, N.C. 27938, (919) 357-1191. Hours: 8:00 a.m to sunset year round.*

101.
Nags Head
Woods

Directions: **Dare County, N.C. From Richmond take I-64 southeast about 100 miles to Norfolk. Take Route 168 south about 34 miles to where it joins U.S. 158; continue south 28 miles to the U.S. 158 bypass. Take the right fork and drive 8 miles to North Ocean Dr. Turn west (right) and go about 1 mile to the preserve.**

Ownership: **The North Carolina Nature Conservancy and the city of Nags Head. Some of the surrounding land is still in private hands. Look for the Nature Conservancy signs.**

This rare stand of great old forest stands in sight of the hodgepodge development of the North Carolina coast. Tucked away behind the neat beach houses is a wild wood of sandhills covered with many species of oaks, wet hummocks of loblolly pine, and freshwater ponds. Northern and southern species, coastal and inland species, all meet here in a blend of plantlife that is unique along the Atlantic Coast. Some of the trees here are as much as 500 years old.

A system of sand roads winds in and out of the woods. Some of them are navigable by car, but the best way to see the area is to walk around, venturing off on side trails from time to time. The preserve covers 700 acres, and adjacent to it are another 600 acres of un-spoiled woodlands, which are privately owned. Since the Europeans first arrived, the land has been in the hands of a few families, who passed it along from generation to generation and protected it from encroaching development.

Covering the old dunes are many types of oaks, including laurel, live, willow, southern red (Spanish), and some white oaks. Many of these oaks cross with each other, making identification a challenge. It is not yet clear whether these crosses are true hybrids which are able to reproduce themselves. It is unusual to find white oak this close to the ocean, but here the high dunes and thick forest protect the trees from salt spray. The dense canopy is an adaption to salt spray. The windblown salt kills the terminal buds on the top branches, stunting vertical growth. Instead the trees grow laterally. Below the canopy the cool, moist microclimate is strikingly different from that of the surrounding scrubland. Another species rarely found on bar-rier islands is American beech. The beeches here are reminders of the last glacial period, when the sea lay far to the east and this forest was part of the mainland (see **Introduction**). Southern red oak is the most common species on the ridgetops. Its long taproot can reach deep into the dune to extract moisture. Loblolly pines and the mar-itime species of live oak, on the other hand, are seldom found far from the sea. In the understory there are also some very large trees, including flowering dogwood, Hercules-club, hophornbeam, and American holly.

The many freshwater ponds scattered through the forest may have developed as a result of winds scouring out hollows in the dunes (see #55). At these low spots the water table is right at the surface, so that rainwater collects in small ponds. All the fresh water on these islands comes from rain. It percolates down through the soil and comes to rest on top of the denser salt water below. These ponds are the only places in North Carolina where all four genera of duckweed are found. Duckweeds are small floating plants that often cover the surface of shallow bodies of water (see #9). In autumn look for the red leaves of the tiny mosquito or water fern in amongst the green duckweed. Mosquito fern is associated with an algae that inhibits the development of mosquito larvae. Each pond has a different mix-ture of vegetation. Some are crowded with willows and sedges; some are crystal clear. Animal activity around the ponds and the depth of the water—as well as other unknown factors—determine these variations.

Around the ponds are hummocks of loblolly pines and lowland southern evergreen or bay forest. Redbay, sweetbay or swamp magnolia, and loblolly-bay look similar but are not closely related. This forest type is an outlier of the tropical evergreen forests to the south. The pine woods (or yellow-lipped) snake reaches its northernmost station in the damp soils of these woods. Confined to the Coastal Plain, this snake often hides under scraps of bark or in decaying tree stumps. Both marbled and red-backed salamanders are found here, even though amphibians are generally uncommon on the barrier islands (see **#56**). The marbled salamander is beautifully marked with white or silvery bands. The female lays her eggs in autumn in a shallow hollow. She stands guard over them until they are covered with rainwater and ready to hatch.

On the eastern face of the dunes, beach heather is an extremely important pioneer shrub, helping to hold the sand in place. This is the southernmost station known for this plant. Live oak, yaupon holly, and golden aster, which are also found at Nags Head, become the primary pioneer shrubs south of here.

Nags Head Woods provide an important harbor to migrant songbirds in both spring and fall. Ornithologists have long known that fall migrants follow the coastline, but the use of this area during the spring flights has been surprising. Most songbirds follow a more inland route northward. Fall raptor migrations are spectacular, with many species in great numbers passing through the region (see **Cape May** and **#32**).

Both parula warblers and pileated woodpeckers nest in Nags Head Woods. These birds are usually associated with inland forests. Wood ducks are attracted to the seclusion of the dense wet forest. Listen for their odd, high-pitched whistling. Listen also for the yellow-billed cuckoo, a common nester in the preserve.

To the west of the wooded dunes, the marsh begins. Loblolly hummocks dot the wetlands. Bobcats, rare east of the Piedmont, have been known to take refuge on these islands.

Remarks: *Please notify the local managers of the preserve before visiting the area. Call or write to Nags Head Woods Preserve Manager, Route 1, Box 631, Manteo, N.C. 27954, (919) 473-5282. Walking is easy. Other activities include swimming and fishing in the ocean, hang gliding off Jockey's Ridge. Camping is available at Cape Hatteras National Seashore to the south and at several private campgrounds along Route 158. Poison ivy grows abundantly throughout the woods. From early spring to first frost be prepared for biting insects and ticks (see **#55** for tick removal).*

102.

Jockey's Ridge State Park
and Natural Area

Directions: **Dare County, N.C. From Richmond, drive southeast on I-64 about 100 miles to Norfolk. Drive south on Route 168 about 34 miles to where it joins U.S. 158; continue south 28 miles to the U.S. 158 bypass. Take the right fork and drive 10.3 miles. The parking area is on the right.**

Ownership: **North Carolina Division of Parks and Recreation.**

Like a desert landscape in miniature, rolling waves of bare sand, rippled and carved by the wind, rise abruptly from the flats of the narrow barrier island known as the Currituck Spit. (See **#55** for barrier island formation.) This dune is about 110 to 140 feet tall, the highest on the Atlantic shore. It lies at the southern limit of a band of inland dunes that extend north to the dunes at False Cape State Park (see **#98**). From unknown sources—onshore, offshore, or some combination of the two—large amounts of sand were at some point swept ashore along this region. One theory is that a period of very heavy storms may have accumulated sediments in offshore bars which then moved gradually onto the beach. The prevailing winds then carried the sand inland and shaped it into dunes. In some places the dunes broke into distinct hills of sand called *medaños*.

If Jockey's Ridge was once covered with vegetation, subsequent disturbance such as fire has destroyed it. It is difficult for plants to reestablish themselves because of the constantly shifting sands. Eventually, however, the sandhills at Jockey's ridge may look like the wooded dunes to the north at Nags Head and False Cape (see **#98**). Although the dunes change shape from day to day, there is only a little net movement to the southwest. This is because the prevailing southwesterly winds from March to August are balanced by northeasterlies the rest of the year. The Nags Head woods may also protect the dunes from the strong winter gales (see **#7** on seasonal winds).

At the fringes of the bare sand, sea oats are beginning to colonize. Here, sea oats have replaced American beach grass as the main stabilizer of the dunes (see #55). Sea oats are not as effective a cover as beach grass, for they do not grow and reproduce as rapidly. Other species in this edge zone include pennywort, croton, sandspurs, and little bluestem. Clusters of shrubs including live oak, redcedar, red-bay, and poison ivy grow in sheltered hollows out of the way of the killing salt spray carried inland from the sea.

Remarks: *Because the sands are bare, this is one of the rare places along the coast where you can walk on the dunes without doing damage. Camping is available at Cape Hatteras National Seashore. There are several private campgrounds in the area. A small interpretative center should shortly be open to the public. Activities include fishing and swimming in the ocean and hang gliding from certain parts of the dunes. Summer is very crowded.*

Recent Changes
in Common Bird Names

The following species have recently been given new common names by the American Ornithologists' Union. As most guidebooks still have the old names, we provide the new designations here rather than in the text.

Old	New
Louisiana heron	tricolored heron
common pintail	northern pintail
common bobwhite	northern bobwhite
common gallinule	common moorhen
American golden plover	lesser golden-plover
northern phalarope	red-necked phalarope
barn owl	common barn-owl
common screech owl	eastern screech owl
saw-whet owl	northern saw-whet owl
common flicker	northern flicker
eastern pewee	eastern wood-pewee
rough-winged swallow	northern rough-winged swallow
northern raven	common raven

Scientific and Confusing Common Names of Marsh Plants

black needlerush: Juncus roemerianus
bulrush, salt-marsh: Scirpus robustus
cordgrass, big: Spartina cynosuroides
cordgrass, salt-marsh: Spartina alterniflora
cordgrass, salt-meadow: Spartina patens
cut-grass, rice: Leersia oryzoides
elder, marsh: Iva frutescens
groundsel bush: Baccharis halimifolia
mallow, rose: Hibiscus moscheutos
mallow, salt-marsh: Kosteletzkya virginica
rose, swamp: Rosa palustris
salt grass: Distichlis spicata
switch grass: Panicum virgatum

Glossary

acidic: Containing an abundance of hydrogen ions. Very acidic soils are poor in nutrients.

alga: Any of a large group of primitive and mostly aquatic plants, ranging from tiny one-celled to large multicelled organisms.

basic: Containing any one substance or a combination of substances that combine with acids to form salts. Slightly basic soils are rich in nutrients and are generally very fertile. Highly basic soils are toxic.

bird of prey: One of the carnivorous birds such as hawks, owls, and eagles.

bog: A wet, soggy area with little or no drainage.

bottomland: Low-lying ground that may be flooded from time to time.

brackish: A term used to describe water that is somewhat salty but not as salty as seawater.

calcite: A mineral made up of calcium, carbon, and oxygen; also known as calcium carbonate.

canopy: An umbrella of trees formed by the tallest trees in a stand.

climax forest: A forest in which the mix of species is relatively stable over time.

competition: Rivalry of plants or animals for the same resources or habitat.

coniferous: Evergreen and cone-bearing.

deciduous: Shedding leaves annually.

disjunct: Set apart from the main distribution of the species.

ecosystem: The interaction of plants, animals, and their environment.

erosion: The process by which the earth's surface is worn away by water, wind, or waves.

habitat: The natural environment of an animal or plant.

Ice Age: A period from about 10,000 to 2 million years ago during which a large portion of the earth was covered by glaciers; also called the glacial epoch.

impoundment: An artificial pond or lake.

interglacial: Warm periods that occurred between the glacial advances when the ice sheets withdrew toward the poles.

intertidal: Pertaining to that part of the shore that lies between the low-tide and the high-tide mark.

larva: The immature, wingless stage of certain insects.

litter: The layer of slightly decomposed plant material on the surface of the forest floor.

marsh: Low, wet land covered by grassy vegetation.

meander: A bend in a river.

migration: The rhythmic seasonal movement of certain birds and other animals.

old field: A stage in the succession of cleared land to forest characterized by grasses, flowering plants, and shrubs.

peat: Partially decomposed plant material common to wet areas with poor drainage.

pelagic: Oceanic.

photosynthesis: The process by which green plants convert water and carbon dioxide into carbohydrates.

pioneer: One of a number of plants that appear early in the process of succession.

Pleistocene epoch: The geological epoch during which the Ice Age occurred.

runoff: Rainwater, melting snow, or groundwater that drains away across the surface of the ground.

secondary growth: The forest that appears after land has been cleared.

shorebirds: Species that frequent coastal areas and inland beaches, such as sandpipers, plovers, and oystercatchers.

shrub: A woody perennial plant that usually has several stems and is generally smaller than a tree.

species: A group of related plants or animals that interbreed to produce fertile offspring.

succession: The process by which the vegetation of an ecosystem changes over time.

swamp: Low, wet forest that is regularly flooded and poorly drained.

tannin: Any one of a variety of large, complex molecules contained in most woody plants.

understory: The trees found growing beneath the canopy species and above the shrub layer.

waterfowl: Aquatic birds, including geese, ducks, and swans.

Bibliography

General Reference

Angel, H., and Pat Wolseley. 1982. *The Water Naturalist*. New York: Facts on File.

Barbour, Michael G., Jack H. Bork, and Wanna D. Pitts. 1980. *Terrestrial Plant Ecology*. Menlo Park, Calif.: Benjamin/Cummings Publishing Co.

Barnes, Robert D. 1968. *Invertebrate Zoology*. Philadelphia: W. B. Saunders Co.

Bascomb, Willard. 1964. *Waves and Beaches: The Dynamics of the Ocean Surface*. Garden City, N.Y.: Doubleday & Co., Anchor Press.

Braun, E. Lucy. 1950. *Deciduous Forests of North America*. Philadelphia: Blakiston Co.

Brown, Lauren. 1979. *Grasses: An Identification Guide*. Boston: Houghton Mifflin Co.

Dickerson, Mary C. 1969. *The Frog Book*. New York: Dover Books.

Eyre, F. H., ed. 1980. *Forest Cover Types of the United States and Canada*. Washington, D.C.: Society of American Foresters.

Fernald, Merritt Lyndon. 1950. *Gray's Manual of Botany*. New York: D. Van Nostrand Co.

Harding, John J., and Justin J. Harding. 1980. *Birding the Delaware Valley Region*. Philadelphia: Temple University Press.

Hunt, Cynthia, and Robert M. Garrells. 1972. *Water: The Web of Life*. New York: W. W. Norton & Co.

Kaufman, Warren, and Orrin Pilkey. 1979. *The Beaches Are Moving*. Garden City, N.Y.: Doubleday & Co., Anchor Press.

Keeton, William T. 1972. 2nd ed. *Biological Science*. New York: W. W. Norton & Co.

315

Kopper, Philip. 1979. *The Wild Edge*. New York: Times Books.

Leatherman, Stephen P. 1979. *Barrier Island Handbook*. Washington, D.C.: National Park Service.

Marx, Wesley. 1981. *The Oceans: The Last Resource*. San Francisco: Sierra Club Books.

Neiring, William. 1966. *The Life of a Marsh*. New York: McGraw-Hill Book Co.

Odum, Eugene P. 1971. 3rd ed. *Fundamentals of Ecology*. Philadelphia: W. B. Saunders Co.

Orr, Robert T. 1970. *Animals in Migration*. New York: Macmillan Co.

Palmer, E. Laurence, and H. Seymour Fowler. 1975. *Fieldbook of Natural History*. New York: McGraw-Hill Book Co.

Perry, John and Jane G. 1980. *The Random House Guide to Natural Areas of the Eastern United States*. New York: Random House.

Petry, Loren C. 1968. *The Beachcomber's Botany*. Chatham, Mass.: Chatham Conservation Foundation.

Press, Frank, and Raymond Siever. 1974. *Earth*. San Francisco: W. H. Freeman & Co.

Ray, Peter Martin. 1972. 2nd ed. *The Living Plant*. New York: Holt, Rinehart & Winston.

Reid, George K. 1976. 2nd ed. *Ecology of Inland Waters and Estuaries*. New York: Van Nostrand Reinhold Co.

Reiger, George. 1983. *Wanderer on My Native Shore*. New York: Simon & Schuster.

Ricklets, Robert. 1976. *The Economy of Nature—A Textbook in Basic Ecology*. Portland, Ore.: Chiron Press.

Riley, Laura and William. 1979. *Guide to the National Wildlife Refuges*. Garden City, N.Y.: Doubleday & Co., Anchor Press.

Shelford, Victor E., ed. 1926. *The Naturalist's Guide to the Americas*. Baltimore: Williams and Wilkins Co.

Stearn, Colin W. and Thomas H. Clark, and Robert L. Carroll. 1979. *Geological Evolution of America*. New York: John Wiley & Sons.

Teal, John, and Mildred Teal. 1969. *The Life and Death of the Salt Marsh*. New York: Ballantine Books.

Terres, John K. 1980. *The Audubon Encyclopedia of North American Birds*. New York: Alfred A. Knopf.

Usinger, Robert L. 1967. *The Life of Rivers and Streams*. New York: McGraw-Hill Book Co.

Vankat, John L. 1979. *Natural Vegetation of North America*. New York: John Wiley & Sons.

Von Frisch, Karl. 1974. *Animal Architecture*. New York: Harcourt Brace Jovanovich.

Welty, Joel Carl. 1962. *The Life of Birds*. Philadelphia: W. B. Saunders Co.

The Chesapeake Bay

Meanley, Brooke. 1975. *Marshes of the Chesapeake Bay Country*. Centreville, Md.: Tidewater Publishers.

Meanley, Brooke. 1978. *Blackwater*. Centreville, Md.: Tidewater Publishers.

Meanley, Brooke. 1982. *Waterfowl of the Chesapeake Bay Country*. Centreville, Md.: Tidewater Publishers.

Schubel, John R. 1981. *The Living Chesapeake*. Baltimore: Johns Hopkins Press.

Delaware

Delaware Geological Survey. 1980. *Delaware: Its Rocks and Minerals*.

Fleming, Lorraine M. 1978. *Delaware's Outstanding Natural Areas and Their Preservation*. Hockessin, Del.: Delaware Nature Education Society.

D.C. Area

Thomas, Bill and Phyllis. 1980. *Natural Washington*. New York: Holt, Rinehart & Winston.

Wilds, Claudia. 1983. *Finding Birds in the National Capital Area*. Washington, D.C.: Smithsonian Institution Press.

Maryland

Amos, William H. 1980. *Assateague Island*. National Park Service, Handbook no. 106. Washington, D.C.: Department of the Interior.

Higgins, Elisabeth A. T., Robert D. Rappleye, and Russell G. Brown. 1971. *The Flora and Fauna of Assateague Island*. Agricultural Experiment Station, Bulletin A-172. College Park: University of Maryland.

Maryland Department of Natural Resources, Wildlife Administration. 1981. *Guide to Public Hunting Areas in Maryland*.

Robbins, Chandler S., and Danny Bystrak. 1977. *Field List of the Birds of Maryland*. 2nd ed. Maryland Avifauna no. 2. Baltimore: Maryland Ornithological Society.

Vokes, Harold E. 1957. *Miocene Fossils of Maryland.* Baltimore: Maryland Geological Survey, Bulletin 20. Helpful guide for collecting
along the Chesapeake Bay.

New Jersey

Bennett, D. W. 1981. *New Jersey Coast Walks.* Highlands, N.J.: Amer-
ican Littoral Society.
Boyle, William J., Jr. 1979. *New Jersey Field Trip Guide.* Summit,
N.J.: Summit Nature Club.
Carlson, Cathy, and John Fowler. 1980. *The Salt Marsh of Southern
New Jersey.* Pomona, N.J.: Center for Environmental Research,
Stockton State College.
Dunne, Peter J. 1977. "Birding at Cape May." *New Jersey Audubon,*
June–July 1977.
Forman, Richard T. T., ed. 1979. *Pine Barrens: Ecosystem and Land-
scape.* New York: Academic Press.
Lester, Thomas. 1977. *The Pine Barrens of New Jersey.* Trenton, N.J.:
Department of Environmental Protection.
Lomax, Joseph L., Joan M. Galli, and Anne E. Galli. 1980. *The
Wildlife of Cape May County, New Jersey.* Pomona, N.J.: Center for
Environmental Research, Stockton State College.
McCormick, Jack. 1970. *The Pine Barrens: A Preliminary Ecological
Inventory.* Trenton: New Jersey State Museum.
McPhee, John. 1968. *The Pine Barrens.* New York: Farrar, Straus &
Giroux.
Parnes, Robert. 1978. *Canoeing the Jersey Pine Barrens.* Charlotte,
N.C.: East Woods Press.
Pinelands Commission. 1980. *New Jersey Pinelands: Comprehensive
Management Plan.* New Lisbon, N.J.
Robichaud, Beryl, and Murray F. Buell. 1973. *Vegetation of New
Jersey.* New Brunswick, N.J.: Rutgers University Press.
Wolfe, Peter E. 1977. *The Geology and Landscapes of New Jersey.* New
York: Crane Russak.

Virginia

Amos, William H. 1980. *Assateague Island.* National Park Service,
Handbook no. 106. Washington, D.C.: Department of the Interior.
Beck, Ruth, and Richard Peake, eds. "Site Guide to Birds of Vir-
ginia." Unpublished. Available through the Virginia Society of
Ornithologists, 520 Rainbow Forest Dr., Lynchburg, Va. 24502.

Higgins, Elizabeth A. T., Robert D. Rappleye, and Russell G. Brown. 1971. *The Flora and Ecology of Assateague Island.* Agricultural Experiment Station, Bulletin A-172. College Park: University of Maryland.

Johnson, Gerald H. 1969. *Guidebook to the Geology of the York-James Peninsula and South Bank of the James River.* Department of Geology, Guidebook no. 1. Williamsburg, Va.: College of William and Mary.

Johnson, Gerald H., Carl R. Berquist, Kelvin Ramsey, and Pamela C. Peebles. 1982. *Guidebook to the Late Cenozoic and Economic Geology of the Lower York-James Peninsula of Virginia.* Department of Geology, Guidebook no. 4. Williamsburg, Va.: College of William and Mary.

Kird, P. K., ed. 1979. *The Great Dismal Swamp.* Charlottesville: University of Virginia Press.

Moore, Kenneth A. 1980. *James County Tidal Marsh Inventory.* Virginia Institute of Marine Science, Special Report no. 188. Gloucester Point, Va.

Moore, Kenneth A. 1981. *Surry County Tidal Marsh Inventory.* Virginia Institute of Marine Science, Special Report no. 187. Gloucester Point, Va.

Silberhorn, G. M. 1976. *Tidal Wetland Plants of Virginia.* Gloucester Point, Va.: Virginia Institute of Marine Science.

Silberhorn, G. M., and A. F. Harris. 1981. *Isle of Wight County Tidal Marsh Inventory.* Virginia Institute of Marine Science, Special Report no. 213. Gloucester Point, Va.

White, Mel. *A Guide to Virginia's Wildlife Management Areas.* Richmond: Virginia Commission of Game and Inland Fisheries.

Field Guides

Audubon Society Field Guide Series. New York: Alfred A. Knopf. The series includes guides to birds, reptiles and amphibians, insects, shells, butterflies, mushrooms, mammals, trees, and wildflowers.

Brockman, George A. 1958. *A Field Guide to Trees and Shrubs.* New York: Golden Press.

Farrand, John, Jr., ed. 1983. *The Audubon Society Master Guide to Birding.* 3 vols. New York: Alfred A. Knopf.

Godin, Alfred J. 1977. *Wild Mammals of New England.* Baltimore: Johns Hopkins University Press.

Klimas, John E., and James A. Cunningham. 1981. *Wildflowers of Eastern America*. New York: Galahad Books.

Newcomb, Lawrence. 1977. *Newcomb's Wildflower Guide*. Boston: Little, Brown & Co. This guide contains an easy-to-follow key for flower identification.

Peterson Field Guide Series. Boston: Houghton Mifflin Co. The series includes guides to birds, reptiles and amphibians, ferns, butterflies, animal tracks, the Atlantic seashore, wildflowers, trees, and shrubs.

Pettingill, O. S., Jr. 1977. *A Guide To Bird Finding East of the Mississippi*. Boston: Houghton Mifflin Co.

Reid, George K. 1967. *Pond Life*. New York: Golden Press.

Robbins, Chandler S., Bertel Broun, and Herbert Zim. 1966. *Birds of North America*. New York: Golden Press.

Watts, M. T. 1963. *Master Tree Finder*. Berkeley, Calif.: Nature Study Guild. An excellent guide for beginners.

Index

Except for bird species, of which every citation is included, the index lists only those plant and animal species that are significantly mentioned or described in detail. *Italic* figures refer to major discussions; **boldface** figures refer to site numbers.

A Note
About the Author

Susannah Lawrence is a graduate of the University of Wisconsin. From 1972 to 1975 she worked as a researcher, writer, and lobbyist on environmental and consumer issues for Consumer Action Now, a public interest group based in New York City. From 1975 to 1980 she was a lobbyist in Washington, first as executive director of Consumer Action Now and subsequently as a staff member of Solar Lobby. She now lives in Manhattan.

Notes

Notes

Notes

Notes

Notes

In order to make subsequent editions of The Audubon Society Field Guides to the Natural Places of America as accurate and up-to-date as possible, users of this guide are encouraged to send corrections, comments, or additions to text and maps as well as suggestions for new sites to: Caroline Sutton, Hilltown Press, % Pantheon Books, 201 East 50th Street, New York, N.Y. 10022.